Toward
Multinational Economic
Cooperation in Africa

B.W.T. Mutharika

The Praeger Special Studies program—utilizing the most modern and efficient book production techniques and a selective worldwide distribution network—makes available to the academic, government, and business communities significant, timely research in U.S. and international economic, social, and political development.

Toward Multinational Economic Cooperation in Africa

PRAEGER SPECIAL STUDIES IN INTERNATIONAL ECONOMICS AND DEVELOPMENT

Praeger Publishers   New York   Washington   London

330.9603
M98t
81100
Dec.1972

PRAEGER PUBLISHERS
111 Fourth Avenue, New York, N.Y. 10003, U.S.A.
5, Cromwell Place, London S.W.7, England

Published in the United States of America in 1972
by Praeger Publishers, Inc.

Library of Congress Catalog Card Number: 71-151955

Printed in the United States of America

To My Mother

Economic cooperation is a very wide subject covering a multiplicity of economic activities, all aspects of which cannot be covered in a book of this kind. However, an attempt has been made to cover at least the most vital issues affecting the development problems of the African countries. For quite some time now, the need has been felt for a more comprehensive book on economic cooperation, written in more simplified terms understandable to the politician and the layman. Quite often, economists have tended to address their writings to university professors and students of economics, and such works failed to carry the message to the people who live with the day-to-day problems of development. As a result, the men responsible for taking vital economic decisions failed to take adequate consideration of the economic realities in the policy formulations or were merely indifferent. As a result, there was lack of coordination between the political and economic principles. This study attempts to provide such coordination.

The book is not confined to the discussion of economic factors, and throughout the text political aspects of economic cooperation have been examined where they were found to contribute to a full understanding of the problems. Chapter 9, in particular, examines the interplay between politics and economics and how the peculiar relationship has governed the vital decisions affecting economic development. It is maintained that a good understanding of the role of politics in economic development would contribute greatly to the solution of the economic problems of Africa in the 1970's.

Throughout this book, the terms "economic cooperation" and "economic integration" are used interchangeably. This usage is deliberate. Although there are some differences in the definitions of the two concepts, since the former is essentially static while the latter is dynamic, it becomes unrealistic to introduce any rigidities in their application and an attempt to draw a clear distinction between them could sometimes lead to absurd results. The peculiarity of the characteristics of the African economies, the development of the economic, social, and cultural institutions and the levels of industrial development in Africa imply that integration, in the strict sense of the word, cannot be said to exist in Africa. For this reason, economic integration must be sufficiently flexible to accommodate the political and economic aspirations of the individual African countries while, at the same time, meeting the requirements for multinational development. In this sense,

vii

there would virtually be no significant differences between the two concepts. Moreover, in practice the two terms are perfectly inter-changeable and when one talks of economic cooperation in Africa what is actually impled is economic integration.

I would like to express my deep gratitude to those who assisted me in the preparation of this book, and in particular to Ann Seidman of the University of Wisconsin (Madison), who kindly agreed to read an earlier draft of the manuscript and made valuable suggestions in matters of substance. To some of my colleagues at the Economic Commission for Africa with whom I discussed parts of this book, I owe much for their useful contributions and helpful comments. I am deeply indebted to Brenda Prouty and Almaz Tedla, who prepared the earlier draft and made valuable contribution to the styling of the book, and to Dagmar Pinto, who worked under great pressure to prepare the final manuscript and without whose patience and cooperation it would have been difficult to complete a book of this size in good time.

Many of the materials that have gone into the preparation of this book were gathered during the course of my duties and assign-ments. I would therefore like to acknowledge the assistance I obtained from the United Nations Economic Commission for Africa (ECA) through the use of its research and other facilities, especially in the preparation of the tables. However, I wish to stress that the views and conclusions made in this book are entirely those of the author and do not in any way reflect the official views of the United Nations Eco-nomic Commission for Africa.

CONTENTS

LIST OF TABLES

Tables   Page

LIST OF ABBREVIATIONS

ADB	African Development Bank
BCEAEC	Banque Centrale des Etats de l'Afrique Equatoriale et du Cameroun (Central Bank of the States of Equatorial Africa and Cameroun)
BCEAO	Banque Centrale des Etats de l'Afrique de l'Ouest (Central Bank of West Africa)
CFA	Communauté Financiére Africanine
COMECON	Council for Mutual Economic Assistance
CPCM	Comité Permanent Consultatif du Maghreb (Maghreb Permanent Consultative Committee)
EACSO	East African Common Services Organization
ECA	Economic Commission for Africa (United Nations)
EEC	European Economic Community

xix

EFTA	European Free Trade Association
FAO	Food and Agriculture Organization (United Nations)
GATT	General Agreement on Tariffs and Trade
LAFTA	Latin American Free Trade Association
OAU	Organization of African Unity
OCAM	Organisation Commune des Etats Africains, Malgache et Mauricien (Afro-Malagasy Common Organization)
OERS	Organisation des Etats Riverains du Sénégal (Organization of the Senegal River States)
TIR Convention	Convention Transit International par Route
UDEAC	Union Douanière et Economique de l'Afrique Centrale (Central African Customs and Economic Union)
UDEAO	Union Douanière des Etats de l'Afrique de l'Ouest (West African Customs Union)
UEAC	Union des Etats de l'Afrique Centrale (Union of Central African States)
UFI	Union des Foires Internationales (Union of International Fairs)
UMOA	Union Monétaire Ouest Africaine (West African Monetary Union)
UNCTAD	United Nations Conference on Trade and Development

I

THE FRAMEWORK
FOR
MULTINATIONAL
COOPERATION
IN AFRICA

1

THE ORIGINS
OF
ECONOMIC
COOPERATION
IN AFRICA

Economic cooperation is an old institution and the need to coordinate production functions as a means of enhancing efficiency and economies of scale was realized even by the classical economists such as Adam Smith in his famous doctrine of the division of labor.[1] In Africa, the need for cooperation was not particularly felt until the countries achieved independence, although economic cooperation in Africa began as a result of the political and economic institutions created by the colonial powers.

The "scramble for Africa" which followed the Berlin Conference of 1884-85, resulted in the fragmentation of the African continent into small colonies and territories whose domestic markets were too limited to permit the level of economic activity which was sufficient to sustain even the lowest rate of economic development. The territorial boundaries which were arbitrarily created during the scramble, became real obstacles to the movement of goods, services, and labor among the countries, especially those belonging to different colonial administrations. In the adminstrative field, the geographical location of these territories caused serious problems and it was subsequently found essential to establish common administrative and financial arrangements comprising groups of these colonial possessions.

As a result of differences in the economic, political, and other objectives of the colonial powers, great disparities occurred in the levels of development between the territories both within the same administration or between two different colonial systems. One basic feature of colonial policies was that the development of these territories was planned primarily to boost up economic activities in the metropolitan countries. Therefore, the events that took place from the early days of European settlement in Africa until the time of

3

independence had profound effect on the development of the present
political, social, and economic institutions of the African countries.
Throughout the colonial period, the external influences not only
hindered the rate of development but also resulted in differences in
policital ideologies, economic thinking, and cultural outlook among
the African people.

ECONOMIC GROUPINGS DURING
THE COLONIAL PERIOD

Until approximately the beginning of the 1960's, the greater
part of Africa was still politically and economically linked with the
European colonial powers. Commercial, monetary, and financial
administration policies for the colonial territories were designed to
make them dependent on the European metropolitan powers. The
creation of the infrastructure had been based on military, political,
and administrative expediency, and economic considerations were
therefore of marginal value. The colonial powers established some
limited forms of economic cooperation between groups of territories
under their control, but these efforts were aimed at easing the
problems of administration and the financing of colonial budgets.
Where economic motives predominated, the development of the
economies was geared mainly to the export of the primary commodities
and other raw materials from the colonial territories to the metropolitan countries. Some of these groupings are briefly examined
below.

French West and Equatorial Africa

The French administrators were quick to discover that the
adoption of a common policy in such matters as currency, trade, and
law enforcement was the most effective means of maintaining control
over their territories. Accordingly, the French possessions in West
and Central Africa were organized into two administrative areas--
French West Africa and French Equatorial Africa.

Each of these two areas constituted a kind of federation with
federal institutions responsible for managing an independent budget.
Each had powers of taxation and was a channel for the distribution
of French financial assistance. A separate monetary system was set
up for each of the two federations, but the French West African franc
and the French Equatorial African franc were freely transferable
between the countries of the respective federations and a par value
was maintained with the metropolitan franc.

As the countries approached independence, these federal and monetary arrangements did not survive, largely because independence was granted not to the federations as such but to the individual countries through a series of bilateral agreements between each of the countries and France. After independence, the powers of legislation and taxation previously enjoyed by the federal assemblies were handed over to the national parliaments. Strangely enough, the breakup of these institutions was supported by some of the countries within these groups, especially the more wealthy countries.

The wealthier countries were naturally the main contributors to the federal funds during the colonial period, and they could not see themselves continuing this role after independence. However, even though the wealthier countries began to implement some programs of industrialization geared to the individual markets, they soon came up against the problem of demand caused by the limitation of these markets. The poorer countries, on the other hand, found themselves with inadequate resources necessary for the carrying out of the normal functions of a sovereign state. In short, there was hardly any prospect for a high rate of industrial development based on the national markets.

In order to safeguard the trading and other interests that had developed embracing all of French West or Equatorial Africa, the countries soon recognized the need to consider the reestablishment of the old economic links. Prior to independence, the colonies had no control over external reserves, which were maintained in Paris, but after independence their ability to maintain the level of imports depended upon the share of foreign exchange reserves maintained in metropolitan France. Joint control of monetary policies was seen as a way of effectively controlling such reserves; therefore, by 1964 the monetary systems of the colonial period had in effect been restored and two central banks backed by French reserves were set up, one each for West Africa and Equatorial Africa: Banque Centrale des Etats de l'Afrique de l'Ouest (BCEAO) and Banque Centrale des Etats de l'Afrique Equatoriale et du Cameroun (BCEAEC).

British West Africa

The British established various forms of integrated economic systems among groups of her territories in West Africa, but in contrast to the French African territories the joint administration was confined to limited areas. Until 1958, a common currency existed throughout British West Africa, these countries had a common income tax policy and administration, and there were some attempts toward harmonizing tariff duties. There were also common education programs, such as the West African Examination Council. The issuing agency, the Bank of West Africa, was partly controlled by the territorial governments but had its own independent reserves maintained in London. On attaining independence, each of the former British West African colonies established a separate currency and adopted independent monetary policies. The fragmentation of the monetary system in the former British West African territories after independence was carried much further than in the former French West African territories. Whereas the former French colonies set up common monetary arrangements, Nigeria, Ghana, Sierra Leone, and Gambia set up independent issuing authorities with their own reserves, and their currencies were no longer convertible with the other countries. Stringent foreign exchange controls were imposed in some of the countries, especially in Ghana. The problem of former British West Africa was mainly that there were no physical means of transportation, largely for geographical reasons. Maritime transport was well developed to connect the area with Europe and other external markets but was not geared to serve development of trade among the countries. Moreover, there appeared to be no incentives for these countries to seriously consider any form of economic cooperation.

The East African Common Market

The East African Common Market is one of the oldest institutions for multinational cooperation in Africa and can be traced as far back as 1917, when Uganda and Kenya formed a customs union.[2] Under the customs union, the two territories constituted a common market which in its later years evolved into an economic organization approximating an economic union. There was complete freedom of exchange between Kenya, Tanganyika, and Uganda, accompanied by a common currency, a common external tariff, and a common income tax. The taxation policies were determined through consultations by the respective governments. Tanganyika joined the customs union in 1927. Since the creation of the union between Tanganyika and Zanzibar in 1964, the former changed its name to Tanzania.

During the 1940's, there was need to reorganize the common market arrangements largely because of the changes in the world economies brought about as a result of World War II. Thus, in 1947 the East African High Commission was established. Although essentially an institution for the administration of common services under the de facto common market, it was an attempt to consolidate the three economies into a closely-knit economic unit. With the approach of independence, problems similar to those encountered by other

systems of economic cooperation in Africa arose for the East African
Common Market. Foremost among the problems was the question of
equalizing industrial development and the general rate of development
in the three countries. By the late 1950's, it had become apparent
that the economic benefits of the common market were not being
distributed equitably among the three partner countries. The development of industries that were geared to serve the East African countries as a whole was largely concentrated in Kenya, while the other
two countries, particularly Tanganyika, served as a market for Kenyan
industries. The common external tariff resulted in loss of revenue
to Tanganyika and Uganda as a result of the diversion of demand from
products manufactured overseas to those manufactured in Kenya. An
attempt was made to devise a system of compensation through direct
financial transfers between the member countries of the East African
Common Market, but this was not sufficient to cover the loss of
revenue, especially in the case of Tanganyika, the least developed
among the three partners. The common external and often protective
tariffs levied by the less favored countries on goods from outside
East Africa were seen as subsidies to Kenyan industries.

By 1961, when Tanganyika got its independence, it had become
apparent that these arrangements could not be sustained for long.
Therefore, the East African Common Service Organization (EACSO)
was established to replace the East African High Commission. Its
main purpose was to rationalize the functions of the various organs
responsible for the operation of such joint services as railways,
postal and telecommunications, and shipping and to administer matters
relating to general transportation, finance, social research, and
economic relations. This was a further attempt to consolidate the
governmental functions that had existed in the past. EACSO was
eventually replaced by the Kampala Agreement, which is examined
in Chapter 8.

The Federation of Rhodesia and Nyasaland

The three territories of Northern Rhodesia (Zambia), Southern
Rhodesia, and Nyasaland (Malawi) came under one political and
economic union in September 1963 with free movement of currency,
common customs and excise legislation, and common economic
policies. It was argued by the federation's proponents that each of
the partner countries would gain as a result of the expanded market;
that the economic association would ensure stability in the prices of
agricultural commodities; that the enlarged market would attract a
greater inflow of capital into the federal area; and that joint economic
planning for development would ensure joint and fuller utilization of
the resources, thereby increasing the national incomes of the three

territories. Although the federation was seen as an economic union, it was argued that the three economies were so complementary and interdependent that the logical step was to create a political union.[3]

Whereas Southern Rhodesia was a self-governing colony with somewhat independent powers of legislation, Northern Rhodesia and Nyasaland were protectorates administered by Britain through the Colonial Office in London. Under the federation, it was intended that the economic development of the area be boosted up by the establishment of infrastructural projects such as the Kariba hydroelectric project and railway and airline projects. Certain economic functions related to customs duties and other trade controls, currency, banking regulations, and such corporations as the Bank of Rhodesia and Nyasaland, the Central African Airways, the Federal Power Board, the Rhodesian Railways, and the joint telecommunications were the responsibility of the federal government. The constituent territories were left with residual powers with regard to such matters as education, agriculture, labor, and social welfare.

However, this economic union was not accompanied by the formulation and adoption of policies to balance the industrial development of the area as a whole and the manufacturing industry was developed in Southern Rhodesia at the expense of the two northern territories. Northern Rhodesia, through its copper exports, accounted for the bulk of the external revenues of the federation, while Nyasaland had hardly any industry of any sort. Just as Kenyan industries were designed to serve Ugandan and Tanganyikan markets under the EASCO agreements, the Southern Rhodesian manufactures were planned to serve Nyasaland and Northern Rhodesia, which spent a great deal of their foreign exchange earnings on the import of consumer goods from Southern Rhodesia at higher prices than could be obtained outside the federation. The federal policies were not designed to grant any compensatory advantages within the federation's integrated market to the two northern countries, and much of the economic development envisaged under the federation would have taken place in any case. The system of allocation of the federal revenues among the member countries and the distribution of industrial development projects offered no incentives for Nyasaland or Northern Rhodesia to remain in the federation. In the political field, the federation was seen by the Africans as an attempt to perpetuate white domination in the three territories, and the nationalists therefore fought relentlessly for the breakup of the federation. Thus, in 1963 the common services, which existed for ten years, were split up. The two northern territories achieved their independence in 1964, and by then separate institutions had been created in the three countries.

The High Commission Territories

The geographical location of Basutoland (Lesotho), Bechuanaland (Botswana), and Swaziland (Ngwane), which constituted the former British High Commission territories, made the position of these three countries somewhat different than that of the rest of the British territories in Africa. The fact that they are surrounded by South Africa apparently made it difficult for Britain to develop the countries at the same pace as the other colonial possessions. The High Commission territories were not administered by the Colonial Office, as were most of the colonies, but came under the Commonwealth Relations Office. The day-to-day administration was subject to the jurisdiction of the British High Commissioner to South Africa, stationed in Cape Town. This was a virtual common market with common market institutions governing banking, currency, and exchange control. The area also had common external tariffs against third countries. There was free movement of labor and capital among the three territories. In 1960, legislative assemblies were established in these territories. The Office of High Commissioner for the three territories was abolished in 1964. Under the High Commission arrangements there was a form of common market in the three territories with free movement of goods, currency, capital, and labor. The three territories, together with South Africa, constitute a customs union under an agreement signed in 1910 between the United Kingdom and South Africa. This is discussed in detail in Chapter 8.

The Ruanda-Urundi Union

The two territories now constituting the independent states of Rwanda and Burundi were formerly administered by Belgium as one unit under the League of Nations mandate, on the same principle as Southwest Africa. The mandate provided that the Belgian government could set up a customs, fiscal, or monetary union, could institute administrative arrangements, or could establish a federation with the adjacent territory of the Congo. In 1925, the Belgian government passed a law under which Ruanda-Urundi was united with the Belgian Congo for the purposes of administration, and a de facto common market of these two units and the Eastern Congo was established.

Subsequently, the two territories were each administered by the "Mwami," who was in charge of "native" affairs. In other areas, of cooperation the two countries formed one economic unit with one currency and common market area. The countries also were linked with the Eastern province of Congo (Kinshasa), which also was under

Belgian rule. There was free movement of capital, labor, and other
services. With the coming of independence, Ruanda-Urundi split into
two separate states, Rwanda and Burundi.

PAN-AFRICANISM AND
MULTINATIONAL COOPERATION

Cooperation among the African countries has long been accepted
as an effective instrument for consolidating the African stand vis-à-
vis the advanced nations of the world, especially the former metropolitan powers. There is evidence of the movement toward African
unity even as early as the nineteenth century. However, the period
in which the concept of African unity actually was given concrete
expression started with the birth of Pan-Africanism, which is the
concept used in the early days of the struggle for independence to
denote the movement toward self-rule and self-determination of the
African people. It expressed the desire of the Africans to rule themselves. It is believed that, although the term appears to have originated in America, it was given its political significance in Nyasaland
(Malawi) and South Africa by Joseph Booth, a Baptist missionary, and
subsequently by John Chilembwe, a political hero of Malawi, himself
a missionary.[4]

The African countries under colonial rule experienced great
hardship and oppression. The deep feelings of dispossession, inferi-
ority, discrimination, and loss of dignity and freedom that resulted
from the treatment of Africans by the European settlers gradually
mounted into a crescendo. The Africans realized that they had a
common enemy to fight--the colonial powers--and that the only way
in which the African personality could be projected was through the
overthrow of the "white masters." This recognition therefore created
a feeling of belonging--a feeling of brotherhood and common bondage
among the African people. Pan-Africanism was therefore a political
instrument rather than a tool for economic development.

The first real step toward unity was the meeting of the Pan-
African Congress in Paris in 1919. This meeting was concerned with
the improvement of the welfare of the African people under colonial
rule. A resolution adopted at this meeting called upon the allied and
associated powers to establish an international code of law for the
protection of the welfare of the "natives" of Africa. The meeting also
called on the League of Nations to establish a permanent bureau
charged with the special duty of ensuring the application of such laws
to the political, social, and economic welfare of the African people.

Another Pan-African Congress, held in Manchester in 1945, recommended the establishment of a West African Economic Union. The meeting noted that there had been systematic exploitation of the economic resources of the West African territories by the "imperialist powers" to the detriment of the economic and social welfare of the indigenous people. It also noted that the participation of the indigenous people in the industrial development of West Africa had been deliberately discouraged and obstructed by the colonial powers, resulting in the perpetuation of the low standard of living of the African people. The meeting further reaffirmed the desire of the African people to map out their own destiny in terms of political, social, economic, and cultural development.

The Bandung Declaration of 1955 adopted by the Afro-Asian Conference also reiterated the need to promote economic cooperation among the African countries. It was held that friendly cooperation in accordance with the principles of the Bandung Declaration would effectively contribute to the maintenance and promotion of international peace and security; and that cooperation in the economic, social, and cultural fields would enhance the economic development of Africa.

The first conference of the leaders of the political parties in Africa was held in Accra in December 1958 and decided to establish a permanent organization, the All-African Peoples Conference. Its objectives were: (1) to promote understanding and unity among the peoples of Africa; (2) to accelerate the liberation of all Africa from imperialism and colonialism; (3) to mobilize world opinion in support of African liberation and to formulate concrete means and methods to achieve that objective; and (4) to develop a feeling of one community among the peoples of Africa, with the object of enhancing the emergence of a United States of Africa. The conference placed great emphasis on the question of economic development as a means of consolidating the independence of the African states from colonial powers. There was a general fear that such powers might plan to substitute economic exploitation for political domination, thereby robbing the newly won independence of African states of its true meaning.

In the field of economic development, it was recognized that the promotion of industrialization and the introduction of agrarian reforms aimed at lifting the masses from subsistence through the modernization of agriculture were logical steps toward such development. In the field of trade, the resolution recommended: (1) the removal of customs and other trade restrictions between the African states; (2) the gradual liberalization of intra-African trade and the conclusion of multilateral payments agreements, with a view to

enhancing economic exchanges and the consequent setting up of an
African Common Market; and (3) the formation of an African Transport Company, for land, sea, and air transportation, to promote trade
among the African states. In other fields of economic development,
it was recommended that regular meetings of economic and finance
ministers should be held in order to coordinate the economic policies
of the African countries. The conference further recommended the
creation of an African Investment Bank and an African Institute for
Research and Training, to promote the development of joint projects.

The second meeting of the All-African Peoples Conference,
held in Tunis in January 1960, endorsed the recommendations adopted
at the first conference and especially emphasized the need for the
African states to work toward economic cooperation. The third All-
African Peoples Conference, held in Cairo in March 1961, particularly
called for the signing of multilateral customs and foreign trade agreements in order to increase exchanges of goods and to strive for the
creation of an African Common Market. Although the need for cooperation in the economic, political, and cultural fields as a means of
strengthening African solidarity and enhancing the economic development of the African countries was fully recognized by the Pan-
African movement, it was not until the late 1950's and early 1960's
that the concept of economic cooperation was given concrete expression. Up to the time of independence, the African peoples, still under
colonial oppression, could not effectively organize themselves into
strong economic or political groupings. It can be noted from the
preceding paragraphs that all the early meetings of the Pan-African
Congress were held outside Africa, and it was only after the attainment of independence by some African states that such meetings were
held on African soil. Furthermore, the basic aim of these meetings
was to intensify the political struggle for independence for those
countries still under colonial rule. As a result, economic development, although of vital importance, could not constitute the principal
policy objectives at that time.

The form of economic cooperation envisaged under Pan-
Africanism was clearly summed up by Nnandi Azikiwe, then Governor-
General of Nigeria, in an address delivered to a meeting of the Committee of African Organizations held in London in August 1961. He
suggested that the African countries promulgate a Convention on
Economic Cooperation that would provide that the member countries
establish a customs union. He further suggested that the formation
of an African Common Market was another economic factor that could
bring about political unity in Africa, and that a common currency for
all countries in Africa should be one of the instruments for achieving
unity. In the field of transport and communications, he envisaged
the formation of a regional road authority, a trans-African railway

system, a telecommunications authority, and a Pan-African Airways.
These developments, he held, formed an integral part of African
unity.

In the link between political and economic development in Africa,
it is essential to point out that, at the time the idea of Pan-Africanism
was given birth, economic cooperation did not feature prominently as
a means of achieving such unity. This was largely because the political emancipation of the peoples of Africa and the consolidation of the
territorial integrity of newly independent states were the prime
concerns of the African leaders. However, after a large number of
African countries had achieved their independence the situation changed
from the fight for political freedom to the need for reconstruction of
the African economies. The need to enhance the rate of economic
progress throughout Africa in order to combat poverty, ignorance,
and disease soon became the major preoccupation of the African
people. But it was soon found that the individual efforts of the African
countries could not induce sufficiently rapid rates of development to
achieve this noble objective. What was needed was to ensure concerted
action by all the African countries through regrouping into more
viable economic units.

Pan-Africanism, however well-conceived it might have been,
failed to bring the African states together in the form orginally
envisaged. In fact, its moving spirit survived only up to the attainment
of independence, because following independence the unifying spirit--
the fight against colonial powers--was no longer strong in some
African states. Therefore, where the spirit of Pan-Africanism failed
to transcend the African states' passionate desire to preserve their
national sovereignty and power of self-determination, there was hope
that economic integration would succeed. The desire to raise living
standards and the politicians' attempts to fulfill their pledges to
improve the economic welfare of the masses soon caused some leaders
in the independent African countries to lose sight of the necessary
link with their brother Africans in other independent states. Moreover, Pan-Africanism failed to translate itself into concrete proposals
for unity because most of the African people conceived African unity
through the political media. It was supposed that, once a kind of
Charter of Unity had been laid down and accepted by the African
leaders, it would be easy to cooperate in fields of economic development. It was not realized then that geographical, cultural, ethnic,
and economic considerations could constitute formidable obstacles
to African unity. What was forgotten was the very important fact
that for any unity to be fruitful there had to be a strong economic
base that would form the common denominator between the African
countries. After the fight for freedom and the spirit of African
nationalism had apparently faded out of the minds of some of the

African leaders, a vacuum was created that could be filled up only by joint economic development efforts.

THE AFRICAN CONCEPT OF
MULTINATIONAL ECONOMIC COOPERATION

Economists have defined economic integration in numerous different ways. Some economists seek to make a clearcut distinction between economic integration and economic cooperation by stating that whereas the former implies the elimination of trade restrictions, the latter denotes the suppression of such discriminatory practices as usually are embodied in trade agreements.[5] Other economists argue that there cannot be integration without cooperation, and that they are merely two sides of the same coin. Therefore, if one proceeds from the premise that both economic integration and economic cooperation are means to an end and not ends in themselves, this distinction becomes merely of academic importance. In practice, there is no clear line of demarcation between them. For this reason, most economists argue that the process of economic integration would, at various stages in its development, embrace some aspects of economic cooperation efforts, such as the establishment of free trade arrangements, customs unions, common markets, and full-fledged economic unions in which wide areas of economic activities are integrated. However, to facilitate the analysis that follows, it is essential at this juncture to examine the definition of economic integration, especially in light of the African conditions.

In ordinary language, to integrate means to bring parts of an object into a complete whole. In economic usage, however, the term would imply, in its narrow sense, the coordination of economic activities within a country for purposes of enhancing the development of that country. Taken in this sense, the economic planning of a country is a process of integration in which the factors of production are directed and coordinated toward the goal of economic prosperity. (For instance, in such countries as India there are national integration plans aimed at coordinating the activities of given sectors of the economy for the purpose of enhancing general economic development.) In its wider sense, economic integration implies the process of coordination of various economies in a given area or region into one single unit for purposes of regional economic development. The process of economic integration implies the pursuit of common economic development policies, at least in the major sectors of common interest, to the mutual advantage of all the participating states.

In the African context the term needs to be redefined to suit
present conditions. The peculiarity of the characteristics of the
African economies and the evolution of political and other institutions
make it unrealistic to apply the term in the same sense as is used in
the developed countries. We shall therefore define the term economic
integration as a process whereby two or more countries in a particular
area voluntarily join together to pursue common policies and objectives
in matters of general economic development or in a particular
economic field of common interest to the mutual advantage of all the
participating states. The essence of this definition is that any scheme
of economic integration must be voluntary and that each state must
demonstrate its willingness to pursue certain policies in close
consultation with the other states. Economic integration in Africa
must be sufficiently elastic to accommodate political aspirations
while taking into account such opportunities as may exist for the
formation of a common market, a payments union, a customs union,
a free trade area, or an economic union. Taken in this sense, economic integration will have to be broadly based and wide in its
application, at least in the initial stages, and sufficiently flexible in
its practical form to embody any social, cultural, political, and economic considerations.

This definition is appropriate because the development of the
economic, social, and political institutions in most countries of the
world, particularly in Africa, has become so complex and involved
that it is futile to try to draw a clear line of demarcation between
them. It is essential that the African countries be quite clear at the
outset as to what they understand by economic integration, and it is
equally important to try to marry the economic propositions with
political dogma. The main reason for this is that it is often difficult
in Africa today to consider economic development problems without
considering the political realities. In the past, it has not been rare
for political problems to make impossible any joint development
proposals, no matter how plausible. This political element is particularly important because economic policies must get the blessing
of the politicians before they can be implemented; as will be noted
in Chapter 9, where political considerations clash with economic
considerations the former usually prevail.

In the developing countries, governments have been forced to
take control of the machinery for planning for economic development
because of such factors as the need to redistribute the wealth and
the desire to channel the factors of production into the most advantageous uses; the need to redistribute income in a more equitable
way; the desire to step up the rate of economic progress to meet the

growing needs of the masses; and the desire to fight ignorance, poverty, and disease. In other words, the laissez-faire type of economy has not been entirely suitable for the African countries because of the concentration of economic power in the hands of a few foreigners. The state has therefore found it necessary to establish firm control of economic policy decisions in order to ensure that the benefits of industrial progress, economic advancement, and indeed the "fruits of independence" are evenly distributed among all the inhabitants of the country. For this reason, the relationship between economics and politics is much more pronounced in Africa than anywhere in the western countries or even in other developing regions of the world. Moreover, the existence of international financial institutions that deal mainly with governments rather than private individuals has increased the rate at which the economic decision-making machinery is being taken over by the state in the newly independent African nations. The relationship between political and economic institutions in Africa may become even more pronounced if the current trend toward the one-party system of government firmly gains ground.

In the initial stages of the process toward economic integration in Africa, the acceptance of the need for joint efforts would be enhanced if integration were confined to the development of somewhat separate individual projects, such as inter-state railways and roads, agricultural projects, hydroelectricity, irrigation projects, and social developement projects involving only a few countries.* At this stage of economic development in Africa it is difficult to envisage any economic projects in which a large number of countries could participate more directly. Hence, the process must involve a few countries or combinations of countries as a nucleus and gradually spread to include other states in a particular area. When the idea of cooperation has fully developed in the minds of the African people and when it has been recognized that economic integration or cooperation is not only desirable but necessary if the rate of advancement in Africa has to be stepped up rapidly, one can envisage wider integration with a certain degree of success involving larger areas, more complex industries, and a greater number of countries. The reason for this rather cautious approach is the fact that the need for closer cooperation in economic development comes at a time when the African people have just freed themselves from colonial rule and when a

---

*It would, however, be advantageous to have as many countries as possible participate in economic integration of a given area because after certain projects are under way it would be more difficult for some countries to join. The experience of Britain's application to the EEC is relevant to this argument.

number of countries in Africa are still under foreign domination.
In fact, the economic base for economic cooperation has not yet been
laid down in Africa. This has made it difficult for the people to
appreciate fully the implications of integration and has caused
some countries to hesitate before committing themselves to agreements about which they understand very little.

Furthermore, because the African states achieved independence
at different times, some states are more developed, while others
have lagged behind. Hence, any move to unite forces, unless
clearly understood by the leaders and their people, is bound to be
accepted with mixed feelings. For this reason, many of the economic associations created during the colonial period were hastily
broken up at the time of independence.

Thus, we must conclude that economic integration in Africa
cannot be achieved by merely setting up codes or signing charters;
recent experience at OAU and even at UNCTAD has demonstrated
beyond doubt that integration cannot be achieved by merely passing
resolutions. What is more, there is no machinery for enforcing
such resolutions among members. The preoccupation of the African
leaders has been and will continue to be the attainment of a high rate
of economic growth in the national economies. Consequently, any
scheme that tends to jeopardize the national interests is bound to be
unacceptable to the African countries. This means that economic
integration will have to be worked out cautiously, step-by-step, until
the African people become fully adjusted to the idea of the existence
of a supranational authority to which their national economies and
national policies must be geared.

During the colonial administration, attempts were made to
foster economic cooperation between groups of countries but the
metropolitan powers were interested primarily in collecting raw
materials for export to Europe and controlling the importation of
manufactures into their colonies. The building of infrastructure,
such as roads, railways, and waterways, was oriented toward these
colonial interests. The situation changed considerably with the
attainment of independence by several African countries, and the
question of economic development acquired special significance. It
was immediately realized that it was essential to establish economic
independence because political would not have true meaning so long
as major economic decisions affecting the development of Africa
were still controlled by the former metropolitan powers. The newly
independent African countries were dismayed to discover that small
domestic markets posed a serious obstacle to the application of
technological innovations of modern economies. Moreover, the acute
shortage of skilled and trained manpower together with the general

inadequacy of the necessary infrastructure for economic development frustrated the efforts of individual African countries to enhance their peoples' standards of living. Under these circumstances, it was only logical to think that economic cooperation would provide the necessary basis for meeting the challenges to economic development.

Although the independent African states still regarded political unity as their ultimate goal, the immediate attainment of such unity presented serious problems. The differences in political institutions and in the level of development were formidable constraints to the attainment of political unity. It was soon recognized that a common base or denominator on which to build African unity had to be found. In other words, the problem was not that of reaching agreement as regards the necessity for unity but that of reaching agreement on how to attain unity. Although the answer to this problem was not the same in the minds of the various African leaders, it soon became clear that economic development through cooperation offered a concrete formula both for consolidating newly won independence and for strengthening the ties between the various states. During the early stages of the movement toward economic cooperation, some African states envisaged multinational cooperation on an all-African basis. In other words, the proponents of political unity, having shifted from the concept of total African unity, thought it possible to initiate projects in which all the independent African states could participate and in which the aspirations of the individual countries could find adequate expression. The resolutions adopted at the earlier conferences of independent African states clearly show that there was a belief that economic development policies embracing all African countries could be devised.

The movement toward regional cooperation was manifested during the First Conference of Independent African States, held in Accra in April 1958, at which the African leaders recognized the need for promoting between the African states economic cooperation based on the exchange of technical, scientific, and educational information, with special regard to industrial planning and agricultural development. The meeting recommended the establishment of a Joint Economic Research Committee, composed of representatives of all independent African states, to be assisted by economic research committees set up within each country to survey that country's economic conditions.

The tasks of the Joint Economic Research Committee were to include the following: to find measures whereby trade among the African countries could be developed and encouraged; to make a detailed investigation of the possibility of coordinating economic planning in each state toward the achievement of all-African economic cooperation; to find ways and means for adopting common industrial

planning procedures within the African states and to examine the
possibility of making joint development of the mineral resources
and other products of the African states; to coordinate the exchange
of information and views on economic and technical matters among
the various independent African states; and to strengthen the cooperation of the African states with the specialized agencies of the United
Nations, and especially the then newly established Economic Commission for Africa.

The idea of economic cooperation was buttressed by the resolutions adopted at the Second Conference of Independent African
States, held in Addis Ababa in June 1960. This conference stressed
the need for creating an organization to be known as the African
Council of Economic Cooperation. The conference also recommended
the establishment of a joint African Development Bank and a joint
African Commercial Bank. It was recommended that, when the
African Council of Economic Cooperation was established, it should
call a committee of experts to review the tariff structure within the
African states and propose concrete measures for the improvement
of customs tariffs administration and for a system of preferential
tariffs among the African states.

The early inter-governmental groupings--such as the Brazzaville
Group, the Casablanca Powers, and the Monrovia Group--aimed at
the creation of one African economic institution. For example, the
African Charter of Casablanca provided for the establishment of the
African Economic Committee, which would be responsible for taking
decisions with regard to economic cooperation in Africa. The
Monrovia Group, on the other hand, adopted a resolution calling for
the promotion of economic cooperation throughout Africa based on
tolerance and solidarity but not the acceptance of one leader for all
of Africa. These resolutions were the ultimate expression of African
aspirations.

However, the complexity of the problems within various states,
the geographical location of the independent countries, cultural and
ethnic considerations, fears of political domination by some of the
African states, and differences in the general level of economic
development rendered impossible the attainment of economic cooperation embracing all the African countries. It was soon recognized
that under existing conditions even economic cooperation could be
achieved only gradually and that, at least in the initial stages, such
cooperation would have to be initiated in a few countries from which
further development would be envisaged. The newly established
governments had to be given ample time to adjust their domestic
policies to fit the multinational set-up, particularly since there was
virtually no economic interdependence or complementarity between

the states. Moreover, as noted earlier, the existing trade and transport structures were oriented toward the establishment and the
strengthening of trade and other economic links with the former
metropolitan powers. To break these traditional links meant dealing
with unknown obstacles. Some African countries were therefore very
cautious, and the old counsel that it is better to deal with the devil
one knows prevailed over their other feelings.

THE RATIONALE FOR
MULTINATIONAL ECONOMIC COOPERATION

In recent years, there has been wide acceptance of economic
cooperation or regional integration as the most effective method of
enhancing economic development in the less developed countries.
Economic cooperation as a tool for economic development does not
have the same impact in the developed countries that it does in the
developing countries. For example, among the developed countries
economic cooperation may be desirable in order to regulate the flow
of certain goods and services or to ensure a monopoly in the production and marketing of certain products. Even in the private sector,
cartels and combines are frequently used to ensure that concerted
action by the investors yields the highest possible returns. In contrast, in the African countries, it has been recognized that there is
an urgent need to consolidate the small and fragmented economies
into more viable economic units through economic cooperation in
order to accelerate the rate of economic development.

Due to the absence of manufacturing industries, the African
countries still depend on the export of primary commodities for a
major portion of their incomes. In most of the African countries,
economic power still lies largely in the hands of the former metropolitan powers. Poverty, ignorance, and disease persist in areas where
some development has taken place as well as in areas where natural
resources remain unexploited. Industrial and agricultural production
is characterized by low productivity, with regard to both labor and
capital. Technological advancement in modern industries requires
the use of expensive and complicated capital equipment, which
precludes the individual African countries from setting up virtually
all categories of heavy industry. Under these conditions, the economic breakthrough that is necessary to set the African economies
on the path to self-sustained growth can be achieved only through
coordinated efforts among the African countries.

The need for economic cooperation among the African countries
is stressed in the United Nations Economic Commission for Africa
study of the rate of economic development in Africa.[6] The study

begins by assuming that average per capita income is $100 in develop-
ing Africa, representing the low-level developing countries; $1,500
in the middle-level developed countries, such as the United Kingdom
or France; and $3,000 in the high-level developed countries such as
the United States or Sweden. The study then poses the question of
how long it would take the African countries to reach the income
level of the developed countries. The answer is extremely interesting:
assuming that the per capita income in the African countries continues
to grow at 1 percent per annum, which is quite realistic, it would
take these countries some 273 years to reach the present income
level in the middle-level developed countries and some 343 years to
reach the income level in the high-level developed countries. Moreover, assuming that income in the developed countries also grew at
the rate of 1 percent per annum over the same period, the gap between
them and developing Africa would widen. This is certainly an over-
simplification of the economic potential of the African countries, and
it is based on the assumption that income would grow at a constant
rate. However, the fact remains that, if the present gap between the
levels of development in the African and the developed countries is
to be considerably narrowed within a reasonable period of time, the
African countries must make additional efforts to increase the
opportunities for economic development.

In order to raise the standard of living within the developing
countries during the second development decade, the United Nations
proposes an average growth rate of at least 6 percent in overall
gross domestic product (GDP) and 3.5 percent in per capita GDP, as
well as growth rates of 8 percent in manufacturing output, and about
7 percent in imports and exports.[7] In recommending 6 percent as
the target overall growth rate for the developing countries, the United
Nations proposed that development strategy be so devised as to enable
these countries to attain a higher rate of growth in the second half
of the second development decade, a rate to be specified on the basis
of a review made in 1975. This target would be a broad indication
of the scope for the concerted efforts to be made during the following
decade at the national and international levels through economic
cooperation. However, the proposed strategy would recognize the
responsibility of each developing country to set its own growth target
in the light of its own circumstances.

It is recommended that the growth rate of the overall sectors
in terms of per capita GDP be about 3.5 percent, with the possibility
of accelerating this rate during the second half of the decade in the
light of the overall increase in the targets suggested above. In countries with very low per capita incomes, the UN study proposed that
efforts be made to double income within 20 years. The 3.5 percent
per capita growth target was suggested on the assumption that the

rate of population growth in the developing countries would be no
more than 2.5 percent annually and on the recognition that each
developing country has the right to formulate its own demographic
objectives within the framework of its national development plan.
An average annual growth rate of 8 percent for the manufacturing
industry was recommended as essential to sustain this rate of overall
growth. The recommendations concerning social objectives related
to employment, education, health, nutrition, housing, and the involvement of youth in the development process, call for measures to
significantly reduce unemployment and under-employment during the
decade; for the enrollment in schools of all children of primary-
school age; and for expanded and improved housing facilities, especially for low-income groups.

For most African countries, it would be impossible to attain
these proposed targets without considerable outside assistance in
terms of capital resources, technical know-how, and skilled manpower.
In some countries, even assuming that these factors were available,
the size of the market would militate against expanding the rate of
development, unless several markets were combined through economic cooperation. This fact strengthens the case for economic
cooperation in Africa.

Economic cooperation acquires special significance for a
number of reasons: (1) a large portion of the population is below a
subsistence level; (2) the level of industrial development is very low
compared with other countries of the world and agriculture predomi-
nates both in overall economic activities and in the volume and value
of exports; and (3) an undeveloped traditional rural sector exists
side by side with a relatively advanced urban sector and the low
general rate of economic developement in the agricultural sector
tends to slow down the overall rate of development. In view of all
these factors, a country must expend vast capital and technical
resources to achieve and sustain a minimum rate of development
and such resources often are beyond the reach of any one country.
Under such conditions, the path toward development lies in cooperation at all levels to ensure that the resources are exploited in the
best interest of the African countries. Thus, the arguments for
economic cooperation in Africa center around the possibilities of
expanding the domestic markets, increasing industrial opportunities,
diversifying agricultural production, and expanding inter-African
trade.

One of the foremost advocates of economic integration in the
sense used in Africa today is Paul Rosenstein-Rodan, who advocated
the application of considerable investment over a wide area comprising
the whole of south and southeastern Europe.[8] In his view, the

institutional framework of the countries was responsible for the
economic backwardness of Europe in the 1940's; this is much the
case in Africa today, where the traditional institutions have been
largely responsible for the slow rate of economic progress.

Paul Rosenstein-Rodan suggested the formation of a political
and economic union for the whole of south and southeastern Europe.
(This could perhaps be regarded as a forerunner of the present
European Economic Community and the Council for Mutual Economic
Assistance, COMECON.) He believed that the need for large applications of capital investment arises as a result of various technical
indivisibilities and external economies. In the developing countries,
the indivisibility of the production function, especially in the supply
of social overhead capital, causes investments to be less profitable
if undertaken by any individual state, largely due to the limitations
in the domestic market. When it is possible for any individual state
in the developing region to undertake large applications of capital
investment, what is called excess capacity or under-utilization of
plant capacity results. To avoid excess capacity, extensive participation in capital investments by a large number of countries is recommended. This argument is relevant to the African situation not only
because it has been difficult for any single state to obtain large
amounts of capital funds from the developed countries but also because,
even where this has been possible, the application of such capital in
isolation often has been uneconomic and wasteful due to the very
underdeveloped nature of the markets. There is considerable excess
capacity in most of the basic industries in Africa, and in some cases
production units are operating below 50 percent of capacity. This is
a very serious situation, and to correct it would call for coordinated
planning and the distribution of capital and its application over a
wider area involving more than one state.

The second setback to economic progress that Paul Rosenstein-
Rodan recognized was the indivisibility of the demand function (or
lack of complementarity), which makes individual investments very
risky due to uncertainty regarding the possibility of finding a market.
This recognition prompted him to advocate the participation of various
governments and international agencies in the investment of capital
over a wide range of industries on a large scale. The arguments
also apply to Africa, where large masses of people live under a subsistence level and where, unless large doses of income are pumped
into the African economies to increase the effective demand, any
individual effort to accelerate the rate of economic progress is
bound to be very limited indeed. It follows therefore that piecemeal
investments will not solve the problems of economic development.

The rate of investment in Africa is generally very low even

compared with other developing countries of the world. According to Ragnar Nurkse, this low investment rate has been due to the low savings rate among the African people, which resulted from low incomes. He further argues that the low incomes are due to low productivity, which results from the low rate of investment due to lack of capital resources, which in turn results from the low rate of savings. This is what Nurkse calls the vicious circle of poverty.9 Any one of the elements in the vicious circle is a serious constraint to development in Africa. Because of this circle of poverty, the African countries in general achieve no substantial rate of economic progress. In other words, any individual effort to accelerate the rate of economic development is like a horse tied to a post--it runs at great speed only to find itself in the same place.

How can the process of economic development be initiated in a situation of this kind so as to enable a country to break through these constraints? Ragnar Nurkse suggests the application of capital investments over a wide range of projects so that the workers of one industry become the consumers of other industries. In a way, this is a refinement of the principle of division of labor developed by Adam Smith. The only limitation to this proposition is that in the African countries the ability for any individual country to diversify invest- ments is so limited that, working in isolation, no development efforts can be sufficient to push the economy out of the vicious circle. What is required is to consolidate the small economies into more viable economic units that would permit the diversification of production both in industry and agriculture.

Thus, in order to attract more capital resources the African investment market must be made more attractive. Where investment decisions still are governed largely by profit motives, there is need to assure the foreign investors of a fair return on their capital out- lays. Needless to say, no single African country is capable of giving this guarantee, especially with regard to the establishment of large- scale industries. Only when the economies are integrated and when risk can be spread over a wide area will the foreign investors be attracted to invest.

Modern technology tends toward specialization, with production carried out by specialized production units employing special and complicated machinery and technical know-how. If Africa is to survive the sharp competition from the advanced countries and if the African economies are to be geared to modern technology, suitable conditions for specialization and large-scale production must be created. With wider market opportunities, it is possible to separate production into specialized processes that ultimately could develop into new industries. There is general consensus among economists

that the African economies have great potential for introducing specialization that could be utilized to the greatest advantage of all Africa.
It can be argued that, even though the African economies by and
large depend upon primary commodities, these products are distributed
in a pattern that could form the basis for specialization. For example,
some countries produce cotton while others produce copper; some
produce coffee or cocoa while others produce timber or iron ore.
Hence, division of labor could be achieved. In fact, even where many
countries produce the same raw materials these could be absorbed
by one industry catering to a group of countries. A typical example
of an industry where specialization could be achieved is the cotton
textile industry.

Thus, certain industries would be allocated to the particular
country within the integrated area that is most suited or has the
greatest advantage in the production of a particular commodity. This
would have to be done on the basis of mutual agreement providing
for the opening up of local markets for that commodity in the
other states. The problem that would arise here is that of determining
the basis for allocation of the industries, which will be discussed at
length in Chapter 5. For the present, it is sufficient to say that the
countries could work out an acceptable solution by taking into account
compensatory factors to balance the short-term disadvantages
resulting when any state leaves a particular industry to the more
suited country.

The ultimate goal of the integrated states should be to achieve
the spread of industrial development and the distribution of benefits
from such industrial progress to all the participating states, thereby
avoiding the concentration of industries in any one particular country. The pattern of industrial development of Africa at present is
dotted by economic islands and the benefits of economic advancement
are enjoyed by only a few. The reallocation of industry, when equitably
achieved, would result in external economies of scale that could be
passed on to the other states in the form of cheaper commodities.
Modern technology also has demonstrated that certain industries
cannot be profitably operated below a given size; this is what is
called the "optimum size" in economic terminology.[10] It simply
means that the cost of one unit of production tends to rise higher than
revenue returns if output is below the optimum level. This optimum
size is becoming so large in most modern industries that no individual
state can afford to set up such industries. This is another strong
reason why it is particularly imperative to initiate a comprehensive
and coordinated planning program involving a number of states.

Various agencies interested in the economic development
problems in Africa have realized that the appropriate strategy for

economic development is through the integration of the various economies to make it viable to establish large-scale industries. The United Nations Economic Commission for Africa has done considerable research on the possibility of integrating the economies of particular regions in Africa. The ECA argues that the harmonization of industrial development programs aiming at overall industrial development for an entire subregion or a group of countries is the answer to the problems of economic development in Africa. The African states themselves must now demonstrate their willingness and capability to work together in close consultation in order to achieve a higher objective. Industrial development formed the basis for rapid economic progress in the now developed countries, and in Africa the long-term objective should be industrial development.

We can now sum up the arguments in favor of economic cooperation in Africa as follows:

1. Economic cooperation is an essential means of accelerating the rate of economic development, and especially of enhancing efficiency in industry. Due to limitations in the size of their national markets, most African countries cannot establish optimum-sized industries that would be capable of withstanding the competition from overseas industries. Even if protection is granted to any such industries, the result will only be to reduce incentives for increasing efficiency. Within the integrated area, individual industries must advance to the stage where they are able to compete with each other. A wider market would sustain a larger number of more efficient industries and would also permit the establishment of heavy industry.

2. Economic cooperation would enable the countries to benefit from economies of scale. Economic diversification through industrialization can be achieved more effectively through coordination of the economic activities in the various countries. It has sometimes been argued that a country's size would not necessarily bar it from attaining a high standard of living. Several countries in Europe, such as Sweden, have been cited as examples. But in the African context the situation is rather different: in contrast to the situation in the developed countries, the national boundaries in Africa pose a real obstacle to the movement of factors of production. In the absence of cooperation, these countries are closed in by tariffs and other trade restrictions. Furthermore, because of the great strides in technological advancement, most of the small African countries are automatically precluded from establishing certain categories of industry. The expansion of markets through cooperation would also enable some existing industries to expand, as would doses of external capital injected into the economies as a whole.

3. Economic cooperation is an essential element in reducing the vulnerability of the African countries to external influences. The high degree of reliance on a few commodities for export earnings in these countries means that their domestic trade policies cannot be totally independent of the trade and development policies in the advanced countries. Fluctuations in the prices of primary products and large increases in imports of manufactured goods render the African countries particularly vulnerable to external influences. In order to change this pattern, the development of industries geared to the manufacture of consumption goods for these countries is a necessary policy objective. This argument is especially pertinent with regard to those countries depending on only one commodity or experiencing an adverse balance of trade. In order to advance industrial development to the stage where these countries attain a certain degree of interdependence, a scheme for development of industries on a multinational scale must be agreed upon.

SOME BASIC PREREQUISITES FOR ECONOMIC COOPERATION

Chapter 2 will show that the economic development of any country or group of countries is not a question of chance but the result of deliberate, sustained efforts, the drive or enthusiasm to improve the economic conditions, and the capability of any given country to take advantage of industrial development and the market structures. Therefore, a country that wishes to develop must strive to create the necessary conditions for such development. In economic cooperation, the capacity to exploit opportunities that come about as a result of the integration of several markets is a major element in achieving the maximum benefits of such cooperation. In addition, the countries wishing to cooperate must fulfill certain basic requirements if the results of such cooperation are to justify the people's efforts. There is no hard and fast rule as to what countries ought to do to create a favorable climate for cooperation; each type or level of cooperation may call for specific measures to be determined according to the main objective of the economic association.

In the case of countries wishing to establish a new economic grouping, there must be absolute certainty as to what the countries seek to achieve. The levels of economic development or industrialization within the prospective partner countries must be studied carefully to determine the areas where there are great disparities and to suggest immediate and long-term measures to correct any such imbalances. If a common market is envisaged, there must be detailed analytical studies of the market structures, transport facilities, customs duties and other trade restrictions, and the general commercial laws and practices of the prospective partners. A carefully worked-out program for coordination would enable the participating states to determine at any stage whether they are indeed moving toward their declared objectives. Some of these requirements will be discussed in detail in subsequent chapters; what must be emphasized here is that an important element of cooperation is not only the willingness of all the partner states to take appropriate policy measures to make such cooperation a success but also the ability of each country to exploit the new development opportunities that may be created. Political will power and sustained adherence to joint decisions also are vital to economic cooperation. It has been said of the EEC countries that their success has been the result not only of increased opportunities in development but also of the determination of the member countries to survive.

Where a country wishes to join an existing economic grouping, as in the case of Somalia, Ethiopia, Zambia, and all other countries that have expressed interest in joining the East African Community, the basic requirement is that the applicant country determine exactly what it seeks to gain by joining the community. Having decided upon its objectives and the type of membership, it would be essential for the country to make a detailed analytical study of its individual position vis-à-vis the community. For example, if a country is interested only in the transport aspects of the community, it must be prepared to take measures to affect the necessary changes in its own transport system to bring it in line with that of the community. These measures might include amendments in traffic regulations and licensing procedures; with regard to railway transport, such factors as the type of gauge used, locomotive train-brake systems, and the kind of carriages or wagons used must be studied and necessary changes made. If the prospective member country is interested in the common market aspect of the community, such factors as levels of trade, customs legislations, trade restrictions, and levels of customs tariffs must be examined in order to pinpoint any major discrepancies and to determine the effect of the liberalization of trade on the general level of economic activity in the prospective member. Where a country has high customs duties in comparison to those in the economic grouping in which it seeks membership, the question of the removal of certain restrictions or the elimination of customs duties may prove difficult. This is especially true where such customs duties constitute a significant portion of government revenues. It should be understood that the current members of an economic grouping may find it necessary to take certain measures to facilitate the entry of new members, but such measures generally are less extensive than those taken by the new members.

OBSERVATIONS

To conclude this chapter, it is worthwhile to sum up the case for economic integration in Africa. Economic integration as a means of enhancing development has been widely recognized and accepted in recent years both in Africa and other parts of the world. It is now recognized in government circles, international organizations, and private institutions that, due to the small size of the African countries, any one state's individual effort to establish large-scale industries would result not only in high costs of production but also in excess capacity. This is due in part to the fact that the low level of income in the African economies results in low purchasing power and hence low demand. It therefore follows that, in order to advance the rate of economic development appreciably, what is required in Africa is a huge dose of capital resources and skilled manpower, the application of scientific and technical know-how on a wide scale, and the establishment of wider domestic markets resulting from increased investments. This implies a large degree of interdependence among the African countries and the integration of the rather small individual markets into more viable economic units. Some important principles emerge from this conception:

1. Since industrialization is the key to economic development in Africa, it is imperative to set up multinational industries if the developing African countries are to push industrialization beyond a certain point and if they are to avoid wasting of resources through industries of uneconomic size operating below capacity with high costs of production. Hence ways must be found to permit the coordination and utilization of the resources in a wider framework through comprehensive schemes of economic integration or cooperation in such fields as trade, industry, transport, natural resources, manpower training, and agriculture. This would involve primarily the harmonization of national development plans and industrial development policies.

2. The expansion and promotion of trade, especially with the advanced countries, is the main objective of the African countries, but recent experience has shown that the mere expansion of exports of primary commodities is not the whole answer. In other words, if the developing African countries wish to increase appreciably their exports to the markets of the developed countries, they will have to develop exports of manufactures and semimanufactures through the establishment of industries that are not only competitive with those of the developed countries but also can withstand competition from other developing countries. Here again, the answer lies in the coordination

of trading activities and the integration of small markets into larger units. This implies the adoption of uniform trading policies and the liberalization of trade among the African countries.

3. There are great limitations on the extent to which African exports especially manufactured and semimanufactured products, can find markets in the developed countries. Therefore, if the African countries wish to develop external trade faster than at the present rate, efforts should be made to expand trade among the African countries themselves as well as trade with the other developing countries. It is now recognized that a number of factors have tended to reduce considerably the scope for increasing trade between Africa and the developed countries, notably the restrictionist policies adopted by the developed countries against manufactured products from developing countries and the great advance in industrial technology in the developed countries, which has resulted in increased use of synthetics and substitutes and decreased use of raw materials per unit of production. The answer therefore lies in cooperation among the African countries and specialization in production units to ensure an increased exchange of goods among the African countries themselves.

4. Agricultural activities constitute the backbone of the economic development structure in the African countries. It follows that any development efforts that do not give adequate attention to the need for increased agricultural production will fail to provide the necessary push toward self-sustained economic growth. A deliberate policy of rural development together with a new drive for the establishment of agricultural manufacturing and other agro-allied industries should constitute an important objective for most African countries that depend upon agricultural raw materials for the major portion of their export earnings. Possibilities should be explored and opportunities increased for cooperation in the field of agricultural development.

5. In order to buttress economic activities in other sectors, there is an urgent need to develop adequate infrastructure, especially transport and communications to connect the African countries within the existing economic groupings as well as with other adjoining states. The present pattern of transport and communications in Africa reveals serious bottlenecks that physically limit the development of agriculture, industry, and trade. It follows that schemes for joint action should include plans for increased capital investment in the transport sector, at both national and multinational levels. The countries should give priority to the development of transport facilities to cater to increased trade under the new multinational economic cooperation arrangements.

NOTES

1. Adam Smith, Wealth of Nations (edited by Edward Cannan), Vol. I (London: Metheun & Co. Ltd., 1961), p. 21 Adam Smith was the first to propound the idea that specialization in production functions is limited by the size of the market. In other words, the wider the market, the greater the opportunities for economies of scale and vice versa.

2. See Jeremy Raisman, East African Report on the Economic and Fiscal Commission (London: Her Majesty's Stationery Office, Cmnd. 1972 February 1961,) p. 7.

3. See Arthur Hazlewood and P. D. Henderson, Nyasaland: The Economics of Federation (Oxford: Basil Blackwell, 1960).

4. See George Sheeperson and Thomas Price, Independent African (Edinburgh: Edinburgh University Press, 1958).

5. See Bela Balassa, The Theory of Economic Integration (London: George Allen and Unwin Ltd., 1965), pp. 1-2.

6. Economic Commission for Africa, A Survey of Economic Conditions in Africa, 1967, E/CN.14/409/Rev. 1, United Nations, New York, 1969 (Sales No. E 68. II. K. 4) p. 5.

7. See United Nations, International Development Strategy for the Second United Nations Development Decade, General Assembly Resolution, A/RES/2626(XXV) (New York, November, 1970), pp. 4-5. The United Nations refers to "gross product" rather than GDP.

8. See Paul N. Rosenstein-Rodan, "Problems of Industrialization of Eastern and South Eastern Europe," Economic Journal, June-September, 1943 Vol. 53, pp. 202-211.

9. Ragnar Nurkse, Problems of Capital Formation in Under-developed Countries (Oxford: Basil Blackwell, 1962), p. 4.

10. For further details see E. A. G. Robinson, The Structure of Competitive Industry (The Cambridge Economic Handbooks) Cambridge: James Nisbet & Co., Ltd., and the Cambridge University Press, 1958, Chapter 2.

2

**ALTERNATIVE
APPROACHES
TO ECONOMIC
COOPERATION
IN AFRICA**

THE CHOICE

The success of any effort to coordinate the economic activities of several countries in a given grouping depends to a great extent upon whether the countries really know what they wish to achieve through such cooperation and especially on how they seek to achieve their goals. Before deciding upon any particular form of cooperation, it must be recognized that economic cooperation is not achieved for its own sake. This being the case, countries may wish to embark on economic cooperation ventures because of a desire to mitigate general constraints to economic development efforts, such as: the inadequacy of the infrastructure; the low level of economic performance in most of the African countries; the low labor productivity, especially in the field of agricultural development, which keeps the majority of the African population below the subsistence level; and the high capital/output ratio in modern industry. The intensity of these constraints differs from one country to another, as does the approach to resolving them.

In almost all the countries of Africa, great changes in the economic variables occur over a relatively short period of time; it therefore becomes extremely difficult to prescribe solutions to the economic problems that can withstand the test of time. In such a situation, it is possible to envisage a number of alternatives to economic development.

Several economic groupings have sprung up in the African continent in the 1960's, with different concepts of both general economic development and the approach to economic cooperation. In the decision regarding economic development strategy three main approaches to cooperation can be distinguished: the multisectoral approach, the sector-by-sector approach, and the project-by-project approach. Within each of these three approaches a number of combinations are

33

possible, depending upon what a given group of countries wishes to achieve. For instance, some African countries see immediate prospects for cooperation through the development and expansion of trade, others consider transport and communications of special significance, and still other countries envisage cooperation by way of industrialization. The differences in the approach emanate from their understanding and interpretation of the concept of economic cooperation and the way they seek to achieve it. Therefore, the development of institutions for cooperation is greatly influenced by the objectives envisaged.

The choice of the type of cooperation depends upon the degree of collaboration that is permissible within the limitations of national aspirations and environments. For example, if it is the countries' intention to create a free trade area, there is no need for major adjustments in other sectors since a free trade arrangement does not necessarily involve the coordination of economic policies. If, on the other hand, the countries want a customs union or a common market, they must be prepared to coordinate their common policies to ensure freedom of movement of capital, technical know-how, and labor. Similarly, if the countries wish to establish a full-fledged economic union, they must adopt joint policies on industrialization, transport and agricultural development, exploitation of natural resources, fiscal and monetary matters, trade expansion, and manpower training; they must indeed be prepared to take the necessary steps to harmonize their national development plans. The following description of the various approaches gives a general indication of the reasons why countries may prefer one system of economic cooperation to another.

The ECA Approach

Since its inception, the Economic Commission for Africa (ECA) work program has been oriented toward the economic development of Africa through joint African efforts. It has been recognized that economic cooperation on an all-Africa basis would be the ideal step toward the solution of the problems arising from the limitations in the size of the domestic markets especially with regard to the establishment of large-scale industries. However, the problems of transport, communication, and the geographical location of the African countries militated against the creation of a single economic unit consisting of all African countries.

According to ECA, the pragmatic approach to the problems of economic development in Africa seemed to be the creation of subregions that took into account geographical contiguity and ethnic and social considerations. (In United Nations usage, the African continent is a region; a subregion consists of any given group of countries lying within the geographical area of the African region.) Therefore, based on the economic, social, and political conditions in Africa in the early 1960's, ECA recommended the division of the African continent into four subregions, one each for East, Central, West and North Africa.

The East African subregion now consists of twelve countries: Ethiopia, Somalia, Uganda, Kenya, Tanzania, Zambia, Malawi, Malagasy Republic, Mauritius, Botswana, Lesotho, and Swaziland. The Central African subregion includes nine countries: Cameroun, Central African Republic, Congo (Brazzaville), Congo (Kinshasa), Chad, Gabon, Rwanda Burundi, and Equatorial Guinea. The West African subregion has fourteen countries: Nigeria, Ghana, Togo, Dahomey, Niger, Ivory Coast, Upper Volta, Mauritania, Liberia, Sierra Leone, Guinea, Senegal, Mali, and Gambia. The North African subregion comprises six countries: Tunisia, Morocco, Algeria, Libya, the United Arab Republic, and the Sudan. Rwanda and Burundi were originally included in the East African subregion, and they both signed the Terms of Association of the Eastern African Economic Community. However, these two countries are now included in the Central African subregion but they have expressed their wish to participate in the activities of both the East and Central African subregions.

As a means of encouraging fruitful cooperation in Africa, ECA advocated the establishment and strengthening of the institutional framework for cooperation at the multinational level, and this was ECA's major occupation during the 1960's. It has been argued that experience has demonstrated that great emphasis should be put on the identification of potential areas of cooperation among the African countries in all aspects of development at multinational level. Therefore, the encouragement of economic cooperation efforts among the African countries as a means of accelerating the rate of economic development constitutes the main policy approach to the strategy for such development.

The creation of smaller groupings was justified on the ground that an economic grouping consisting of about a dozen countries with somewhat common social, cultural, historical, and economic background could easily develop into a viable unit for purposes of economic development. It was further recognized that it was necessary that each subregional group have a concrete and acceptable program for development of multinational projects and that each member state fully subscribe to such a program. For this purpose, the ECA advocated that clear definitions for determining whether projects were suitable for multinational development should be agreed upon and a set of priorities established for implementation at subregional level.

To understand fully the basis of this approach, it is essential to

MAP 2.1

The ECA Subregions

ECA Headquarters
Subregional Offices
North Africa
West Africa
Central Africa
East Africa

Source: ECA Cartography unit.

examine ECA's terms of reference, which state, inter alia, that ECA
"shall initiate and participate in measures for facilitating concerted
action for the economic development of Africa, including its social
aspects, with a view to raising the level of economic activity and levels
of living in Africa, and for maintaining and strengthening the economic
relations of countries and territories of Africa, both among themselves
and with other countries of the world; to assist in the formulation and
development of coordinated policies as a basis for practical action in
promoting economic and technological development in the region."[1]

In line with the terms of reference, ECA identified the problems
of economic development in the African region. As a means of accelerating the rate of development, multinational cooperation in all fields
of economic activity is considered to be the ideal strategy. The political and economic fragmentation of the African continent resulting from
the creation of small states at the time of independence has hampered
the economic advancement of the African countries. The national
markets are too small to allow the rapid rate of economic expansion
necessary to raise the standard of living. Economic cooperation and
regional integration among the African states are therefore the best
practical means of creating viable economic units in the African region.
Within this framework, a policy approach emerged, therefore, that in
order to lend meaning to economic cooperation the African countries
will have to establish or strengthen their multinational institutional
machinery within which discussions and decisions on common policies
and projects can be made. Such institutions should be given adequate
powers to ensure the implementation of joint decisions.

From ECA's point of view, the essential issues in this approach
were: (1) that each subregional group have an agreed program of multinational development in which each member country would find some
reasonably equitable benefits; (2) that the areas for possible joint programs be studied at a level of technical and economic detail that would
make it possible for groups of countries to negotiate for final commitments toward cooperation; (3) that, as economic cooperation developed
further, the various programs be subject to careful scrutiny so as to
retain the cohesiveness of the subregional group; and (4) that subregioal
economic cooperation presupposed the establishment of joint institutions
for planning and implementing concrete projects at the subregional
level.

These considerations suggested a number of conclusions regarding ECA's work program for the beginning of the next development
decade. In order that cooperation be successful, ECA held the view
that there should be a suitable machinery for joint policy action. In
the final analysis, the countries themselves must take appropriate
action to implement their programs for development. In this regard,

the African countries will have to set up or strengthen the multinational institutional machinery within which they can discuss and make decisions on collective policies and projects. An essential part of the multinational machinery should be a joint civil service organ with the task of advising on the promotion and execution of joint undertakings, and that the African countries should agree on, and find the material means for implementing, any such concrete development projects as would increase economic contacts between their countries.[2] ECA's approach to economic cooperation in the 1960's concentrated on the establishment of subregional institutional arrangements responsible for the joint decisions. Toward the end of the 1960's, however, a shift of emphasis began emerging toward direct assistance to the existing economic groupings in Africa.

The Multisectoral Approach

In the efforts to solve the problems of economic development common to a group of countries, such countries may find it to their mutual advantage to integrate more than one sector at a time. Where this approach to economic integration is desirable, countries might wish to adopt common policies and joint action in the key sectors of their economies but leave out sectors that, due to their nature or through rigidities in domestic policy, are best left for action at the national level.

Some economists speak of a global approach to economic integration, implying that it is feasible or even desirable to have economic cooperation involving all sectors of the economies of a group of countries or an entire continent. This is erroneous and unrealistic because countries may not always find it to their advantage to coordinate activities in all sectors of economic development. Even where economic integration is fairly advanced, as in the EEC, there are still sectors such as agriculture where development takes place largely at the national level. Because of these difficulties, we shall develop the concept of multisectoral approach to economic cooperation. This approach implies that, depending on the levels of development of the intending partners, countries might decide to adopt joint action in a group of sectors where there are immediate or clear advantages for cooperation while reserving other sectors for national action.

The multisectoral approach to integration describes a situation where the key sectors of the various economies in the integrated area are considered in the negotiations for cooperation. The basis of this approach is that, if all key sectors are developed together, the group of countries will move to a higher general equilibrium since the process of economic expansion generated in these sectors will spread to the remaining sectors. The argument is that the multisectoral approach offers a greater chance for adjustments to be made in the various economies so as to counteract any losses resulting from the surrender of any industry to the most suited partner state. There would be a jointly accepted formula for the allocation of multinational projects in the various sectors based on the comparative cost-advantage principle. This would minimize the problem of sharing gains from cooperation because negotiations for allocation of multinational projects among the member countries would generally involve a wider range of such projects.

Both the Central African Customs and Economic Union (UDEAC) and the East African Community (EAC) have adopted the multisectoral approach to integration. In East Africa, there was a discrepancy in the rate of economic development between Kenya on the one hand and Uganda and Tanganyika on the other; hence, the multisectoral approach was regarded as a method of redressing such imbalances, especially in trade and industrial development. The preamble to the EAC Treaty states that the countries became aware that there were differences in the levels of industrialization and that the time had come for them to introduce measures intended to ensure balanced development on the three states.

The UDEAC Treaty, on the other hand, was governed by the desire to extend national markets and coordinate their development programs in order to improve the standard of living of the people of this area. It will thus be noted that, whereas the question of balancing the levels of development was of prime importance to the EAC so as to remove the disparity of industrialization, especially between Tanzania and the other member states, the UDEAC countries sought an equitable distribution of industry as a measure for enhancing the general level of development.

The Maghreb economic cooperation provides another example of the multisectoral approach to integration. There were three possible solutions to the Maghreb's economic integration problems--the minimum solution, the intermediate solution, and the maximum solution.

The minimum solution called for the countries to pledge to work toward the gradual establishment of an economic union. There would be no legal commitments, and cooperation would essentially be limited to regular participation in negotiations on tariff or quota concessions on trade in locally produced goods. In this solution, economic union would have been approached through individual projects.

The intermediate solution would have involved commitments spread over a period of three to five years, during which time the

Maghreb countries would commit themselves to a linear reduction of customs tariffs at an agreed level and of quantitative restrictions on products originating in the Maghreb. The countries enumerated the industries that no Maghreb country would set up without prior consultations with and the approval of the other member countries; the products of such industries would enjoy free circulation and exemption from duties in the Maghreb market. A Maghreb integration bank was established to finance future renovation of existing industries and the establishment of new industries. The harmonization of trade policies toward third countries, so as not to endanger the establishment of a common external tariff at a later stage, was considered the major element of the Maghreb economic union.

The maximum solution would have involved the immediate signing of a treaty instituting the Maghreb economic union, including in particular the development of a schedule for the total elimination of customs duties and quota restrictions; the progressive standardization of external tariffs; the adoption of a common agricultural policy; and the setting up of common institutions with decision powers. The countries did not seem to be ready for this kind of cooperation.

The minimum solution had the advantage of simplicity of application: the yearly negotiations on tariff and trade concessions would deal with each product separately. However, in the absence of a wider perspective, the negotiations on the establishment of new industries would run into difficulties because of the absence of a mechanism for adjustment in the remaining sectors. This problem actually arose with regard to metallurgy, assembly plants, and glassware industries. The maximum solution, which would institute in one move the Maghreb economic union, had the advantage of avoiding the drawbacks inherent in the adoption of the minimum solution. However, the time was not ripe for negotiation of a treaty instituting a Maghreb economic union, with all its supranational implications. Moreover, such negotiations would necessarily extend over a long period, during which time the Maghreb countries, each pursuing its own independent national policy of economic development, might destroy the chances for Maghreb integration.

Accordingly, the Maghreb tried the intermediate solution, which aimed at counteracting some of these problems. It was believed that the intermediate solution had the additional advantage of taking into account special economic situations such as that of Libya. It was a agreed that, if there were no positive results at the end of the period of five years, the way would nevertheless be open to the gradual creation of the Maghreb economic union and the countries would have the chance to choose a more suitable form of cooperation.

The difficulty in the multisectoral approach is that the harmonization of national development plans is an essential feature without which efforts toward the coordination of industrial development could not be easily achieved If the countries intend to adopt this approach, it might be advisable to set up joint planning consultative machinery to direct the common development policies. UDEAC, the East African Community, and the Maghreb do not have machinery for joint planning but merely an expression of their desire to harmonize the development plans (see, for example, Articles 47-50 of the UDEAC Treaty), and the UDEAC Treaty gives very vague powers to the Directing Committee for this purpose. The treaty for East African Cooperation is not explicit in this regard, although it provides for the establishment of an Economic Consultative and Planning Council. (The need for establishing a joint planning has been recognized in East Africa, and new efforts are being made to define the functions of such an organ more clearly.) It must be pointed out here that the vagueness of these treaties in this respect has resulted in difficulties in the adoption of joint industrial development decisions and their implementation.

Another problem arising under the multisectoral approach is the fact that the national development plans were launched at different times, for different objectives, and with different durations. As a result, the harmonization of development plans becomes extremely difficult and even if it were possible it would disturb the planning mechanisms already established. Moreover, in recent years, planning has come to be identified with the political thinking of the leaders in power. Since important economic decisions have gradually shifted to the governments, the setting up of planning priorities may be governed not by economic considerations so much as by the desire to satisfy political aspirations. Another difficulty is that the politicians have not yet accepted the idea of a supranational organ vested with sufficient powers to make decisions binding upon the member states of the economic associations. Even in cases such as the EEC where the foundations of cooperation are fairly well established, the question of multinational planning still poses serious problems.

Multinational planning is difficult to achieve because countries often are less willing to enter into agreements that limit their freedom of action in a wide area of economic activities. Moreover, the problems of geographical location, political considerations, past colonial background, and ethnic and cultural conditions limit the adoption of wider measures for cooperation. Therefore, at this stage it would appear that countries would not normally be ready to adopt extensive plans involving a large number of sectors, although there is evidence of acceptance of the multisectoral approach in some African countries.

The Sector-by-Sector Approach

Because, for various reasons, countries would not be keen to adopt the multisectoral approach, the other alternative to cooperation is the adoption of the sector-by-sector approach. The sectoral approach to integration involves the coordination of policies and development efforts in respect of one particular sector at a time, such as trade, agriculture, industry, or transport. The main principle of this approach is that countries might readily agree to establish the conditions for joint action where only one sector is considered. The countries would seek to integrate a given sector at each successive stage of negotiations, and the participants would be free to make adjustments in the non-integrated sectors. In this way, the countries would be given the opportunity to decide whether to extend cooperation to other sectors.

It is often argued that, through inter-sectoral dynamism, the growth in the integrated sector (or sectors) would lead to growth in the remaining sectors through the expansion of demand for other commodities as a result of forward and backward linkages.[3] For instance, if the industrial sector is integrated, the increase in income of industrial workers would increase their demand for, e.g., such agricultural products as foodstuffs. In this way, the multiplier effect in industry also would generate income in the agricultural sector. There is evidence of wide acceptance of the sectoral approach in a number of economic groupings in Africa, and proposals often are put forward to integrate such individual sectors as industry, transport, trade, and agriculture. The main attraction of this approach lies in the simplicity of cooperation agreements. Countries can cooperate in single sectors while maintaining their power of self-determination in general economic policy decisions. There are numerous instances of sectoral integration in Africa; the OERS, the Niger River Basin Commission, and the Lake Chad Basin Commission are outstanding examples. This approach offers the necessary flexibility to induce the African countries to enter into negotiations for specific sectors.

Typical examples of the sectoral approach to integration are the African countries' efforts toward trade liberalization. The countries within a given economic grouping might set up minimum targets for reduction of trade barriers by identifying specific trade aspects or individual products for which they could commit themselves not to erect barriers to mutual trade and to remove existing trade obstacles. This might be done for the products of existing industries; in the case of products from new industries to be set up, it might be necessary to negotiate a new set of agreements (see Chapter 6). In the scheme for trade liberalization, a given group of countries might find it feasible to formulate certain intermediate targets for complete elimination of trade barriers. Alternatively, they might agree to reduce trade barriers on a selected list of imports from the partner states, especially where customs duties are high, and to establish a ceiling for protection on such imports.

The sectoral approach to integration has its own limitations, and a number of objections to it have been raised. For example, it is argued that simultaneous integration of a number of sectors would provide ample opportunity for making complementary arrangements, whereas measures toward integration in one sector might lead to disturbances of equilibrium in the integrated sector as well as the remaining sectors. Where a country suffers losses because of contraction of production capacity in the newly integrated sector, it normally has no compensation until the next phase of negotiations and there is no guarantee that its position will be improved even at the next round of negotiations.

Moreover, under the sectoral approach every step toward integration tends to result in a new level of prices, costs, and resource allocation and, hence, a new level of equilibrium. It follows therefore that production and investment forecasts made on the basis of a given level of prices will be unrealistic since the equilibrium is disturbed by sudden "jumps" and "shocks" at every phase of negotiations.

Furthermore, sector-by-sector integration places additional burdens on the balance of trade and payments of the partner countries, especially where the integrated sector has high production costs. In such cases, integration is less attractive, particularly if identical products can be obtained from third countries more cheaply. Unless sufficient exchange control measures are introduced, this approach places serious strains on foreign exchange reserves in some partner states while increasing the reserves of other partners. As a result, the less privileged countries might in fact be subsidizing economic activities in the stronger partner states.

In addition, in the absence of proper coordination of monetary, fiscal, and other policies, under the sectoral approach differences in economic policy often could lead to adverse movements of commodities and factors of production, quite often against the least industrialized partner states. For example, an imbalance in the integrated sector would occur if inflationary policies were followed in one country while deflationary policies were adopted in other countries, and any trade restrictions would prevent adjustments in other sectors. Hence, the sectoral approach could operate more successfully where a common market is created.

It is further argued that under the sectoral approach the general wage structure tends to be higher in countries with protective tariffs. This in turn tends to reduce the volume of production and hence reduce employment in the integrated sector. An attempt to freeze the wage rates in the integrated sector could only lead to such undesirable social effects as a reduction in the standard of living. In the African experience, however, it would appear that this form of cooperation is readily acceptable under present conditions if only because it is less involved. The pertinent conclusion is that countries tend to be more willing to enter into limited agreements involving individual sectors that to commit their general economic policy.

The Project-by-Project Approach

There are instances of efforts toward cooperation on the African continent where countries join together in single enterprises. We will call this form of cooperation the project-by-project approach. Under this approach, the countries agree to adopt joint action in the exploitation of a single project in the transport, industrial, or agricultural sectors. The basis of this approach is that, although cooperation at the sectoral level may not be attainable for various reasons, joint efforts still can be initiated even in specific development projects within a given sector. The participating states would retain a large degree of freedom of action insofar as the entire sector is concerned but would cooperate where cooperation brings short- or medium-term advantages. A railway line between two countries is an example of the project level approach in the transport sector. This approach has the further attraction that a single venture can be carried out without elaborate agreements.

There are a number of instances in Africa where countries have preferred the project-by-project approach, largely because it is possible to cooperate without involving high-level political considerations. The OERS, the Council of Understanding (Conseil de l'Entente), the Niger River Basin Commission, and the Lake Chad Basin Commission originally were single venture economic cooperation projects within specific sectors. In East Africa, a good example of this kind of cooperation is the Zambia-Tanzania rail link, a single project in the transport sector. The sugar agreement in the Ocam, the West African Rice Development Association, the African Peanut (Groundnut) Council, and the Cocoa Producers Alliance are instances of single project cooperation in the agricultural sector. The simplicity of these arrangements is not only the great attraction but also accounts for the success of these cooperation efforts.

TYPES AND DEGREES OF MULTINATIONAL COOPERATION IN AFRICA

The nature of the African economies and their historical background provides numerous alternatives for economic cooperation. At the simplest level, one can indentify bilateral trade agreements and

other simple cooperation efforts involving one sector of the economy
or even a single project within a given sector, such as the Association
of African Airlines and the Association of African Central Banks.
Some of these associations do not call for firm commitments on the
part of the member states so long as countries express their willingness
to cooperate. At the highest level of cooperation there are more elaborate forms approximating common markets or economic unions, such
as the East African Community which envisages the coordination of
development policies including consultations in national planning,
industry, agriculture, and transport and communications. Between
these two extremes a variety of combinations have been attempted
among groups of African countries with varying degrees of success.
A general characteristic of the African economic associations is that
they all regard the establishment of a common market between the
member states as a major objective. This interesting phenomenon
is probably explained by the fact that the development of Africa is
seen to depend on the expansion of external trade.

Free Trade Arrangements

A group of countries may wish to enhance the expansion of trade
among them through the elimination of trade barriers. Toward this
end, they may wish to establish a free trade area. In a free trade
area, the member states often agree to suppress or gradually eliminate
all trade restrictions. Tariff and other trade restrictions between the
member countries and third parties remain unaffected by this arrangement, and members are free to impose any level of tariffs against nonmember countries. The principal goal of a free trade area is to
gradually achieve a state of perfect competition among the industries
of the member states. For example, the countries in the European
Free Trade Association (EFTA) agreed to promote in the free trade
area as a whole and in each member state a sustained expansion of
economic activity, full employment, increased productivity, and the
rational utilization of resources; to ensure that trade among the
member countries takes place in conditions of fair competition; and
to contribute to the harmonious development and expansion of world
trade. Beginning on July 1, 1960, the member countries agreed to
reduce their duties on each other's goods by 20 percent as specified
in the agreement. Thereafter, the reduction was to progress by 10
percent each year until, by January 1, 1969, the duty stood at 10 percent. After that date, the member states agreed not to apply any import
duties on each other's goods. The conditions upon which the reduced
duties were applied were: (1) that the goods were wholly produced
within the area; (2) that they fell within the description of goods listed
in the Annex to the Agreement; and (3) that, where imported materials
were used, the value of such materials should not exceed 50 percent
of the export value of the finished goods.

In Latin America, the Treaty of Montevideo, signed in February 1960, established the Latin American Free Trade Association (LAFTA) providing for free movement of goods among the member states. The agreement called for the gradual elimination of trade barriers in respect of substantially all their reciprocal trade; no duties, charges, or restrictions were to be applied to imports of goods originating in the territory of the member states. During the first three years of the agreement, the countries committed themselves to reduce by 8 percent annually the import duties on goods originating in the member states until such duties were completely eliminated.

The essence of a free trade area is that the countries recognize the importance of the development of trade through the elimination of intra-regional barriers as a means of accelerating economic development in the member states. An interesting point to note is that the agreements do not call for the immediate removal of all customs and other trade restrictions. The countries often agree on a period of, e.g., ten to fifteen years during which all tariffs on goods from the partner states are to be removed completely. This gives ample time for the industries to set themselves on competitive footing.

There are no free trade areas as such on the African continent, but by implication some of the agreements lead to the creation of limited free trade arrangements. There are, however, a large number of bilateral trade agreements and most African countries participate in one or more such agreements. Because a free trade arrangement does not involve the coordination of economic policies, one has the impression that the African countries would readily agree to establish free trade associations. The general expectation is that a free trade arrangement would increase the flow of trade between the member states. Although this may be true in the developed countries, the African countries generally cannot increase trade among themselves simply through the creation of free trade arrangements. This is because, as will be shown in Chapter 6, intra-African trade constitutes barely 5 percent of total external trade; hence, such arrangements would not lead to economic development. A free trade arrangement supported by appropriate industrialization policies would seem to be the answer for the expansion of intra-African trade.

Customs Unions

There are instances where a group of countries might wish to adopt certain customs and import regulations to govern transit arrangements between coastal and land-locked countries. The countries might enter into agreements whereby the former grant port and harbor facilities to the latter. Although such an arrangement may serve the purpose, quite often administration and collection of tax becomes cumbersome and the land-locked countries may not always get the assurance that these arrangements will be respected by the coastal countries. To solve these and allied problems, such countries might find it to their mutual benefit to consider the creation of a customs union. A customs union is an association of a group of countries governed by an agreement to remove tariffs levied on imports from member countries while establishing common external tariffs on imports from nonmember countries. In general, a customs union combines the elements of free trade arrangements with policies of protection since it provides for freedom of movement of goods between the partner states while protecting the market within the union from competition from third countries. A customs union is distinguished from a free trade area in that the member countries of a free trade area are at liberty to fix their own individual tariffs on imports from third countries.

It is customary to expect the member countries of a customs union to agree to refrain from introducing any new customs duties among themselves that would have the effect of increasing duties above the levels existing at the time of the agreement. If this were to happen, the basis for continuing the customs union would not remain attractive to some member countries. Quite often, the countries make firm commitments to reduce tariffs gradually over a given period of time at the end of which there is to be complete freedom of movement of goods originating in the partner states. The reduction in the tariffs is made by adopting an arithmetic average of duties to be applied each successive year. An annual rate reduction between 8 and 10 percent seems to be generally acceptable as a fair basis for starting negotiations toward the total abolition of customs duties. To avoid harming the weaker partner states, especially in cases where the removal of customs duties would expose a given industry to severe competition from the stronger partners, it is often prudent to prepare several lists of goods with each list subject to different levels of customs duties. This procedure enables some industries to be accorded more favorable treatment and is conducive to a more favorable rate of industrialization of the least developed partner states.

The economic argument for the establishment of a customs union is as follows: that both countries A and B produce a given commodity but A produces it more cheaply than B, the elimination of customs duties between the two countries and the adoption of a general tariff toward third countries would compel B to shift consumption from higher-cost domestic products to lower-cost products imported from A. The case for the customs union would be strengthened if B would abandon its production in favor of A as this would result in economies of scale. If certain goods for the enlarged market are produced at a lower cost in country A, consumption of similar goods originating from third countries will be further reduced or eliminated, since the local demand is met by goods from the partner country A. This constitutes the trade creation effect of the customs union.[4] In such cases, there will be savings in country B on the real cost of goods that previously were produced locally at a higher cost and now are imported from country A at a lower cost. The difference between the total outlay paid by country B and the new outlay on goods from country A represents the consumers' surplus for country B. This would be a real gain from cooperation. This argument is further based on the assumption that the price elasticity of demand in country B for the goods from third countries is zero, since where elasticity is greater than zero a substantial reduction in the price of a given commodity from a third country would imply that country B would gain by maintaining its imports from the third country. In this case, it would appear less attractive for country B to continue membership in the customs union unless other compensatory factors were introduced.

The customs unions that have been established in Africa have treaty provisions for the removal of trade restrictions, the erection of a common external tariff, and the coordination of import and export regulations. UDEAC and the West African Customs Union are fair examples of this form of cooperation.

The problems of the existing African customs unions generally are twofold. In the first place, due to the high cost structure of most African industries, it still would be advantageous for some countries to import goods from third countries. This is sometimes the case regardless of whether the economies of scale have been fully exploited, due largely to technological factors, import content of raw materials, and the organization of the market structure. In the second place, difficulties have arisen in the collection and distribution of customs revenues. Due to the lack of adequate and reliable statistics and the difficulty encountered in the adoption of formula for sharing customs revenues that would satisfy the land-locked countries, it often has been difficult to determine the total revenue collected and ensure its fair and equitable distribution. As a result, time and again the inland countries have erected tariff walls, contrary to original commitments, in order to protect their industries or for revenue purposes.

Common Markets

Where trade constitutes an important source of the GDP, countries often find it expedient to adopt measures aimed at the expansion of export trade. Since the movement of goods and services among any number of countries is restricted when the countries adopt different trade and commercial policies and practices, it becomes essential to

establish a common market. In a common market, in addition to the
free trading arrangements and common external tariffs envisaged in
customs unions, there is implied free movement of factors of production
--such as capital, labor, managerial skills, and enterprise--among the
member states. Although the countries may not have a common currency, there often is free convertibility between the currencies of the
partner countries. Free competition between productive units in the
partner states is also implied.

A common market is therefore a higher level of economic
cooperation than a free trade area or a customs union. For example,
the EEC countries were prompted, inter alia, by the desire to strengthen
the unity of their economies and to ensure their harmonious development
through the reduction of existing differences. This was to be achieved
through the elimination of customs duties and quantitative restrictions
between the member states with regard to goods originating in the
member countries. The countries also agreed to establish a common
customs tariff and a common commerical policy toward third countries.
There are no obstacles to the free movement of persons, services, and
capital in the EEC. The common market was established gradually
over a period of twelve years. It was agreed that the transitional
period would be divided into three stages of four years each, but the
length of each stage could be modified according to treaty provisions.
The object of introducing these stages obviously was to give ample
opportunity for adjusting the economies to the needs of the community,
especially for the least developed member states.

The Central American Common Market established by a treaty
signed at Managua on December 13, 1960, provided for the creation
of a common market that was to be brought into full operation within
a period of not more than five years from the date the treaty went into
effect. (It is interesting to note that, whereas the EEC thought a period
of twelve years was required to bring about a full common market, the
Central American countries thought that they could achieve this goal
in five years). The countries agreed to grant one another free trade
treatment in respect of all products originating in their respective
territories. Such goods also were to be exempted from all quantitative and other restrictions. Certain categories of goods were subject
to special interim treatment exempting them from the immediate free
trade treatment. This meant that countries could still impose customs
duties on these goods for a period of five years, at the end of which these
these duties would be removed. Thus, it was felt necessary to protect
certain industries for a limited period, after which they were expected
to stand on their feet and face competition from similar industries in
the partner countries.

Some of the elements of a full common market are absent in

existing common market arrangements in the African region. For
instance, in the East African Common Market there is provision for
the "abolition generally of restrictions of trade between the partner
states" and the establishment and maintenance, subject to certain
conditions, of common customs and excise tariffs. The common market
arrangements are to run for a period of fifteen years, at the end of
which time the treaty is subject to review. Freedom of movement of
factors of production has been difficult to implement in East Africa.
The free movement of factors of production has gradually been restricted, especially in recent years, and the adoption of a common
external tariff has not been fully implemented. However, due to
increased dependence on external trade for a substantial portion of
income in the African countries, there is a growing desire to establish
common markets involving a number of countries. This is regarded
as a means of ascertaining independence from overseas trade and
increasing intra-African trade. Virtually all economic associations
in Africa today aim at the creation of a common market among the
member states.

Economic Unions

A group of countries might decide to tackle all problems of
development through joint action. In such cases, it would be advisable
to create an economic union. An economic union comes into existence
when countries agree to integrate all their economic activities and to
undertake joint decisions in all aspects of economic development policies. It therefore embraces wider implications than a customs union
or a common market. Countries must be willing to adopt joint economic
policies in all sectors and at all levels of economic development.
Achieving this objective requires harmonious political relationships
and identity of political ideologies. In short, for a full economic union
to be successful, experience suggests a need to create conditions
approximating a full political union.

Elements of an economic union do exist in the known types of
economic cooperation, but none of them comes close to a full economic
union even in cases where it is the declared intention of the parties to
establish such a union. For instance, in the EEC there is provision
for the application of procedures permitting the coordination of the
economic policies of the member states and the correction of disequi-
libria in their balances of payments. The COMECON Charter seeks,
by uniting and coordinating the efforts of the member countries, to
promote the planned development of the national economies, the
acceleration of economic and technical progress in the member countries, and the raising of the level of industrialization in the industrially
less developed partner countries in order to ensure a steady increase

in labor productivity and a constant improvement in the welfare of the peoples in the member countries. These objectives fall within the definition of an economic union, but neither the EEC nor the COMECON really satisfies all the conditions.

In the treaties for cooperation in Africa, such as the East African Community, there are provisions for the coordination of economic planning and industrialization and considerations for the adoption of common agricultural and transport development policies. The UDEAC Treaty clearly states that it is the intention of the member states to create a full economic union. The countries agreed to take the necessary measures for the creation of arrangements for consultation and harmonization procedures on fiscal systems, development plans, and the regulation of foreign and domestic investments. However, in all these instances the level of cooperation is nowhere near a full economic union.

Moreover, the broad objectives of economic unions in Africa are not defined clearly. Most of these unions embrace ad hoc arrangements for joint action and could fall within any of the forms of cooperation enumerated earlier. Some economic unions in Africa are no more than simple economic agreements covering individual sectors of the economy. However, in most of the economic associations in Africa there is now a marked trend toward the desire to coordinate the overall economic development policies.

There are numerous other forms of economic associations that cannot be classified within any of the four categories of economic cooperation described above, largely because their objectives are not clearly laid down in the agreements. These agreements call for cooperation in one limited field or project within the larger economic sectors. In this type of economic association, the level and degree of cooperation does not generally call for the establishment of elaborate institutional framework, and joint decisions are carried out through simple arrangements and consultations. A good example of this type of cooperation is the Scandinavian Airlines System, which provides for the development of air transportation among the Scandinavian countries without coordinating other economic activities. In the African continent, the African Civil Aviation Commission, the Association of African Airlines, and the Association of African Central Banks are also good examples. In Eastern Europe, the COMECON is an example of this type of cooperation where joint action is envisaged in single venture projects carried out within a wider institutional framework for cooperation.

OBSERVATIONS

Nearly all the approaches to cooperation described above have been adopted, with varying degrees of success, in one or the other of the intergovernmental economic organizations in Africa. Some of these organizations possess elements of a customs union, a common market, and an economic union irrespective of their designation or treaty objectives. The African countries do not seem to be guided by any economic rationale in their choice of approach to cooperation. In a majority of cases, political motivations, with a mixture of socio-economic factors, have influenced the establishment of these organizations. This phenomenon can be explained largely due to lack of adequate and accurate information on the economic conditions in the African countries and the absence of concrete analytical studies of the opportunities for cooperation and the implications of cooperation on the national economies. Thus, we find that a number of these organizations, having initially adopted a multisectoral approach to cooperation, subsequently discover that the economic conditions in the member countries cannot permit the degree of economic cooperation originally envisaged.

Since politics play a decisive role in the economic life of the African people, the choice of the approach which a group of countries may adopt will be governed by the intentions of these countries. Nonetheless, factors such as the levels of economic development of the constituent countries, and the anticipated gains from cooperation weigh heavily in decision-making and should be given adequate consideration. Where countries are prepared to coordinate their overall development policies, an economic union would be the ideal form of cooperation. On the other hand, where countries wish to establish a common market, a customs union, or a free trade area, it would normally not be imperative to coordinate policies in fields of economic activity other than the adoption of common trade and commercial policies, common external tariffs, and such other policy measures to ensure freedom of movement of such factors of production as capital, labor, and technology.

In the African experience, it is unrealistic to advocate the establishment of the all-embracing types of cooperation. This is because of the lack of a generally acceptable formula for the distribution of gains from economic cooperation and the absence of an effective method of allocating multinational industries or projects among the partner countries in an economic organization, especially where such projects or industries fall within the key sectors considered by each country to be of vital importance to its economic development. In addition to this, the inadequacy of the means of transport and communication links even among countries of the same economic organization, and the traditional rigidities in the production and trade patterns of the African countries in general, complicates the calculation of the benefits from cooperation and the assessment of the impact of cooperation on the development of the individual economies. Moreover, the wider the range of economic activities included in cooperation agreements, the greater the demands on the member countries' resources and the greater the need to make profound adjustments in the internal economic policies of each country to support the joint development efforts.

From the foregoing we are led to conclude that in Africa, the time is not yet ripe for the creation of an all-embracing framework for cooperation, especially where simpler and less sophisticated forms of cooperation would achieve the desired objectives. Countries would generally find it easier to cooperate in individual sectors or projects while leaving the larger area of development policies outside the economic cooperation commitments. The rather limited sectoral or project cooperation seems to have greater chance of success than the all-embracing types. The small beginnings toward cooperation adopted in organization such as the Lake Chad Basin Commission, the Organization of the Senegal River States (OERS), the Council of Understanding (Conseil de l'Entente), and joint ventures such as the Zambia-Tanzania rail link, lay firm foundations for wider cooperation. It is more realistic for the African countries to concentrate their effort on the joint development of an individual sector or project where chances of success are readily determinable than to enter into a wider range of cooperation commitments especially if the available financial, technical and skilled manpower resources do not justify such commitments.

This conclusion is based on the recognition that the level of economic acitivity in most African countries does not permit the adoption of wider cooperation commitments as is generally envisaged in some of the cooperation treaties. It should, however, be stressed at this stage that the development policies of the partner countries in an association should be oriented so that the sectoral or project-by-project approach eventually leads to the adoption of a general strategy for cooperation. Through the backward and forward linkages, especially in the leading sectors, the development process will gradually spread to the remaining sectors. As the countries become more industrialized and the transport and communication facilities between the African countries generally improve, a larger number of multinational projects will emerge and can readily be identified. New sectors will also emerge in which countries can see immediate advantages for joint development, and the existing sectors originally excluded from cooperation would lend themselves for coordinated action. It should then be more realistic and advantageous for countries to move to higher degrees of cooperation. The main point to bear in mind is that the sectors or projects which are integrated should be geared to long-term development perspectives. This is because it would be essential to integrate a good number of sectors of the economies, especially the key sectors, at some stage in the development process in order to correct the disequilibrium that is inherent in the sectoral or project-by-project approach.

NOTES

1. Economic Commission for Africa, Annual Report, E/4354, (New York, 1967), p. 309.

2. Economic Commission for Africa, A Venture in Self-Reliance, E/CN.14/424, United Nations, Addis Ababa, 1968, pp. 32-33.

3. See, for example, W. W. Rostow, The Process of Economic Growth (Oxford: Clarendon Press, 1960), pp. 261-62. Rostow argues that a rapid rate of economic growth in any leading sectors would lead to a general increase in the rate of growth of the entire economy.

4. For a complete analysis of the theory of customs union, see Harry G. Johnson, Money, Trade and Economic Growth (London: George Allen and Unwin, Ltd., 1964), pp. 46-62; Jacob Viner, The Customs Union Issue (London: Stevens and Sons, Ltd., 1950), pp. 41-78.

3

THE INSTITUTIONAL
MACHINERY
FOR
ECONOMIC COOPERATION
IN AFRICA

THE NEED FOR EFFECTIVE
DECISION-MAKING MACHINERY

In the quest for economic cooperation in Africa, the development of adequate institutional machinery is an essential condition for successful coordination of development policies. In addition to providing a forum in which opinions on matters of common interest can be exchanged, these institutions are of particular importance in the implementation of joint decisions for cooperation. The coordination of industrial development policies and the harmonization of national development plans cannot be achieved if there are no adequate institutional arrangements to take the coordinating role.

Economic cooperation at any level implies the delegation of power to a supranational body entrusted with the task of safeguarding the interest of both the multinational grouping as well as those of the individual member countries. Quite often, the scope of jurisdiction conferred on the supranational organs reflects the intentions of the member states. It is not a matter of accident that the most successful economic groupings both inside and outside Africa have adequate and elaborate institutional arrangements for economic cooperation. It was recognized that, where differences in national interests were likely to be an obstacle to cooperation, it was necessary to establish an institution that would be able to smooth these differences so as to enable a harmonious relationship to exist among the partner states.

The establishment of adequate institutional machinery for cooperation is an essential condition for successful coordination of development policies. Such institutions are necessary for making joint decisions affecting the multinational grouping, for ensuring the implementation of such decisions, and for following up. The determination of an institutional arrangement in any grouping depends largely upon the objectives of the member states. It is sometimes noted that, the less defined the objectives for cooperation, the more vague are the powers conferred upon the multinational body, vice versa. Where the final decision lies with the respective national assemblies of the member states in a given economic grouping, the countries often confer extensive powers on a multinational institution. On the other hand, where it is intended to give the multinational body powers to make binding decisions, such powers often have been very limited both in scope and application.

Where the member states have equal representation and voting powers and where the principle of unanimity is strictly adhered to in final decisions, the member governments tend to be more willing to confer wider powers on the institutions created to serve them since, in any event, a country can exercise its veto power to prevent any decision that might be detrimental to its interests. In Africa, some of the economic groupings do not consider it necessary to set up elaborate institutions for cooperation. More often, an economic grouping may be served only by a council of ministers assisted by a committee of experts. In contrast, the East African Community has the most elaborate common institutions on the African continent. Some of these institutions are listed in Figure 3.1 which, although not entirely exhaustive, serves to give an indication of the extent to which it has been found necessary to establish institutional machinery.

Executive Functions

The ability to take appropriate decisions regarding joint efforts in a particular venture depends to a great extent upon the degree and level of political involvement in the venture. The political involvement in turn depends upon the form of cooperation that the countries wish to have. The economic situation within the group of countries wishing to cooperate also may have influenced the setting up of these institutions. In the EEC, for instance, the Assembly, which is composed of parliamentarians from the member states, is the supreme organ and exercises the advisory and supervisory powers conferred upon it by the treaty. The heads of state are not directly involved in the decision-making of the EEC. The member countries of the EEC are not equally represented in the Assembly. Three countries, West Germany, France, and Italy each have 36 representatives; Belgium and the Netherlands each have 14 representatives; and Luxembourg has 6 representatives. The Assembly's decisions involve rather complex arrangements. It is provided that the most important decisions should be unanimous but that other decisions be governed by an absolute majority of the votes cast, and the quorum is laid down in the rules of procedure.

FIGURE 3.1

East African Community: Institutional Machinery

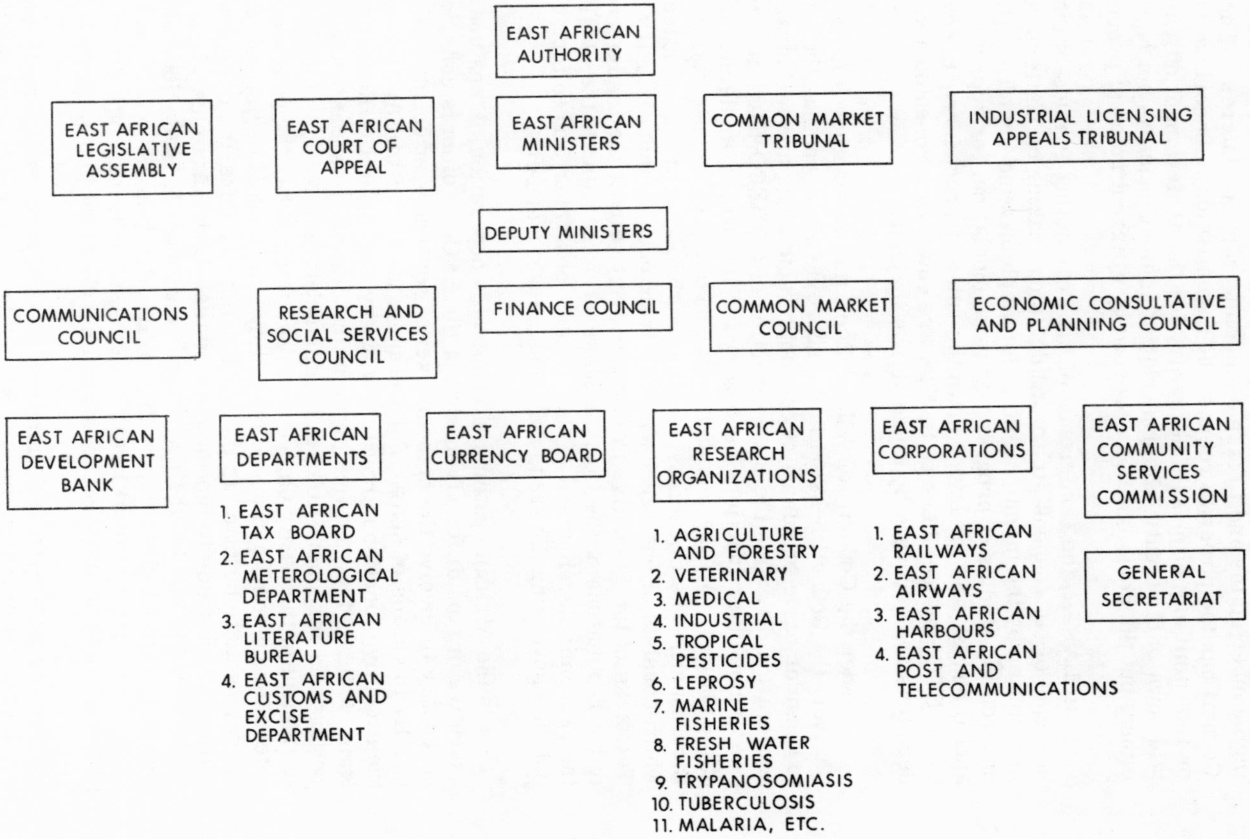

EAST AFRICAN LEGISLATIVE ASSEMBLY

COMMUNICATIONS COUNCIL

EAST AFRICAN DEVELOPMENT BANK

EAST AFRICAN COURT OF APPEAL

RESEARCH AND SOCIAL SERVICES COUNCIL

EAST AFRICAN DEPARTMENTS

1. EAST AFRICAN TAX BOARD
2. EAST AFRICAN METEROLOGICAL DEPARTMENT
3. EAST AFRICAN LITERATURE BUREAU
4. EAST AFRICAN CUSTOMS AND EXCISE DEPARTMENT

EAST AFRICAN AUTHORITY

EAST AFRICAN MINISTERS

DEPUTY MINISTERS

FINANCE COUNCIL

EAST AFRICAN CURRENCY BOARD

COMMON MARKET TRIBUNAL

COMMON MARKET COUNCIL

EAST AFRICAN RESEARCH ORGANIZATIONS

1. AGRICULTURE AND FORESTRY
2. VETERINARY
3. MEDICAL
4. INDUSTRIAL
5. TROPICAL PESTICIDES
6. LEPROSY
7. MARINE FISHERIES
8. FRESH WATER FISHERIES
9. TRYPANOSOMIASIS
10. TUBERCULOSIS
11. MALARIA, ETC.

INDUSTRIAL LICENSING APPEALS TRIBUNAL

ECONOMIC CONSULTATIVE AND PLANNING COUNCIL

EAST AFRICAN CORPORATIONS

1. EAST AFRICAN RAILWAYS
2. EAST AFRICAN AIRWAYS
3. EAST AFRICAN HARBOURS
4. EAST AFRICAN POST AND TELECOMMUNICATIONS

EAST AFRICAN COMMUNITY SERVICES COMMISSION

GENERAL SECRETARIAT

57

The Assembly is assisted by the Council, an executive body whose task is to ensure the coordination of the general economic policies of the member states and to take decision of common interest. The Council has the power to request the Commission to undertake studies or to submit any proposals necessary for the achievement of objectives laid down in the treaty. Representation in the Council is not equal either, but the decisions are governed by different rules of procedure.

In LAFTA, the Conference of the Contracting Parties is the supreme organ responsible for all decision-making on matters requiring joint action by the member states, for implementing the treaty, for undertaking studies of progress on implementation, for approving the annual budget, and for laying down the rules of procedure. In contrast to the EEC, the members of LAFTA are equally represented and their decisions are governed by a two-thirds majority.

Under the Council for Mutual Economic Assistance (COMECON) Charter, the Council Session is the supreme organ and has the power to consider basic problems of economic, scientific, and technical cooperation, to define the main direction of COMECON activity, and to exercise other functions necessary for the proper implementation of the charter. All the member states have equal representation in the Council. The Council is assisted by the Executive Committee, which consists of one representative from each member country. The tasks of the Executive Committee are to direct the implementation of the resolutions of the Council Sessions, to coordinate the plans for the economic development of the member countries, and to formulate policies governing the trade relations among members.

In the African systems of economic cooperation, the nature of executive organs differs from that of the EEC. It often is considered necessary to involve the highest level of political representation, usually the heads of state. For example, under the UDEAC Treaty, the executive functions are carried out by the Council of Heads of State, which is the supreme organ of the organization and has wide powers and responsibilities in the formulation of policies for the attainment of the treaty objectives. The Council has the power to determine customs and economic policy and to make decisions regarding the payments to be made to the Joint Solidarity Fund and the distribution of such funds to the member states. Under Articles 17 and 18 of the UDEAC Treaty, the Council has the power to make decisions regarding tax policies, import duties, fiscal duties and other charges, harmonization of internal fiscal systems, coordination of industrial projects, and coordination of national development plans.

In the East African Community, before the present treaty came into force, the executive functions were the responsibility of the High

Commission, composed of the British governors of Uganda, Kenya, and Tanganyika. Under the East African Common Services Organization, the supreme executive organ was the Authority, which was composed of the principal elected ministers responsible to the legislatures of the three respective territories. After all three East African countries attained independence, the heads of state of the three countries became the Authority. The various agreements and constitutional changes* provide that within the countries the Authority have the capacity of a body corporate with perpetual succession and the power to acquire, hold, and dispose of land and other property, and the power to sue and be sued.

Under the present East African Treaty, the East African Authority is the supreme organ of the East African Community and is composed of the three presidents of Kenya, Uganda, and Tanzania. It is responsible for the general direction and control of the economic decisions in accordance with the provisions of the treaty. Unlike the High Commission or the Authority under the EACSO, the present East African Authority does not in itself possess the status of a body corporate. It is now the East African Community that has the legal capacity and personality required for the performance of the treaty functions. The Authority is assisted in its decision-making functions by the East African Ministers and the Common Market Council, which are basically political bodies with equal representation from each of the three countries. The East African Ministers do not hold ministerial posts in their respective countries but have offices at the seat of the East African Community. In addition to these bodies, the East African Customs and Excise Departments and the East African Income Tax Department can take certain decisions affecting their areas of jurisdiction.

The Charter of the OCAM provides that the Conference of Heads of State and Government is the supreme organ of the organization. It is composed of the heads of state and government of the member states or their duly accredited representatives. It has the power to make studies and take decisions of common interest in accordance with the charter. Its decisions are governed by a majority of the votes cast, and each state has one vote.

---

*The Tanganyika East African Common Services Organization Agreement (Implementation) Ordinance No. 52 of 1961; the Kenya East African Common Services Organization Ordinance (Chapter 4 of the Laws of Kenya); and the Uganda East African Common Services Organization Ordinance No. 22 of 1961.

In some of the groupings in West Africa, such as the West African Customs Union (UDEAO), Conseil de l'Entente, and the Organization of the Senegal River States (OERS), the heads of state or the Council of Ministers do not enjoy powers as wide as in the case of the East African Community, and the decisions of the joint organs are subject to ratification by the legislative bodies in each country. For instance, Article 10 of the UDEAO Treaty provides that the majority decision of the Council of Ministers shall be binding and enforceable in each member state, but in practice the Council could not enforce its decisions on the member states.

Legislative Functions

The establishment of a supreme organ in any economic grouping presupposes the acceptance of the idea of supranationalizm and hence the surrender of some decision powers to a multinational body. It therefore becomes necessary to define the areas in which such a body will have jurisdiction to enact laws that are recognized as such in the member states. The legislative powers and functions differ from one organization to another, and there is no single formula for deciding the extent to which the laws enacted within the multinational insti- tutions may override the national laws enacted under the national constitutions. Because of this lack of clarity, in some economic groupings conflicts have arisen between the interest of an individual country and that of the group or between national and community laws.

In the UDEAC Treaty, the two organs, the Council of Heads of State and the Directing Committee, have indirect powers of legislation. Under Article 9 of the UDEAC Treaty, the Council of Heads of State is empowered to take unanimous decisions on matters related to economic, customs, and fiscal legislation. Such decisions are subject to ratification by the national legislative assemblies of the member states but have the force of law in the member states one day after their publication in the official gazette of the Organization. The Directing Committee, through authority delegated by the Council of Heads of States, may take decisions by a unanimous vote on matters related to customs laws and regulations, investment code, and tariffs and related matters; such decisions have the force of law in the member states. The Directing Committee also may cause appropriate amendments to be made in the existing national laws, and its recom- mendations are taken seriously by the Council of Heads of State.

The East African Legislative Assembly has full competence to legislate on a wide range of subjects related to implementation of the Treaty for East African Cooperation. The enactment of the laws for the East African Community is done by means of bills passed by the

Assembly following the normal procedures. Such bills must, in accordance with the provisions of Article 59 of the treaty, have the assent of the three heads of state of the partner countries acting on behalf of the EAC.

During the interim period before the East African Legislative Assembly first met, the East African Authority was empowered to take such measures and to make amendments to existing laws where this appeared necessary or expedient in order to bring the law in line with the treaty provisions. To make the amendments effective, it was necessary that they be incorporated, through the normal legislative procedure, in the laws of each individual member country. The laws in existence prior to the treaty in respect of such common services as were retained by the EAC were incorporated into the East African Community Laws. In addition to the Assembly, the East African Customs and Excise Department and the East African Income Tax Department were incorporated as autonomous bodies of the East African Community. These departments are staffed by EAC civil servants who are free from national direction or interference and are responsible for implementation of the East African Community laws within the constituent states. Under the EAC laws, these departments also have discretionary powers to modify, in limited cases and where appropriate, the jurisdiction of the national courts in matters relating to their respective fields. This is an interesting aspect not generally found in economic associations in Africa; it developed as a result of the peculiar arrangements that existed during the colonial days.

Under the Treaty of Rome, the laws of the EEC are automatically binding upon the member states, and the directives of the Assembly and the Council of Ministers do not require national legislation to become effective in the member states. Although the European Assembly has no legislative powers, it is empowered under Articles 143 and 144 of the treaty to debate the Annual Report submitted to it by the Commission, and it can cause the resignation of the Commission by a vote of no confidence. When taken by an absolute majority of the votes cast, its decisions and recommendations may have the effect of law in the member states. It is an agreed practice in the EEC that national laws cannot override EEC laws. This matter is not clearly defined in any of the treaties for cooperation found in Africa.

Judicial Functions and Settlement of Disputes

When countries decide to come together to pursue a common objective, there must be laws to govern their conduct, to safeguard the member states from unscrupulous behavior, to redress injustices done to any member state, and to settle disputes between them. Differences in the interpretation of the provisions of the agreements for cooperation may raise serious problems of implementation. Therefore, it becomes necessary to have a multinational body that can guide the economic grouping in any matters that may result in a conflict of interests. Some economic associations attach little importance to the need for a separate organ responsible for enforcing community laws, whereas others regard this as essential. The EEC has the European Court of Justice, whose task is to ensure the observance of the community law, and the interpretation and application of the Treaty of Rome. The European Court of Justice has jurisdiction over the member states and possesses power to make decisions on any disputes arising between the member states. In the COMECON, the Council Session possesses juridical personality and has the capacity to conclude agreements, to acquire lease and dispose of property, and to engage in legal proceedings. This arrangement is similar to that of LAFTA, where there is no special organ but LAFTA itself possesses complete juridical personality and has the power to contract and institute legal proceedings.

In the East African Community, the East African Court of Appeal has jurisdiction to hear and determine such appeals from the courts of each member states as provided by the laws in force in that particular state. In the common market aspects of the treaty, the judicial functions are undertaken by the Common Market Tribunal which does not, however, have the characteristics of a court of law. Nevertheless, it has the competence to accept and adjudicate all matters that may be referred to it by the member states, and its decisions are not subject to appeal. Articles 37 and 41 of the East African Treaty provide that any decision delivered by the Common Market Tribunal in accordance with the powers conferred on it by the treaty shall not be subject to appeal, and its decisions often are delivered in public. Where the partner states have agreed to refer a dispute concerning the interpretation or application of the treaty insofar as it affects the common market aspects to the Common Market Tribunal, they shall not submit the dispute for any mode of settlement other than through the tribunal. In addition to the Common Market Tribunal, the East African Industrial Licensing Appeal Tribunal adjudicates matters relating to the application of the industrial licensing regulations of the member states.

UDEAC does not have a specific body to enact the common laws, but any decisions of the Council of Heads of State, insofar as they affect economic cooperation between the member states, have the force of law within the states. However, it is provided that the decisions of the Council of Heads of State and the Directing Committee must be ratified by the national parliaments of the member states in accordance with their own procedures before they can become laws of the UDEAC. In the OCAM, there is no specific mention of judicial functions, but it is provided that all decisions related to the interpretation or the implementation of the OCAM Charter must be taken by a two-thirds majority of the member states of the organization if they are to be binding upon the member states.

The question of arbitration has been tackled in different ways in the various economic groupings in existence in Africa and in other parts of the world. In the UDEAC, for example, the Directing Committee is responsible for settling disputes arising from the implementation of the treaty. The members of the Directing Committee meet basically to support the policies of their respective governments, and disputes that they cannot solve are referred to the Council of the Heads of State, where such disputes may be settled through the spirit of brotherhood and friendly persuasion.

In such other economic groupings as the OCAM, the OERS and the Maghreb, the treaties are not explicit on these matters, and often disputes arising between member states are left to be solved through a series of dialogues and consultations. The East African Community has an impartial body known as the Common Market Tribunal, whose main task is to ensure the observance and interpretation of the Community Law, especially insofar as it affects the common market aspects of cooperation. The Common Market Tribunal is competent to accept and adjudicate all matters under the treaty and treaty obligations. It sits in plenary and delivers its decisions in public. As previously noted, the decisions of the Common Market Tribunal are not subject to appeal; when a member does not agree with the majority decision, it has the right to deliver a dissenting opinion and can record the dissent in public. It is believed that this provision ensures complete impartiality and thus safeguards the interests of the East African Community.

The EEC Court of Justice has the power of arbitration and of settling disputes arising from the interpretation of treaty provisions. If a member state believes that another member state has not fulfilled its obligations under any provision of the Treaty, of Rome, it has the right to refer the matter to the Court of Justice. However, this can only be done after the matter has been referred to the Commission, which may deliver its considered opinion after hearing petitions from each of the parties in dispute. If the Court of Justice is convinced that a member state has indeed failed to meet its obligations under the treaty, it has the power to take judgment and require the state to take appropriate action for the implementation of the judgment of the Court of Justice.

One of the major defects in the institutions for cooperation in Africa today is that the question of implementation is not fully tackled. There are clear provisions as to who makes the decision, but there does not appear to be sufficient provision for implementation of such joint decisions. This problem has come up in some economic groupings in Africa in recent years. For example, problems arose within the OCAM in regard to the provisions of the Sugar Agreement; since there is no machinery for the settlement of disputes or for the interpretation of the Sugar Agreement, the countries have found it difficult to solve the question of the sugar quotas. Similarly difficulties arose in the implementation of the treaty in the case of the UDEAC and in regard to the collection and distribution of the revenue from customs duties in UDEAO. These problems arose largely because due to the absence of a multinational institution charged with clearly defined powers to take joint decisions, the member states meet basically to support their individual interests and therefore the principle of impartiality, which is an essential element in international relations, becomes ineffective. Where it has been difficult to reach consensus on any pertinent issue, the absence of an impartial body, such as the East African Common Market Tribunal, has greatly reduced the scope for cooperation.

Statutory Bodies

Where countries wish to cooperate in a wide range of areas, the need for the creation of other statutory organs cannot be overemphasized. Specific fields of economic activity require special studies and methods of implementing common decisions. Thus, in addition to the councils of heads of state and other organs, there are often other bodies created for specific functions. UDEAO has a Committee of Experts, consisting of representatives from member states, whose function is consisting of representatives from member states, whose function is to formulate proposals, recommendations, and opinions based on the studies and other information submitted by the Secretary-General. In the Maghreb, several committees have been created to deal with development issues related to specific fields, such as posts and telecommunications, maritime, road and air transportation, hotels and tourism, and esparto grass. An industrial studies center was also established to conduct studies and make proposals for joint industrial development. In the UDEAC, the Directing Committee makes all proposals in respect of joint policies and each committee member is supported by at least four experts from his own country.

In the East African Community, a number of organs that existed as autonomous bodies under the former de facto common market were incorporated in the treaty. These are the East African Airways Corporation, the East African Harbors Corporation, the East African

Posts and Telecommunications Corporation, and the East African Railways Corporation. In addition to these corporations, the treaty also created the Communications Council, the Finance Council, the Economic Consultative and Planning Council, and the Research and Social Council. There also are semistatutory bodies, such as the East African External Telecommunications Services which is owned by the three countries and a British company.

ADMINISTRATIVE FUNCTIONS

The EEC has elaborate secretariat arrangements that facilitate its day-to-day functioning. The secretariat in Brussels has facilities to cater to any conceivable requirement of the member states. The Commission, whose main function is to ensure the application of the treaty provisions in regard to the orderly development of the common market, may also submit recommendations or opinions to the Council or Assembly on matters relating to provisions of the treaty in which it has competence. One other function of the Commission is to prepare the general report of the activities of the EEC. In these functions, the Commission is assisted by the Economic and Social Committee which is composed of representatives of the various categories of economic and social life, such as producers, farmers, transport operators, workers, merchants, artisans, and the professions. Other general interests are also represented in the Committee. This Committee acts as the consultative body of the EEC, and its broad representation ensures that all aspects of life in the EEC are adequately safeguarded. There are also provisions for the establishment of such subcommittees as may be required for the proper implementation of the treaty.

The COMECON has established standing commissions whose task is to work out measures and to prepare proposals for the implementation of the decisions of the Council. The commissions are assisted by the secretariat, which prepares for Council meetings, undertakes surveys of the economic conditions in the member countries, and prepares proposals on the scientific problems of the work of the Council. The secretariat also is responsible for drafting the multinational agreements on economic and technical cooperation among these countries, for maintaining records of the execution of the recommendations and decisions of the organs of the Council, and for generally implementing the various charter provisions.

In most of the African economic organizations, the Council of Ministers (generally composed of foreign affairs ministers or finance and economic planning ministers) is responsible for policy measures affecting the organization's day-to-day functioning. UDEAC has a

Directing Committee that conducts studies and makes the general recommendations for the consideration of the Council of the Heads of State. In the OCAM and the OERS, councils of ministers perform similar functions. In the East African Community, the East African Ministers control the day-to-day functioning of the Community. Figure 3.2 lists the functions of the various institutions under the East African Treaty. Unlike the councils of ministers in the other economic groupings in Africa which give their first loyalty to the countries that they represent, the East Africa Ministers in principle owe their loyalty to the Community. This is an interesting factor not found in many East African economic groupings. The East African Treaty, also established the East African Service Commission, which makes appointments to the offices in the service of the East African Community, and exercises powers of disciplinary control and dismissal over persons in the Community's employ. The Central Secretariat undertakes work and studies and performs other services related to common market matters that are assigned to it by the Common Market Council.

The question of the establishment of adequate secretarial facilities does not seem to have been fully considered in some of the economic groupings in Africa. For most of these groupings, there seems to be a feeling that once the agreements for cooperation have been reached there is no need for elaborate secretariat arrangements. For example, the Conference of East and Central African States has virtually no secretariat arrangements. There is a provisional rotating secretariat that moves each year to the city where the Summit Conference of the Heads of State is held. This situation may have stemmed from the difficulties of recruitment and staffing of the secretariat with fully trained and experienced personnel. Because of this limitation, a large number of the economic associations in Africa have in the past found it difficult to conduct the necessary studies and to implement the joint decisions for cooperation; eventually, this may also be the case for the Conference of East and Central African States. Therefore, it seems essential that any group of countries wishing to cooperate seriously give adequate consideration to the question of creating a good secretariat. In fact, the establishment of a sound secretariat is as important as the decision-making institutions themselves. Even for the existing groupings, consideration must be given to expansion of the existing facilities to make them effective instruments for carrying out joint decisions for economic cooperation.

THE ECA SUBREGIONAL
INSTITUTIONAL ARRANGEMENTS

The ECA has played a vital role in fostering the economic development of Africa through economic cooperation. Its contribution

FIGURE 3.2

East African Community:
Responsibilities of Ministers and Secretary General

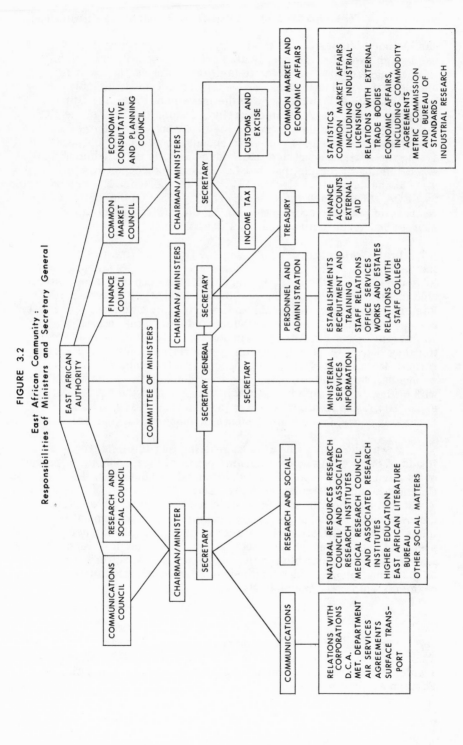

Source: EACSO, Treaty for East African Co-operation, 1967. Eastern African Literature Bureau.

67

has included studies aimed at identifying areas in which development can be achieved through coordinated action. From its inception, the ECA recognized that, in order to facilitate joint decisions, it is essential that an institutional machinery be set up at the multinational level. Its role will increase with the movement toward greater co-operation among the African countries. During the 1960's, the ECA directed its efforts mainly toward the creation of machinery for economic cooperation. In order to encourage economic cooperation among the African countries, ECA advocated the establishment and strengthening of the institutional framework for cooperation, particu-larly at the subregional level. ECA's own experience has demonstrated that ECA should place more and more emphasis on the identification of areas of possible cooperation among the African countries at the subregional level in all respects of development.

In the East African subregion, the first step toward the estab-lishment of a subregional institutional machinery was taken in October-November 1965 at the meeting on subregional economic cooperation held in Lusaka. The meeting recommended that the governments of Eastern Africa formally establish the Economic Community of Eastern Africa* under a treaty to be drawn up and that in the interim period an Interim Council of Ministers be set up to draw up the treaty and to carry out measures of economic cooperation pending treaty ratifi-cation. It was agreed that the proposed treaty should commit the member governments to enter into joint consultations and negotiations with a view to ensuring integrated development of the subregion, especially in the fields of industry, agriculture, transport and communications, trade and payments, manpower, and natural resources.

It was decided at the Lusaka meeting that the Conference of Heads of State would be the supreme organ of the Economic Community of Eastern Africa, supported by the Council of Ministers, the Economic Committee, and a Permanent Secretariat. The Council of Ministers would include one minister from each member state. It would be empowered to set up, if necessary, subsidiary committees at either ministerial or official level to work out programs and agreements in specified areas of economic cooperation. The Council of Ministers also would be responsible for the negotiations of specific agreements on individual projects and requirements in respect of trade and payments among the member states.

---

*The East African Community is made up of Uganda, Kenya and Tanzania, whereas the Economic Community of Eastern Africa has a wider membership that includes all the countries constituting the Eastern African Subregion.

The implementation of joint decisions taken in the organs of the Economic Community of Eastern Africa was in general to be the responsibility of individual governments. In other words, any executive institutions set up under the proposed treaty would have no powers to enforce its decisions on the member countries, but in adopting its own program for development, each country should ensure that it honors obligations in respect of joint decisions duly ratified by it. It was also agreed in this regard that efforts should be made by the member countries to incorporate the jointly agreed projects in the national development plans and that budgetary and other resources within each member country should be provided for the implementation of these projects.

The first meeting of the Interim Council of Ministers established an Economic Committee, which was the technical organ under the Council of Ministers and was composed of officials and experts in national planning and economic development. This body was responsible for advising the Council of Ministers on all aspects of its work, especially the formulation of general policies of integrated development, the drawing up of work programs for the Council of Ministers and any subsidiary bodies that it may set up, the elaboration of the principal outlines for specific agreements between member governments, the harmonization of national development plans in the areas chosen for integrated development, and the supervision of the work of the Permanent Secretariat that was to be created. The Permanent Secretariat would be responsible for the day-to-day functioning of the Economic Community. In the initial stages and until the Economic Community recruited its own personnel, it was agreed that the Economic Commission for Africa would provide secretariat facilities.

The aims of the Economic Community of Eastern Africa were laid down in the Terms of Association as: (1) to promote, through the economic cooperation of the member states, coordinated development of their economies, especially in industry, agriculture, transport and communications, trade and payments, manpower, and natural resources; (2) to further the maximum possible interchange of goods and services among the member states and, to this end, to progressively eliminate customs and other barriers to the expansion of trade among them as well as restrictions on current payment transactions and movement of capital; (3) to contribute to the orderly expansion of trade between the member states and the rest of the world and, to this end, to take measures to render their products relatively competitive with goods imported from outside the Economic Community and to seek more favorable conditions for their products in the world market; and (4) by all these efforts to make a full contribution to the economic development of the continent of Africa as a whole.[1]

ECA made similar attempts to establish an institution for co-operation in the Central African subregion, but the countries were not ready for the type of cooperation then envisaged. The meeting on economic cooperation in the Central African subregion held in Brazza-ville in April 1966 examined the question of closer cooperation among the member states in the fields of transport, agriculture, and trade development and the establishment of institutional machinery to further economic cooperation in the subregion. No major decisions were taken on the pertinent issues, but the Executive Secretary of ECA was asked to conduct studies in all fields of development and these studies were to form the basis for future meetings. The governments of the subregion asserted that it was the policy of their countries to encourage closer mutual economic cooperation and brisker trade but that since the decision in this respect was the responsibility of sover-eign states, further studies of the matter were necessary. With regard to the establishment of institutional machinery for the subregion, the meeting recommended that the heads of state set up an interministerial committee to study problems related to economic cooperation among member states of the subregion and to propose appropriate action.

Since that meeting, there has been little activity in the Central African subregion but, following the report of the ECA mission on economic cooperation in Central Africa and the report of an expert group on the study of transportation in Central Africa sponsored by Belgium, it was proposed to hold a conference on transport to establish a coordinated and phased program of transport development for the years 1970-90 and to consider possible arrangements for permanent cooperation on transport development in the subregion. Therefore, the second meeting on economic cooperation was held in Kinshasa in November 1969.[2] The meeting reviewed developments in the fields of trade, transport, agriculture, industry, manpower and training, and natural resources, based on a number of papers presented by ECA. The meeting did not discuss the question of the establishment of subregional institutional machinery for economic cooperation but recommended that a meeting be held at the technical level to discuss matters relating to the coordination of industrial development in the subregion. This meeting was to be followed by another meeting at the ministerial level to take decisions in this field.

In the West African subregion, ECA organized the first meeting on economic cooperation at Niamey, Niger, in October 1966. At this meeting, several recommendations were adopted regarding the establishment of economic cooperation among the member states of the subregion. It was recommended that the governments of the subregion approve the draft Articles of Association establishing a West African Economic Community. In the field of transport develop-ment, the meeting recommended the establishment of a permanent transport committee within the framework for subregional economic cooperation. The task of this committee would be, inter alia, to study and ascertain possibilities for financing programs for instituting new transport systems, that would improve and connect the various networks in order to achieve a more complete integration of the transport systems in the subregion; to study the possibilities for standardization of transport equipment in order to determine a technical basis for further integration of subregional transport services; and to encourage the local manufactures of such equipment. Another recommendation adopted by the meeting was related to the establishment of an energy committee to define an integrated development policy for energy in the West African subregion; to undertake studies in this field; and to make recommendations with a view toward more integrated prospecting for primary energy resources in the subregion.

A second conference on economic cooperation in the West African subregion was held in Accra in April-May 1967. The conference was convened pursuant to the recommendations adopted at the October 1966 subregional meeting on economic cooperation in West Africa. The Accra meeting adopted the Articles of Association setting up the Economic Community for West Africa.[3] The aims of the Economic Community for West Africa were: (1) to promote, through the economic cooperation of the member states, a coordinated and equitable development of their economies, especially in industry, agriculture, transport and communications, trade and payments, manpower, energy, and natural resources; (2) to further the maximum possible interchange of goods and services among the member states; (3) to contribute to the orderly expansion of trade between the member states and the rest of the world; and (4) by all these efforts and endeavors to contribute to the economic development of the continent of Africa as a whole.

The institutional organs of the Economic Community for West Africa included the Council of Ministers, but until the treaty came into force there would be an Interim Council of Ministers composed of members from all countries of the subregion. The principal responsibility of the Interim Council of Ministers was to draft the treaty governing the Economic Community for West Africa; it was given power to establish a provisional Secretariat, an Interim Economic Committee, and any other appropriate subsidiary bodies. It also was to have power to determine the areas of economic development to be undertaken jointly by the member states, the manner and degree of such development, and the time required to achieve it. A provisional Executive Secretariat also was established to undertake administrative functions during the interim period. The first meeting of the Interim Council of Ministers was held in Dakar in November 1967. The meeting made recommendations for economic cooperation in various fields of development. In particular, recommendations were adopted for the liberalization of trade and payments in the West African subregion. The meeting also discussed the outline of the proposed treaty.

In the North African subregion, ECA sponsored a meeting on economic cooperation in June 1966 attended by representatives of Algeria, Tunisia, Libya, Morocco, the United Arab Republic, and the Sudan. The meeting was in accordance with resolution 142(VII) adopted at its Seventh Session, which recommended to the member states "to set up at an early date at the subregional levels inter-governmental machinery charged with the responsibility for the harmonization of economic and social development in the subregion, taking into account the experience of similar institutional arrangements inside and outside Africa."[4] The June 1966 meeting discussed various questions related to economic cooperation in the subregion. No recommendations were adopted regarding the establishment of an institutional arrangement embracing all six countries in the subregion. (The four Maghreb countries--Tunisia, Algeria, Libya, and Morocco--already have created an effective institution for cooperation):

However, the countries agreed, to keep each other informed of reciprocal possibilities in the development of maritime transport and to compare experience and derive any lessons therefrom that might increase cooperation in this field; and to grant the necessary traffic rights to the companies of the subregion to enable them to provide air links. With regard to future action by the countries of the subregion, the meeting recommended that an inventory be made of the sectors in which economic cooperation was necessary and feasible. Following these recommendations, the ECA secretariat proposed studies covering the fields of education, maritime transport, air transport, energy, agriculture, industry, tourism, statistics, and family planning. No further meetings sponsored by ECA have been held in the subregion since 1966.

ECA is now shifting its emphasis from attempts to initiate the establishment of all-embracing institutional arrangements covering an entire subregion to direct assistance toward strengthening the already existing multinational economic groupings.[5] It is considered more effective to work with the existing multinational economic groupings in addition to attempting to create new forms of economic association. It is envisaged that the existing groupings will constitute part of the enlarged subregional machinery. Although in the past the existing economic groupings did not directly object to the proposals to create subregional machinery, they nevertheless gave their first loyalty to their own institutional arrangements. ECA's policy for the 1970's is to work as closely as possible with existing groupings both in terms of work programs and priorities and in formulating general strategy for economic development in Africa.

OBSERVATIONS

The experience of the existing economic groupings indicates that there cannot be any hard and fast rule regarding the kind of institutional machinery any form of economic cooperation should endeavor to create. In fact, as noted in the previous paragraphs, there are even some groupings in Africa, such as the Conference of East and Central African States, that seem to believe that, given good will and the desire to cooperate, the member countries can initiate joint economic projects without creating any institutions that would give rise to legal obligations through a treaty. The introduction of treaty obligations frightens some countries because of the possibility of surrender of some powers of self-determination.

Although the creation of large and all-embracing institutional machinery would be ideal when a group of countries moves from simple to higher levels of economic cooperation, examples are numerous in Africa where less cumbersome organs for joint action have proved to be just as effective in promoting joint development efforts. In some instances, the machinery for cooperation is confined to the level of technical experts. For this reason, some African countries have expressed some misgivings in the past about the structure and composition of the existing subregions. While accepting the idea of a subregional approach to economic cooperation as a sound proposition for solving the problems of the limitation in the size of the national markets, some countries wish to see a review of the working of these subregions. They hold the view that these subregions are not sufficiently flexible and do not constitute coherent economic entities that would permit achievement of the necessary rate of development to raise the standard of living of the African people. It is argued that there is need to reorganize these subregions to make for a more effective translation of their aspirations into economic realities.[6] It should be stressed, however, that the ECA subregional groupings were never meant to be water-tight compartments, nor was economic cooperation intended to be confined to each of these areas. When they were established, these subregions were found to be the most pragmatic approach to the solution of the economic development problems facing Africa.

It ought also to be stressed that the existing subregions have seemed ineffective in the initiation of joint economic projects partly because of the lack of sustained adherence to the joint economic decisions and partly due to the geographical location of the countries composing the subregions. Moreover, within these subregions there are smaller pressure groupings that sometimes make economic cooperation difficult as a result of conflicts of interests between these groupings.

The lack of adequate infrastructure, especially transport and communications facilities, has contributed to the problem of creating effective subregional institutional machinery for cooperation. It is for this reason that some economists argue that such smaller inter-governmental economic groupings as the East African Community, the Lake Chad Basin Commission, the Conseil de l'Entente, and the Maghreb Permanent Consultative Committee seem to have better chances of survival under present conditions in Africa than those composed of a large number of countries. In fact, it is sometimes stated that, with the exception of OCAM, a great majority of the more forward-looking economic groupings comprise no more than six countries. One would therefore conclude that, the fewer the countries composing any given economic grouping, the fewer their problems and differences. By the same analogy, the greater the number of countries, the more complex the problems. Although this may be true, the point to note is that, taking into account total population, investment opportunities, GDP, and overall purchasing power, none of the present economic groupings in Africa can economically sustain large-scale industrial and other development projects. This is equally true of the larger ECA subregions. Hence, the groupings should not be regarded as the end goal of efforts toward cooperation but rather as springboards for larger economic groupings.

Although the idea of establishing an institutional machinery for economic cooperation has been widely accepted in Africa, there are still problems of making such institutions into effective instruments for joint development. The idea of supranationalism still worries a number of countries. Nevertheless, as will be emphasized throughout in this study, the efforts toward economic cooperation in Africa are beginning to show positive results. To enhance this trend, additional efforts are required to strengthen the present institutional arrangements to meet future requirements. ECA has identified numerous alternative permutations for economic cooperation at different levels. What is now required is for the African governments to take positive action to lend support to ECA's development efforts, through individual country policy measures as well as through action within the existing multinational economic groupings.

Finally, the experience gained in some existing groupings, such as the East African Community, is of importance in the search for effective institutional machinery for cooperation. In the East African Community, each department or sector, although eventually responsible to the East African Authority, has its own administrative machinery with somewhat autonomous powers to make decisions affecting its field of responsibility. The activities of the various departments are then synchronized in the Council of East African Ministers. The other economic groupings in Africa do not possess this level of

institutional arrangements. In the UDEAC, the Directing Committee
is responsible for making the vital decisions affecting the group's
day-to-day functioning; in the OERS, the Council of Ministers exercise
similar functions. However, there are no departments equivalent
to those in the East African Community in these two organizations or
in any other grouping in Africa.

The conclusion drawn from the lessons of experience in Africa
and elsewhere in the world is that, since in the development process
there is a tendency for each of the leading sectors to develop itself
into rather specialized units, it might be necessary for some of the
economic groupings that seek multisectoral cooperation to consider
establishing institutions similar to those of the East African Community.
In economic groups where cooperation is envisaged at project level,
such as the lake and river basin development projects or such com-
modity-oriented economic groupings as the West African Rice Development Association, the need for elaborate machinery may not arise
since in most cases decisions are purely technical and can be resolved
at the level of experts. In this regard, it is useful to stress that,
whatever the degree or level of economic cooperation, it is essential
to create an effective institutional machinery for taking joint economic
decisions.

NOTES

1. See Economic Commission for Africa, Report of the First
Meeting of the Interim Council of Ministers of the Proposed Eastern
African Economic Community, (Addis Ababa, May 1966) E/CN.14/352,
Annex V, Article I, pp. 1-2.

2. See Economic Commission for Africa, Report of the Central
African Subregional Meeting on Economic Cooperation, E/CN.14/CA/
ECOP/13.

3. See Economic Commission for Africa, Report of the West
African Subregional Conference on Economic Cooperation (Addis Ababa,
May, 1967), E/CN.14/399, Annex IV, pp. 1-6.

4. Economic Commission for Africa, Compendium of Resolutions
(Addis Ababa, August 1967), E/CN.14/DOC/2/Add. 12.

5. Economic Commission for Africa, Report of the Second
Meeting of the Executive Committee, E.CN.14/ECO/18 (Addis Ababa,
November, 1969), pp. 51-52. Following comprehensive studies conducted by ECA on the possible alternative combinations for economic
cooperation and after a long period of experimentation with different

types of approaches, the countries seem more responsive to the
proposals for closer collaboration with ECA.

6. See Economic Commission for Africa, Summary of Proceedings
of the Tenth Anniversary and the Ninth Session of the Economic
Commission for Africa (Ten Years of ECA) (Addis Ababa, February
1969), p. 22.

A PLAN
FOR COOPERATION
IN THE
MAJOR
ECONOMIC SECTORS

4

COOPERATION

IN

AGRICULTURAL

DEVELOPMENT

THE CASE FOR COOPERATION
IN AGRICULTURE

The need to transform agriçulture from subsistence to market
production as an initial step toward the economic development of
Africa provides the a priori case for cooperation in agriculture. The
problems of agricultural development in Africa need to be tackled
from two angles. First, there is a need to rescue the masses from
the bondage of subsistence. This should be done through the adoption
by the African governments of positive policies and measures for the
development of the rural areas. Second, there is a need to introduce
new production methods in agriculture and to explore areas in which
new manufacturing or agricultural processing industries can be established, in order to reduce Africa's dependence on exports of agricultural raw materials.

The transformation from subsistence can be done largely on a
national basis. Since this transition is basically dependent on the
growth of the domestic markets as a result of the growth of industries,
it is essential that the governments take deliberate measures to enhance
agricultural development, especially in areas that are predominantly
traditional. In order to achieve this goal, it is essential that there
be developed adequate transport and marketing facilities to enable the
rural communities to bring their produce to the urban centers. The
governments would do well to assume responsibility for providing
adequate market facilities, e.g., warehousing and storage, price support systems, provisions for tractors, new brands and seeds, fertilizers, and direct assistance to the national grain marketing boards.

The establishment of manufacturing in agriculture is essential because any economy that develops industry without giving adequate consideration to agriculture is merely walking on one leg. One cannot speak of development when a major portion of the population still lives below a subsistence level. An interesting illustration that strengthens this point is the case of LAFTA, which started with heavy and extensive industrialization geared to import substitution as a way of redressing the balance of payments problems of the member countries. Industry in the member states was developed on an ad hoc basis, and agricultural development was left out of the integration program. The result was a situation where a highly modernized industrial sector existed side by side with a highly traditional agricultural sector in which the majority of the population remained below subsistence. The imbalances in the development of the urban and the rural populations that resulted from this situation could only aggravate the problems of economic development.

In the African economies, the development of agriculture should be regarded as one of the fields in which economic integration should be envisaged, although this is the field in which cooperation will be most difficult to achieve.* The fact to be noted is that most of the economic prosperity in Africa has been achieved in the field of agricultural development, especially the export of agricultural raw materials. Almost all the African countries depend on the export of raw agricultural commodities for the major portion of their national income. Any major plans for economic progress, therefore, cannot ignore the importance of the development of agriculture through the diversification of production. Hence, any progress in the scheme of economic integration essentially must have roots in the agricultural sector.

Of the total wealth of an African economy, nearly 85 to 90 percent is derived from agriculture. It is estimated that Africa south of the Sahara comprises about 15 percent of the world's total land surface including water. The share of arable land in Africa is about 20 percent of the world's total arable land. Africa has 15 percent of the world's total forest land and about 18 percent of the world's pasture land.

---

*It is realized that, as a result of the lack of complementarity in agricultural production in the African states, there would be difficulties in the initiation of joint economic cooperation plans. However, to start on the premise that cooperation in agriculture is not at all possible for this reason, is to lose sight of the real requirements of economic development in Africa.

This represents about 200 million hectares of arable land, 450 million hectares of pasture land, and about 640 million hectares of forest land. However, Africa has only about 5 percent of the world's total population. Nearly 70 percent of the total area is cultivated by indigenous farmers, mainly for subsistence. Agriculture therefore cannot be ignored.

Agriculture plays an important role in the development of Africa, and this fact has been recognized by the African countries. As shown in Table 4.1, over 30 to 40 percent of total investment is alloted to agriculture in such countries as Upper Volta, Dahomey, Tunisia, Morocco, and Niger. Chad, Togo, Mauritius, Ethiopia, Senegal, and Sudan also attach great importance to the development of agriculture. When the gross domestic product of Africa is broken down by origin, agriculture, in general terms, makes a much larger contribution to GDP than any other single field of economic activity.

Between 1960 and 1966, agricultural output in Africa measured in terms of value added (at 1960 factor cost) grew at an annual rate of 1.3 percent, which was slower than the rate of growth of production in such other sectors of the economy as industry and transport. Although the share of agriculture in GDP fell from about 40 to less than 36 percent between 1960 and 1966, the weight of agriculture in total economic activity remained quite high, underlining the fact that adequate increases in agricultural productivity remain a sine qua non of the general strategy of economic development in Africa. Furthermore, agricultural commodities provide at least 60 percent of total export earnings in developing Africa and about three-quarters of the population of Africa lives in rural areas and is engaged mainly in agriculture. The share of agriculture in GDP was highest in West Africa, where its contribution was as high as 54 percent, followed by North Africa, where it was 24 percent. These statistics underline the need for concerted action in the development of agriculture.

AFRICA'S MAJOR CROPS

The need to diversify agricultural production in Africa through economic integration will be greatly appreciated when it is recognized that in most of the African countries agriculture accounts for about 80 to 90 percent of total exports and that the bulk of these exports are in the form of raw materials or semiprocessed commodities. The most important crops in Africa are coffee, cocoa, cotton, palm oil, tobacco, tea, bananas, sugar, and groundnuts. The distribution of these raw materials is not even throughout Africa, although a few

TABLE 4.1

Share of Agriculture in Total Investment in Development
Plans of Selected African Countries
(percent)

Country	Plan Period	Share of Agriculture in Total Investment	Share of Agriculture in Public Investment	Planned Annual Increase of Agricultural Production
North Africa				
Morocco	1965-67	34	29	3
Tunisia	1965-68	31	45	2.8
Sudan	1961/62-1970/71	21	27	4
Libya	1963/64-1967/68	--	20	--
West Africa				
Dahomey	1966-70	34	--	--
Gambia	1964-67	--	21	--
Ivory Coast	1967-70	--	30	5.3[a]
Mali	1961-65	--	20	9
Mauritania	1963-66	9	17	2
Niger	1965-68	31	--	3.3
Nigeria	1962-68	--	14	--
Senegal	1965/66-1968/69	20	42	5.4
Sierra Leone	1962/63-1966/67	6	8	--
Upper Volta	1963-64	40	--	--
Togo	1966-70	23	26	3.5
Central Africa				
Cameroun	1966-71	19	17.7	3.3
Chad	1966-70	28	--	5.1
Congo (Braz-zaville)	1964-68	6	--	1.7
Gabon	1966-70	1[b]	--	3.5
Central African Republic	1965-70	18	--	5.9
Eastern Africa				
Ethiopia	1962/63-1966/67	21	15.3	2.3
Kenya	1966-70	4	26	4.8
Madagascar	1964-68	12	31	5.9
Mauritius	1962-65	24	29.7	--
Tanzania	1964/65-1968/69	15	28	4
Zanzibar	1964-67	--	8	--
Uganda	1966-70	13	27	5.2
Zambia	1966-70	10	15	4.7

[a]This rate refers to industrial agriculture only. For traditional agriculture the rate is 2.8 percent and for forestry 20 percent.
[b]Excludes investment in forestry.

Sources: Government agencies, national development plans.

crops are grown in almost all the African countries. But, as shown in Table 4.2, from the commercial point of view only one or two countries possess sufficiently large potential for the development of any particular agricultural industry.

Coffee

Total African coffee production has expanded considerably in recent years. According to the data in Table 4.3 between 1961 and 1967, production grew from 753,800 metric tons to 1,196,700 metric tons (see Table 4.3), an average annual increase of 11.1 percent, while exports as a percentage of production fell from 87.4 percent in 1961 to about 71.3 percent in 1967. The widening gap between production and exports reflects the problems on the international coffee market and the tendency for production in the principal producing countries to exceed actual consumption. The International Coffee Agreement concluded in 1962 regulates coffee exports through periodically revised quota restrictions. The coffee-producing countries in Africa and elsewhere had been troubled by excessive coffee stocks that resulted in a decline in the prices, and the quota system is a means to prevent this decline. The International Coffee Agreement has resulted in a general improvement in coffee prices, especially for robusta coffee, which accounts by volume for more than three-quarters of total coffee exports from Africa. The major coffee-growing area in Africa is East Africa, where Ethiopia, Kenya, and Tanzania produce arabica coffee and Uganda and Madagascar produce robusta. There has been a marked increase in output, particularly in Uganda, Kenya, and Tanzania in recent years; in 1965, output rose by more than 20 percent in Tanzania and Uganda and by more than 30 percent in Kenya, but output declined in 1967. Exports from Ethiopia, which has a sizable domestic consumption, increased by some 10 percent per annum between 1961 and 1967, largely due to improvements in marketing facilities. In West Africa, the Ivory Coast is the main producer and exporter; its exports grew from 154,700 metric tons to 185,700 metric tons between 1961 and 1965. In Central Africa, there was a slow growth in production in Congo (Kinshasa) followed by a decline in exports; this had a considerable effect on total exports from the area. Elsewhere in Africa, production in Angola was stable between 1961 and 1967.

Cotton

Much of Africa's cotton production is carried out in North Africa.

TABLE 4.2

Production of Selected Agricultural Crops
in Africa, 1961 and 1963-66
(thousands of metric tons)

	Production			
	1961	1963	1964	1965
North Africa				
Raw sugar	321*	426	457	418
Wine	1,733	1,718	1,482	2,161
Bananas	76	66	60	74
Citrus fruits	1,192	1,442	1,677	1,525
Groundnuts	181	341	337	367
Olive oil	83	163	149	130
East Africa				
Raw sugar	1,188*	1,466	1,336	1,576
Wine	1	1	1	1
Bananas	289	336	352	383
Citrus fruits	100	107	112	121
Groundnuts	347	445	425	434
Copra	30	37	43	37
West Africa				
Bananas	182	263	236	242
Citrus fruits	172	188	193	197
Cocoa beans	707*	764	1,047	743
Groundnuts	2,900	3,132	3,068	3,575
Palm kernels	639	614	602	598
Palm oil	730	712	732	750
Copra	10	8	13	9
Central Africa				
Raw sugar	48*	62	58	69
Bananas	406	391	397	387
Citrus fruits	18	19	19	19
Cocoa beans	121*	135	146	136
Groundnuts	388	477	500	509
Palm kernels	167	135	158	132
Palm oil	268	286	271	207
Copra	6	5	6	6
Total Africa				
Raw Sugar	2,850*	3,436	3,434	3,321
Wine	2,020	2,069	1,833	2,164
Bananas	1,023	1,122	1,146	1,169
Citrus fruits	1,929	2,281	2,519	2,459
Cocoa beans	828*	899	1,193	879
Groundnuts	4,119	4,719	4,598	5,139
Palm kernels	816	767	777	744
Olive oil	83	163	149	130
Palm oil	1,017	1,016	1,022	975
Copra	111	112	119	91

*Production for 1961/62.

Source: FAO, Production Year Book, 1966.

TABLE 4.3

Production of Coffee by Principal
Producing Countries in Africa, 1961-67
(thousands of metric tons)

	1961	1962	1963	1964	1965	1966	1967
Uganda	95.5	120.2	164.8	184.9	223.1	166.6	157.5
Ethiopia	130.0	132.0	134.0	136.0	138.0	150.0a	150.0a
Madagascar	44.5	28.6	51.5	51.2	52.4	52.0	82.0
Kenya	27.8	61.0	44.2	39.4	52.1	26.0	24.4
Tanzania	20.2	27.4	32.4	36.6	44.2	44.8	51.3
Total East Africa	318.0	309.2	426.9	448.1	509.8	439.4	465.2
Ivory Coast	96.8	194.8	261.2	202.0	271.0	130.0	288.0
Guinea	15.0	13.0	12.3	13.5	9.3	7.2	10.2
Togo	10.3	10.6	13.8	12.0	13.5	5.7	13.8
Total West Africa	133.0	218.4	298.7	241.2	308.1	142.9	312.0
Congo (Kinshasa)	54.0	66.0	66.0	57.0	60.0	54.0b	60.0b
Cameroun	40.3	42.6	43.2	47.0	54.7	63.3	66.0
Rwanda and Burundi	23.3	19.5	21.3	22.5	25.8	22.9	29.3
Total Central Africa	134.2	128.1	153.7	143.3	160.7	140.2	155.3
Angola	168.6	185.0	168.0	186.0	168.0	198.0b	204.0b
Total other Africa	168.6	185.0	168.0	186.0	168.0	198.0	204.0
Total Africa	753.8	937.3	1,047.3	1,018.6	1,146.6	987.7	1,196.7
Total world	4,423.2	4,610.6	4,224.9	3,521.1	4,524.9	3,839.6	4,267.8

aFAO estimates.
bUnofficial estimates.

Sources: FAO: Production Yearbook, 1963, 1966, and 1968.

Table 4.4 shows that more than half of the cotton grown in Africa is produced in the United Arab Republic and the Sudan. Between 1961 and 1967, production in North Africa increased at an annual rate of more than 10 percent. In 1967, output in this area was some 7 percent lower than in 1965, partly due to a reduction in acreage and partly to heavy damage caused by the bollworm in Egypt. The volume of exports grew more slowly over this period, largely due to increasing domestic demand, particularly in the Sudan. Uganda and Tanzania are the principal producers in the East African subregion, and output in Tanzania increased steadily at an annual average rate of 18.6 percent between 1961 and 1967. Taking the area as a whole, the production in East, Central, and West Africa showed a decline between 1965 and 1967.

The fall in output and exports in Congo (Kinshasa) affected the total exports for the Central African subregion. In Chad and Cameroun, however, there was appreciable increases in both production and exports, especially in 1966. Nigeria is the main cotton producer in West Africa; although Nigeria experienced some fluctuations in production between 1961 and 1967, there was an increase in output in 1967. Exports for Nigeria declined as a result of the expansion of textile manufacturing in the country. Elsewhere in Africa, production grew very rapidly, especially in 1967; production in Mozambique fluctuated considerably in 1961 and 1967. Much of the output of cotton in Africa is consumed by local textile industries, which have expanded considerably in recent years.

Natural Rubber

Nigeria and Liberia are the main producers of natural rubber in Africa. Although production figures for Liberia are not available, according to ECA's analysis the export data suggest that output grew slowly between 1960 and 1967. There were violent fluctuations in production in Nigeria during this period, but there was an overall increase of some 27 percent in 1967. In the Ivory Coast, production and exports grew remarkably from a very low base, and by 1965 the Ivory Coast accounted for about 4 percent of total West African production. In Central Africa, output and exports declined in Congo (Kinshasa) but increased considerably in Cameroun, and between 1960 and 1965 exports from Cameroun increased at an annual rate of almost 24 percent.

Exports of natural rubber from developing Africa are threatened by severe competition from synthetic rubber, leading to a general

TABLE 4.4

Production of Cotton (lint) by Principal
Producing Countries in Africa, 1961-67
(thousands of metric tons)

	1961	1962	1963	1964	1965	1966	1967
U.A.R.	336	696	442	504	520	455	437
Sudan	116	217	163	102	150	159	179
Total North Africa	455	913	611	613	678	614	616
Uganda	67	33	65	69	79	78	78
Tanzania	34	39	48	53	67	80	68
Total East Africa	111	72	126	141	172	158	146
Congo (Kinshasa)	20	16	13	7	5	7	8
Chad	16	33	38	36	31	45	39
Cameroun	10	13	16	17	19	19	17
Total Central Africa	59	62	80	72	67	71	64
Nigeria	50	28	49	44	44	43	50
Mali	6	7	10	18	20	10*	11*
Total West Africa	64	35	72	75	78	53	61
Mozambique	37	43	29	39	29	38	42
South Africa	5	6	11	11	17	15	15
Angola	4	7	5	4	7	7	9
Total other Africa	48	56	47	56	55	60	66
Total Africa	937	943	936	957	1,050	1,036	1,041
Total world	9,835	10,537	11,282	11,428	11,769	10,716	10,380

*Unofficial estimates.

Sources: FAO, (United Nations) Production Yearbook, Vol. XX, 1966 and Vol. XXII, 1968.

87

decline in the price of natural rubber in recent years; in 1966, the average price of natural rubber was at its lowest in the 1960's. This price drop was accounted for, to some extent, by release from stock-piling of the American authorities, who sold 240,000 long tons of natural rubber from stock at less than market prices in 1966.

Sisal

Although sisal is of great importance in a number of individual countries, particularly Tanzania, sisal exports account for less than 1 percent of the foreign exchange earnings of developing Africa. In East Africa, which dominates the production and export of sisal in Africa, output and exports increased very slowly between 1960 and 1965 and output actually fell in 1966, but production and exports rose considerably in Madagascar, which accounted for about 8 percent of East African production in 1965. Exports from Mozambique rose by 2.3 percent between 1960 and 1965, and in 1966 production fell sharply. For most African countries, there was a general decline in output of sisal in 1966.

Like most primary commodities, sisal faces mounting competition from synthetics and substitutes, and this has resulted in the lowering of sisal prices on the world market. This price drop is cause for particular concern to Africa, which accounts for more than half the world's sisal. To mitigate this problem, the FAO Study Group on Hard Fibers recommended in September 1967 an indicative price for sisal of $176.40 plus or minus $12 per long ton and a reduction of almost 5 percent in 1968 export quotas. This recommendation was subsequently approved by representatives of the governments and the hard fiber industry. At the time the agreement was made, the market price for sisal was $139.20 per long ton, and in January 1968, despite the curtailment of production and a reduction in exports, the price was only $56 per long ton.

Tea

Tea has no great weight in total exports from developing Africa, but for Malawi and Kenya it constitutes about 29 and 13 percent re-spectively of total export earnings and it is increasingly important in a number of other African countries. The East African subregion accounts for 75 percent of Africa's tea, and production increased at an annual average rate of 7.0 percent between 1960 and 1965. During the period 1960-67 total exports from the area grew by almost 11 percent annually. In Central Africa, output in Congo (Kinshasa) changed little between 1963 and 1967 but in Mozambique both output and exports expanded steadily over the same period. The expansion of tea production in East Africa was accompanied by a decline in unit values, and in 1967 export earnings from tea were about 20 percent less than in 1964 although there was an increase of 7 percent in the volume of exports.

Future Prospects

The development of the agricultural industry is the most difficult task faced by the newly independent African states in their efforts to uplift the masses from poverty. The present development pattern shows that there are no sizable manufacturing or processing industries in Africa, and trade with the outside world consists mainly of the export of raw materials. At the same time, there are large imports of foodstuffs, which indicates that food production has not received adequate attention in the past. Food shortage is now a regular feature in some of the African countries, which has resulted in serious malnutrition problems that have greatly retarded the economic productivity of the labor force. The problem of reliance on exports of primary commodities has been aggravated by the fact that most of the African states are dependent on one or two crops for most of their income.

In order to overcome these difficulties and to transform the agricultural sector from subsistence to money economy, there is a strong case for diversification of production in the agricultural industry; this can be best accomplished if the African economies are properly integrated. The climatic factors coupled with the absence of complementarity in agriculture have resulted in the development of agriculture virtually in isolation and without due regard for the need for concerted action. The absence of diversification of agricultural production in Africa may prove disastrous in the future if the price of primary commodities continues to fall in the world market and if the present rate of development of synthetics and substitutes is maintained in the developed countries. In fact, in recent years this problem has been faced by producers of a number of commodities. As technology advances, there are growing fears in the developing world that there will be increased use of synthetics and substitutes, resulting in a considerable fall in the demand for primary commodities in the advanced countries. Therefore, there is urgent need for joint action in planning for the development of agricultural production. Any degree of cooperation in agriculture would constitute a useful step toward enhancing the general rate of development in Africa.

FOOD-PROCESSING INDUSTRIES

The development of trade is discussed in great detail in Chapter 6, but it is useful at this stage to point out that most of the African countries import very large quantities of foodstuffs. This is paradoxical because the African economy is primarily agricultural, and some experts hold the view that Africa could be self-sufficient in food requirements and that with proper development policies Africa could become a net exporter of foodstuffs.

However, in some African countries imports of foodstuffs have constituted about 20 percent of total imports throughout the 1960's, and this pattern is likely to persist unless radical measures are taken to correct it. Since it is technically possible for the African countries to step up the rate of food production, efforts should be made toward this objective through integration. In the past, the markets of the individual states were closed to other African imports as a result of tariff and other barriers. It therefore follows that legislation and trade policies will have to be coordinated in order to ensure that the agricultural products of the newly integrated industries find a market. However, food-processing industries will not be easy to establish in the face of very sharp competition from the industrialized countries that use raw materials from the African countries because setting up processing plants must mean the diversion of raw materials from these countries. In the initial stages, experience suggests that the development of agricultural industry will have to begin with plants for processing raw materials, followed by the production of finished agricultural goods.

Chapter 6 shows that agricultural commodities account for a high proportion of Africa's export earnings and that the proportion of agricultural products in the total import bill also is quite large. In this chapter, it is sufficient to state that in 1965 food, live animals, and crude materials accounted for about 44 percent of total agricultural exports while food and live animals accounted for 62 percent of total agricultural imports.

Due to the introduction of new techniques in production, there were changes in the trade patterns of the different commodities and total agricultural exports from developing Africa increased in value by 42.2 percent while agricultural imports grew in value by 26.7 percent between 1963 and 1964. For beverages and tobacco, the value of exports went up by 24 percent as compared to an increase of 11 percent in the value of imports; the value of exports and imports of food and live animals both increased by about 22 percent during this period.

In the North African subregion, imports of agricultural products rose in value by some 25 percent and exports rose by 21 percent between 1960 and 1964. In East Africa, between 1962 and 1965 total agricultural imports increased in value at twice the rate of exports. The highest increase was for beverages, tobacco, and animal and vegetable oils. In West Africa, in value terms exports increased by 24 percent and imports by 11 percent. Imports of foodstuffs are much greater than exports for most African countries, but net consumption of imported beverages and tobacco declined from $33.8 million to $33.2 million between 1962 and 1965.

As noted earlier, much of Africa's agricultural production is on a subsistence basis. Although production for the market has been expanding in recent years, it is probable that subsistence production still accounts for more than 50 percent of total agricultural output. Very little is known of the market responsiveness of the subsistence farmer. Although the African economy is generally described as a dual economy, it would be impossible to imagine that the agricultural sector of the African economy can be divided into water-tight compartments comprising subsistence production on the one hand and production for the market on the other, nor is it always easy to draw a clear distinction between production for domestic consumption and production for export. Despite these difficulties, however, it is possible to group African foodstuffs into two broad categories: those produced mainly for domestic consumption and those for which exports represent a fairly large proportion of production. The first group comprises mainly cereals, starchy roots, and pulses, although it should be noted that these same crops also are sold extensively in local markets. The second group covers the cash crops for which export markets are important even though some part of total production may be consumed by the farmers themselves. Since much of the agricultural output comes from subsistence farming, it is difficult to ensure statistical reliability, and much of the available data is based largely on estimates of production and consumption in the subsistence sector.

As shown in Table 4.5, the combined production of cereals, starchy roots, and pulses increased by about 2.6 percent per annum for the whole of Africa between 1961 and 1967. The total production for all Africa rose from 99.041 million metric tons to 117.046 million metric tons in this period. This probably is not a spectacular increase when one takes into account the fact that population has grown at

TABLE 4.5

Total African Production of Cereals, Starchy Roots, and Pulses, 1961-67
(thousands of metric tons)

Crop	1961	1962	1963	1964	1965	1966	1967	Percentage Increase 1961-67
Wheat	4,358	4,358	6,382	6,242	6,082	8,749	9,699	122
Barley	1,748	3,172	3,433	2,844	2,917	1,779	2,593	48
Rice	4,404	5,562	5,809	5,800	5,419	5,665	6,696	52
Maize	14,518	16,586	16,457	14,848	15,314	17,969	22,157	52
Sorghum and millet	19,463	20,091	20,890	21,089	21,320	20,687	23,303	19
Total cereals	44,491	52,586	52,971	50,823	51,052	61,732	64,596	45
Potatoes	1,709	1,800	1,958	1,876	2,121	1,856	2,064	20
Sweet potatoes and yams	20,956	21,386	21,883	22,475	23,050	23,911	23,600	12
Cassava	28,308	26,991	28,353	28,982	29,519	30,467	30,518	7
Total starchy roots	50,973	50,177	52,194	53,333	54,690	56,234	56,182	10
Pulses	3,577	4,942	4,060	4,302	4,302	4,148	4,956	38
Total cereals, starchy roots, and pulses	99,041	102,213	109,225	108,458	110,044	107,048	117,046	18

Source: FAO, (United Nations) Production Yearbook, Vol. XX 1966 and Vol. XXII 1968.

a rate of about 3 percent. The data for subregions shown in Table 4.6 indicates that the composition of staple foodstuffs production varies considerably from subregion to subregion, depending largely on food habits. In West Africa, the bulk of the population is heavily dependent on such starchy roots as sweet potatoes, yams, and cassava.

The output of wheat expanded rapidly between 1961 and 1965 but still accounted for little more than 2 percent of total cereal production in 1965. Rice is not a staple food for the East African subregion, but it is important to particular countries, especially Madagascar, which accounts for some 90 percent of the subregion's rice production. Among the root crops, sweet potatoes, yams, and cassava increased by more than 9 percent between 1963 and 1965.

As in the East African subregion, cereals constitute the main staple food for North Africa, and in 1965 they accounted for more than 85 percent of staple foodstuff production. Wheat alone accounted for 31 percent of the total; maize for some 15 percent; and rice, barley, sorghum, and millet for between 12 and 14 percent each. These crops often are subject to fluctuations in total output due to bad weather conditions. For example, drought affected the Tunisian barley crop in 1965 although for the subregion as a whole barley output increased by 3 percent. Good harvest crops in maize in Egypt accounted for the 5 percent increase in subregional output of maize. Egyptian rice production was low in 1965, and since Egypt is the principal rice producer of the continent this was reflected in a decline of 9 percent in the subregional output.

In the Central African subregion, as in West Africa, starchy roots are the principal staple foodstuffs; in 1965, these accounted for more than 80 percent of total food production. Among the cereals, sorghum and millet are the leading crops, but production was rather slow and grew little more than 1 percent between 1961 and 1965. Maize production showed a decline in 1965 compared to 1963 and 1964 but was still some 14 percent higher than it had been in 1961 and the same was true of rice. Wheat production grew steadily over the period, but in 1965 it still constituted a negligible proportion of total food output for the subregion.

Raw Sugar

Almost half of the raw sugar in Africa is produced in East Africa, particularly in Mauritius, Reunion, and Southern Rhodesia. Between 1961 and 1965, the production of raw sugar increased by more than

TABLE 4.6

Production of Cereals, Starchy Roots,
and Pulses in Africa, by Subregion,
1961 and 1963-65
(thousands of metric tons)

	1961	1963	1964	1965
North Africa				
Wheat	3,028	5,013	4,654	4,870
Barley	946	2,595	2,013	2,066
Rice	1,165	2,245	2,062	1,885
Maize	1,739	2,538	2,290	2,400
Sorghum and millet	2,336	2,570	2,331	2,172
Total cereals	9,214	14,779	13,350	13,393
Potatoes	835	956	831	1,031
Sweet potatoes and yams	105	100	106	104
Cassava	115	120	120	124
Total starchy roots	1,055	1,176	1,057	1,259
Pulses	545	781	990	1,016
Total cereals, starchy roots, and pulses	10,814	16,736	15,397	15,668
West Africa				
Rice	1,589	1,774	1,886	1,787
Maize'	1,763	2,039	2,165	2,217
Sorghum and millet	9,340	10,618	10,995	11,012
Total cereals	12,692	14,431	15,046	15,016
Potatoes	3	6	5	5
Sweet potatoes and yams	16,663	17,979	18,060	18,518
Cassava	11,908	13,237	13,011	13,440
Total starchy roots	28,574	31,222	31,076	31,963
Pulses	1,096	1,197	1,197	1,203
Total cereals, starchy roots, and pulses	42,362	46,850	47,319	48,182
Central Africa				
Wheat	8	9	11	13
Rice	113	116	118	107
Maize	650	789	768	745
Sorghum and millet	1,590	1,534	1,504	1,608
Total cereals	2,361	2,448	2,401	2,470
Potatoes	100	106	156	168
Sweet potatoes and yams	1,576	1,428	1,723	1,839
Cassava	11,049	9,650	9,815	10,133
Total starchy roots	12,725	11,184	11,694	12,140
Pulses	401	499	523	471
Total cereals, starchy roots, and pulses	15,487	14,131	14,618	15,084
East and Southern Africa				
Wheat	364	403	435	461
Barley	763	796	788	817
Rice	1,281	1,297	1,429	1,312
Maize	4,481	4,441	4,688	4,778
Sorghum and millet	4,916	5,679	5,078	5,134
Total cereals	11,805	12,716	12,418	12,502
Potatoes	435	457	467	478
Sweet potatoes and yams	2,579	2,306	2,518	2,520
Cassava	3,952	4,011	4,674	4,380
Total starchy roots	6,966	6,774	7,659	7,378
Pulses	1,355	1,376	1,433	1,431
Total cereals, starchy roots, and pulses	20,126	20,866	21,510	21,311

Source: ECA, A Survey of Economic Conditions in Africa, 1967,
E/CN. I4/409/Rev.I.

7 percent per annum. In 1965, output increased by 18 percent as a result of a general increase in output in all producing countries in the subregion except Madagascar, where production declined by 29 percent due to drought conditions. Exports of sugar, both raw and refined, increased by more than 9 percent per annum between 1961 and 1965, and much of the exports came from Southern Rhodesia.

About 12 percent of the raw sugar produced in Africa in 1965 was grown in North Africa, mainly in Egypt, but exports of sugar declined very substantially between 1961 and 1966, partly due to an increase in domestic consumption.

The Central African subregion is a modest producer of raw sugar; it accounted for less than 3 percent of total African output in 1965. In recent years, however, production has grown significantly in the two Congos. For example, in Congo (Brazzaville) output increased at an annual rate of 18 percent between 1961 and 1965 and by nearly 94 percent in 1966. In Congo (Kinshasa), an increase of about 27 percent was achieved in 1965. The Central African subregion does not export sugar--all the sugar produced in Central Africa is consumed locally.

Citrus Fruits and Wine

In 1965, North Africa accounted for almost 83 percent of total wine production in Africa; Algeria is the major producer. Algerian and Moroccan production both increased considerably during the first half of the 1960's, but because of the decline of Algerian exports to France wine exports from North Africa declined sharply between 1961 and 1964.

North Africa also supplies more than 60 percent of the citrus fruits grown on the African continent, and between 1961 and 1964 both production and exports grew markedly. South of the Sahara, South Africa is an important producer of wine and citrus fruits, supplying the Southern African market.

Cocoa

West Africa produces some 85 percent of all the cocoa beans grown in Africa. Ghana and Nigeria are the principal West African producers, followed by the Ivory Coast, which has contributed significantly to the increases in production recorded in recent years.

Between 1961 and 1963, production grew by a little over 4 percent per annum, but output increased by almost 37 percent in 1964 and by about 29 percent in 1965. In 1966, the production of cocoa beans in Nigeria and the Ivory Coast increased by 44 and 24 percent respectively, while in Ghana output declined by 8 percent as a result of continued bad weather conditions and the incidence of black pod. Despite the decline in production, exports of cocoa beans were constant throughout 1961 and 1963 and increased quite rapidly between 1963 and 1965.

In the organization of food production, whether at the national or multinational level, the main problem is that fresh food is perishable and therefore the provision of quick and adequate means of transportation together with other marketing facilities is of utmost importance. If food cannot reach its destination in good time, storage becomes essential. Therefore, one of the plans for integration in the development of food industries would be the coordination of market facilities in a given area comprising several countries. In food grains, there is need to establish multinational grain marketing boards through the coordination of the activities of the existing national grain marketing boards. As has been stressed elsewhere, the African countries, in collaboration with the FAO, should conduct an inquiry into the availability of different kinds of food and foodstuffs, including staple food. An African food census could be undertaken so as to enable the distribution of food, especially to areas where food is scarce. In certain cases, governments might find it useful to study ways and means of introducing new kinds of staple foods in the famine-stricken areas.

FISH PRODUCTION

The development of fisheries is an important aspect of economic development since the population must have access to adequate sources of protein. Africa at present suffers from lack of high-grade protein, which shows that the fish industry, which is the major source of protein, is not yet fully developed.

The growth of fisheries in Africa is often underestimated largely due to lack of statistics. Much fishing is done by traditional fishermen who do not maintain records of their catches. Much of the fish caught on a commercial basis, especially in Eastern and Southern Africa, is manufactured into fishmeal, most of which is exported to Europe as cattle feed. High-grade fish often is canned or frozen for export, while dried fish is usually for the local market. In the traditional sector, dried fish is an important item of trade, especially in the areas far away from the sea or lakes.

Much of the fish in Africa is found on the continental shelf. Between 1961 and 1965, fish catches in Africa by weight increased by 6 percent per annum. About one-half of the fishing is carried out in Southwest and South Africa. In West Africa, Senegal is the subregion's largest producer, while in North Africa Morocco is an important producer. The use of traditional means of fishing greatly reduces fish production.

Inland fisheries provide significant proportions of the total African catch, particularly in West, Central and East Africa, but the lakes are not yet fully exploited. Much of the fishing on a commercial scale is done by foreign-owned enterprises. The U.S.S.R., Japan, Greece, Portugal, Italy, and France are among non-African countries engaged in the fishing industry in Africa, especially in off-shore fishing.

Africa's fish production does not account for any large share of world trade in fish products. In fact, the African countries import large quantities of fish, both frozen and canned. In 1965, exports of fish products from Africa declined compared with 1961, largely due to the slow increase in fish production in 1965.

Imports of fresh, frozen, and canned fish into Africa increased by some 3 percent per annum between 1961 and 1965. The principal importers are Congo (Kinshasa), the U.A.R., Southern Rhodesia, Reunion, Zambia, and Kenya. On balance, developing Africa is a net importer of fish products.

Joint action, especially between the inland and the coastal countries, should be given greater importance in the development of the fish industry. Through arrangements involving the cold storage boards in a number of countries, fish could be transported from the coastal to the inland areas; this clearly is an area in which the countries can cooperate. Since provision of cold storage facilities is an expensive venture, it is essential that groups of countries work together for the establishment of joint shuttle services for the transportation of fish among them. In the development of water reservoirs for providing water for irrigation and harnessing to provide electricity, consideration should be given to the joint development of the fish industry by the countries bordering the dams. The possibility of developing the fish industry on the man-made lakes should be given adequate consideration. In the areas of the lakes, especially in East Africa, there is great potential for the development of the fish industry on a multinational scale, and this potential should be fully exploited.

VEGETABLE OIL AND OILSEED PRODUCTION

The development of oilseeds in Africa is of significance to economic cooperation largely for two reasons. (1) oilseeds constitute an important source of foreign exchange in a number of African countries and (2) these countries face stiff competition from oilseed production in the advanced countries and are therefore subject to tight import restrictions. Africa is the second largest producer of oilseeds in the world. These oil-producing seeds include groundnuts, palm kernels, cotton seed, linseed, coconuts, sunflower seed, and soya beans. Total world production of oilseed was around 86 million metric tons in 1965, of which 10 percent was produced in Africa. On the African continent, Nigeria produces half the palm kernels and about one-third the groundnuts in Africa. The second largest producer of palm kernel is Congo (Kinshasa), while Senegal is the second largest producer of groundnuts.

The East African subregion accounted for some 8 percent of total African groundnut production in 1965, and between 1961 and 1965 its production of groundnuts increased at an annual rate of almost 6 percent. Uganda is the main East African producer, followed by Southern Rhodesia and Malawi. Some 70 percent of all Africa's groundnuts are grown in West Africa; output was 10 percent higher in 1963 than in 1961 but is subject to regular fluctuations. Nigeria and Senegal are the main exporters of groundnuts. In Cameroun and Chad, groundnut production rose significantly between 1961 and 1965, at annual rates of 18.6 and 3.6 percent respectively. In 1966, however, there was no change in output in Chad while in Cameroun production declined by almost 20 percent.

Palm kernels and palm oil are produced mainly in the West African subregion. There was a general decline in production and exports of palm kernels in the period between 1961 and 1965. Some 10 percent of Africa's copra is produced in West Africa, principally in Nigeria, but because of the political situation in that country production and exports of copra have declined in recent years. Congo (Kinshasa), Chad, and Cameroun are the main groundnut producers in Central Africa, but since 1961 the groundnut crop in Congo (Kinshasa) has been declining.

In developing the oilseed-processing industries, several problems will be encountered. First, as stated earlier, there is competition from industries in the developed countries that operate behind high tariff walls, as evidenced by tariff on oilseeds in the EEC. Second, the price of oilseed on the world market fluctuates considerably, adversely affecting foreign exchange earnings. Thirdly, the industry requires highly skilled personnel, which is not often available in the oilseed-producing countries in Africa. In terms of capital requirements, oil-processing demands expensive equipment and is capital-intensive; this factor alone prevents individual African countries from setting up oilseed-processing industries.

The importance of the processing industries is that there is a choice in exports between crude oil, refined oil, and oilcakes, which do not always go to the same market, thereby providing the necessary diversity in markets. Moreover, the processing industry provides a base for other manufacturing industries, such as soap, margarine, and animal feed production. Along with the development of processing industries, there is a need to open up the market of the African countries for these products through granting special preferences.

LIVESTOCK AND THE MEAT INDUSTRY

The lack of statistical data on the number of herds, especially in rural areas and remote parts of Africa, makes it difficult to form an accurate estimate of the livestock population in Africa. However, it is estimated that all the African countries taken together had an estimated 1965 livestock population of 128 million head of cattle and 267 million sheep and goats. The number or density of the livestock population varies greatly among the African countries, largely due to climatic and topographic conditions. There has not been any substantial increase in the size of cattle herds in recent years; between 1960 and 1964, the rate of growth was estimated at less than 2 percent per annum, while the average takeoff from cattle herds has been between 7 and 9 percent.

The East African subregion is the dominant cattle-producing area in Africa. Ethiopia, the main producing country in the area, has a cattle population almost as great as that of the whole of West Africa taken together. There has not been a substantial increase in cattle herds in Ethiopia in recent years, due to poor methods of livestock production and husbandry and the continued presence of livestock diseases. The cattle herds in the other countries of the subregion have increased very slowly, especially in the early years of the 1960's, and in Kenya and Southern Rhodesia the cattle population declined between 1960 and 1965. In Madagascar, however, the number of cattle grew by more than 7 percent per annum between 1960 and 1964, and it is believed that Madagascar now surpasses Ethiopia in terms of cattle per person.

In West Africa, there has been considerable growth in the cattle population; between 1960 and 1964, the rate of growth was 4.5 percent per annum. Much of the increase in the number of cattle occurred in Mauritania, where the size of the herd is believed to have doubled in 1960-64, followed by Mali and Senegal. The highest cattle density in Africa is found in Namibia (Southwest Africa) and Botswana; it is estimated that Namibia possesses 4 head of cattle per person and Botswana more than 2 head of cattle per person. These figures are significant when compared with the African average of 41 head of cattle per 100 persons and with the world average of 32 cattle per 100 persons. With the exception of Chad, which is the largest cattle-raising country in the subregion and has sizable numbers, Central Africa has a cattle density generally lower than most parts of Africa.

As regards the sheep and goat population in Africa, there has been an increase of 2.6 percent per annum over the 1960's. Much of this increase took place in West Africa, especially in the Ivory Coast, Togo, and Mauritania. In the North and Central African subregions, the average annual increases were less than 3 percent, while in other parts of Africa there has been little or no change in the size of sheep flocks and goat herds.

From the data available, there is evidence to suggest that meat does not constitute a large item in the trade among the African countries. In the majority of African countries, the meat from cold storages and abattoirs serves very limited urban centers. However, livestock--especially cattle, sheep, and goats--for a long time has been the basic item of exchange in the traditional trade among the African countries. The data on meat production from indigenous animals in Table 4.7 indicates that Ethiopia and Uganda are the principal meat-producing countries in East and Southern Africa. In Central Africa, Cameroun produces sizable quantities of meat. In West Africa, Nigeria is the main producer, followed by Upper Volta, Senegal, and Niger. In North Africa, Egypt, Sudan, and Morocco are the principal meat producers. Elsewhere in Africa, the Republic of South Africa produces large quantities of meat, followed by Southern Rhodesia, Namibia (Southwest Africa), and Angola.

Trade in livestock constitutes one of the oldest forms of cooperation among the African people. From times immemorial, the African countries traded in cattle, sheep, goats, hides, and skins. There is no evidence to suggest that modern development should disregard this form of trade. On the contrary, since livestock is of great importance to the African economy, measures should be instituted to develop this industry on modern lines. In the initial stages of

TABLE 4.7

Production of Meat in Selected
African Countries, 1961-65
(thousands of metric tons)

	1961	1962	1963	1964	1965	Annual Rate of Growth 1961-65 (percent)
North Africa						
Algeria	76	61	61	62	64	4.2
Morocco	130	129	130	134	137	1.3
Tunisia	35	38	40	42	43	5.3
U.A.R.	210	197	232	249	254	4.9
Sudan	124	130	135	140	148	4.5
West Africa						
Mali*	16	16	17	17	17	1.5
Senegal*	29	29	31	31	32	2.5
Upper Volta	23	26	28	33	35	11.1
Niger*	26	27	30	30	31	4.5
Ghana*	22	22	22	23	25	3.2
Nigeria	149	150	153	169	174	4.0
Central Africa						
Cameroun*	75	60	60	60	60	-5.4
Chad	20	23	25	23	24	4.7
East and Southern Africa						
Ethiopia	280	297	301	312	319	3.3
Somalia	22	15	22	22	22	0.0
Kenya	31	38	33	32	31	0.0
Uganda	149	132	116	122	127	-3.9
Tanzania	88	85	87	89	91	0.8
Madagascar	80	81	83	86	88	2.4
Botswana*	21	21	21	21	21	0.0
Lesotho*	22	22	22	22	22	0.0
Southern Rhodesia	70	76	78	78	76	2.1
Angola*	53	53	53	53	53	0.9
Namibia*	64	64	64	64	64	0.0
South Africa	525	535	550	565	574	2.2

Note: Meat includes beef, veal, pork, mutton, and lamb.
*FAO estimates.

Source: FAO, Production Yearbook, 1966, ECA, A Survey of Economic Conditions in Africa, 1967, E/CN.14/409/Rev.1.

development, the processing industries could be started on a coordinated basis involving groups of countries in meat processing and such other related industries as tanning and the manufacture of shoes, leather goods, and other meat products. The problems in this industry that should be tackled on a multinational basis are the scarcity of technical know-how and managerial skills; the absence of concerted action by the countries developing livestock industries; the problems of disease, especially foot and mouth disease; and the eradication of the tse-tse fly in those areas where this pest is rampant. There is also a need to provide adequate transport and storage facilities for the preservation of meat. In this respect, the policies and actions of the national cold storage boards should be harmonized to ensure uniformity in the prices and quality of meat products. Governments may find it necessary to give more direct assistance through the provision of adequate transport and storage facilities.

FORESTRY AND FOREST-BASED INDUSTRIES

There is ample evidence that timber and wood product industries are increasingly important elements of industrialization in some African countries. Africa possesses considerable timber reserves, accounting for about 17 percent of the world's total. In the dense savannah forests, penetration is difficult, and except in areas along the rivers and the coast there is no full exploitation of the forestry resources. Moreover, because of the extreme dispersion of useful species, the yield per hectare of natural forest is much smaller than that derived from the specially planted areas. African forestry production has increased steadily in recent years, at an average annual rate of about 2 percent. In 1965, total forest products had reached a level of 213.2 million cubic meters, which represents almost 11 percent of the world total.

The main African producers are Nigeria, Ethiopia, the Sudan, and Botswana. African production of industrial wood grew by 4.4 percent per annum between 1961 and 1965; in 1965, output of industrial wood was 26.8 million cubic meters. The largest suppliers of industrial wood in Africa are the Ivory Coast, Nigeria, Ghana, Gabon, and Congo (Brazzaville).

Several African countries are now becoming increasingly aware of their timber potential, and plans are under way to exploit these resources. In Gabon, for example, about 25 percent of total capital investment under the 1966-70 development plan was for forestry development. Output of plywood, wood pulp, and pulp products has grown quickly in recent years as efforts to develop wood-based processing industries become a feature of African economic activity. Arrangements have been made for training personnel in a number of African countries with assistance from the United Nations Special Fund. These arrangements have included forestry training and demonstration centers in Congo (Brazzaville) and the Central African Republic; a forestry research and training center in the Sudan; a reforestation institute in Tunisia; a national forestry institute in Gabon; a forestry section at the University of Ibadan (Nigeria); and a project for forestry development in Togo.

The forestry reserves in the Central African subregion have special significance in the development of timber, paper pulp, and other wood-based industries. The area has reserves estimated to be in the neighborhood of 160 million hectares; almost half the total surface area is covered by dense forests. Timber plantations do not play a significant role in the forestry industry since most of them were established during the 1960's and the trees have not yet reached the harvesting stage. The largest timber plantation areas are located in Congo (Kinshasa), Gabon, Congo (Brazzaville), Cameroun, Central African Republic and Chad. Logging operations, usually in integrated operations in Central Africa, are carried out almost exclusively by private enterprises mainly for export, although local industries also increasingly account for a fair share of the total demand. There are 335 logging operations in the subregion, the majority of which are found in Congo (Brazzaville) and Gabon; more than two-thirds of the total log output is produced by a few large firms.

The importance of the production of logs for export varies from country to country. For instance, while production for export is of secondary importance in Congo (Kinshasa), it accounts for 85 percent of forest output in Gabon. In 1961, there were 104 sawmills in the subregion, with an output per mill of about 4,000 cubic meters of sawnwood and sleepers. In the production of paper and paperboard, on account of the small local consumption, much of the expansion of this industry is still geared for export markets.

Veneer and plywood mills are located mainly in Gabon with 2 mills, Congo (Brazzaville) with 2 mills, and Congo (Kinshasa) with 5 mills; the largest plywood mill is located in Port Gentil, Gabon. Current production has been estimated at 60,000 cubic meters of plywood, and Central Africa ranks among the world's most important producers. In addition to Gabon, plywood is produced in the Congo (Kinshasa). A plant in Congo (Brazzaville) that was established in the early 1950's started plywwod production initially but in later years

switched over to veneer production exclusively. In 1962, the subregion's plywood and veneer mills accounted for 95 percent of Africa's
and 14 percent of the world's veneer exports; for plywood, the figures
were 62 percent and 2 percent respectively. Much of the plywood
and veneer industry is almost exclusively export-oriented.

The demand for paper and paperboard in Central Africa is
expected to rise to about 45,000 metric tons by 1975. There are no
pulp and paper factories in the area, but a number of pulp mill projects
have been under consideration for some time. In view of the small
consumption of paper and paperboard in the area and the relatively high
plant capacity required for an economically sized pulp mill, there is
a strong case for orienting production to serve the entire subregional
market. The minimum economical size for a paper mill is generally
lower than that of a pulp mill, but for technical reasons a paper mill
can produce only a limited range of the different paper and paperboard
grades required in a given country. Hence, in order to increase the
production range, consideration should be given to joint ventures by a
group of countries in this industry. In any case, another difficulty is
that the local wood in the subregion does not seem to be suitable for
producing chemically prepared or semichemically prepared paper
pulp, and the production requires blending with imported long-fiber
pulp. Taking the Central African subregion as a whole, raw materials
for paper production are available as follows: papyrus in Chad, euca-
lyptus in Congo (Brazzaville) and the Kivu area, reeds and bamboo
in Katanga, and megass in the Niari Valley of Congo (Kinshasa).
These are believed to be adequate for supporting a multinational paper
industry.

There are good prospects for the development of forestry industry in Africa. According to the demand projections based on current
consumption (see Table 4.8), in West Africa the demand for sawnwood
will rise by over 100 percent in 1975, with demand for paper products
rising from 0.06 million cubic feet to 0.15 million cubic feet and
demand for paper and paperboard rising from 0.08 to 0.26 million
cubic feet. For Africa as a whole, the demand for sawnwood, paper
products, fuel wood, and paper and paperboard will rise considerably
by 1975, justifying joint development by a group of countries. Thus,
taking 1959-61, as the base year, the index for 1975 for sawnwood is
177, for paper products 265, for roundwood 129, for fuel wood 129
and for paper and paper products 246. The overall demand projections
show great increases that justify action at the multinational level.

There is evidence that the demand for wood for fuel and for
building will increase considerably in the early years of the 1970's.

TABLE 4.8

Annual Consumption of Wood Products in Africa in 1959-61 and Estimated Requirements in 1975

	Sawnwood	Panel Products	Roundwood Products	Fuelwood	Paper and Paperboard (millions of tons)
		(millions of cubic meters)			
1959-61 Consumption					
West Africa	1.10	0.06	4.9	80.4	0.08[a]
East Africa	0.82	0.07	4.8	89.6	0.11[a]
North Africa	1.00[a]	0.11[a]	0.4[a]	4.4[a]	0.31[a]
Southern Africa	1.08[b]	0.13[b]	1.8[b]	2.5	0.39[a]
African Region	4.00	0.37	11.9	176.9	0.89[a]
Requirements in 1975					
West Africa	2.39	0.15	6.6	105.2	0.26
East Africa	1.62	0.20	6.6	113.6	0.28
North Africa	1.74	0.33	0.7	6.2	0.81
Southern Africa	1.34	0.30	1.5	3.4	0.86
African region	7.09	0.98	15.4	228.4	2.21
Index African region 1959-61 = 100	177	265	129	129	246

[a]Data for 1960-62.
[b]Consumption data for 1959.

Source: United Nations, Industrial Development in Africa ID/CONF.1/RBP/1.

In the development of this industry, there will be a need for concrete measures for import substitution, especially in areas importing non-wood products where local wood products could serve. The level of exports will have to be expanded through the opening up of new markets in Africa. There should be measures to coordinate forestry development programs in order to take advantage of economies of scale that will arise from increased production. One way to achieve this goal is to introduce standard production and grading rules and to negotiate for the gradual removal of tariffs and other restrictions on trade in forestry products, especially the processed wood products. The forestry development policy should be oriented toward development in other sectors, especially in such social overheads as housing for urban areas.

SOME EFFORTS TOWARD COOPERATION
IN AGRICULTURE

The process of integration of agriculture will require due recognition of two fundamental principles. First, that it is essential to develop the agricultural industry if Africa is to step up the rate of economic progress; this need stems from the recognition that economic development through industrialization on the lines of the western countries is a long-term consideration and is therefore bound to be limited at least in the early stages of economic integration. Secondly, that even in the field of agriculture the scope for expansion is bound to be limited if the African states continue to rely on the markets of the advanced countries, which use fewer and fewer raw materials per unit of output as a result of great improvements in technology. The invention of synthetic substitutes for rubber, plastic, nylon, and beverages also has greatly reduced the demand for raw materials in the advanced countries. This is indicated by the small increase or even decline in the imports of the advanced countries from the primary producing countries during the 1960's (see Chapter 6). This means that agricultural development in Africa can be envisaged not by increasing exports of raw materials to the industrialized countries but by creating new markets within Africa. In other words, the expansion of economic activities in Africa must be considered of prime importance.

In order to expand the agriculture, new measures should be taken to expand agricultural trade among the African countries through specific trade agreements or other economic cooperation measures. New trade links and trade agreements giving special preference to agricultural products must be created during the process of economic integration in order to increase the flow of commodities among the African states. It is encouraging to note that, despite the difficulties in achieving cooperation in the field of agriculture, efforts are in progress to increase such cooperation in limited sectors of agricultural production. Among these associations are the West African Rice Development Association, the Cocoa Producers Alliance, the Inter-African Coffee Organization, and the African Peanut (Groundnut) Council.

Cocoa Producers Alliance

The Cocoa Producers Alliance (CPA) was established in 1964 with headquarters in Lagos, Nigeria. The member states are Ghana, Nigeria, Ivory Coast, Cameroun, Togo, and Brazil. Although Brazil is not an African country, its interest in cocoa qualified it for member-ship. The objectives of the CPA are contained in the agreement signed on September 19, 1964, at the CPA's second annual meeting in Rio de Janeiro. They are: (1) to make adjustments between production and consumption where normal market forces have failed; (2) to prevent excessive price fluctuations; (3) to protect foreign exchange earnings of member countries; (4) to assure adequate cocoa supplies at renumerative prices for growers; and (5) to facilitate the expansion of cocoa consumption and to regulate its production accordingly. The CPA agreement is administered by a board composed of one representative from each member state. The agreement was to remain in force for three full years and would be renewed for an additional period upon the board's decision. It could be terminated at any time by a two-thirds majority. The agreement is still in force.

Inter-African Coffee Organization

The Inter-African Coffee Organization (IACO) was established by the main African coffee producers, Burundi, Congo (Kinshasa), Ethiopia, Kenya, Nigeria, Rwanda, Sierra Leone, Tanzania, Uganda, and the eight OCAM countries--Cameroun, Central African Republic, Congo (Brazzaville), Dahomey, Gabon, Ivory Coast, Madagascar, and Togo. The purpose of the IACO as laid down in the agreement is "to study common problems concerning African coffee, in particular its production, processing, and marketing, in order to ensure the smooth disposal of production and the optimum level of selling prices, the consumption of these coffees, and the publicity to be undertaken in order to increase the demand. . . ."

The organs of the IACO include a general assembly that consists

of one delegate from each member country. Each delegate has a
deputy and advisers. The assembly has the power to elect the president, vice-president and other members of the executive committee.
It meets annually in ordinary session, approves the budget, and controls revenues and expenditures. Other bodies are the executive
committee which has a minimum of six and a maximum of seven
members, including the president and vice-president of the assembly.
The president nominates a secretary-general after consultation with
the executive committee. Subscriptions are made by members according to the amount of production expected.

West African Rice Development Association

Fourteen countries of West Africa--Dahomey, Gambia, Ghana,
Guinea, Ivory Coast, Liberia, Mali, Mauritania, Niger, Nigeria,
Senegal, Sierra Leone, Togo, and Upper Volta--met in September 1969
to consider ways to coordinate their rice-growing program. For this
purpose, they agreed to establish the West African Rice Development
Association (WARDA); all West African countries were to be eligible
for membership. Countries in other parts of Africa wishing to join
WARDA also would be eligible. A committee was appointed to draft
an association agreement. At the second meeting, held in September
1970, the agreement establishing WARDA was signed. The countries
concerned will have to ratify the constitution.

The objectives of WARDA are: (1) to initiate research into the
growing, processing, storage, and marketing of rice; (2) to study the
patterns of international trade in rice; (3) to arrange for an exchange
of information among rice-growing countries; and (4) to give technical
assistance and training to farmers. WARDA expects to develop a
rice research center in West Africa. It was agreed that, in the interim
period, FAO would be in charge of organizing WARDA's activities
through the FAO Regional Office located in Accra, Ghana; during this
period, the FAO regional representative in West Africa was to act as
the executive secretary of WARDA. WARDA's headquarters will be
located in Monrovia, Liberia.

African Peanut (Groundnut) Council

Some West African countries established the African Peanut
Council (APC) in 1964. The members include Niger, Nigeria, Senegal,
Gambia, Congo (Kinshasa), and Mali. The constitution and bylaws
were initialed on June 18, 1964, following two years of conferences.

The first meeting of the APC was held in Dakar, Senegal, on February 22-26, 1966. APC's main objectives are: (1) to ensure, through joint action, remunerative prices for peanuts and peanut by-products in world markets; (2) to promote the expansion of production; (3) to organize the exchange of technical and scientific information; and (4) to establish continuous liaison, to discuss problems of mutual interest, and to advance social and economic relations among contracting parties. At a meeting held in July 1966, a committee was appointed to study and make recommendations on the possibilities of establishing a common selling office for member states.

In recent years, there has been discussion of expanding the activities of APC to include all oilseed production in Africa. The main oilseed products other than peanuts are oil palm, sesame, and cotton seeds. The African exports of these commodities represent a high percentage of the world total production, increasing competition from synthetics poses serious problems to future expansion in production and trade. In recognition of these problems, the FAO and UNCTAD took specific measures for expanding trade in these commodities. Progress was achieved at the technical level, but there were political difficulties for which no real solution has been found. At the African level, APC's aim is to coordinate the policies of oilseed-producing countries through the establishment of a scientific and technical department to follow developments in the field of research.

PROBLEMS OF AGRICULTURAL
DEVELOPMENT IN AFRICA

Before any plan of integration in agricultural development can take shape in Africa, a number of problems must be solved to ensure success. The integration will involve far-reaching changes in the concept of land tenure and agricultural production, and these changes will result in permanent reorientation of the people's social and cultural outlook. Most African peasants grow crops primarily for home consumption because the market economy is not yet fully developed. To overcome this situation, resources must be channeled into the most productive uses and the rural communities must be educated and reconditioned to the changes. Many factors must be taken into account, and to effect any changes in agricultural production African attitudes toward land tenure should be adjusted to the modern concept of land holding in order to make new industrial production techniques possible.

The decision of whether production should be carried out on

plantations or on small-scale holdings involving a large number of peasants is not a matter for immediate concern but will be decided according to the nature of the crop and production envisaged. It is difficult to set any hard and fast rule as to whether plantation farming necessarily will be most effective under the integration plan, although prima facie one might be tempted to arrive at this conclusion. However, the most important consideration is not how production will be carried out under the plan of economic integration but that, whatever the method adopted, agricultural production must be integrated and the policies pursued by the states participating in such integration must be coordinated. The problems of agricultural development are briefly outlined below.

Lack of Capital Resources

One of the most important considerations in integrating agricultural production is that huge amounts of capital must be invested in agriculture, which has not been the case previously. The main problem is that the indigenous farmers lack capital resources and have no means of raising capital from domestic sources. This fact has been largely responsible for the persistence of subsistence agriculture in Africa. Most of the modern agricultural production is carried out by foreigners who bring in capital from abroad. Capital is needed to develop irrigation facilities; to provide means for the farmer to transport his produce to the market; to buy the necessary equipment and implements, seeds, and fertilizers and to pay for labor. However, the greatest problem is that in the past agriculture has not been sufficiently attractive to induce foreign investors to stake huge resources. The limitations of the local markets, the difficulty of expansion of such markets, and the absence of complementarity limited the production of major crops. Local African markets are so small and the barriers between them so rigid that any commodities produced in one country can only be consumed locally or exported to the advanced countries. This situation reduces the scope for expansion of agriculture, both individually and on a coordinated basis.

Primitive Farming Methods

Another setback to the development of agriculture in Africa has been the use of primitive farming methods. The lack of knowledge of the new production techniques and the lack of capital resources have limited the productivity of peasant farming. As a result, the peasant farmer does not always have production for marketing in mind when

he begins his planting operations. The use of the old farming methods
has resulted in considerable soil erosion, which has reduced soil
fertility. Brush burning, shifting cultivation, and the unsettled nature
of some peasants in the past resulted in extensive leaching in certain
areas and serious drainage of fertile soil. These factors, accompanied
by drought in some areas, not only have reduced vast areas of Africa
to waste but also have resulted in frequent famine and chronic shortage
of food in many parts of Africa.

Lack of Education

African peasant agriculture has been very unproductive in the
past not only because of poor soils but also because of lack of the
education that is essential to make the farmer aware of better farming
methods to improve yield in terms of output per acre and in terms
of quality. Lack of education has had considerable influence on decisions about the type of crops to be grown and how to grow them.

It is also essential to adjust the thinking of the African peasants
with regard to the market economy. One of the reasons for the African peasants' slowness in reconditioning themselves to production
for sale is the lack of proper knowledge of the market conditions
and of available facilities. Although the colonial powers started
agricultural institutions in certain countries, progress toward educating
the African peasants was slow. Even where market facilities are
available, lack of knowledge of world market prices usually means
the ordinary man must be satisfied either with the price given by
middlemen or with production for his own consumption. The plan for
economic integration would include education programs through intensive training courses and such mass information media as radio and
television to train the African farmer in the use of modern production
techniques in agriculture. In the initial stages, this would entail the
improvement of existing schools at the national level and the establishment of new joint training institutions for a group of countries
in a given area.

Climatic Factors

Although a major portion of Africa lies in the tropics, there
are large expanses of land that do not receive sufficient rainfall.
These areas tend to have scanty population and are characterized
by very frequent droughts and famines. To develop such areas,
huge sums of money must be spent on irrigation, sums that tend to

be out of reach of any individual African state. Even if any government considered it expedient to establish large irrigation schemes
over a wide area, the available resources would not permit this
since there would be other more pressing priorities. Moreover,
even if a government could afford to raise the capital required for
such projects, the geographical location of these schemes may be
such that one or more other states would naturally benefit. The
obvious answer in such cases is to have the project established jointly
by the countries likely to benefit, and this offers one field in which
economic cooperation in agriculture can be exploited. In certain areas
of Africa, the problem of agriculture insofar as climatic factors are
concerned is not lack of rainfall but too much rainfall. In such areas,
the main problems affecting the soil are extensive leaching and soil
erosion, which reduce soil fertility and hence agricultural productivity.
In such instances, the major problem is to provide proper drainage,
terracing, and other facilities to check the loss of soil.

Agricultural Policies During the Colonial Period

Foreign administrators during the colonial period played an
important role in influencing agricultural development and thereby
shaping the mode of agriculture for the indigenous African peasants.
Such crops as cotton, coffee, and tobacco were grown largely by
European farmers, sometimes through deliberate government policy.
It is not essential to go into any detail about the colonial agricultural
policies; it is sufficient to say that agriculture in most parts of Africa
was geared to the raw material requirements of the metropolitan
countries and that only as much food as was absolutely essential
was allowed to be produced in Africa, with much food imported from
the developed countries.

The import of food in Africa has reached alarming proportions
in recent years, partly because of the subsistence nature of traditional
agriculture, diversity in eating habits among different African cultural
groups and adverse climatic conditions and partly because of the
absence of specific policies for encouraging food production. Thus,
indigenous production was confined to immediate consumption requirements.

Due to these policies and other factors, the new African governments must initiate new hopes and enthusiasm among the indigenous
farmers and take concrete steps to improve the condition of the
present farmers to justify these hopes. In plans for economic integration, the initial stage would be to redistribute existing supplies of

food from the areas where food is in abundance to the areas where it is in short supply. Further steps must take the form of direct assistance to indigenous farmers so that they can obtain fertilizer and good seed, diversify production, and ensure self-sufficiency in food production.

Marketing Problems

The underdeveloped nature of the African markets and their limitations due to various barriers are among the most serious problems in the development of agriculture in Africa. There are several factors contributing to this problem. First, as has been noted, a large portion of the peasants are ignorant of the marketing facilities available in their countries and do not understand the world market. They therefore must depend on the many middlemen who are not always honest and often exploit the peasants. As a result, the ultimate price that the peasants receive is so low that it discourages them from increasing production and also reduces their incomes, thereby reducing the general purchasing power of the rural sectors of the African economies.

The second problem is the lack of transport facilities, especially to connect the remote rural areas with the commercial urban centers. Many peasants who would otherwise have become producers are discouraged by the difficulty in bringing their produce to the market centers. Although in recent years cooperative movements and produce marketing boards have greatly assisted farmers in the rural areas, their efforts have been directed only at existing production and have not been conducive to increasing productivity.

The third and perhaps major problem of marketing, and one that will greatly hamper the process of economic integration, is the apparent absence of complementarity in agriculture. This is especially pronounced in food production; staple food habits differ in each subregion of Africa, which implies that increased food production for the local inhabitants often cannot be sold elsewhere. This situation makes the move to diversify agricultural production more difficult: unless the African countries are fully compensated by other advantages, it would be difficult if not impossible to expect any state to abandon the production of a given commodity for the sake of diversifying production in a particular economic grouping. However, this problem could be solved by establishing a processing or manufacturing industry using a given raw material. This will be particularly advantageous in cases where the raw material is produced by a number of states but the output of any individual state is not sufficient to support an industry able to serve the entire grouping. In such a case, one or two production units could be established in the subregion with the agreement that all the states would supply the required raw materials on an agreed basis in return for a guaranteed price. At the same time, the states would undertake to open up their national markets to the new product by giving it preference over similar products from outside the subregion. In this way, the participating states will have a double advantage: (1) there will be a guaranteed market for the raw materials and (2) the finished product will be obtained at a cheaper price as a result of economies of scale, and the reduction of transport costs from abroad.

The main difficulty in the process of economic integration is to increase production under existing market conditions. It is one thing to step up production and it is quite another thing to sell the entire product. Due to the limited nature of the domestic markets and the fact that these markets were closed in the past, it has not been possible for the African countries to expand production beyond the requirements of the individual markets. At the same time, it has not been possible for the African countries to increase exports of raw materials to the industrialized countries. To overcome the marketing problems, radical departures from the existing policies of individualism and isolation must be made in the field of agricultural development.

PROSPECTS FOR AGRICULTURAL DEVELOPMENT IN AFRICA

In view of the importance of agriculture in the African economies and its contribution to the gross domestic product, agricultural development must feature significantly in the process for economic cooperation. In some parts of Africa, the countries may have no choice but to develop agriculture on a large scale. However, it must be recognized that, to establish any sizable agricultural industry that would be fairly competitive with the products of the advanced countries, production techniques must be so advanced as to produce the quality of products to which the African countries are already accustomed. The productive processes must be such that the prices of the finished products are fairly low; otherwise, the consumers will still prefer to import such products from abroad, in which case the plan for integration in agriculture might defeat its own purpose. In the preliminary stage, instead of three or four countries competing by trying to establish the same industry at the same time, some form of "division of labor" could be worked out. For example, some states, especially the small producers, could grow, spin, and dye cotton, while one or two countries in a given area could set up a weaving factory to absorb the cotton from the other states. The advantages of specialization in agriculture in any multinational grouping are substantial, but due to the levels of development in these countries the potential has not yet been fully exploited. In a more advanced form, several countries could come together and decide to leave the entire cotton textile industry to one state that was particularly suited for it. In this way, the remaining states could divert their meager resources to other more pressing and profitable uses.

In developing the food industries, greater consideration should be given to the question of balancing the distribution of foodstuffs. In particular, ways should be found to obtain a better balance between food supply and demand, particularly in the subsistence sector, in order to eliminate periodical shortages. In certain countries, efforts should aim at meeting the demand of the urban workers and miners in order to reduce food imports. In a wider sense, special measures would take the form of stressing complementary arrangements with the coastal zone, developing the traditional exchanges in livestock, fish, cola nuts, and modernizing and diversifying production of grain and pulses. In the field of trade in agriculture, efforts should be made to ensure maximum outlets for export commodities by cutting production costs and fixing local prices that compare favorably with world prices.

One important measure for developing agriculture is the establishment of research facilities. Thus far, the development of research in agriculture has received little encouragement from governments and other agencies. In such areas as food products and food technology, there is urgent need for action. Research is required in determining the best fertilizer doses and formulas; research into animal production is needed; and genetic research is necessary for certain crops threatened by competition, such as rubber, cotton, sisal, and coffee. There also should be extensive research on cultivation techniques and such related fields as weed killers, pesticides, and improved tools.

Sociological research should be conducted for the better preparation and application of programs for integrated development. Prior to implementation of such programs, investigations should be carried out by teams of experts in the various branches of science, including sociologists, nutritionists, and economists, to ensure a smooth transition from subsistence to a modern economy, especially where the traditional methods of production are deeply rooted.

If the change in concepts of agricultural production is to be
attractive to the indigenous farmers, it must be accompanied by a
comprehensive scheme of incentives. One such incentive is the price
received for the products. The marketing policy for products intended
for multinational markets should consider two factors: (1) the inadequacy of the marketing system in most African countries to serve the
growing demand for agricultural products and (2) the adverse ratio
between the cost of inputs and the value of production. It is essential
to stabilize producer prices throughout the year through the creation
of buffer stocks and, possibly, to subsidize the prices paid to the
farmers for a certain period. Dealing with this problem calls for
concerted action at the multinational level. It must be borne in mind
that agricultural commodity prices are still governed by constraints
outside Africa. It is therefore largely by improving intra-African
marketing channels and rationalizing agricultural processing industries that the African governments can influence world market prices.
These objectives require resources that can be available only through
multinational programming of investments in agricultural development.

In order to effectively adopt the measures suggested above, the
question of specialization must be given greater significance. It is
quite possible to envisage a situation in which such countries as
Ghana and Nigeria, for example, could supply the entire cocoa and
palm oil required by the whole of West Africa and other parts of
Africa as well. Instead of a situation in which cocoa beans and paste
are exported to the developed countries and then come back to Africa
in cans at exorbitant prices, cocoa could be manufactured in Ghana
and all the other African countries could import cocoa from Ghana
rather than from Europe. Such countries as Uganda and Ethiopia, for
example, could supply all the coffee required by the entire Eastern
African subregion, while Zambia could supply copper and the Sudan
and Egypt could supply cotton. In this way, the multiplier effect
generated as a result of increased incomes from increased employment in these areas of production would not be exported out of Africa
in the form of payments for imports and other services but would
remain in Africa to activate an upward spiral in the growth of incomes.
The net result would be a general increase in incomes for all the
states in Africa.

The above are but a few examples of the possibilities that could
be exploited in the plan for economic integration. Integration of the
agricultural industry could therefore take any form, and each area
of cooperation would require specific measures. Because agriculture
at present forms the core of income-earning activities in most African
countries, there must be a careful assessment of agricultural

productive capacities in order to determine the areas in which complementarity is feasible and the areas that require immediate joint
action. Some of these measures are suggested below.

The first major step toward integration in agriculture could be
the supply and distribution of already existing foodstuffs within a
given area. Due to disparity in climatic conditions and other factors, some parts of Africa frequently experience famine and drought.
These states could be supplied by other states where food is abundant.
The states within a given area could come together through the United
Nations to assess the food situation and to arrange for distribution of
food to the hunger-stricken areas. Such action not only would save
millions of lives but also would form the basis for mutual understanding.

The second step would be to determine the allocation of industries
in the agricultural sector. In some developed countries, the comparative cost principle can be used to determine the basis for the
establishment of certain agricultural industries, but this is quite
difficult to envisage in the African context because of the lack of complementarity and the traditional orientation toward markets in the
industrialized countries. Furthermore, for a variety of reasons among
which are the traditional rigidities in the domestic agricultural policies,
countries are generally not readily prepared to subject their agricultural industries to outside competition. This is true even of advanced
countries such as within the EEC or EFTA.

The third major step in the process of economic integration
would be the establishment of industries in the agricultural sector
through coordination of existing agricultural projects. The various
states likely to gain from a given project--e.g., desert locust control
or the establishment of plants for chemical fertilizers--could come
together to determine the exploitation of the project to their joint
advantage. In certain cases, plantation farming could be jointly
exploited by two or more states. Even where production of a given
crop must of necessity be confined within the boundaries of one state,
other states could participate by providing the necessary raw materials or skilled labor and personnel or by opening up their markets.
In most cases, rivers form common boundaries and it would be to the
advantage of the bordering states to jointly exploit the harnessing of
hydroelectricity, the provision of water for irrigation over large areas,
and perhaps the establishment of a fishing industry. Such projects
as the Volta dam in Ghana and the Kariba dam jointly owned by Zambia
and Rhodesia are concrete examples of cooperation in the supplying
of energy or in irrigation plans.

The integration of agricultural development is of vital importance for the advancement of the African economy, especially in the initial stages of economic development. The establishment of such basic industries as iron and steel, although of extreme importance for economic development, would best be tackled as a long-term objective after the agricultural industry has gained firm roots. It therefore becomes imperative for the states to consider the development of agriculture as having prime importance. It should be emphasized that between 75 and 95 percent of the incomes of most African countries is derived from agriculture; the importance of this agriculture therefore cannot be overemphasized. The advantage of establishing agriculture-based industries is that most of the production processes tend to develop into specialized industries. For example, in the cotton industry ginning, spinning, dyeing and weaving are all distinct processes; therefore, cooperation could prove advantageous for the overall development of the cotton industry.

5

COOPERATION

IN

INDUSTRIAL

DEVELOPMENT

THE APPROACH TO INDUSTRIALIZATION

The case for industrialization as a strategy for the economic development of Africa is so widely accepted that it is not necessary to spell it out in any detail here. Even in the case of the already developed nations of the world, industry continues to play a vital role in the economic life. The major requirement in the development strategy for the 1970's is a rapid structural transformation of the individual economies in Africa from the basically traditional pattern of production to the modern industrial economy. Along with this change, it is necessary to shift the pattern of Africa's external trade from the production of primary commodities to the manufacture of intermediate and capital goods with a strong bias toward the production of consumer goods. There is evidence to suggest that, as the rate of development increases, the share of manufacturing industry in gross domestic product increases. Moreover, labor productivity tends to be higher in industry than in any other sector of the economy. These factors suggest that the people's average income would increase through industrialization.

Although the contribution of industry to GDP is relatively less than agriculture in the African economies, its importance is becoming increasingly felt, especially in light of the efforts to develop external trade. The data for GDP by industrial origin (see Table 5.1) shows that agriculture made the greatest contribution throughout the period 1960-66, followed by commerce and manufacturing. This shows that agriculture plays and will continue to play a significant role in the economic development of Africa. It is nevertheless recognized that if the present trade patterns with the industrialized countries are to

119

TABLE 5.1

Gross Domestic Product by Industrial Origin at Current Factor
Cost in Developing African Countries in 1968
(percentage)

	Agri-culture	Mining	Manu-facturing	Cons-truction	Com-merce	Transport and Communi-cations	Other Services	Public Administration and Defense
North Africa	23.9	16.9	13.2	5.5	11.1	6.4	12.3	10.7
Morocco	33.7	4.7	14.5	4.7	15.2	5.7	9.7	11.8
Algeria	17.0	20.3	10.7	6.5	13.3	5.8	10.6	15.8
Tunisia	17.1	2.5	20.2	7.7	13.6	9.2	12.1	17.6
Libya	2.4	59.0	1.9	8.5	6.9	3.7	10.2	7.4
U.A.R.	27.6	3.5	21.5	3.5	9.9	9.0	17.7	7.3
Sudan	54.5	0.1	6.8	4.6	10.0	4.8	6.8	12.4
West Africa	46.7	4.4	9.3	4.1	15.8	4.9	7.0	7.8
Mauritania	38.3	24.5	2.2	2.8	10.0	3.3	5.0	13.9
Senegal	32.6	0.3	13.7	3.6	23.8	4.5	6.6	14.9
Mali	48.2	--	7.3	5.3	17.2	3.3	4.6	14.1
Ivory Coast	37.2	0.3	12.3	5.8	16.2	9.0	8.2	11.0
Upper Volta	51.0	0.4	8.9	4.9	14.2	3.6	8.9	8.1
Dahomey	53.2	--	6.9	5.0	11.0	7.8	5.0	11.0
Niger	58.7	--	7.0	5.4	11.9	3.8	5.8	7.4
Gambia	59.0	--	5.1	--	15.4	2.6	10.2	7.7
Guinea	34.7	13.0	6.9	4.7	11.7	4.4	5.7	18.9
Sierra Leone	29.7	19.4	8.0	3.2	16.5	8.5	10.0	4.7
Liberia	25.1	31.2	4.5	4.5	10.6	5.8	6.7	11.5
Ghana	--	2.4	7.1	--	--	--	--	5.5
Togo	42.8	6.1	17.1	2.6	14.4	5.7	3.9	7.4
Nigeria	54.9	2.6	9.0	3.7	15.7	3.7	6.8	3.6
Central Africa	37.1	4.4	10.9	3.7	16.6	4.9	7.6	14.8
Cameroun	45.9	0.1	8.1	2.5	21.0	5.9	4.0	12.5
Chad	47.8	--	5.3	5.3	18.6	1.3	10.2	11.5
Central African Republic	36.7	7.7	8.9	3.0	17.1	2.4	4.1	20.1
Gabon	25.5	23.6	6.6	8.0	10.8	7.1	4.7	13.7
Congo (Brazzaville)	34.5	1.7	13.6	4.5	16.4	6.2	6.2	16.9
Equatorial Guinea	67.2	--	4.7	6.2	6.2	1.6	3.1	10.9
Congo (Kinshasa)	19.3	6.0	17.8	3.0	16.9	6.1	12.1	18.8
Rwanda	69.3	2.2	2.9	7.3	7.3	0.7	1.5	8.8
Burundi	71.7	--	4.2	2.4	8.5	1.2	6.6	5.4
East and Southern Africa*	27.1	9.6	10.1	1.9	17.8	3.9	19.5	10.1
Botswana	44.2	--	8.2	4.9	14.8	8.2	14.8	4.9
Lesotho	66.7	1.4	1.4	1.4	5.5	1.4	12.5	9.7
Swaziland	35.6	16.1	10.4	5.8	6.9	8.0	9.2	8.0
Mozambique	29.2	0.3	14.7	1.5	19.3	1.9	22.4	10.7
Namibia	15.4	47.5	6.5	3.6	5.7	7.5	8.4	5.4
Zambia	7.8	35.3	11.1	8.0	15.6	6.0	10.9	5.3
Southern Rhodesia	15.2	5.7	24.7	5.9	17.5	8.3	17.3	5.4
Malawi	47.7	0.3	10.4	5.3	11.9	7.3	9.4	7.7
Madagascar	37.8	0.7	4.6	6.0	17.6	8.7	9.1	15.5
Mauritius	26.1	--	17.7	5.9	12.4	12.4	19.6	5.9
Tanzania	50.0	1.9	7.4	3.8	14.5	5.1	9.4	7.9
Uganda	56.4	2.5	9.1	2.4	10.0	3.4	11.6	4.6
Kenya	34.8	0.5	13.7	5.1	14.1	8.3	18.1	5.4
Ethiopia	56.9	0.3	9.9	5.9	8.3	3.6	9.9	5.2
Total Africa	28.0	10.5	14.6	4.5	14.6	6.7	11.5	9.6
Total Developing Africa	33.3	10.3	11.7	4.8	13.6	5.7	11.2	9.4

*Excluding South Africa.

Source: ECA, A Survey of Economic Conditions in Africa, 1969 (E/CN. 14/480,/Rev.1 pp.25-26

120

be changed significantly, Africa must step up its rate of industrial development geared to the requirements for wider markets at multi-national level. Because of the smallness of the domestic markets, most if not all the African countries cannot set up optimum-sized industries. Therefore, it has become essential that, in planning for industrial development, priority be given to the establishment of industries that are capable of supplying the requirements for manu-factured goods in a number of countries.

In adopting policies for industrialization in Africa, two factors should be taken into account. First, the vast majority of the African population still lives at or below the subsistence level. At this level, the local production is engaged mainly in producing handicrafts and perhaps other simple tools and agricultural implements. It is there-fore essential that, at the early stages of industrialization, adequate consideration be given to the establishment of small-scale industries, especially in areas that are predominantly agricultural. Secondly, it has often been argued that, in order to expand the rate of development in Africa, it is essential to set up large-scale industries. In other words, it is believed that the best strategy for economic development is through industrialization in a wide range of productive activities.

One school of thought seems to argue that the establishment of such basic industries as huge iron and steel complexes would enable the employment of a large number of people and therefore would greatly contribute to the reduction of unemployment and underemploy-ment, especially in rural areas. It is held that industrialization would result in a general increase in the people's level of income, thereby increasing the effective demand and, through forward and backward linkages, increasing production in other sectors. It is believed that the best way to tackle the problem of economic development in Africa is not by "piecemeal" efforts but through comprehensive schemes of industrialization covering an entire subregion.[1] The argument behind this approach is that, apart from the vast employment opportunity such a plan would offer, the large industries would result in economies of scale that eventually would lower prices of finished goods. If locally produced articles are cheaper than imported articles, the people will switch their demand to the former, assuming other things remaining the same. Such a development would reduce the volume of imports and result in savings on foreign exchange.

It is further argued that industrialization should be given preference because large industries would offer opportunities for a number of countries to participate in one project, thereby reinforcing the spirit of unity and cooperation in Africa. This approach is based on

the argument that in almost all the advanced countries of the world
the heavy basic industries were established initially, followed by
agricultural development. Therefore, without a solid industrial base
the economic development of the African countries cannot be expanded
significantly.

Another related argument in favor of industrialization is that
for a long time the African countries have depended on the industrialized
countries to supply their entire requirements for industrial and manufactured goods, including some foodstuffs. Throughout the colonial
period, the industrial development in the African territories was geared
to supply cheap raw materials for the industries of Western Europe
and, unless drastic measures are taken to correct the situation, this
position is likely to persist for a long time to come. Some such
measures would include the launching of comprehensive schemes of
industrialization, especially in industries geared to domestic consumption and import substitution.

These arguments appear to be valid under the following assumptions: (1) that the size of the market and, therefore, the demand is
given; (2) that the quality of the goods produced by the new industries
is of the same standard as the goods to which the African countries
are now accustomed; (3) that there are adequate transport facilities
to serve the proposed heavy industrialization; (4) that all the African
countries agree to impose a common tariff and duties on imports from
outside the integrated regions; and (5) that capital resources are
available to finance these comprehensive schemes of industrialization.
If these assumptions do not hold, the whole argument falls to pieces
under present conditions.

It is plausible to argue that the advanced countries of the world
started with heavy industrialization; however, these countries did not
experience the difficulties that Africa faces today. There was no acute
shortage of foodstuffs in most of these countries when they started to
industrialize; there was virtually no competition from more developed
industries; demand for their products was virtually guaranteed since
any surplus could be diverted to the colonial territories; and these
countries had adequate capital resources at their disposal. In Africa,
the position is entirely different, and the problems of industrialization
are unique in that the continent is starting to industrialize at a time
when the countries are very susceptible to adverse external factors,
the world food supply, and the world population explosion. In fact,
experience in other regions of the world indicates that schemes of
heavy industrialization without corresponding development of the
other vital sectors of the economy would fail to bring the required
boost to economic development.

The other view is that, although large-scale industrialization is vital to economic growth, adequate attention also should be given to the role of small-scale industries in the economic development of Africa. This is because the majority of the African population lives under subsistence production and hence the establishment of small-scale industries would provide the necessary leverage for transforming the rural communities from subsistence to the market economy. The development of small-scale industries could be considered from two angles: (1) what it can contribute to the desired change in the economic and social structure of the African countries and how much any new industries can contribute to the expansion of export earnings and (2) the extent to which industrial development could contribute to the reduction of unemployment. An export-oriented program for the development of industries on multinational basis, especially in the small and medium ranges, could increase the rate of economic development in the African countries. Since in certain economies it is unrealistic to envisage a sudden jump from subsistence to large-scale industry, the small and medium-sized industries would facilitate the emergence of indigenous African enterprise, which could prove an effective means of ensuring development of the middle- and lower-income groups.

The objective of development planning in any economy is to make the economy self-supporting, either through an increase in export earnings that would reduce the import bill or through the expansion of production of goods for domestic consumption. In the African countries, there is a strong case for small-scale industries, and this proposition is equally true where a group of countries is involved. To achieve this, it is essential that the development of small-scale industry be supported by coordinated programs for financial and technical assistance to the small entrepreneurs. Such programs could include intergovernmental measures for the provision of favorable credit facilities, especially in marketing, training, modernization of equipment, and the provision of technical know-how and other capital requirements.

PATTERNS OF INDUSTRIAL GROWTH
IN AFRICA, 1950-68[2]

The level of manufacturing industries is very low, as shown throughout this chapter. However, the output of manufacturing industries in the African countries increased by over 170 percent from 1950 to 1968. There were several reasons for this increase in output, which was quite spectacular. First, total demand for manufactures increased from 1950-68 largely as a result of the general improvement in economic conditions in newly independent Africa. Second, the growth in the demand for manufactured goods increased opportunities for

development in other sectors, producing some favorable effect on the
general rate of development. Third, there was considerable progress
in efforts toward import substitution, especially in consumer goods
industries. Finally, exports of manufactures and semimanufactures,
although relatively small, provided some push in industrial growth.

In assessing the patterns of industrial development, it is important to note that at the beginning of the last decade a large majority
of the African countries had very small industrial bases. For example,
in a group of 41 African countries, in 9 countries the contribution of
industry to GDP in 1960 was less than 5 percent; in 20 countries it
was between 5 and 9.9 percent; in 7 countries it was between 10 and
14.9 percent; and in only 5 countries it was more than 15 percent.
For the continent as a whole (excluding South Africa), the proportion
of GDP originating in manufacturing was around 10 percent. Much of
the industrial contribution to GDP--in many countries 50 percent or
more--originated in handicrafts and artisan workshops. The position
had greatly improved toward the close of the 1960's, as can be seen
in Table 5.1.

The manufacturing industry was concentrated in a few countries.
For example, about 60 percent of Africa's total manufacturing activity
was in the U.A.R., Algeria, Congo (Kinshasa), Southern Rhodesia, and
Nigeria. Of the total value added to GDP by manufacturing industries
in 1960, North Africa accounted for 50 percent; East Africa accounted
for 17 percent; West Africa for 16 percent; Central Africa for 13 percent; and other Africa (excluding South Africa) for 4 percent. Generally, manufacturing in Africa, regardless of the size of the manufacturing sector, was concentrated in a few major urban centers. This
tendency to locate industries in those countries where external economies of scale are greatest is a common feature of underdevelopment,
and in itself strengthens the case for cooperation through planned
distribution of these industries.

During the period 1960-66, the contribution of manufacturing
industry to GDP (measured at current prices) increased at an average
annual rate of 9.3 percent. In most African countries, the manufacturing industries laid emphasis on import substitution and some
processing of agricultural and mineral products for export. There
was no significant progress in the production of intermediate goods.
Basic cement industries were established in a large number of African
countries, and they reduced the level of cement imports. The development of various building material industries expanded considerably.
The number of petroleum refineries increased from 4 in 1960 to 20
in 1967, and the number of petroleum or petroleum-gas based

industries also increased, especially in some North and West African countries. The development of manufactures in most countries was reflected in changes in the pattern of African trade. The most striking feature of the development of imports in the late 1960's was the general increase in imports of machinery and transport equipment. On the export side, there were substantial exports of petroleum products, cocoa products, pulp and wastepaper veneer and plywood, prepared or preserved vegetables, preserved fruit, tinned meat and prepared meat products, and miscellaneous non-ferrous metals.

From the available statistical material, it appears that the North African subregion is the most industrialized of the four subregions, with a very long tradition of organized manufacturing industries. There is a wide range of manufacturing industries, with a clear advancement over the level of mere subsistence. The planners have given great emphasis to investment in heavy industry in the past, but recently the consumer goods sector has become increasingly predominant in the industrial structures of all countries in the North African subregion. As in the rest of Africa, the industries are not primarily export-oriented, although some specific industries that already have been established or are under construction reflect the increasing importance of the need to develop exports. Between 1965 and 1967, the output of industries in the subregion increased by nearly 16 percent, but because of adverse factors operating in the U.A.R. in the following years, output is believed to have declined. Great discrepancies exist in the production patterns of the North African countries, reflecting differences in endowments with natural resources, demand conditions, and development targets and priorities.

The West African subregion as a whole appears to be the least industrialized area in Africa, although for individual countries there was a rapid increase in industrial output in the late 1960's. There has been a fairly rapid rate of industrial growth, and in the years 1965-67 levels of output in almost all countries were up to 60 percent higher than in 1964. This rapid rate of increase reflected increased industrial activity in Ghana, Ivory Coast, Nigeria, and Senegal, the most industrialized countries in the subregion. The general output continued to expand in the years after 1967, except in Nigeria where the political situation brought industrial production to a virtual stand-still. Apart from the petroleum refineries, a few fertilizer plants, cement factories, and export-oriented wood industries, the West African subregion has laid relatively less stress on heavy industries than North Africa, and most industrial production has been directed toward consumer goods.

The East African subregion showed upward movement in industrial production during 1965-67, with the exception of Burundi and Rhodesia in 1967. The overall increase in output between 1964 and 1967 ranged between 40 and 50 percent. The political climate in Southern Africa affected the countries' level of output, and in 1967 this level was probably much lower than in the previous years. There was a conscious drive toward import-substitution industries (e.g., textiles, sugar, petroleum refineries, cement, fertilizers) in a number of countries. In some of the countries of the Eastern African subregion, including Kenya, Uganda, and Southern Rhodesia, there was emphasis on such export-oriented industries as petroleum refineries, chemical fertilizers and cement. A significant feature of the industries was the diversification of production, especially in the small- and medium-sized plants.

The countries of the Central African subregion showed general increases in output in manufacturing industries between 1965 and 1967, with the level of output in the latter year nearly 30 percent higher than in 1964. The increase in total output reflected the new capacity in countries other than Congo (Kinshasa), where the growth of output between 1965 and 1967 was largely a result of increased utilization of existing capacity. In Congo (Kinshasa), industrial output is oriented primarily to the domestic market and industrial efforts have been directed toward attempts to reestablish pre-independence levels of output; in contrast, much of the industrial development in the other countries of the Central African subregion has been export-oriented. The import-substitution industries generally have been confined to such small-scale industries as textiles, sugar refining, cement, and motor vehicle assembly.

The question of the allocation of industries in a multinational set-up has presented considerable difficulties in the industrial development of the existing economic groupings. One major problem in this respect is that currently some countries in Africa seem more industrialized or better placed to industrialize than others. Therefore, there is fear that, unless special safeguards are taken, the industrialized states will tend to industrialize more than the other states, aggravating the disparity in levels of development. Furthermore, the problem of distribution of industries would become acute because no formula has yet been found for the effective or rational allocation of new industries. It will be necessary to carry out many pre-feasibility studies; allocation of new industries can be rationally carried out only under the principles of comparative cost advantage. The following sections provide information on some of the major existing industries, indicating existing capacity and potential for development, the subregional demand for the various industries, and the opportunities that exist in selected industries based on the availability of raw materials and on demand. Due to lack of adequate and reliable statistics, the question of transport costs and such other factors as the cost of production are not discussed here. It follows, therefore, that the suggestions for allocation of industries can only be tentative.

THE IRON AND STEEL INDUSTRY

The development of the iron and steel industry has come to be regarded as one of the most important aspects of industrialization in Africa. Consumption of iron and steel products increased considerably over the 1960's, and it is estimated that it will continue to increase in the coming years.

Given the slightest available opportunity, most African countries would seriously consider the establishment of an iron and steel plant. In order to understand the implications of any rational allocation of the iron and steel industry, it is essential to examine the matter according to the various geographical areas of Africa: East and Southern, Central, West, and North Africa. Total iron and steel production figures for Africa are not available, but the principal iron ore producing countries are shown in Table 5.2. Small-scale production of steel goods is carried on in most African countries.

East and Southern Africa

In East and Southern Africa, the present demand for iron and steel products is estimated at 450,000 tons, 33 percent of which represents bars, rods, and light sections, while about 25 percent consists of cold reduced sheets and coils. About 15 percent of the total consumption of these products is produced locally. Consumption has increased by about 3 percent annually, but according to ECA estimates, the future growth in consumption will increase by about 8.9 percent per annum.

From scattered data, it is further estimated that by 1980 annual demand will have risen to about 1,635 million tons, 40 percent of which will constitute bars, rods, and light sections, with another 20 percent made up of cold reduced sheets and coils. There are three major areas in which iron deposits are found, which constitute potential markets for iron and steel goods. The first area includes Southern Rhodesia, Zambia, and Malawi. Within this area Que-Que, lying about

TABLE 5.2

Production of Iron Ore by Principal Producing Countries in Africa, 1960-68
(thousands of metric tons)

Country	1960	1961	1962	1963	1964	1965	1966	1967	1968	(1968 Index 1960 = 100)
Liberia	2,192	2,139	2,653	3,715	8,843	10,985	11,538	12,575	14,713	671
Mauritania	--	198	656	841	3,239	3,875	4,638	4,846	5,008	2,529a
Algeria	1,788	1,491	1,072	1,028	1,424	1,637	916	1,335	1,566	-12
Sierra Leone	881	1,029	1,186	1,147	1,196	1,286	1,382	1,259	1,900	215
Tunisia	563	479	413	476	512	609	684	501	558	-8
Morocco	874	815	675	609	525	567	602	683	486	-44
Guinea	338	271	350	279	454	378	305	350	--	103b
Swaziland	--	--	--	--	38	642	1,003	1,098	--	2,889c
Angola	409	504	470	398	562	509	494	712	2,034	497
Southern Rhodesia	98	241	384	406	597	824	830	450	160	163
South Africa	1,965	2,535	2,838	2,859	3,157	3,745	4,366	4,910	5,057	257

a1968 over 1961.
b1967 over 1960.
c1967 over 1964.

Source: ECA, (Statistics Division) Yearly Statistics of Industrial Production, 1968.

130 kilometers southwest of Salisbury in Southern Rhodesia, has total deposits of nearly 11 million tons, with 50-64 percent iron content, and Buhwa, 200 kilometers south of Salisbury, has about 130 million tons of iron ore deposits with 60 percent iron content. In Zambia, iron ore deposits occur at Nambala, about 11 kilometers west of Lusaka, where there are over 211 million tons of iron ore with about 57 percent iron content. In this area, iron and steel industries potentially could be established in Zambia and Rhodesia.

The second potential market is made up of Tanzania, Kenya, Uganda, Rwanda, and Burundi. Iron ore deposits occur at Liganga, about 120 kilometers from Njombe in Tanzania, with about 45 million tons containing about 40 percent iron and about 12.8 percent titanium dioxide. In Uganda, iron ore deposits are found at Sukulu, north of Tororo, with 200 million tons containing 62 percent iron and at Kigezi, in the southwest area, with 30 million tons of about 63-68 percent iron content. These deposits could be exploited on a multinational basis to serve the market.

The third potential market is made up of Ethiopia, Somalia, and the coastal areas of Kenya. There are about 20 million tons of iron ore deposits with 60 percent iron content in an area 40 kilometers east of Asmara in Ethiopia. Another area is Bar Acaba, lying 150 kilometers northwest of Mogadishu in Somalia, with deposits of nearly 200 million tons having 35 percent iron content. The deposits in Somalia could provide a sound base for iron and steel industry to serve this area.

Coking coal available at Wankie in Southern Rhodesia could be used for iron ore smelting plants in Rhodesia and Zambia, and coal of a slightly inferior quality is found in Zambia. In Tanzania, there are large coal deposits in the vicinity of the iron ore deposits, but the coal is of non-coking quality and, since the iron ores in this area have a high titanium content, this coal could not provide a base for large-scale iron and steel works. In Ethiopia, the iron ores lie close to the harbor of Massawa and it is believed that coking coal could be imported. Kenya has large resources of charcoal, which would be the best fuel supply for an iron and steel plant at Tororo; for processing the Kigezi iron ores, methane gas from the depths of Lake Kivu eventually could be used. Limestone deposits of sufficient quality and quantity occur in most countries in East and Southern Africa; some of them already are being worked for cement production at places near the potential locations of iron and steel works. Deposits of sufficient quantities of fire clay, silicium sands, magnesite, and dolomite exist in various countries, and deposits in Southern Rhodesia and Zambia already are being explored.

TABLE 5.3

Growth in Consumption of Iron Ore and Steel Products in
Africa, 1953–63
(thousands of tons)

	North Africa	West Africa	Central Africa	East Africa[a]	Other Africa[b]	Total Africa
1953	450	220	180	170	1,300	2,320
1954	560	230	190	240	1,390	2,610
1955	670	250	230	350	1,510	3,010
1956	680	250	230	350	1,550	3,060
1957	620	320	240	370	1,760	3,310
1958	820	310	150	320	1,650	3,250
1959	920	370	130	290	1,300	3,010
1960	1,130	360	90	380	1,620	3,580
1961	1,100	450	110	420	1,810	3,890
1962	1,050	500	110	430	1,770	3,860
1963	1,070	530	140	430	1,980	4,150
Percentage change $\frac{1963}{1953}$	138	140	-22	153	52	78

Note: Steel products include finished steel, iron products, and cast iron pipes.

[a]Includes Mozambique, Comoro Islands, Reunion, Seychelles, and Burundi.
[b]Botswana, Lesotho, Swaziland, Namibia, and South Africa.

Source: United Nations, Industrial Development in Africa ID/CONF. 1/RBP/1

An integrated iron and steel works exists in Southern Rhodesia, and the Rhodesian Iron and Steel Company has its own coking plant. Pig iron production is about 300,000 tons per annum and the two 75-ton Siemens-Martin furnaces have a total capacity of around 130,000 tons per annum, producing 4-ton ingots. The rolling mill consists of 38-inch, 21-inch, 12-inch, and 10-inch mills with a capacity of 45,000 tons per annum, and the range of products covers rods, bars, and light sections up to 3 inches. Small steel plants consisting of electric arc furnaces and small rolling mills are operating at Jinja in Uganda, owned by the East Africa Iron and Steel Company, and at Akaki near Addis Ababa, owned by the Ethiopian Iron and Steel Company. The bulk of production is reinforcement bars. There are three galvanizing and corrugating plants in operation at Mombasa in Kenya, at Dar-es-Salaam in Tanzania, and at Akaki in Ethiopia. Wire is produced at Que-Que and, to a limited extent, at Akaki. Pipes (seamed and seamless) are produced at Que-Que and at Luanshya in Zambia. Most of the steel finishing plants in the whole area operate at about 50 percent of capacity. Mass production of iron and steel foundries is carried out only in Southern Rhodesia and Zambia; in the other countries, the foundries concentrate on jobbing and repair work.

According to statistical projections based on the availability of raw materials, the centers of distribution, transport facilities, and the optimum economic sizes of iron and steel smelters and rolling mills, it is estimated that plants with annual production of 500,000 tons would be economical for the Eastern African subregion. It is therefore envisaged that, in planning for an East and Southern African iron and steel industry, the Que-Que plant could supply Southern Rhodesia, Botswana, Lesotho, Mozambique, Madagascar and Mauritius. A new plant could be set up near Lusaka to supply Zambia, Malawi, and parts of Tanzania. Another plant could be set up in Uganda to supply the East African market plus Somalia, Ethiopia, and, probably, the Eastern Congo (Kinshasa) and the southern Sudan. In such cases, the small rolling mills in Madagascar and Ethiopia could then produce bars, rods, and light sections out of billets supplied by the Que-Que and Tororo plants respectively.

Central Africa

In Central Africa, possibilities for establishing the iron and steel industry are already being explored. There are no detailed estimates of consumption of finished steel products, but preliminary studies give some positive indications that a growing supply of steel locally produced is likely to be of major importance in the development of the area. It is estimated that the total steel consumption in Congo (Kinshasa) stood between 61,000 and 128,000 tons annually between 1953 and 1960. Congo (Kinshasa) has large reserves of high-grade ore in Katanga and in Eastern Congo (Kinshasa). There are also considerable quantities of high-grade ore deposits in Congo (Brazzaville), the most important of which are the Sengha deposits, 150 miles from Mekambo.

The main obstacle to the establishment of iron and steel industries in Central Africa is the lack of coking coal. Except in Katanga, where non-coking coal deposits are available, iron and steel production would depend on imported ore as well as coking coal. There are ample quantities of high-grade ore available in a number of countries in West Africa, and this ore could be shipped cheaply to plants located in the coastal areas in Central Africa. In addition, cheap power from Inga could strengthen the case for iron and steel production. High-grade iron ore (64 to 65 percent) could be obtained from Mauritania while anthracite for electrodes would have to be imported, but opinion is that this could not prevent the establishment of fair-sized iron and steel works in this area. Limestone deposits are available near Lusaka, the Inga region is rich in silica, and manganese ore can be obtained from Beceka manganese.

For these countries, the proposed iron and steel works would be located in the coastal areas, but it would also be possible to locate these works near Kinshasa at Kimpoko, based on iron ore from Congo (Kinshasa). This location would have the advantage of supplying steel less expensively to the northern part of Congo (Brazzaville), the Central African Republic, and Chad. It is also believed that there are possibilities for setting up an iron and steel works at Pointe Noire, based on either Zanaga ore brought down by rail or Sengha ore brought through the Owendo-Balinga railway (provided that this line is extended) and then by sea to Pointe Noire. The development of iron and steel production in Central Africa would require a long-term perspective and careful study of the possibilities of Pointe Noire or Bangui as potential sites.

West Africa

For West Africa, it is estimated that the total demand for iron and steel would increase from 1 million tons in 1970 to 2.4 million in 1980. Bars, rods, sections, and wire rods represent over 40 percent of this projected demand. Nigeria will require about 40 percent of the total demand and Ghana approximately 20 percent. Iron ore deposits are available in practically all the countries, with the richest deposits found in Liberia, Sierra Leone, and Mauritania--these are already being worked for export to Europe and the United States. Except for Nigeria, where non-coking coal is found, none of the countries in this area possesses coal. There are limestone deposits in Mali, Niger, Ghana, Senegal, the Ivory Coast, Dahomey, Guinea, and Nigeria. The deposits in Senegal and Dahomey and those at Lokoja in Nigeria seem the best situated for shipment by sea. Manganese deposits are found in Upper Volta, Mali, Ghana, Senegal, the Ivory Coast, and Nigeria. The deposits at Tambao in Upper Volta are of very high quality but are not at present being worked. The Yakau deposits in Ghana, situated near the coast, were already being worked during World War II, but the reserves are limited.

Groups of countries could envisage integrated iron and steel works with capacities varying from 350,000 to 970,000 tons. The projection of demand in 1980 could justify the construction of two integrated iron and steel works, with rerolling mills. In the short run, there can be only a single integrated iron and steel works with a capacity of 700,000 tons, which would manufacture simple rolled products. However, by 1980 an electrical steel works could be set up in the West African subregion using cheap hydroelectric energy produced in Ghana or electric energy from natural gas in Nigeria.

North Africa

In the North African subregion, average annual consumption of iron and steel products in 1961-63 amounted to about 1.1 million tons, of which the U.A.R. accounted for 42 percent and Algeria for about 22 percent. Future demand is estimated at 4.5 million tons in 1980, of which bars and rods would account for 50 percent. As development progresses, the engineering industries also would expand, leading to a rise in the demand for cold reduced sheet.

Iron ore deposits containing about 240 million tons of iron ore are found in Morocco, Algeria, Tunisia, and the U.A.R. The total production of iron ore in 1962 was 4.5 million tons. Morocco, Algeria, and Tunisia exported all their steel, while the U.A.R. deposit of around 460,000 tons at Aswan was used largely to meet the demand of the domestic iron and steel works. The Maghreb iron ore deposits have an iron content between 51 and 62 percent, while the Aswan ore contains only 44 percent iron. Known deposits amount to 220 million tons; the Beharya deposits near Cairo are the most important. Good coking coal is available only in Morocco, while in the U.A.R. additives

have been used to improve coal quality. In Algeria, the coal deposits
are of low quality, and no deposits are known to exist in Tunisia, Libya,
or the Sudan. However, there are substantial limestone deposits
in every country of the subregion, the largest being found in the Sudan.

The U.A.R. has the most developed iron and steel industry, and
the integrated iron works at Helwan has a capacity of 200,000 tons,
producing flat material and light and medium sections. In addition,
three other semi-integrated plants produce 180,000 tons of bars. In
Algeria, an integrated iron and steel works at Bons has a capacity of
380,000 tons; it uses imported coke but employs sintering facilities
and oil injection to keep the coke rate low. Other works based on
scrap produce reinforcing bars and light sections and have a capacity
of 300,000 tons per annum. In Tunisia, a small integrated works at
Menzel-Bourgiba has a capacity of 80,000 tons per annum; the plant
is based on imported coke and produces mainly reinforcing bars and
light sections. Morocco, Libya, and the Sudan at present do not have
iron and steel works. The U.A.R. plans to expand the Helwan works
to a capacity of 1.5 million tons of ingots, and a strip mill with a
capacity of 700,000 tons was completed in recent years. A second
integrated iron and steel works is planned at Aswan, to produce 400,000
tons of bars employing the electric reduction process. The existing
semi-integrated plants in the U.A.R. will double their capacity, with
one plant specializing in special alloy steels. Morocco plans to
establish a rerolling mill at Casablanca with a capacity of 120,000
tons per annum. This plant will use imported billets and will produce
bars, rods, and light sections. If the plans for economic integration
of the subregion were successful, the U.A.R. could serve as the center
for a multination iron and steel industry.

Future Prospects

In the projections for future development of iron and steel industry in Africa, in most countries considerable emphasis is laid on
the manufacture of metals. A number of new factories are proposed:
tractor assembling could be establsihed in Uganda; combustion engine
assembling in Zambia; steam boilers and gas cylinder manufacturing
in Uganda and Kenya; and grain milling machinery manufacturing in
Southern Rhodesia. Factories for pumps and valves are planned for
Ethiopia, Tanzania, Kenya, Rhodesia, and Zambia; while weighing
machines could be manufactured in Ethiopia, Uganda, Southern
Rhodesia, and Zambia. The manufacture of transport equipment,
especially trailers and bus and truck bodies could be undertaken in
Ethiopia, Tanzania, and Uganda. Railway freight cars could be made

in Kenya and Southern Rhodesia.. With regard to electrical engineering goods, manufacturing or assembling of the following articles on a multinational basis is recommended: radios, refrigerators, bulbs, dry cells, electric motors between 0.5 and 10 horsepower, and switch-gears.

Two issues are involved in the development of the iron and steel industry. The first consideration is that, since the industry is capital-intensive and high cost, the question of the location of the industry as dictated by the availability of raw materials will have to be balanced against the cost of transportation of other raw material components and the distribution of the finished product. Based purely on raw material considerations, a number of African countries produce iron ore and therefore have the potential to develop iron and steel industry, but whether it would be in their interest to do so, even if it were fea-sible, is quite another matter. The second consideration is that the location of plants in any part of the country also must be governed by such factors as the cost of manufacturing iron and steel products from the local smelters and the extent of the market for iron and steel goods in any given subregion. The question of how well the new iron and steel industries in Africa could withstand competition from over-seas manufacturers is another issue that must be taken into account.

The desirability of establishing iron and steel industry on a multinational basis cannot be disputed. The large capital requirements, high optimum level, and limitations in the national markets support the suggestion for joint action in the development of this industry. The major problem will be to decide to whether a single huge plant can satisfy a group of countries or whether several smaller plants located in different countries should be considered. Given the absence of reliable statistical data on this industry, it is rather difficult to resolve this issue.

However, the existing trend in the development of iron and steel industry in Africa suggests that one or two integrated plants producing a wide range of products to supply a given subregion should be given serious consideration. This is particularly important if economies of scale and hence reduction in production cost are to be achieved. The manufacture of such smaller iron and steel goods as rods, plates, and steel wires would continue to be carried out within the national markets. For such heavy iron and steel goods as heavy plant, rails, heavy steel sheets, and heavy iron rods and bars, even a subregional market may be inadequate to sustain the establishment of an optimum plant; therefore, it may be prudent to consider establishing this or part of the industry on a regional basis or serving at least two

subregions. This observation necessarily must be tentative pending
further detailed investigation and analysis of the market structure
and production possibilities.

THE FERTILIZER AND BASIC
CHEMICAL INDUSTRIES

The fertilizer and basic chemical industries constitute an important area of industrial development in Africa. Due to the increased
importance attached to the development of agriculture in recent years,
there has been a significant increase in the demand for fertilizers and
insecticides. There is a direct correlation between the use of fertilizers and the policy of rural development: in countries where great
emphasis is placed on the development of rural communities, the
demand for fertilizers and insecticides has risen considerably. The
differences in the climatic conditions and the types of crops grown
in the various parts of Africa also account for the uneven distribution
of fertilizers. It is not easy to suggest any pattern of location for the
projected fertilizer plants, due largely to the lack of comprehensive
statistical data. Table 5.4 gives an indication of the major phosphate
producing countries in Africa, those with deposits capable of satisfying
a number of countries.

East and Southern Africa

The present demand for fertilizers in East and Southern Africa
is estimated at about 60,000 tons of nitrogen and 50,000 tons of phosphoric acid. Potash consumption is estimated at about 25,000 tons.
The main consuming countries are Southern Rhodesia, accounting for
about 48 percent, Mauritius for 19 percent, and Kenya for over 15
percent. There is considerable demand for ammonium sulphates and
single superphosphates. The demand for compound fertilizers also
has increased in recent years. The local production of phosphoric
acid accounts for nearly 75 percent of the demand. Although all the
governments are making great efforts to intensify the utilization of
fertilizers by informing and subsidizing farmers, the present use of
fertilizer varies considerably from country to country. The demand
in the subregion is expected to increase to 250,000 tons of nitrogen,
190,000 tons of phosphoric acid, and 110,000 tons of potash by 1980.

Potash salts are known to exist at Dallol in the Danakil Depression of Ethiopia; apatite at Sukulu near Tororo in Uganda; and crude
phosphate at Dorowa in Southern Rhodesia and Mijingu Hill near Arusha

TABLE 5.4

Production of Phosphates by Principal Producing
Countries in Africa, 1960 and 1963-68
(thousands of metric tons)

	1960	1963	1964	1965	1966	1967	1968
Morocco	7,492	8,549	10,098	9,827	9,438	10,545	10,572
Tunisia	2,101	2,365	2,751	3,040	3,534	3,157	3,753
Senegal	198[a]	596	798	1,038	1,135	1,276	1,270
Togo	476	441	801	974	1,152	1,139	1,139[b]
U.A.R.	566	644	613	594	661	683	680[b]
South Africa	268	455	579	610	1,063	1,152	1,565

[a]Figure for 1963.
[b]Estimate.

Source: ECA, (Statistics Division) Yearly Statistics of Industrial Production, 1967, 1968, and 1969.

137

in Tanzania. Pyrite is found at Kilembe, near Kasese in Uganda, in
the vicinity of Geita in the Lake Victoria district of Tanzania, and at
Mazoe near Salisbury in Southern Rhodesia. Anhydrite is found near
Kilwa in Tanzania. These minerals constitute the materials on which
the fertilizer industry can be based. The basic materials for ammonia
production are coke, natural gas, or petroleum feedstocks. In addition
to the coke from Wankie in Southern Rhodesia, the industry can utilize
light virgin naphtha from the refineries in Assab (Ethiopia), Mombasa
(Kenya), Dar-es-Salaam (Tanzania), Tamatave (Madagascar), and
Umtali (Southern Rhodesia).

In Uganda, the Tororo Industrial Chemical and Fertilizers Company is exploiting the apatite deposit at Sukulu, which is estimated at
200 million tons containing 12 to 15 percent phosphoric acid. The
present capacity is about 25,000 tons of single superphosphate, but
there are plans for extending the capacity to 100,000 tons annually.
Sulfuric acid is produced at a rate of 10,000 tons per year using imported sulfur. Plans are known to exist for a sulfuric acid plant at
the Kilembe copper mines in western Uganda based on the pyrite
deposit there.

In Southern Rhodesia, the African Explosives and Chemical
Industries (Rhodesia) Limited processes local phosphates from Dorowa
and the capacity of single and triple superphosphates is about 50,000
tons each year. The capacity of the sulfuric acid plant is about 122,000
tons, and the same plant also produces compound fertilizers. Factories
for mixing compound fertilizers are being constructed at Port Louis
in Mauritius and Nekuri in Kenya. A potash fertilizer plant with a
capacity of 1.5 million tons per year using potash salts from Dallol
in the Danakil Depression in Ethiopia is being considered.

Taking into account the location of raw materials, the transport
network, the demand, and the market structure, two ammonia plants
are often suggested, and economically the best locations are at Umtali
in Southern Rhodesia and Mombasa in Kenya. If the Lake Kivu gas
proves to be industrially exploitable, a plant could be located in Uganda.
Another plant has been considered at Dar-es-Salaam to supply Tanzania
and the islands; it would use crude phosphate from Minjingu Hill and
imported sulfur pending the exploitation of the pyrite or anhydrite
deposits.

Sulfuric acid and caustic soda together constitute the most important basic chemicals in the production of fertilizers. Caustic soda
also is used with chlorine in the manufacture of other industrial products. The market for chlorine in the area is mainly in the production

of polyvinylchloride, such insecticides as DDT and BHC, and pulp and paper. Caustic soda also is used by the soap and textile industries. The present demand for caustic soda is about 20,000 tons. The consumption of DDT and BHC is not known exactly, since import statistics only mention pesticides and insecticides, but it is expected to increase to 17,500 tons in 1980. The consumption figures of plastics, both polyvinylchloride and polyethylene, is estimated at 68,000 tons in 1980.

Chlorine, a by-product of the production of caustic soda, is produced in salterns at various places in Ethiopia, Somalia, Kenya, Tanzania, Madagascar, and Mauritius. Salt is obtained from Lake Magadi in Kenya and Lake Katwe in Uganda, and brine is found at Uvinsa in Tanzania. Light virgin naptha and other petroleum feedstocks could be obtained from the refineries that are situated at various points in the area, while benzene is produced in coking plants in Southern Rhodesia. Recognizing that the availability of abundant and cheap electric energy is an essential element of the fertilizer industry, it is feasible to locate such industries at Koka, southeast of Addis Ababa in Ethiopia; Jinja in Uganda; Nairobi in Kenya; Dar-es-Salaam in Tanzania; Umtali in Southern Rhodesia; and Livingstone in Zambia.

West Africa

The market for nitrogenous fertilizers is primarily made up of Nigeria, Ghana, the Ivory Coast, and Senegal. The demand was 16,440 tons of nitrogen in 1965 and is estimated to grow to 94,500 tons in 1975. Natural gas exists in abundance in Nigeria, but cheap electricity is available only in Ghana. With regard to phosphate fertilizers, the bulk are found in Nigeria, Ghana, the Ivory Coast, and Senegal. The demand was 16,390 tons of P_2O_5 in 1965, but it is estimated that this demand will rise to 108,100 tons in 1975. The largest phosphate deposits are found in Senegal and Togo. No potassium deposits have yet been discovered in West Africa, and potassic fertilizers will therefore have to be imported. Resources for phosphate fertilizers are known to exist in the Tilemsi valley in Mali, where there are reserves of 2.5 million tons of a phosphate with a 26-28 percent phosphoric acid content. Pallo in Senegal has deposits of 40 million tons of ore containing 28-30 percent phosphoric acid. The Taiba deposit, 110 kilometers from Dakar, contains some 115 million tons of ore containing 57 percent of tricalcic phosphate, which can be enriched to obtain 40 million tons of 37.5 percent phosphoric acid. These deposits are now being worked, and present annual capacity is 700,000 tons. Phosphate deposits also are found in Dahomey, but they are too poor for working. There is a large phosphate deposit in Togo with reserves of more than 100 million tons.

North Africa

The fertilizer industry of North Africa is the most advanced in
Africa. The U.A.R. has the largest and most diversified fertilizer
industry in North Africa, followed by Morocco and Tunisia, where
the industry is based on phosphate and sulfate resources. While the
U.A.R. produces its own requirements of ammonia, all other countries
rely on imports. The countries of the North African subregion consumed
245,000 tons of pure nitrogen, 99,000 tons of phosphoric acid, and
29,000 tons of potash in 1961/62, and this constituted nearly 75 percent
of total consumption in developing Africa. The demand has risen
tremendously, and 1980 demand is estimated at 900,000 tons of nitrogen,
600,000 tons of phosphoric acid, and 200,000 tons of potash. About
135,000 tons of nitrogenous fertilizers and 140,000 tons of phosphates
were produced by local factories in 1961/62. Raw materials for the
production of both phosphatic and nitrogenous fertilizers are abundant.
Phosphate deposits in Morocco are estimated at 30 billion tons, while
Algeria, Tunisia, and the U.A.R. have smaller resources. Natural
gas is available in all these countries.

Future Prospects

The development of fertilizers has been hampered in the past
for a number of reasons. In the first place, a great majority of the
African farmers are peasants producing on a traditional basis mainly
for home consumption. As a rule, such farmers do not use fertilizers
and since consumption of fertilizers is mainly by the few plantation
farmers, there has not been significant increase in their demand for
fertilizers. Second, there have been inadequate supply facilities in
most African countries, especially in the remote rural areas, and
very little is known about the use of fertilizers in these areas. Third,
the lack of information regarding the kind of fertilizers to be used
for a given crop also has reduced the demand for this product. Finally,
fertilizer production is capital-intensive and high cost in most of the
producing countries, and the price of fertilizers is often too high for
the peasant farmer. Moreover, the lack of transportation facilities
increases the cost of distribution of fertilizers.

In the plan for development of this industry, there is need for
government action, especially in the education of peasant farmers in
the use of modern methods of agriculture. This is particularly important in countries where the government has adopted deliberate
policies for the development of the rural communities. Related to
this issue is the need for providing research facilities and extension

services to the peasant farmers. In addition, the governments should adopt favorable pricing policies for fertilizers. In certain cases, it may even be necessary for governments to distribute free fertilizers to the peasant farmers, especially those who cannot afford to buy them. There also should be an effective system of distribution of fertilizers. This can be done through the establishment of pricing support systems and farm credits toward the development of certain cash crops.

Since any improvement in the methods of farming or the use of fertilizers would generally increase productivity in the rural areas and hence increase output, it is essential that, along with these measures, the governments establish a sound marketing system so as to enable the farmers to sell their produce at the most profitable prices. There is nothing more damaging to the morale of the peasant farmers than for the governments to encourage increased production of a given crop but fail to provide the basic facilities that would enable the farmers to bring their crops to the markets.

THE PETROLEUM INDUSTRY

The prospects for the petroleum industry in Africa increased so much during the 1960's as to provide an economic breakthrough in some countries, especially Libya and Nigeria. The discovery of large quantities of crude oil and natural gas provided the necessary push in this industry, resulting in tremendous increases in the national incomes of these countries. The main petroleum producing countries in Africa are Libya, Algeria, Nigeria, the U.A.R., and Gabon. There was a rapid expansion in the production of crude petroleum, especially between 1960 and 1968 (see Table 5.5). In Libya, for example, the production rose from a mere 692,000 metric tons in 1960 to over 125 million metric tons in 1968. In Nigeria, production expanded very rapidly up to 1967 but declined considerably thereafter due to the Nigerian political crisis. Similarly, production in the U.A.R. declined following the June 1967 Middle East War.

Petroleum output has increased due to favorable production conditions in these countries and the geographical proximity of most of the oil wells to ports and harbors, and due to the favorable price conditions of petroleum in the world market. Most of the manufacture of petroleum products is carried on in the U.A.R., Algeria, and Morocco. In West Africa, Senegal and Upper Volta are the principal producers, while in East and Southern Africa Kenya, Tanzania, Southern Rhodesia, and South Africa are the major producers. The number of petroleum refineries has expanded extraordinarily in recent years,

TABLE 5.5

Production of Crude Petroleum by Principal Producing Countries in Africa, 1960-68
(thousands of metric tons)

	Libya	Algeria	United Arab Republic	Nigeria	Gabon
1960	--	8,632	3,319	850	800
1961	692	15,660	3,819	2,271	774
1962	7,852	20,498	4,676	3,328	827
1963	22,039	23,641	5,592	3,772	890
1964	41,476	26,227	6,354	5,933	1,058
1965	58,803	26,025	7,129	13,531	1,264
1966	72,540	33,264	6,264	21,000	1,447
1967	82,540	39,072	5,716	15,588	3,444
1968	125,216	40,776	8,995	7,023	4,642

Source: ECA, A Survey of Economic Conditions in Africa, E/CN. 14/401; ECA, (Statistics Division) Yearly Statistics of Industrial Production, 1968.

largely due to increased demand for petroleum products in the African countries. In 1964, there were 10 refineries on the continent, but in 1969 there were 31 with a total capacity of over 40 million tons (see Table 5.6).

The most important petroleum products are fuel oils, which account for nearly 69 percent of the total production in Africa; followed by gasoline, 20.5 percent; and kerosene, 10.2 percent. Petroleum products constitute an important import item for most African countries, but the geographical distribution of consumption is uneven. In 1965, for example, about 70 percent of the total African production of petroleum goods was consumed in North Africa; 14.9 percent in West Africa; 11.7 percent in East and Southern Africa; and 3.8 percent in Central Africa. The U.A.R., South Africa, and Algeria together accounted for about 55 percent of the total African consumption.

Data on production and consumption of petroleum products in Africa is reported in Table 5.7. There is a marked discrepancy between production and consumption in most of the African countries. The main producing countries generally produce more than they consume. For example, in 1965 Algeria produced 2.2 million metric tons but consumed only 1.2 million metric tons, while in the U.A.R. production stood at 7.7 million metric tons but consumption was only 5.5 million metric tons. In East Africa, in 1965 Kenya's production was around 1.7 million metric tons but its consumption was only 0.7 million metric tons. These data support the notion that there is considerable overproduction of petroleum in most African countries.

There is no detailed statistical material to show trade in petroleum products among the African countries. Most of them import these products from overseas in large quantities. As part of the plan for economic cooperation, surveys should be made of the production and consumption patterns in the various African countries. On the basis of the data obtained, negotiations could be started toward the promotion of trade in petroleum goods. In recent years, a number of refineries have sprung up without due regard to the need for coordinating production of existing petroleum and petrochemical industries in different countries. A number of these refineries cannot be sustained by their domestic markets alone, and it therefore becomes prudent for the countries producing these products to consider cooperation in this industry.

THE ALUMINIUM INDUSTRY

Aluminium is a new metal, and the development of aluminium industry for commercial purposes gained importance only since the

TABLE 5.6

Location and Capacity of Oil Refineries
in Africa, 1969

	Location	Capacity (millions of tons of refined oil per annum)
North Africa		
Algeria	Arzew	1.25
	Maison Caree	2.50
	Hassi Messoaud	0.10
Morocco	Mohamedia	1.25
	Sidi Kacem	0.25
Canary Islands	Tenerife	5.00
Tunisia	Bizerte	1.00
Libya	Marsa el Brega	--
	Waha	--
U.A.R.	Alexandria	2.25
	Suez	3.00
Sudan	Suez	3.80
	Port Sudan	1.00
West Africa		
Senegal	Dakar	0.06
Ivory Coast	Abidjan	0.70
Ghana	Tema	1.20
Nigeria	Port Harcourt	1.50
Central Africa:		
Gabon	Port Gentil	0.70
Congo (Brazzaville)	Kinlao	0.70
Congo (Kinshasa)	Moanda	0.60
East and Southern Africa		
Angola	Luanda	0.55
Ethiopia	Assab	0.50
Kenya	Mombasa	1.80
Tanzania	Dar-es-Salaam	0.60
Southern Rhodesia	Umtali	1.00
Mozambique	Lourenco Marques	0.60
Madagascar	Tamataye	0.60
South Africa	Boksburg	0.20
	Durban	2.90
	Durban	3.40
	Cape Town	1.50

<u>Source</u>: ECA Cartography Unit.

144

TABLE 5.7

Production and Consumption of Petroleum
Products in Africa, 1960-65
(thousands of metric tons)

	Production				Consumption			
	1960	1963	1964	1965	1960	1963	1964	1965
North Africa								
Algeria	40	360	1,680	2,190	1,480	1,310	1,250	1,390
Morocco	180	870	940	1,000	790	910	960	1,060
Tunisia	---	60	650	660	430	570	730	630
Libya	--	--	--	--	240	280	340	350
U.A.R.	4,050	6,030	7,240	7,730	4,890	5,270	5,670	5,490
Sudan	--	--	90	460	390	480	550	620
West Africa								
Mauritania	--	--	--	--	10	20	30	30
Mali	--	--	--	--	40	50	60	60
Senegal	--	10	260	430	200	260	310	350
Guinea	--	--	--	--	130	230	230	230
Liberia	--	--	--	--	50	120	160	180
Gambia	--	--	--	--	10	10	10	10
Sierra Leone	--	--	--	--	60	130	100	100
Ivory Coast	--	--	--	170	140	190	240	380
Upper Volta	--	--	--	--	20	30	40	50
Niger	--	--	--	--	10	30	30	30
Ghana	--	170	800	740	420	500	570	510
Togo	--	--	--	--	20	40	40	40
Dahomey	--	--	--	--	50	40	50	50
Nigeria	--	--	--	170	580	820	960	1,150
Central Africa								
Cameroun	--	--	--	--	100	110	150	160
Chad	--	--	--	--	20	30	30	30
Central African Republic	--	--	--	--	30	20	20	30
Gabon	--	--	--	--	50	50	60	60
Congo (Brazzaville)	--	--	--	--	70	80	90	80
Congo (Kinshasa)	--	--	--	--	380	440	310	390
Rwanda	--	--	--	---	20	30	30	30
Burundi	--	--	--	--	20	20	20	20
Equatorial Guinea	--	--	--	--	--	--	--	--
East and Southern Africa	--							
Ethopia	--	--	--	--	100	130	140	130
Somalia	--	--	--	--	30	30	40	40
Uganda	--	--	--	--	120	130	150	180
Kenya	--	130	1,480	1,750	700	700	790	700
Tanzania	--	--	--	--	300	310	330	370
Zambia	--	--	--	--	130	140	150	150
Malawi	--	--	--	--	40	50	50	50
Madagascar	--	--	--	--	120	130	140	160
Mauritius	--	--	--	--	50	60	80	80
Botswana	--	--	--	--	--	--	--	--
Lesotho	--	--	--	--	--	--	--	--
Swaziland	--	--	--	--	--	--	--	--

Source: ECA, A Survey of Economic Conditions in Africa, 1967, E/CN.14/409/Rev.1.

early 1950's. Therefore, the African policy makers had doubts about how much effort should be put into the development of the aluminium industry and how profitable it would be. However, the trend in world production of aluminium is quite encouraging. Between 1900 and 1960, world production of aluminium doubled every seven years. The consumption of aluminium in Africa shows an upward trend and therefore has great potential for development. There are more than 44 aluminium fabricating plants scattered all over Africa. Nigeria and South Africa each have 6 plants (see Table 5.8). The principal products from aluminium are household and hospital utensils, roofing sheets used in the housing industry, and electrical goods and insulating materials such as those used in cold storage chambers.

Bauxite, the basic raw material for the production of aluminium, is found in large quantities in Africa; the total African reserves are estimated to be about one-third of the total world reserves. The largest deposits of bauxite in West Africa are found in Guinea, Ghana, the Ivory Coast, Mali, and Upper Volta, in Central Africa, in Cameroun and Congo (Kinshasa); in East and Southern Africa, in Madagascar, Malawi, Mozambique, and Southern Rhodesia. Africa has abundant supplies of electrical energy, which is required in aluminium industry. It is therefore estimated that there will be substantial increase in consumption as well as exports of aluminium in the coming years.

The demand for aluminium in Africa was 24,000 tons in 1963, and it is estimated that demand will grow to 114,000 tons by 1980. The total consumption of aluminium in Africa was about 51,000 tons in 1963. About 27 percent was consumed in West Africa, 19 percent in North Africa, and about 11 percent in East Africa and the remaining was distributed in Central and outer Africa, including South Africa. World demand grew from 4.22 million tons to 5.52 million tons between 1960 and 1963, an increase of about 25 percent. It is estimated that the world demand will have grown to 11 million tons by 1975.   Much of this demand will undoubtedly be in the advanced countries. There is a wide gap between the production and demand of aluminium in the world market, which should present the African countries with great opportunities for expanding production, especially in bauxite, alumina, and crude aluminium.

In 1967, Africa's production capacity for aluminium was estimated to be around 165,000 tons, whereas demand (including South Africa) was on the order of 50,000 to 60,000 tons. West Africa has good potential to produce crude aluminium on a large scale.

In Central Africa, Cameroun is the major producer of aluminium metal, with a total of about 53,000 tons in 1963. Production is based

TABLE 5.8

Aluminium Fabricating Plants in Africa, 1965

Country and Location of Plants	Number of Plants	Principal Products	
		Utensils	Sheet
Algeria	5	x	x[a]
Cameroun	1	x	
Congo (Kinshasa)--Jadotville, Bukavu	4	x	
Ghana--Tema	2	x	x[b]
Ivory Coast	1	x	
Nigeria--Lagos	6	x	x
Sudan--Khartoum, Omderman	2	x	
U.A.R.	3	x	
Burundi--Bujumbura	1	x	x[c]
Rwanda	1	x	
Ethiopia--Asmara and Addis Ababa	3	x	
Kenya--Mombasa	2	x	
Uganda--Kampala	2	x	
Tanzania--Dar-es-Salaam	3	x	x[d]
Zambia--Lusaka	1	x	
Southern Rhodesia--Salisbury	1		x
South Africa	6	x	x[cd]

[a]One rolling mill and four corrugating plants, one of which also makes utensils.
[b]Windows, ladders, furniture, and castings also.
[c]Corrugated sheet.
[d]Extrusions, wire, and cable also.
[e]Includes rolling mills processing ingot.

Source: ECA, A Survey of Economic Conditions in Africa, 1967, E/CN.14/409/Rev.1.

147

on cheap power from Edea and imported alumina, but it is hoped that bauxite and alumina will be obtained within Cameroun in the future.

Although there are prospects for stimulating consumption of aluminium products in Africa, the future production of aluminium metals will depend for some time to come on markets outside Africa.

Since the aluminium industry is relatively new, projections for production and use generally are difficult to formulate. However, as new uses are discovered its significance will increase. In order to promote this industry, it is essential to adopt more policies that look outward in the development of the aluminium products. The countries interested in the development of this industry should come together to formulate concrete measures for the promotion of aluminium products and to determine areas for concerted action. As in other industries, the adoption of liberal trade policies will be a major step toward the expansion of the aluminium industry.

THE TEXTILE INDUSTRY[3]

The case for cooperation in the development of the textile industry lies largely in the fact that consumption far outstrips local production and hence the major portion of such consumption must be met with imports. The production of textiles in Africa rose from 681 million square yards in 1948 to nearly 2,000 million square yards in 1965. Consumption of textiles was estimated to have risen from 2,000 million square yards to 5,100 million square yards over the same period, leaving a gap of about 3,100 million square yards between production and consumption. In other words, economic cooperation efforts mean attempts to fill this gap through the development of import substitution industries. The major products of the African textile industries are yarns, cotton (staple and mixed), cotton prints, blankets, sewing threads, woolen and synthetic fibers, and ready-made garments of all kinds.

In East Africa, cotton and rayon constitute the major items both in consumption and production. In recent years, there has been an appreciable shift in favor of lighter fabrics and ready-made clothing. Production in the countries varies greatly. Ethiopia has about 9 textile establishments of which 5 are spinning, weaving, and finishing units and one carries out knitting as well. Ethiopia also has two other factories, one for knitting wool and one for making blankets. Uganda has one single composite textile mill situated at Jinja, which produces a wide range of products. Kenya has a few knitting factories, one of which carries out spinning using local fibers. Tanzania has three cotton-weaving factories and two rayon-weaving plants and a few smaller knitting factories. In Madagascar, there is one composite mill carrying out spinning and weaving as well as finishing functions. Malawi, Zambia, Somalia, and Mauritius do not have textile mills, but Malawi has one blanket factory.

In Central Africa, there is a large textile market made up mainly of Congo (Kinshasa), followed by Cameroun. Congo (Kinshasa) has a well developed textile industry: there are 3 exclusively spinning units, 2 weaving units, and 4 combined spinning and weaving plants; there also are 2 units that combine spinning, weaving, and printing, 2 that produce sacks, and 1 that is devoted exclusively to printing. The Central African Republic, Chad, Gabon, Rwanda, Burundi, Equatorial Guinea, and Congo (Brazzaville) each have one textile mill that produces goods for export to neighboring countries. Cameroun does not have a textile industry, but Cameroun and Chad produce large quantities of cotton.

In West Africa, the market is made up largely of Nigeria and Ghana, which together account for about 60 percent of total consumption in the area. Although Nigeria has a few composite units, it still imports large quantities of textiles. In West Africa as a whole, local production accounts for only 20 percent of the consumption, and the remainder is met with imports. Thus, there is great potential for the development of textile industries.

In North Africa, the U.A.R., the Sudan, and Morocco are the main markets for textiles, and cotton constitutes the largest single item accounting for about 71 percent of the total fabric consumption in the subregion. Egypt has the most developed textile industries in Africa, with some 1.4 spindles and over 23,000 looms. Wool, yarn, and woolen fabrics also are manufactured in the area, especially in the U.A.R. and Morocco.

The main obstacle to expansion of domestic production in the textile industries is the localized nature of the production units. The vast majority of the textile mills are oriented largely toward the domestic market. Thus far, there has been no effort to coordinate production, and a number of countries produce cotton mainly for export overseas. The second limitation to the expansion of textile production is the use of relatively obsolete machinery and equipment in some plants, especially in Eastern Africa. Moreover, investment cost per unit of equipment is generally much higher in the African countries than in such developing countries as India and Pakistan, and therefore African textile goods find it difficult to compete with the cheaper imports. These two factors reduce the competitiveness of African textiles with similar imported goods.

There are prospects for the expansion of the textile industry. For example, Table 5.9 shows that the future consumption of textiles is expected to increase significantly by 1975. In order to meet domestic demand for textile products, it is estimated that Africa will need investments on the order of $1,300 million per year up to 1975. Obviously, there is a strong case for joint action in the development of this industry. The magnitude of the difference between current production and consumption (see Table 5.9) strengthens the case for coordination of production and investment in the textile industry.

SMALL-SCALE INDUSTRY

There is no generally accepted definition of a small-scale industry. What may be termed a small-scale industry in one country may not be small-scale in another. For instance, small-scale industries were once defined by the number of persons employed. In the United Kingdom and the United States, any production unit employing fewer than 100 persons was regarded as small-scale, while in Korea the number was under 200 and in Japan under 300. In India, any manufacturing enterprise employing fewer than 50 persons and with capital equipment worth less than U.S.$100,000 was considered small-scale. In Pakistan, firms with or without the use of motive power employing fewer than 20 persons fell in this category, whereas in the U.A.R. the number was as low as 10 persons. According to ECA:

> Small industries comprising small-scale and handicraft undertakings are understood to mean establishments for manufacturing, processing and service activities which differ from larger enterprises inter alia, by a significant lack of specialization in management. Such undertakings vary from craft shops in which the self-employed owner works together with his family to the small mechanical factory which may employ up to some 50 workers.[4]

In regard to the establishment of small-scale industries, two main considerations should be stressed here. In the first place, the importance of small-scale industry must be seen in light of its impact on the economic and social structure of the African countries. This category of industry provides a certain range of consumer goods. It also provides employment opportunities, although they are limited

TABLE 5.9

Production and Consumption of Textiles in Africa, 1962
(millions of square yards)

	East Africa	Central Africa	West Africa	North Africa
Output 1962	200	102	220	--
Demand	870	262	1,050	--
Difference covered by imports (demand minus output)	670	160	830	--
Production target 1975	1,300	276	1,125	--

Source: ECA, Textile Industries In Africa, E/CN.14/AS III/24, January, 1966.

151

in terms of the total number employed in any one country. In the second place, small-scale industries should be seen as contributing to the increase of purchasing power of the low-income groups and as the mainstay of intra-African trade. In economies where subsistence agriculture is predominant, the development of small-scale industry will provide the necessary bridge between the urban and the rural communities. Indeed, such industry provides the necessary stage for adjustments in the people's thinking from the purely traditional outlook to the modern concept of society.

Small-scale manufacturing includes a wide range of products that enter the day-to-day consumption list of the middle-class and low-income groups. Some of the common items under this category are examined below, but the list is by no means exhaustive and is used only to give an indication of the extent of small-scale industry.

Products of Small-Scale Industry

Ceramic, Glass, Clay, and Cement Products

This includes kitchen utensils and such tableware as cups and saucers, jugs, tea and coffee sets, and plates. It also includes bricks, mirrors, thermos flasks, glass beads, marbles, ashtrays, and bangles.

Chemical and Allied Products

There is a long list of goods produced in chemical and allied industry. Among them are sealing wax, printing inks, detergents, disinfectants, laundry and toilet soaps, and dry-cell batteries. Paints include varnishes and allied products, of which the chief items are distemper, floor polish, and aluminium paints. Paper products include carton boxes, paper bags, envelopes, letter pads, exercise books, registers, and toilet paper rolls. Next in this list are pesticides and such pharmaceutical products as sanitary towels and surgical cotton wool. Plastic products are becoming increasingly popular items in the modern household. These products include footwear, insulated wire and cable, foam plastics, buckets, bowls, tumblers, coat hangers, polythene bags, handbags, overalls, and raincoats. Next in importance in this group are the rubber products, which include such footwear as rubber and canvas shoes, rubber boots, bath and door mats, gloves, insulated wire and cable, garden and fire hoses, bicycle tires and tubes, and mountings for industrial machinery. Among the toilet preparations and cosmetics produced are face powder and cream, toothpowder and toothpaste, hair oil and cream, lipstick, nail polish, shampoo, perfume, eau de cologne, and shaving soap and cream.

Electrical Fittings and Accessories

The range within this group is rather limited. However, production includes such items as neon signs, lamp shades, cables and electric wiring, and miniature and electric bulbs.

Food and Food Preparations

There is a wide range of food and foodstuffs manufactured by the small-scale firms. These include sausages, bacon and ham, fresh, condensed, and powdered milk, vinegar, syrup, chutney, jam, fruit juice, toffee and other candies, biscuits, macaroni, spaghetti, and vegetable soup. There are also large quantities of vegetable oils, including peanut oil, margarine, and palm kernel oil. Alcoholic beverages, including wine, cider, vermouth, and gin, also are produced on a small scale.

Hosiery and Ready-to-Wear Garments

There are small production units of hosiery and ready-to-wear clothing in almost every African country. The products range from socks, vests, briefs, and stockings to knitted jerseys, corsets, blouses, and dresses. Ladies' clothing also includes petticoats, knickers, panties, and brassieres. Menswear includes shirts, dressing gowns, jackets, suits, bush shirts, and raincoats. Other items in this category are mosquito curtains, blankets, towels, pillow-cases, sheets, and rugs.

Leather and Leather Products

The leather industry has become widespread in the African countries. Most of these countries have factories producing all kinds of shoes, mainly for the local market. Among the popular leather goods are wallets, handbags, purses, shoes, sandals, slippers, suitcases, briefcases, attache cases, and carryalls. Industrial leather products include belting, buckles, hydraulic presses, gloves, bicycle saddles, and washers.

Mechanical Engineering Products

Because mechanical engineering products are somewhat specialized items, the range is rather limited. The main products in this category are plows, harrows, weeders, and cultivators. The smaller items include spades, pickaxes, shovels, knives, and pedal pumps. Hardware produced includes locks and padlocks, wire nails, woodscrews, nuts and bolts, chains, curtain rails, and door handles.

Foundry and fabricated products include brass, bronze and copper castings; iron and steel castings; wire drawing and barbed wire; gates, doors, windows; electro-coating; and such machine parts as mountings, weights, and measures. The lighter engineering products include pressure and wick stoves, lanterns, torch cases, umbrellas, tin containers, barrels, and pails. Among the most popular household items are frying pans, saucepans, buckets, and dustbins. Office equipment produced in the small-scale industries includes paper pins, staples, paper weights, steel furniture, desks, chairs, cabinets, racks, stools, and cash-boxes. Among the heavier building items are metallic grills, window grills, cots, beds, meat safes, and wheelbarrows.

Timber and Wood Products

Wood products are important both for building and household uses. The main wood products are radio cabinets, beds, wardrobes, chairs, dressing tables, drawers, cupboards, and window and door frames. Coat hangers, wooden toys, picture frames, and trays are also important items. The heavier wood products include railway sleepers, parquet flooring, and bus and truck bodies.

Prospects in Small-Scale Industry

It will be noted from the preceding paragraphs that there is a wide range of production in the small-scale industries. The question of economic cooperation in the small-scale industry therefore raises important issues. Since many of these operations are rather localized and serve the small markets centered around urban and industrial areas, the case for economic cooperation appears, on the face of it, to be rather weak. It is sometimes argued that the small-scale industries should be left out of integration plans because they are too small to serve a multinational market. The point to note, however, is that, since these products constitute the bulk of the consumption goods of a large portion of the African population, measures should be taken to investigate ways to make consumers aware of the products manufactured in adjoining states. Although manufacturing is carried out on a wide scale, there are still considerable imports of these goods in most of the African countries. One way in which intra-African trade could be encouraged is through the creation of small-scale industrial fairs and exhibitions.

The small-scale entrepreneur could be assisted in another way through training programs in management and modern production techniques. Governments also could institute measures to provide

easy credit facilities to owners of small firms. The advantage that
the small-scale producer has over the larger firms is that he can
easily adjust his production methods to fit changing conditions. The
introduction of machinery and other equipment in the production of
the small-scale units are essential measures toward the development
of this sector, but such measures are beyond the reach of most
potential entrepreneurs. It is therefore essential that the African
governments provide all necessary encouragement to the development
of the small-scale industries as part of the efforts toward economic
cooperation.

BALANCING INDUSTRIAL DEVELOPMENT

Several methods for the balancing of industrial development
can be envisaged. Such methods, including the use of fiscal policies,
tariffs, taxes, and quantitative restrictions, have been tried with some
measure of success in a number of economic groupings. Fiscal policies
can be used to ensure greater equity among the member states through
direct financial transfers from the economically stronger to the weaker
states. However, as in the case of the Kampala Agreement, this method
is not generally acceptable politically because countries with adequate
funds are not always willing to entertain the idea of subsidizing
development efforts in other countries while potential recipient countries do not wish to be beggars in an economic cooperation grouping.
However, where countries adopt this method they may make adjustments in their fiscal policies, especially in the monetary and investment fields, or may create a payments union through which the central
bank can operate to provide credit facilities for the financing of
multinational industries.

Development banks have been found to be effective instruments
for balancing the development of industries. For example, in the
EEC the European Investment Bank was created with the specific
purpose of ensuring the balanced and smooth development of the
European Common Market and of facilitating the financing of (1)
projects for developing less developed partner states; (2) projects
for modernizing or converting enterprises or for creating new activities necessary for the gradual establishment of the common market
in cases where the projects could be financed by individual member
states; and (3) projects of common interest to several member states
that, by their size or nature, could not be financed with funds available
within the individual member states.[5] The East African Development
Bank also was created to provide financial and technical assistance
to promote the industrial development of the partner states. It is

required to give priority to industrial development in the relatively less industrially developed partner states, thereby endeavoring to reduce the substantial imbalance. The charter of the East African Development Bank also provides that wherever possible, the bank encourage the development of projects designed to make the economies of the East African countries increasingly complementary in the industrial field.

The second method that could be used to balance industrial development is the use of tariffs. Through adjustments in tariff rates the weaker partner states may be granted a longer period in which to make tariff reductions or eliminations toward the creation of a common external tariff. This can be achieved by agreeing that tariffs should be reduced pari passu with the development of industry and trade. This method need not be used in a general way but could be employed through the item-by-item negotiations. For example, the LAFTA contracting parties may authorize any partner state that is at a relatively less advanced stage of economic development to apply, as a temporary measure, appropriate non-discriminatory measures designed to protect the domestic production of specified industries. The EFTA Convention provides that, if reducing tariffs might cause serious problems for a given product in any member state, that state may be allowed to adopt alternative arrangements in respect of tariff reductions for that particular product.

The third method of balancing industrial development is by the use of transfer tax, as in the East African Community. This method is discussed in detail in Chapter 8.

Finally, the least developed partner state can apply quantitative restrictions or industrial licensing on imports of goods from the more advanced partner states. This method was tried in East Africa between 1964 and 1967 but had to be abandoned when the new treaty came into force. Objections often have been raised against this method because it is difficult to administer and is subject to much abuse. Countries could use the method not as means of protecting infant industries but as a mode of retaliation against any other partner state for any reason whatsoever. Moreover, quantitative restrictions have disruptive effects on the movement of trade among the member states and are thus contrary to the concept of a common market or free trade area.

Use of the allocation of industries as an element for balancing industrial development would be facilitated if the states had effective control of investments. Since the profit motive governs the investment decisions of the private entrepreneur, the absence of an effective machinery for controlling investment decisions might well result in the concentration of industries in the already more industrialized partner states. In order to institute effective control over industrial investments, countries might consider state participation in the key industries. Another formula is to create a general industrial development fund from which multinational industries could be financed. Loan finance also could be created from the general funds to assist in the development of private enterprises especially the indigenous entrepreneurs. This would be particularly desirable for industries that fall outside the multinational agreements but have a sufficiently large level of production to make substantial impact on the development of the individual states. Multinational industrial corporations also could be established to finance multinational industrial projects. Finally, the allocation of industries could be facilitated by the establishment of industrial promotion councils that would be responsible mainly for carrying out negotiations for the allocation and financing of the various aspects of industrial development, especially where the coordination of industrial planning is envisaged.

PROBLEMS IN THE COORDINATION OF INDUSTRIAL DEVELOPMENT

Industrial development in most African countries still is concentrated largely on consumer goods and a limited range of intermediate products, especially building materials. These industries include textile manufacturing, sugar refining, cement production, flour milling, petroleum refining, brewing and soft drink production, and the production of fertilizers, cigarettes and matches, footwear, soap, and vegetable oils. Production for export still accounts for a relatively small proportion of total industrial output, but there has been a marked increase in the exports of primary products in a more processed form. An encouraging feature of industrial development is the emergence of joint ventures involving two or more African countries, as in the Maghreb countries where there have been joint studies aimed at reaching an agreed allocation of particular industries. Industrial coordination, although not yet actually achieved, constitutes the main development efforts of the countries of the East African Community, UDEAC, OERS, Chad and Cameroun, and Togo and Dahomey.

A problem that is of foremost importance in initiating a plan for economic integration is the fact that all the African leaders aspire to raise the living standards of their people through the launching of comprehensive schemes of economic development. As a result, planners have become preoccupied with the national economies, and

more often than not they give hardly any thought to the need for concerted action. The problem in the quest for economic integration is
to ensure that the industrial plans under economic integration are
compatible with the national aspirations. This is not easy to achieve,
largely because of the great disparities in the levels of industrial
development and also because it is difficult for states to maintain
absolute self-determination in matters of economic development and
at the same time achieve greater cooperation with other countries.
If industrial coordination is to be successful, there inevitably must
be some degree of give and take. To what extent this will appeal to
the African leaders is quite another matter. Because of the individu-
alistic approach to questions of industrial planning and development,
the coordination of national policies has caused considerable difficulty.

The pressures brought about by independence in Africa have
prompted the African states to explore new areas of industrial development to combat the problems of economically raising the masses.
Most African states apparently feel that the formulation of national
development plans is the most effective means to achieve these
aspirations. However, formulating development plans means taking
into account the availability of natural resources, trained manpower,
technology, and other requirements without due consideration of what
happens across national frontiers. The problem has been that of
attempting to look at matters not only in terms of national interests
but also in terms of the interests of the other states with which economic
cooperation is envisaged. The experience in the EEC shows very
clearly that, even in countries that already are economically advanced,
the immediate switch from nationalism to multinationalism is difficult
to attain. This problem of uniting national and multinational policies
is more pronounced in Africa, where the race for economic development
has gathered momentum in recent years.

Problems of Industrial Financing

Industrial financing in Africa has been one of the greatest problems
of economic development. The availability of capital funds for economic
development has greatly influenced the extent to which industrialization
has been achieved in the countries of Africa.

This problem would become more acute in the financing of economic
integration. The problem is basically twofold: First, the countries of
Africa have very low incomes and hence very low savings. They therefore find it extremely difficult to raise funds from domestic resources.

In certain countries, capital formation from domestic resources is so meager that nothing can be done to industrialize without huge capital doses from abroad. This problem has been aggravated by the lack of investment opportunities and by the virtually complete absence of local money and capital markets that are necessary to stimulate savings and investments and to channel such savings to the most productive uses. Foreign borrowings often have been made on very favorable terms, and this has resulted in the multiplier effect by which such investment fails to generate the required incomes within the African countries and consequently the rate of economic development is slowed down. The problem of increasing domestic savings and investment has been considerably worsened by the growing increase in the value of imports in the African countries during the 1960's; there has been a constant drain of domestic resources that has been reflected in the chronic balance of payment deficits in many African countries.

Second, although the volume of foreign aid is believed to have increased in recent years, this increase has fallen short by far of the expectations of the African countries since it has not kept pace with capital requirements.* Both foreign aid and foreign investments have been selective and do not often coincide with the actual needs of the recipient countries, due largely to the strings attached to such aid offers. Investment decisions have been governed mainly by the profit motive, and where profits have not been attractive foreign capital has shied away. Even where loans have been obtained, the cost of servicing these loans has been so high as to constitute heavy burdens on the young African economies. Another problem related to foreign investment is that, due to the acute demand for investments, there often has been keen competition among the African countries in their efforts to attract capital from the developed countries. This competition is indicated by the large number of investment laws enacted in the 1960's in the newly independent states. Many countries have been forced to offer very attractive terms to foreign investors, even where such terms are not to the best advantage or interest of their economies.

---

*During the first United Nations Development Decade, hope was expressed at UNCTAD that the developed countries would transfer at least 1 percent of their national incomes to aid the developing countries. The developed countries did not accept this approach, and in fact aid from some developed countries declined in recent years.

In economic integration, two major problems can be easily distinguished. First, if the participating states decide that the financing of jointly owned industrial projects must be left to an intergovernmental body, the participating states no longer will be able to canvass for foreign investments in certain fields individually. This will imply the existence of two aspects of industrial financing, one for the development of industries that are purely national in character and the other for multinational industries. The problem that will arise here is where to draw the line between the national and multinational agencies. The main point to note is that, unless there is adequate joint state control, foreign investors will continue to determine the shape of investment decisions even in the multinational set-up. If this happens, the results of economic integration may benefit the foreign investors and not necessarily the local inhabitants.

If foreign loans and investments are obtained by a multinational economic grouping for an entire region or subregion, the other problem that will immediately arise will be the determination of the extent of liability to be incurred by each state. Past experience indicates that coordinated action is needed with regard to investment decisions so as to introduce the necessary institutional changes to end domination by a few foreign private oligopolies created during the colonial period. Where loans must be guaranteed by the states individually or collectively for such multinational industrial projects as interstate highways, railways, airlines, and hydroelectric schemes, the African countries would be concerned about the extent to which each state should guarantee these loans. If guarantees must be on an equal basis, would there be any assurances that the benefits from such industrial projects would be equitably distributed among the member countries? If some disparity in the distribution of benefits from such schemes emerged, what compensation would be given to member countries that, by their geographical location and other factors, were likely to benefit less than the others?

On the other hand, the problem of industrial financing would emerge in a different context if the countries decided that the financing of projects under integration should be undertaken separately. For instance, if a road or railway is desired to join two or three countries and each country is to undertake the financing of the portion of the road or railway that lies in its territory, the problem would arise as to whether all the countries could afford the building of the railway or road as against other national projects. If one of the states were unable to finance its part of the project, the entire project might well be futile. The essential point that emerges here is that even in the financial field concerted action is essential for the control of investments as well as other foreign funds in a multinational set-up.

Problems of Training and Industrial Research

It is necessary to emphasize the lack of trained and skilled man-power in Africa today. The problem is prominent not only in industry but also in all fields of economic development and in administration. There are no adequate institutions for training the technicians required to service the various projects in economic development. All economic activities in Africa are characterized by acute shortages of personnel at all levels. By and large, a very large percentage of the total pop-ulation is engaged in the subsistence sector, whose contribution to economic development is almost negative. The question of training manpower becomes essential especially when the establishment of in-dustry on a very large scale to serve several countries is envisaged. In the past, the recruitment of the required skilled personnel from overseas resulted in a considerable portion of capital resources being exported back to the advanced countries in payment of salaries. The situation is disturbing when one considers that it has been estimated that between 1964 and 1975 Africa will require about 9,700 senior technicians at the university level; 23,700 junior technicians; 30,000 engineers and scientists and 83,000 technicians in the industrial sector alone; and 128,000 skilled workers for the East African subregion alone.[6] This is a very formidable problem that calls for the immediate attention of all African countries.

The research facilities in industrial development provided in the past have not been adequate to meet the growing needs of the African countries. Much of the research undertaken so far as has been done overseas, where the economic and social conditions are not the same as in Africa. What appears feasible in the advanced countries is not necessarily feasible in Africa. At present, there are only a few re-search centers on the African continent, and these cannot adequately meet the requirements of Africa. The African states would do well to consider establishing joint industrial research institutions as a prerequisite for industrial development. It is of vital importance to determine exactly what industries are required and to what extent various factors of production will be employed before such industries are set up. In fact, it is necessary to conduct research in the quality of the goods to be produced under economic integration, the standard-ization in production within the African economic groupings, and the prices of manufactured goods. Small-scale research institutions, especially in the field of agriculture, have been set up in most African countries, but it is necessary either to expand these institutions so that they will be able to serve a given group of countries or to establish new research institutions to meet the growing demand.

PROSPECTS FOR INDUSTRIAL DEVELOPMENT IN AFRICA

A conscious scheme of industrialization constitutes an essential element of the general strategy for economic development. As has been stressed elsewhere, one of the most important constraints on the rate of industrialization in Africa is the limited size of national markets, which are still too small to support industrial plants of an economic and competitive size. Generally, at very low income levels a large proportion of consumption expenditure is on the acquisition of the bare necessities for subsistence, such as food and shelter. The size of the population is one of the factors determining the size of the market, but the crucial factor in Africa is the level of per capita consumption of industrial goods. The per capita consumption of manufacturers in Africa is very low, largely because the low per capita income reduces the purchasing power of a large portion of the population.

In this situation, measures designed to accelerate the rate of industrialization should aim at raising the level of per capita income as well as increasing the gross domestic product. However, raising per capita income is difficult to attain in the short run since it can be achieved only through raising overall productivity. Therefore, the most practicable way to accelerate the rate of industrialization would be to integrate national markets in order to serve multinational industries. It is recognized that some industries could be viable without access to larger markets outside national boundaries. However, within the modern concept of development the list of such industries is small and would almost inevitably exclude the heavy industries. In a majority of the heavy industries, further expansion on an efficient scale can be done only through coordinated industrial development efforts.

A quick glance at the pattern of industrialization in Africa indicates the problems that arise from the proliferation and duplication of industrial plants, often at high cost and behind high tariff walls. Moreover, the protection of industries through indirect taxes is a common feature in the African economies, and this seems to be the case in many developing nations. Although the main objective of cooperation and integration in Africa is to set up new industries that would not be viable without cooperation, measures should be taken to increase the efficiency of those industries through competition. It can therefore be argued that the mere duplication of plants in such fields as textile factories, for example, does not indicate a lack of economic advantages in integration of national markets because the introduction of competition would tend to increase efficiency. In fact, it can also be argued that the existence of excess capacity in certain industries would strengthen the case for economic integration since any expansion of these industries would depend on the widening of the market comprising a group of countries. This is one of the reasons why even developed countries seek to integrate their markets even though in certain instances they might be producing similar goods. Careful planning at the multinational level will be required if competition is to be ensured in any scheme of industrialization.

An important aspect of any industrialization effort is that complementarity in industrial development can be achieved if there is adequate integration of production policies of the various states. Within the limited national markets, only two kinds of industries can be established: industries producing final or semimanufactured goods mainly for the local market and industries engaged in the processing or semiprocessing of primary commodities destined for export. In both instances, the backward and forward linkages are weak and, because of the general absence of the multiplier effect, such industries generally do not boost up economic development. This was the industrial pattern during the colonial period, a result of the peculiar economic relationship that existed between the African and metropolitan countries. Individual efforts to alter this pattern have not often yielded the expected results. In any multinational grouping, the expansion and diversification of industrial development programs through the coordination of industrial investments is an essential step toward ensuring a balanced distribution of industries and a decrease in dependence on external trade, reducing the balance of payments problems. In some parts of Africa, the production of intermediate industrial goods for the domestic market is one step toward achieving balanced industrial growth.[7] Toward this end, it is suggested that countries adopt a more detailed development policy with concrete provisions for the development of each branch of industry and an accurate assessment of such elements as size, location, and complementarity with other branches of the same industry.

The case for coordination of industrial development lies in the fact that, in most African countries, industries are characterized by excess capacity, especially such industries as chemical fertilizers, petro-chemical industries, textiles, and iron and steel. This is a direct result of the high optimum levels in these industries and the size limitations of the national markets. The expansion of such industries often is inhibited by the high cost structure, which in turn reduces the product's competitive position vis-à-vis similar products imported from overseas. In such a situation, common sense shows that the path toward industrialization in Africa lies in coordination of development planning, cooperation on industrial investments, and integration of the national markets into more viable economic units.

In this regard, one of the main constraints to industrial development in Africa is not so much the lack of financial resources and technical know-how as the absence of consultation on investment policy and decisions affecting vital fields of industry. This is largely due to the absence of multinational planning authorities responsible for taking joint decisions on industrialization in a given group of countries. The ability to adapt the modern application of science and technology, manpower planning, and the assessment of the availability of natural resources is generally limited by a number of factors of which the size limitations of the domestic market is the most important.

In order to industrialize rapidly, it is essential to provide trained manpower at different levels of production; to undertake extensive industrial research in order to diffuse new production techniques and to ensure standardization not only in the end product but also in the kind of machinery and equipment employed; and to expand and adjust the domestic institutions to fit into the wider framework for industrial development. Few African countries can take these steps without extensive aid from abroad. This fact further strengthens the case for cooperation.

NOTES

1. Economic Commission for Africa; Report of the Sub-regional Meeting on Economic Co-operation in East Africa, E/CN.14/346, Annex IV, p. 3.

2. Economic Commission for Africa; A Survey of Economic Conditions in Africa, 1967 E/CN.14/409/Rev.1, pp. 62-63.

3. See Economic Commission for Africa, Textile Industries in Africa, E/CN.14/AS/III/24 (1966).

4. Economic Commission for Africa, Small-Scale and Handicraft Industries, E/CN.14/INR/9 (1962).

5. Treaty establishing the European Economic Community and connected documents, Article 130.

6. United Nations, Training of National and Technical Personnel for Accelerated Industrialization of Developing Countries, E/3901/Add.1, June 1964, pp. 26-29.

7. United Nations Economic and Social Council; Economic Co-operation and Integration in Central Africa, E/AC.54/L.26/Add.3, p. 75.

THE CASE FOR TRADE LIBERALIZATION

The development of trade constitutes one of the most important objectives of the economic policies in the developed and the developing countries. In Africa, the expansion of trade has become particularly important because of the great dependence on export earnings as the major source of exchange earnings and government revenues. This has been true from the colonial period up to the present time. Although little is known about the past trade patterns among the African countries, especially before the Great Depression of the interwar period, the available data indicates that external trade earnings contributed a significant portion of the GDP. During the colonial period, export proceeds from primary commodities provided the major means for financing imports of manufactured goods and foodstuffs. The main policy objective of the colonial powers in the general development of their possessions was to create an independent budget for each of the territories and the development of external trade was seen as a means of achieving this objective. Moreover, the colonial administrations found it difficult in certain instances to levy income and other personal taxes, and trade became a major source of government revenue. Therefore, development of such economic institutions as commercial banking, insurance, transportation, and shipping reflected the predominance of external trade in the economic activities in the colonies.

These policies had an impact on the pattern of trade in the African countries, which revealed several important general characteristics. First, there was a high degree of dependence on exports for the major portion of national income. In certain countries, one or two commodities provided the major portion of export earnings.

Exports were mainly made up of primary raw materials and semi-processed products; there was almost total lack of exports of manufactured goods. Second, there was a high degree of import of manufactured goods including foodstuffs. The export earnings were hardly sufficient to cover these imports. Consequently, there were persistent adverse trade balances for these countries. Third, a certain degree of specialization developed on the part of the metropolitan powers on the one hand and the colonies on the other hand. The former concentrated on manufactured products that were exchanged for primary products from the colonies; this was a deliberate policy adopted by the colonial administrations. The trading arrangements with the colonial territories were buttressed through the imposition of preferential tariffs and the establishment of common currency zones. These characteristics are still reflected in the development of trade in post-independence Africa.

In the newly independent African states, the development of trade not only has lagged behind that of the other developing countries but also has been increasingly unfavorable, due to the tendency to increase the production of raw materials which has reduced the world prices of such raw materials. Increased imports, especially of capital equipment to sustain the newly instituted development plans, has increased the adverse balance of trade. The reliance on one or two primary products has made the African states more vulnerable to cyclical movements in the industrialized countries. To overcome this difficulty, the development of intra-African trade is now generally accepted as one of the essential aspects of economic progress in Africa.

Chapters 4 and 5 have shown that there is considerable potential for the development of the African market. However, unless the African production and manufacturing industries are diversified so as to enhance the exchange of commodities, this market will continue to be exploited by the advanced nations of the world and Africa will remain a supplier of raw materials.

The immediate problem is how to expand the domestic markets to serve economic development. In other words, what can Africa do to exploit its market potentials? The layman's answer generally is that tariff walls must be abolished and other trade restrictions should be removed. This is normally followed by the suggestion that the flow of trade within Africa could be increased by the formation of an African payments union or customs union. Others advocate the establishment of an African common market as the best strategy in tackling the problems of economic development in Africa. That all these steps are essential elements in the expansion of trade among the African states cannot be disputed, but they do not in themselves constitute a solution because, before advocating these steps, one must first answer the following questions: where are the commodities in which the African states are to conduct trade? In other words, since all the African states have primary products to offer with no complementarity between them and since there are no manufacturing or processing industries in Africa to absorb the raw materials, will the mere formation of a payments union or a common market necessarily enhance the flow of trade in Africa?

The solution to the problems of trade in Africa does not lie merely in providing a mechanism for facilitating payments; it lies fundamentally in increased production of goods and services through specialization. The prerequisite for economic progress in Africa is therefore the establishment of industries and the diversification of industrial and agricultural production. Hence, the formation of an African common market or a payments union without the necessary improvement in production structures would not yield the desired effect on the African economies, since in themselves such arrangements cannot result in increased economic activity. Such measures would merely facilitate the flow of trade by removing barriers and providing means for settlement or effecting international payments. It is useful to note that some of the African countries have had bilateral trade and payments agreements for some time and yet no significant change in the share of inter-African trade to total world trade has been achieved. The coordination of manufacturing activities envisaged under economic integration would be a more realistic step to enhance intra-African trade.

It is true that in Europe the formation of the EEC and EFTA were intended to increase trade among the European nations, but the situation in Europe is entirely different from that in Africa. The rate of industrialization and the rate of economic development are high in most of the countries of Europe, and the creation of the EEC merely catered to trade in the existing products. The EEC nations are able to offer products for mutual exchange. Furthermore, it is possible for the EEC nations to switch their markets to the partner countries in substitution for the loss of outside markets. Since a common market has the effect of trade diversion, the initial steps taken by the EEC were to fill up the gaps in trade with the goods from the member countries. This cannot be done in Africa, since the African countries must first create an economic base on which the other institutions can be built.

Therefore, contrary to the once popular notion that the

prerequisite for trade development in Africa is the formation of an African common market, it is suggested here that the best way to achieve such development is to look at the fundamental requirements for development. The basic requirement is to set up new industries on the basis of division of labor so as to diversify production in both industry and agriculture and step up the rate of production in the existing industries. The increase in the income of the rural areas would result in an increase in their purchasing power, which would increase the general demand for manufactured goods. Such a situation will generate forces that will tend to work in an upward spiral and in turn accelerate the rate of industrialization.

Efforts must be made to set up complementary industries so as to widen domestic markets and thereby diversify the commodities that the African countries can offer for trade. Recent experience in the EEC and EFTA has shown that, despite the high rate of economic advancement in Western Europe, it is still extremely difficult to work out a comprehensive scheme of cooperation in trade and marketing through the formation of a common market. This clearly demonstrates that the problem goes deeper. Africa should learn from the experience of others that an attempt to solve African economic problems by merely decorating the surface with a payments union or a common market will only frustrate development efforts. The problem in the expansion of trade is, therefore, not the creation of means of payment but the creation of commodities in which to trade.

In any scheme for trade liberalization among the African countries, it must be recognized that the main purpose of liberalizing trade is not merely to increase the flow of goods among the African countries but to accelerate the rate of economic development in these countries. The abolition of obstacles to trade is an essential part of the plan for multinational economic cooperation but, due to the absence of a wide range of manufactured goods in the African countries, trade liberalization efforts should be based not on the assumption of a spontaneous increase in traditional trade in agricultural goods but rather on the adaptation of existing and future industrial structures toward the general increase in the manufacture of consumer goods currently imported from overseas. In the consideration of commitments with regard to trade liberalization, account must be taken of the inequalities of the distribution of trade benefits, the losses of revenue from goods previously subject to duties that will now enter a given country duty-free from other partner countries, and the distortions resulting from the competition arising therefrom.

AFRICA'S DEPENDENCE ON EXTERNAL TRADE

From the years immediately preceding World War II, to the present, the total external trade of the African countries has expanded considerably, both in volume and value. Table 6. 1 shows that between 1938 and 1967, Africa's exports to the rest of the world grew from above $1,000 million to well over $10,300 million, an increase of nearly ten times, while imports grew from over $1,500 million to over $10,800 million. This rate of growth compares favorably with that of the other developing regions of the world, namely Asia and Latin America. The large expansion of African exports generally is attributed to the increase in demand for primary commodities that was initiated during World War II. After the end of the war, African exports of primary commodities were considerably affected by the reconstruction of the war-devastated economies of Western Europe, which boosted up the economic activities of most of the developed countries, and the Korean War in the early 1950's. Political factors also contributed to the expansion of African exports. For example, the advent of independence for a large number of African countries, especially in the early 1960's, followed by the launching of new economic development efforts strengthened the drive toward the expansion of exports to finance the increased imports. The other factor responsible for the rapid expansion of African exports was the general increase in the price of primary commodities in the world market over this period. Moreover, the discovery of petroleum and other valuable minerals in such African countries as Libya, Nigeria, and Gabon, contributed considerably to the rapid expansion of total African exports.

Although great efforts have been made to diversify the external trade relations of most African countries, the general trade pattern that developed during the colonial era continues to reflect the influence of past traditional links with the former metropolitan powers. The former French territories in Africa continue to trade largely with France and the other EEC member states, while the Commonwealth countries still trade mainly with Great Britain. Hence, much of the external trade of the African countries is still conducted with the countries of Western Europe. If the diversification of trade relations is a policy objective of the African countries, it is suggested that the development of intra-African trade would be the real issue in these countries' development efforts.

TABLE 6.1

Development of Exports of African Countries, 1938-67
(value in millions of U.S. dollars)

Country	1938	1948	1953	1959	1960	1961	1962	1963	1964	1965	1966	1967	System
North Africa													
Algeria	162	420	397	366	394	368	--	759	727	637	621	724	S
Libya	6	12	10	12	11	22	141	336	620	797	995	1,178	G
Morocco	43	178	269	329	354	342	348	384	432	430	428	424	S
Tunisia	39	61	111	142	120	110	116	126	127	120	140	149	S
U.A.R.	153	607	409	461	568	486	398	520	537	604	604	560	S
Sudan	30	99	128	192	182	179	228	227	198	196	204	215	S
West Africa													
Mali	--	--	--	--	--	14	10	11	17	16	13	17	S
Mauritania[a]	--	--	--	--	--	2	3	16	46	58	69	--	S
Senegal[ab]	19	84	105	116	115	124	124	111	123	129	149	137	S
Guinea	3	10	23	29	52	62	45	55	43	--	58	--	G
Gambia	2	9	8	8	8	9	10	9	14	14	--	--	G
Sierra Leone	11	22	33	55	83	82	58	81	95	89	83	70	G
Liberia	2	16	31	67	83	62	68	81	126	131	146	153	S
Ivory Coast[ac]	11	42	109	137	151	191	193	230	302	277	311	325	S
Upper Volta[ac]	--	--	5	5	4	3	7	11	13	15	16	18	S
Togo	2	10	16	18	15	19	18	18	30	27	36	32	S
Dahomey[a]	3	12	15	12	18	15	11	13	13	14	11	15	S
Niger[a]	1	6	10	12	13	16	20	22	21	25	35	26	S
Ghana	32	202	224	286	294	292	291	273	293	291	244	278	G
Nigeria	47	252	348	458	475	486	472	531	601	751	795	677	G
Central Africa													
Chad[d]	--	--	14	17	13	21	17	23	27	27	24	27	S
Cameroun[de]	7	36	75	108	97	98	103	135	140	139	145	158	S
Central African Republic[d]	--	--	14	15	14	14	15	22	29	26	31	29	S
Gabon[d]	--	--	22	45	47	56	59	72	90	96	100	120	S
Congo (Brazzaville)[d]	--	--	6	14	18	20	34	42	47	47	43	48	S
Congo (Kinshasa)[f]	52	245	398	489	503	--	331	318	343	336	461	435	S
Equatorial Guinea	--	--	--	--	--	--	--	--	--	--	--	--	
Rwanda	--	--	--	--	--	--	--	--	--	--	--	--	
Burundi	--	--	--	--	--	--	--	--	--	--	--	--	

East and Southern Africa													
Ethiopia	--	33	68	72	73	76	80	90	105	116	111	101	G
Somalia	--	--	--	20	23	26	25	32	30	27	30	28	S
Uganda g	40	105	94	121	120	116	115	153	186	179	188	184	G
Kenya g	15	63	64	107	112	117	126	142	150	145	174	166	G
Tanzania g	4	8	79	129	155	138	147	179	197	176	235	222	G
Zanzibar	--	--	22	13	16	12	13	14	11	11	14	16	G
Zambia	--	--	--	329	362	335	335	361	470	532	691	658	G
Malawi	--	--	--	22	25	26	29	30	35	40	49	57	G
Botswana													
Lesotho													
Swaziland													
Madagascar	24	50	85	76	75	78	94	82	92	92	98	104	S
Mauritius	14	44	58	61	39	62	64	90	77	66	71	64	G
Other Africa													
Republic of South Africa h	163	557	830	1,214	1,233	1,328	1,329	1,400	1,458	1,485	1,688	1,898	G
Angola	15	60	123	125	124	135	148	163	204	200	221	238	S
Mozambique	8	40	56	66	73	95	91	101	106	108	112	122	S
Southern Rhodesia	--	--	--	161	173	200	204	210	374	442	273	264	G
Reunion	6	20	31	29	36	37	33	38	37	34	39	36	S

Note: G= general trade; S = special trade.

aTrade with the countries of former French West Africa is excluded prior to 1959 for Dahomey and Guinea; prior to 1960 for Niger; prior to 1961 for Mali, Mauritania, Upper Volta, and Ivory Coast; prior to 1962 for Senegal.

bUp to 1960, data includes trade for Mauritania and Mali.

cData for Upper Volta included with Ivory Coast for 1938 and 1948.

dTrade among the members of the UDEAC excluded.

ePrior to 1963, data is for East Cameroun only.

fPrior to 1961, data includes trade for former Ruanda-Urundi.

gInterterritorial trade among the three states excluded.

hImports f.o.b., data adjusted to approximate trade of present customs area with Botswana, Lesotho, and Swaziland.

Source: United Nations, Yearbook of International Trade Statistics, 1967. (ST/STAT/SER. G/18)

The Expansion of African Exports

Far-reaching measures to expand exports of the developing African countries have been carried out vigorously, especially following independence. The importance of these measures is seen in the impact of exports on the growth of GDP in these countries. For instance, in 1965 the share of exports in GNP exceeded 75 percent in Libya and Zambia; exceeded 50 percent in Gabon, Liberia, Somalia, and Mauritania; exceeded 25-40 percent in Congo (Kinshasa), Algeria, Tanzania, and Malawi; fell within the range of 10-15 percent in some eighteen countries; and was below 10 percent in Mali, Dahomey, Upper Volta, Rwanda, and Burundi. With regard to imports, in the majority of the African countries the share of imports in GNP was between 25 and 50 percent in 1965; only in a few countries, such as Congo (Kinshasa), Liberia, and Zambia, did the share exceed 50 percent. Over the period 1960-66, the balance of trade was predominantly adverse in a majority of African countries and only twelve had a favorable balance of trade.[1]

The Direction of Exports

The pattern of exports follows the general trade pattern described earlier: the largest market for African exports is the EEC. This is especially true of former French Africa, while Britain remains the most important trading partner for former British Africa. Among the centrally planned economies, the largest outlet for African exports is Eastern Europe, especially the U.S.S.R. There also is growing trade among the African countries themselves. For example, African exports to other developing Africa accounted for 7.6 percent of the total exports in 1966, as against 4.1 percent to Asia and only 0.6 percent to Latin America. This is an interesting indication that trade among the developing regions of the world still is very underdeveloped.

The biggest market for African exports is the EEC; France, the largest buyer, accounted for about 42.4 percent of total African exports to the EEC in 1965; followed by West Germany 28.2 percent; Italy, 12.0 percent, Belgium-Luxembourg, 9.8 percent; and the Netherlands, 7.6 percent.[2] Other destinations for African exports include the EFTA, which ranks second in importance; the United Kingdom is the principal importer with over 75 percent of total African exports to the EFTA area, originating mainly in the Commonwealth African countries. The main importers of African products outside Europe are Japan and the United States. In the countries of Eastern Europe, the Soviet Union is the principal importer of African commodities. The pressures on the African economies brought about by independence have prompted some African countries to explore new primary commodities for

export so as to increase foreign exchange earnings. Great successes
have been realized, especially in petroleum and such minerals as
gold and uranium; the discovery of these products has further under-
lined the reliance of the African countries on external trade.

The Commodity Composition of Exports

The commodity composition of exports indicates that primary
commodities constitute the bulk of Africa's exports and accounted
for about 80 percent of exports in 1965. Within this category, raw
materials, food, beverages, tobacco, and fuels were the most important
items of export. Between 1960 and 1965, the share of these items
(except fuels) in total exports declined somewhat. With regard, to
imports the structure is very interesting. Despite the fact that Africa
is generally agricultural, the share of food in total imports is very
significant, although in recent years it is believed that the share has
declined. Industrial goods, machinery, and transport equipment
constitute a major share of total imports to the African countries.

In recent years, considerable progress has been made in the
diversification of the structure of exports. However, in most African
countries one or two primary commodities still constitute a substantial portion of total exports (see Table 6.2).

The Problems in Expansion of African Exports

Agricultural raw primary commodities constitute the bulk of
exports of the African countries. Hence, the most difficult problem
facing Africa in its efforts to promote exports to developed countries
is the diminishing demand for these primary commodities. There is
ample evidence that the demand for these commodities in the developed
countries has reached the saturation point, which implies that further
African exports can be achieved only if there is a considerable population increase in these countries. However, demographic data show
that the rate of population growth tends to be very low in the developed
countries, implying that the expansion of Africa's external trade
cannot be envisaged through increases in exports to the advanced
countries.[3]

Furthermore, African exports continue to meet stiffer tariffs
and other trade restrictions in the advanced countries; in recent
years, such restrictions have made it increasingly difficult for the
African countries to penetrate these markets. In addition, for most

TABLE 6.2

Africa's Dependence on Primary Commodities for
Export Earnings, Selected Countries, 1965
(percentage)

Commodity	Exporting Country	Share in Total African Exports [a]	Share in Country's Total Exports [b]
Petroleum	Libya	53	99
	Algeria	32	69
	Nigeria	13	26
	U.A.R.	1	3
	Gabon	1	14
Copper	Zambia	76	91
	Congo (Kinshasa)	17	32
	Uganda	4	13
	Southern Rhodesia	3	4
Cotton	U.A.R.	56	56
	Sudan	15	47
	Uganda	8	27
	Chad	4	88
	Tanzania	6	19
	Mozambique	3	18
	Central African Republic	1	19
Coffee	Uganda	16	48
	Ivory Coast	20	38
	Ethiopia	14	66
	Kenya	7	30
	Madagascar	5	32
	Cameroun	6	22
	Togo	1	22
Cocoa	Ghana	46	61
	Nigeria	29	16
	Ivory Coast	11	16
	Togo	2	26
	Cameroun	7	22
Groundnuts	Nigeria	51	14
	Senegal	18	29
	Niger	6	48
	Gambia	3	54
	Guinea	1	50
Wood and timber	Ivory Coast	36	27
	Gabon	16	34
	Congo (Brazzaville)	9	38
	Ghana	17	11
Iron ore and concentrates	Liberia	49	73
	Mauritania	27	94
	Sierra Leone	8	20
Diamonds	Sierra Leone	26	62
	Angola	17	16
	Congo (Brazzaville)	11	43
	Central African Republic	8	54

Commodity	Exporting Country	Share in Total African Exports[a]	Share in Country's Total Exports[b]
	Tanzania	11	11
	Congo (Kinshasa)	13	7
	Ghana	11	6
Phosphates	Morocco	70	25
	Tunisia	15	20
	Togo	6	33
	Senegal	7	9
Citrus fruits	Algeria	46	9
	Tunisia	4	4
	Morocco	48	14
Sugar	Mauritius	50	95
	Reunion	22	79
	Mozambique	8	9
	Madagascar	4	5
Palm nuts and kernels	Nigeria	72	10
	Dahomey	2	14
	Sierra Leone	8	11
Palm oil	Nigeria	60	5
	Congo (Kinshasa)	24	5
	Dahomey	5	21
Groundnut oil	Senegal	60	41
	Nigeria	32	4
Rubber	Nigeria	41	4
	Liberia	39	22
	Congo (Kinshasa)	12	3
	Cameroun	7	4
Sisal	Tanzania	56	23
	Kenya	15	8
	Angola	14	5
	Mozambique	8	6
	Madagascar	7	5
Manganese ore	Gabon	45	28
	Ghana	22	4
	Morocco	17	2
	Congo (Kinshasa)	7	1
Tea	Kenya	34	13
	Malawi	22	29
	Mozambique	14	7
	Uganda	14	4
	Tanzania	8	2
Tin	Nigeria	86	6
	Congo (Kinshasa)	10	12

[a]Denotes share of individual country's exports in total African exports of the particular commodity.
[b]Denotes share of each commodity in total exports earnings of each individual country.

Source: ECA, Africa's Trade: Trends Problems and Policy Issues, E/CN.14/UNCTAD III.

African agricultural primary commodities the competition from synthetics and substitutes in the developed countries has increased, further
reducing demand for these commodities. Finally, the African countries
also face competition from the other developing countries of Asia and
Latin America in the export of certain commodities, such as rubber,
natural fibers, coffee, tin, and copper. There has been a policy of
overproduction of most of these commodities in the developing countries, aggravating the problems of access of these commodities to
the markets of the advanced countries. This policy has only served
to lower prices of these commodities. Moreover, the fluctuations in
world market prices for primary products have created severe problems for the foreign exchange earnings of most African countries,
and more particularly for countries that depend on one or two primary
commodities for a substantial portion of export earnings.

These problems have led to growing fears in the African countries that during the 1970's export earnings in most African countries
might become insufficient to meet import requirements, adversely
affecting development efforts. This has been recognized as a problem
facing all developing countries and is now being vigorously examined
by the United Nations organs, especially UNCTAD, which has become
an important forum for the discussion of general problems affecting
exports from the developing to the developed countries. The major
issues include the access of primary commodities, semimanufactures,
and manufactured goods into the markets of the developed countries;
quotas for certain categories of primary commodities, such as coffee,
sugar, and copper; and the need for the developing countries to adopt
a general strategy in negotiations with the developed countries for
better conditions of trade. Several committees and study groups on
the international scale have been established to deal with problems
specific to certain commodities.

The developing countries have requested that, as a step toward
easing these problems, the developed countries agree on a general
system of preferences for primary and manufactured products from
the developing countries in line with the general trend toward the
liberalization of world trade and that the developed countries give
greater priority to the special and pressing problems of export
promotion in the developing countries. The main objective of the
general system of preferences is to ensure that the developed countries do not grant preferences to some developing countries so as to
discriminate against the rest of the developing countries. The developing countries of Africa, Asia, and Latin America see this as a major
step toward more favorable conditions for access of their products
into the developed countries.

In addition to international measures, the African countries should consider other measures for enhancing their trade. In this connection, there is an urgent need for restructing Africa's trade in order to counteract the impact of general world trade problems on the African economies. The African countries should reexamine their general trade promotion policies to ensure that trade will continue to make a more positive contribution to their economic development.

Thus, in line with the general development efforts, the African countries should take appropriate measures to ensure that the production structures are transformed from the traditional primary producing basis to the establishment of a more diversified pattern of agricultural and manufacturing industries on a multinational scale. Ideally, such measures would include, in the short run, the standardization of customs legislation, the harmonization of commercial laws and practices, and the gradual reduction or elimination of customs duties and other trade restrictions on products originating in the African countries. In the long run, more far-reaching measures should include the harmonization of general economic policies and the coordination of industrial development efforts, especially with regard to industries oriented toward import substitution and the promotion of intra-African trade. This is important because the African countries cannot expect to advance their rate of economic development by depending on the existing market structures in the developed countries. Rather, they must develop their economies through the exploration of the possibilities and opportunities for trade expansion among themselves. To put such a program into effect, it would be necessary to institute radical changes in policy orientation with regard to industrialization and trade development.

The Growth of Imports Into African Countries

The African countries' high dependence on the advanced metropolitan countries for nearly all their requirements of consumer and industrial goods is the direct result of the lack of manufacturing industries in Africa. The relevant factor in this respect is that it has become increasingly difficult for the African countries to finance their imports with export proceeds. This implies that trade is being subsidized from other sources of revenue, impeding development in the other sectors. The major imports into Africa include industrial goods, machinery, transport equipment, and such durable consumer goods as automobiles, radios, refrigerators, cooking stoves, and furniture. Food and foodstuffs also constitute a large proportion of the import bill in the African countries, although the share of food in total imports has decreased since 1967 over the past six years.

The imports into the African countries are shown in Table 6.3. Between 1938 and 1967, imports have expanded at a phenomenal rate in some of these countries.

In the Eastern African subregion two groups of countries--the East African Common Market and the Southern African Customs Union*--have had considerable mutual trade. The volume data for external trade is somewhat underestimated since the trade within these groups is generally omitted from the general trade statistics. However, there was considerable growth of imports during the years 1938-67.

The Source of Imports Into Africa

In certain countries, imports have grown faster than exports. Although in recent years there have been remarkable efforts toward the diversification of the sources of imports, the pattern of imports is similar to that of African exports. Most imports come from Western Europe, especially the EEC and EFTA countries, which together accounted for over 54 percent of total African imports in 1966; among these countries, France, the United Kingdom, Italy, and Belgium are the principal suppliers, mainly to their former colonial territories. In recent years, imports from the United States, Japan, West Germany, and South Africa have expanded substantially. In 1966, the United States accounted for 11.2 percent of the total African imports while Japan accounted for 7.3 percent, Eastern Europe for 7.4 percent, and developing Asia for 8.3 percent.

The Structure of Imports

There is a direct correlation between the development of manu-facturing industries and the expansion of external trade, especially imports, in Africa. As a result of the slow rate of industrialization, Africa imports almost all her requirements of manufactured goods and there is a high degree of imports of industrial goods, machinery, transport equipment, and durable consumer goods. Basic materials,

---

*The Southern African Customs Union was established by South Africa, Botswana, Lesotho, and Swaziland in the early part of the twentieth century and was modified recently. See also Chapter 8.

mineral fuels, and chemicals make up a small portion of the African imports. Paradoxically, there is a high proportion of imports of food-stuffs, which accounted for over 16.5 percent of total African imports in 1965. The African countries are net importers of finished goods, and taken together they had adverse balance of trade with most countries of the world throughout the period 1961-66 but maintained a favorable balance with the countries of Western Europe. However, except for those countries with rich mineral resources, most African countries experienced persistent adverse trade balances throughout this period, causing serious problems in some of these countries.

THE MAIN FEATURES OF INTRA-AFRICAN TRADE

Throughout this text, intra-African trade will be construed to mean the movement of goods produced within the African countries themselves across the national frontiers; the tables in this section refer only to domestic exports and do not include transit trade or re-exports. This restrictive definition is essential because it is this category of goods that could lead to the development of fruitful economic relationships among the African countries.

One of the salient feature of intra-African trade is that it consists of a great portion of traditional exchanges that remain largely unrecorded. For example, in 1959 the total value of unrecorded trade in Africa was about $133 million, which constituted nearly 28 percent of total intra-African trade. This implies that the statistical material must be interpreted with some caution since it tends to underestimate the level of development of intra-African trade.

The second feature of this trade is that it has tended to develop rather slowly in the past. In the first half of the 1960's, the share of intra-African trade in total trade was extremely low, and conservative estimates put it at around 5 percent. In 1966, the proportion of intra-African trade to total trade was about 7.6 percent, compared with a level of 11 percent among the Latin American countries and 24 percent among the Asian countries. Moreover, there is less diversification of intra-African trade compared with the general trade of the African countries, which underlines the fact that to a large extent trade among the African countries is still carried out in traditional goods. Much intra-African trade consists of food, beverages, tobacco, sugar, cattle, and meat. There is also a good deal of reexport trade, especially between the coastal and land-locked countries.

Third, intra-African trade is influenced by the economic and other links that were developed during the colonial period. Hence,

TABLE 6.3

Growth of Imports (c.i.f.) into African Countries, 1938-67
(value in millions of U.S. dollars)

	1938	1948	1953	1959	1960	1961	1962	1963	1964	1965	1966	1967	System
North Africa													
Algeria	143	482	579	1,140	1,265	1,024	--	683	703	671	639	639	S
Libya	47	22	31	114	169	149	206	239	292	320	405	477	G
Morocco	63	389	489	326	397	440	423	447	456	445	476	517	S
Tunisia	45	179	172	153	189	209	216	223	244	245	249	260	S
U.A.R.	188	674	516	638	667	701	740	916	953	933	1,070	792	S
Sudan	32	92	146	169	183	238	261	285	274	208	222	213	S
West Africa													
Mali a	--	--	--	--	--	36	46	34	37	43	36	52	S
Mauritania a	--	--	--	--	--	31	36	30	16	24	23	--	S
Senegal ab	29	115	176	178	179	155	155	156	172	160	155	158	S
Guinea a	5	16	36	62	50	73	66	46	49	n.a.	53	n.a.	G
Gambia	2	9	6	9	9	13	13	12	12	16	n.a.	n.a.	G
Sierra Leone	7	20	31	66	74	91	85	84	99	108	100	90	G
Liberia	2	9	19	43	69	91	113	108	111	105	113	125	S
Ivory Coast ac	9	34	71	115	120	169	156	170	238	236	257	263	S
Upper Volta ac	-	-	8	8	11	28	35	38	38	37	38	36	S
Togo	2	7	12	15	26	26	27	29	42	45	47	45	S
Dahomey a	3	10	16	18	31	25	27	33	31	34	34	44	S
Niger a	1	3	8	7	13	19	28	24	34	38	45	46	S
Ghana	38	127	207	317	363	394	333	365	341	445	352	307	G
Nigeria	42	169	303	500	605	625	569	581	711	770	718	626	G
Central Africa													
Chad d	n.a.	n.a.	18	25	25	25	30	29	35	31	30	38	S
Cameroun de	6	42	80	82	85	96	102	128	133	153	147	180	S
Central African Republic d	n.a.	n.a.	13	17	20	22	25	26	30	28	31	40	S
Gabon d	n.a.	n.a.	14	28	32	36	41	48	56	63	66	67	S
Congo (Brazzaville) d	n.a.	n.a.	40	56	70	79	65	62	65	65	70	82	S
Congo (Kinshasa) f	37	191	363	308	308	n.a.	253	254	288	321	337	263	S
Equatorial Guinea	n.a.	n.a.	n.a.	n.a.	n.a.	n.a.	n.a.	n.a.	n.a.	n.a.	n.a.	n.a.	
Rwanda	n.a.	n.a.	n.a.	n.a.	n.a.	n.a.	n.a.	n.a.	n.a.	n.a.	n.a.	n.a.	
Burundi	n.a.	n.a.	n.a.	n.a.	n.a.	n.a.	n.a.	n.a.	n.a.	n.a.	n.a.	n.a.	

East and Southern Africa

Country													Trade type
Ethiopia	n.a.	45	56	79	84	90	104	119	123	150	162	143	G
Somalia	n.a.	n.a.	n.a.	30	30	32	38	45	55	50	42	40	S
Uganda[g]	35	155	72	72	73	74	73	87	92	114	119	116	G
Kenya[g]	14	81	145	172	196	193	195	206	214	249	314	298	G
Tanzania[g]	5	11	80	97	106	111	112	113	123	140	178	182	G
Zanzibar			16	15	15	15	15	15	10	12	13	8	G
Zambia	n.a.	n.a.	n.a.	n.a.	n.a.	n.a.	n.a.	n.a.	219	295	345	429	G
Malawi	n.a.	n.a.	n.a.	n.a.	n.a.	n.a.	n.a.	n.a.	40	57	86	80	G
Botswana	--	--	--	--	--	--	--	--	--	--	--	--	
Lesotho	--	--	--	--	--	--	--	--	--	--	--	--	
Swaziland	--	--	--	--	--	--	--	--	--	--	--	--	
Madagascar	17	78	129	119	111	103	122	127	135	138	142	145	S
Mauritius	12	41	53	60	70	68	68	70	87	77	70	78	G

Other Africa

Country													Trade type
South Africa[h]	464	1,424	1,194	1,368	1,556	1,410	1,418	1,698	2,156	2,459	2,304	2,690	G
Angola	10	49	85	131	128	114	136	147	164	195	209	275	S
Mozambique	22	71	80	120	128	137	136	142	156	173	208	199	S
Southern Rhodesia	n.a.	n.a.	n.a.	n.a.	n.a.	n.a.	n.a.	n.a.	303	335	237	262	G
Reunion	8	25	37	44	52	58	63	70	89	97	105	116	S

Note: G = general trade; S = special trade.

[a] Trade with the countries of former French West Africa is excluded prior to 1959 for Dahomey and Guinea; prior to 1960 for Niger; prior to 1961 for Mali, Mauritania, Upper Volta and Ivory Coast; prior to 1962 for Senegal.

[b] Up to 1960, data includes trade for Mauritania and Mali.

[c] Data for Upper Volta included with Ivory Coast for 1938 and 1948.

[d] Trade among the members of the UDEAC excluded.

[e] Prior to 1963, data is for East Cameroun only.

[f] Prior to 1961, data includes trade for the former Ruanda-Urundi.

[g] Interterritorial trade among the three states excluded.

[h] Imports f.o.b. data adjusted to approximate trade of present customs area with Botswana, Lesotho, and Swaziland.

Source: United Nations, Yearbook of International Trade Statistics, 1967.

trade among the African countries has tended to concentrate within the common currency and trade zones that were developed between African countries. For instance, in East and Southern Africa three such currency zones can be distinguished. The first area consists of Kenya, Uganda, and Tanzania, which have constituted a common market since the beginning of the twentieth century; the second area comprises the former Federation of Rhodesia and Nyasaland, (Zambia, Malawi, and Southern Rhodesia); and the third group consisted of the former High Commission Territories, Botswana, Lesotho, and Swaziland, which are now linked in a customs union with South Africa by a series of agreements. Malawi, Rhodesia, Angola, and Mozambique also maintain trade ties with South Africa. The countries of the Central African Customs and Economic Union (UDEAC), Cameroun, Gabon, Central African Republic, and the Congo (Brazzaville) constitute a trade grouping, and although Chad is not a member of the UDEAC, it maintains trade links with this grouping. Congo (Kinshasa), Rwanda, and Burundi constituted another common currency area during the colonial period. These trade patterns are shown in Table 6.4.

In West Africa, the former French West African countries established the West African Customs Union (UDEAC) providing for free movement of goods. The former British West African territories did not constitute a free trade area as such, but had a common currency board that facilitated the flow of goods and services. In North Africa, the Permanent Consultative Committee of the Maghreb (CPCM), made up of Algeria, Morocco, Tunisia, and Libya, constitutes another trade grouping. Elsewhere in the area, Sudan and the U.A.R. have developed considerable mutual trade.

Finally, except in a few instances such as trade between Rwanda and Burundi, and trade within the East African Community, and trade between Ghana and Nigeria and the French West African countries, the French African countries generally have little trade with British African countries, even where they share common boundaries. Although this pattern is slowly changing, the direction of inter-African trade is still in isolated and concentrated small pockets. In developing Africa as a whole, the share of inter-African trade in total trade is on the average only about 7 percent.

INTRA-AFRICAN TRADE IN NORTH AFRICA

There are two distinct trade flows in the North African subregion, one made up of the four Maghreb countries and the other consisting of Sudan and the U.A.R. Within the Maghreb, there is a great deal of exchange, especially between Algeria and Morocco (see Table 6.5). Outside the North African subregion, Morocco's main African trading partners are the Ivory Coast, Cameroun, and the UDEAC countries. Algeria's other trading partners outside North Africa are Senegal, Ivory Coast, and Nigeria. The remaining countries of the subregion have little trade with the other African countries.

Trade between the North African countries consists of food, chemical and pharmaceutical products, textiles, cement, tobacco, tires, gut, crude and refined oil, clothing, footwear, vegetables, leather goods, wine, fresh fruit, and mules.

Intra-African Trade in West Africa

The West African subregion has three distinct trade flows, one made up of the OERS countries, the second made up of the Conseil de l'Entente, and the third made up of the UDEAC countries. (Trade statistics are not available for Gambia, Guinea, and Liberia, and these countries have therefore been excluded from the analysis.) There is no high degree of interdependence in trade within these groups, and the concentration of trade is found mainly in the UDEAC (see Table 6.6). For example, in 1966 of the total imports of over $28 million into Ivory Coast from all African countries, Senegal accounted for over 25 percent, followed by Upper Volta and Mali, both of which are members of the UDEAC. Trade among Senegal, Mali, Upper Volta, and Ivory Coast also is fairly well developed.

The countries comprising OERS generally have very little mutual trade, although there is some trade between Mali and Senegal and between Senegal and Mauritania. Within the Conseil d'Entente, Ivory Coast and Upper Volta have developed strong trade relations and Togo and Dahomey have large exchanges. Taking West Africa as a whole, Ivory Coast and Niger have more diversified trade than the rest of the countries.

Intra-African Trade in Central Africa

Trade of the countries of Central Africa with other African countries is very limited. Much of the trade is confined to areas that had trade and other economic links during the colonial period, notably the UDEAC. Other main trading partner countries outside this area are mainly Nigeria, Sudan, Kenya, Uganda, Tanzania, Zambia, South Africa, and the U.A.R. There are three major reasons for these trade characteristics. In the first place, the exchange of goods during

TABLE 6.4

Intra-African Trade by Country, 1966-68
(thousands of U.S. dollars)

	Imports (c.i.f.)			Exports (f.o.b.)			Balance		
	1966	1967	1968	1966	1967	1968	1966	1967	1968
North Africa									
Morocco	32,304	15,619	16,414	24,532	14,435	16,669	-7,774	- 1,184	+ 255
Algeria	--	--	--	--	--	--	--	--	--
Tunisia	5,456	3,827	1,866	13,435	12,107	16,219	+7,797	+ 8,280	+14,353
Libya	10,053	12,974	18,920	3,344	973	575	-6,709	-12,001	-18,345
U.A.R. [a]	--	32,304	25,707	18,559[a]	39,498[a]		--	-13,745	+13,791
Sudan	16,548	12,457	15,504	9,350	9,332[a]	8,249[a]	-7,198	- 3,125	- 7,255
West Africa									
Mauritania	942	--	--	1,628	--	--	+ 686	--	--
Senegal	22,041	--	--	12,054	--	--	-9,987	--	--
Mali	7,614	8,585	--	12,220	14,068	--	+4,579	+5,483	--
Ivory Coast	26,866	28,441	42,839	28,427	32,576	37,581[a]	+1,561	+4,135	- 5,258
Upper Volta	13,683	--	--	11,817	--	--	-1,866	--	--
Dahomey	2,484	5,252	--	2,001	2,436	--	+ 483	-2,816	--
Niger	--	--	--	--	--	--	--	--	--
Guinea									
Sierra Leone	3,538	2,755	5,600	357	163	400	-3,181	-2,592	- 5,200
Liberia	--	1,805	--	--	2,437	--	--	+ 632	--
Ghana	14,082	12,845	11,399	4,566	4,970	2,695	-9,516	-7,875	- 8,704
Togo	4,481	4,693	4,212	1,417	1,752	1,994	-3,001	-2,941	- 2,218
Nigeria	7,782	7,165	8,500	12,866	7,872	8,200	+5,084	+ 707	- 300
Gambia									
Central Africa									
Cameroun [c]	8,126	13,213	18,546	8,567	5,333	18,028	+ 441	-7,880	- 818
Chad	1,857	3,631	16,471	5,095	4,711	6,365	+3,238	-8,342	-10,106
Congo (Kinshasa)	60,289	--	--	19,250	--	--	-41,039	--	--
Equatorial Guinea	--	--	--	--	--	--	--	--	--
Rwanda	4,196	4,414	5,597	416	1,148	1,878	-3,780	-3,266	- 3,719
Burundi	2,435	2,510	--	706	--	--	-1,729	--	--
Congo (Brazzaville)	4,387	5,260	--	2,005	4,382	--	-2,382	- 878	--
Gabon	2,636	3,462	--	6,158	7,045	--	+3,522	+3,583	--
Central African Republic	2,083	2,353	--	385	770	--	-1,698	-1,583	--

186

East and Southern Africa									
Ethiopia	1,569	1,467	2,524	6,019	4,353	4,853	+ 4,450	+ 2,886	+ 2,329
Somalia	4,371	--	--	1,558	--	--	- 2,813	--	--
Kenya	4,639	4,132	3,147	15,062	15,117	19,021	+10,423	+10,985	+19,133
Uganda	930	605	554	3,581	5,660	6,154	+ 2,651	+ 5,055	+ 5,600
Tanzania e	3,271	3,621	2,052	20,300	23,357	25,242	+17,029	+19,736	+23,190
Zambia	156,556	169,554	--	54,215	47,511	--	-102,341	+22,043	--
Malawi	31,517	26,898	24,836	11,600 [a]	13,131 [a]	11,460 [a]	-19,917	-13,767	-13,376
Botswana	--	--	--	--	--	--	--	--	--
Lesotho	--	--	--	--	--	--	--	--	--
Madagascar	8,640	6,535	9,698	12,505	22,209	24,104	+ 3,865	+15,674	+14,406
Swaziland	--	--	--	--	--	--	--	--	--
Mauritius	9,766	11,400	11,557	1,311	1,578	2,150	- 8,455	- 9,822	- 9,407
Other Africa									
South Africa	--	198,200	168,600	--	315,900	348,700	--	+117,700	+180,100
Southern Rhodesia	--	--	--	--	--	--	--	--	--
Angola	10,042	10,936	14,584	16,078	13,772	18,356	+ 6,036	+ 2,836	+ 3,772
Mozambique	33,110	32,778	--	22,522	28,364	--	-10,588	- 4,414	--
Portuguese Guinea	--	1,172	--	--	97	--	--	- 1,075	--
Reunion	12,317	17,909	--	785	--	--	-11,532	--	--

a General exports.
b Imports exclude petroleum for refining.
c East Cameroun only.
d Includes Zanzibar.

Sources: United Nations, Foreign Trade Statistics of Africa, E/CN.14/ STAT/SER.A/14 and E/CN.14/STAT/SER.B/14, 15, 16, and 17.

TABLE 6.5

Trade Among the Countries of the North African
Sub-region, 1967
(thousands of U.S. dollars)

	Algeria	Morocco	Tunisia	Libya	U.A.R	Sudan	Total Intra-African Trade
Algeria							
Exports		7,253	998	363	3,926	--	n.a.
Imports		4,114	1,354	723	3,092	616	n.a.
Balance		3,139	-356	360	n.a.	+897	n.a.
Morocco							
Exports	4,802		749	591	--	--	14,435
Imports	6,373		350	391	--	--	15,619
Balance	-1,571		+399	+200	--	--	-1,184
Tunisia							
Exports	1,252	216		8,932	2	--	12,107
Imports	877	952		78	32	--	3,827
Balance	+375	-736		+8,854	-30	--	+8,280
Libya							
Exports	1	423	42		46	--	973
Imports	122	531	9,691		1,500	44	12,974
Balance	-121	-108	-9,649		-1,454	--	-12,001
U.A.R.							
Exports*	2,546	301	25	1,647		8,059	18,558
Imports	5,173	334	5	373		15,187	32,304
Balance	-2,627	33	+20	+1,274		-7,128	-13,745
Sudan							
Exports	521	20	117	47	8,438		9,274
Imports	--	--	--	--	9,523		12,457
Balance	--	--	--	--	-1,085		-3,183

Note: Exports f.o.b.; imports c.i.f.

*General exports

Source: United Nations, E/CN.14/STAT/SER.A/14.

the colonial period was encouraged only between the territories and the metropolitan powers. This was true in all colonial territories. In the second place, these territories produced largely agricultural and mineral raw materials that were exported to the industrialized countries in exchange for manufactured goods and foodstuffs. Finally, as a result of the interplay of the two factors mentioned above, no manufacturing industries were established in the area to permit the growth of trade among the countries.

The Pattern of Trade Among The Countries of Central Africa*

Cameroun

Cameroun has wide trade contacts with other African countries. Its main African trading partners outside the UDÉAC are Algeria, Guinea, Morocco, Nigeria, and Senegal. Between 1960 and 1966, the largest amount of imports came from Guinea, followed by Senegal and Morocco. Cameroun's imports from African countries in 1966 constituted roughly 6 percent of its total imports. Between 1960 and 1966, most of Cameroun's exports went to Gabon, Morocco, Nigeria, and Algeria.

Central African Republic

The main African trading partners for Central African Republic are Congo (Kinshasa), Morocco, and Senegal. Central African Republic also has some trade with South Africa. It did not have as much trade with Cameroun as with other countries before 1966. The bulk of the exports go to Congo (Kinshasa), Morocco, and South Africa. The Central African Republic has a generally adverse balance of trade except with South Africa, where exports were much higher than the imports between 1960 and 1966.

Congo (Brazzaville)

Congo (Brazzaville) has wide trading relations with African countries. The main trading partners are Mauritania, Senegal, Tunisia, and South Africa, which were also the source of bulk of

---

*This section excludes trade between the UDEAC countries; Cameroun joined the UDEAC in 1966.

TABLE 6.6

Trade Among the Countries
of the West African Subregion, 1966
(in thousands of U. S. dollars)

Country	Mauri-tania	Mali	Senegal	Gambia	Guinea	Liberia	Sierra Leone
Mauritania							
Exports		--	1	--	--	--	--
Imports		--	264	--	--	597	--
Mali							
Exports	161		2,582	--	23	72	--
Imports	82		1,110	--	191	62	82
Senegal							
Exports	1,292	75		--	136	192	343
Imports	6	571		--	27	2	5
Sierra Leone							
Exports	--	1	1	--	8	2	
Imports	--	--	470	--	21	51	
Ivory Coast							
Exports	13	1,777	7,443	--	12	125	25
Imports	1	420	5,320	--	4	173	--
Upper Volta							
Exports	--	617	3	--	--	--	--
Imports	--	2,882	1,336	--	--	--	--
Ghana							
Exports	16	--	1	--	--	8	78
Imports	8	3,177	219	--	--	34	61
Togo							
Exports	--	1	23	--	1	1	--
Imports	--	4	535	--	3	4	--
Niger							
Exports	1	205	45	--	2	--	--
Imports	--	2	1,560	--	1	--	--
Dahomey							
Exports	1	--	64	--	22	40	--
Imports	--	--	265	--	--	--	--
Nigeria							
Exports	1	3	436	--	11	500	664
Imports	--	21	113	--	65	168	138

Note: Exports f.o.b.; imports c.i.f.

Source: United Nations, Foreign Trade Statistics for Africa E/CN.14/STAT/SER.A/14

Ivory Coast	Upper Volta	Ghana	Togo	Niger	Dahomey	Nigeria	Total Intra-African Trade
--	--	10	--	--	--	7	1,628
8	--	--	--	--	--	--	942
4,704	991	3,108	2	206	--	4	12,220
2,870	165	429	1	67	190	5	7,614
1,301	24	111	407	85	791	111	12,054
6,684	9	26	8	1	57	85	22,041
--	--	1	--	--	--	16	357
15	--	192	375	--	--	683	3,538
	2,154	120	245	1,024	702	475	28,427
	412	9	10	353	204	940	26,866
8,141		2,423	--	304	329	--	11,817
8,463		476	--	216	--	--	13,683
432	10		116	2	1	2,020	4,566
571	3,921		179	1,246	3	3,307	14,802
81	2	391		27	584	51	1,417
249	83	1,735		116	825	318	4,481
668	278	555	107		739	6,066	n.a.
1,941	151	401	19		298	665	n.a.
99	1	61	847	139		514	2,001
58	--	6	732	47		695	2,484
1,424	3	2,229	225	401	217		12,866
553	--	695	27	76	26		7,787

imports to Congo (Brazzaville) between 1960 and 1966. There were
also sizable imports from Angola during this period. Exports went
mainly to South Africa and Congo (Kinshasa). Other countries importing from Congo (Brazzaville) were Reunion, Ivory Coast, and
Cameroun.

Gabon

Gabon imported most of its goods from Morocco, Cameroun,
and Tunisia. Gabon's imports from African countries steadily increased over the period 1960-66. The bulk of its exports to other
African countries went to Senegal, Cameroun, and Ivory Coast.
Between 1962 and 1966, Gabon's exports to Ivory Coast rose from
$1.094 million to $25.522 million; to Senegal from $2.430 million to
$15.313 million; and to Morocco from $3.524 million to $4.578 million.
In other words, Gabon's exports more than doubled over this period.

Chad

Chad has the largest trade with Nigeria, Sudan, and Cameroun.
Cameroun, Nigeria, and Chad are members of the Lake Chad Basin
Commission. Most of Chad's imports from within Africa came from
Nigeria, followed by Senegal and Cameroun; the bulk of Chad's exports
in Africa went to Nigeria, Morocco, and Sudan. Between 1960 and
1966, Chad's exports to Nigeria increased from $26.817 million to
$33.502 million and to Morocco from $2.836 million to $5.590 million.
Chad's exports to other African countries, such as Algeria, Cameroun,
and Niger, declined substantially over this period.

Congo (Kinshasa)

Congo (Kinshasa) had considerable trade with the former area
of the Federation of Rhodesia and Nyasaland, especially Zambia. In
1965, most African imports to Congo (Kinshasa) came from South
Africa, Angola, Canary Islands, and Congo (Brazzaville). Between
1960 and 1965, imports from South Africa grew from $10.938 million
to $64.452 million and imports from the former Federation of Rhodesia
and Nyasaland grew from $5.874 million to $84.748 million. There
were also substantial imports from Angola. Exports from Congo
(Kinshasa) went mainly to South Africa, and between 1960 and 1965
they grew from $6.9 million to $47.9 million. Other importers were
the three East African countries, Angola, Congo (Brazzaville), and
Zambia.

Trade between Congo (Kinshasa) and the UDEAC area constitutes a small portion of her total intra-African trade. Between 1960 and 1965, the growth of this trade was sluggish. The principal trade partners are the Central African Republic, Chad, and Congo (Brazzaville). There is virtually no trade with Gabon and Cameroun. The imports of Congo (Kinshasa) from the UDEAC consist of meat, fish, rubber products, cotton, timber, plywood and veneer, and her exports to these countries include coffee, tea, palm oil, textiles, cement, jute sacks, bottles, barrels and boats.

Rwanda

Rwanda imports considerable quantities of products from its immediate neighbors, mainly the three East African countries, Burundi, and Congo (Kinshasa). Her exports to other African countries are small indeed, reflecting the virtually complete absence of manufacturing industries. The main importers of Rwanda's goods are Burundi, Congo (Kinshasa) and Uganda.

Burundi

Like, Rwanda, Burundi imported considerable quantities of goods from Kenya, Tanganyika, Rwanda, Congo (Kinshasa), and Southern Rhodesia in 1964; these are Burundi's principal suppliers. Its exports went mainly to Congo (Kinshasa), Rwanda, and Tanganyika. Kenya and Egypt also imported some products from Burundi, but in limited quantities.

Trade Among the UDEAC Countries
Under Taxe Unique *

Trade among the countries of the UDEAC is very advanced indeed and only trade within the East African Community is comparable. The total flow of trade under taxe unique is shown in Table 6.7. The producing countries are on the horizontal axis; the consuming

---

*The taxe unique is a production tax levied on all domestic manufactured goods destined for consumption within UDEAC. The tax is collected by the producing or exporting country and is distributed to the member states in proportion to the volume of the goods consumed by each state. The purpose of this tax is to compensate the consuming country for the duty it lost as a result of importing the commodity duty-free.

TABLE 6.7

Production and Consumption of Goods Under Taxe Unique
in the UDEAC Countries, 1967 and 1968
(value in thousands of U.S. dollars)

Importing Country	Year	Producing Country					
		Cameroun	Central African Republic	Congo (Brazzaville)	Gabon	Chad	Total
Cameroun	1967	47,140	386	1,819	337	12	49,696
	1968	41,807	350	1,802	385	102	44,449
Central African Republic	1967	1,683	6,196	3,150	95	62	11,188
	1968	2,349	6,608	2,725	86	157	11,927
Congo (Brazzaville)	1967	959	225	9,329	203	4	10,722
	1968	1,124	531	10,058	155	52	11,922
Gabon	1967	2,106	64	2,450	861	1	5,486
	1968	2,069	38	1,385	1,181	3	4,679
Chad	1967	1,724	2,254	4,455	114	6,040	14,590
	1968	1,583	1,330	4,658	94	8,115	15,811

Source: UDEAC Secrétariat Générale, Le Commerce Extérieur de l' UDEAC, 1967 and 1968.

or importing countries are on the vertical axis. Trade under the
taxe unique has constituted one of the most important aspects of
economic cooperation in these countries.

In summing up the trade situation within UDEAC, one important
point comes to light: due to the differences in the levels of development
and industrialization in these countries, three countries - Congo
(Brazzaville), Cameroun, and the Central African Republic - are the
principal suppliers of goods under the taxe unique. Gabon supplies
mainly wood products, timber, and lumber while Chad exports relatively smaller quantities of goods to its trade partners. The principal
items of exchange among the UDEAC countries are beer, refined sugar,
perfumes, matches, cigarettes, textiles, leather goods, plastic shoes,
motorcycles, and bicycles. The progress toward import substitution
is fairly rapid in this area, and this should increase trade among the
UDEAC countries in the 1970's.

Trade Among Countries of the
Eastern African Subregion

Like other areas, the countries of the Eastern African subregion
have, in the past, supplied mainly raw materials and minerals to the
developed countries and have imported all their requirements of
manufactured goods, especially capital goods, machinery, transport
and equipment and heavy agricultural implements. For purposes of
this section, these countries include, Ethiopia, Kenya, Somalia,
Uganda, Tanzania and Zambia, but Rwanda and Burundi are also included due to their special trade and transport links with the East
African Community countries. During the colonial period, virtually
no manufacturing industries were encouraged, and where this was
found necessary, it was merely to convert certain raw materials to
semifinished or processed goods for ease of transportation to Europe.
This accounted for the very small exchange of goods among the countries in this area. One significant characteristic of trade in East
Africa is that, where a country succeeded in penetrating the markets
of the other colonial territories, that country usually exported only
one or two commodities without necessarily importing anything in
return. The result has been that the more industrialized leading
countries (e.g., Kenya and Southern Rhodesia) usually were able to
maintain a favorable lead over their neighbors.

Another significant feature of East African trade is that in the
past no defined efforts were made by any country in the area to
expand or promote trade with its neighbors. Trade developed as a

matter of chance, not as a result of deliberate policy. Until quite
recently, there were no trade missions to other countries in the area
and trade fairs were far apart and confined mainly to agricultural
shows. As a result, in general there was little or no information
regarding trade opportunities in the neighboring states. Table 6.8
shows the trade of the individual countries, indicating the concentration
of trade between a few countries.

The Pattern of Trade Among the Countries
of East Africa

Ethiopia

Exports from Ethiopia in 1967 consisted mainly of primary products; the only exports of manufactured goods were carpets exported
to Kenya. Ethiopia's main export items to Somalia were chat and salt;
to Kenya, Uganda, and Tanzania, lentils, chickpeas and beans. Other
exports included oilseeds (linseed and sesame), gum arabic, spices
(including chilies and pepper), hides and skins, cereals, and potatoes
and other vegetables. Ethiopia's other African trading partners are
Libya, the U.A.R., Sudan, and Mauritius.

Somalia

Somalia's exports to other countries of the subregion consist
mainly of a few primary products such as fish, rice, feed, dyeing
and tanning extracts, and small quantities of perfume, cosmetics,
dressed furs, cotton textiles (bleached), and textile fibers. Other
African trading partners for Somalia are the U.A.R. and Sudan.

Kenya

Kenya's exports to the subregion cover a wide range of items,
but in 1967 the major items were cement and petroleum products,
mainly fuel oil shipped to Mauritius and natural gas to Madagascar.
Meat and tea are also important export items, mainly to Somalia,
Zanzibar, and Ethiopia. Butter was exported to eight countries in
the subregion and constitutes an important export item for Kenya.

Kenya also exports sizable quantities of other foodstuffs, including cornmeal to Zanzibar and coffee to Somalia. Kenya also
exports eggs, cheese, bakery products, potatoes and potato flour,
beans, pepper, and coconuts to various other countries of the subregion. Other trade items include paper bags, bottles, cordage,

TABLE 6.8

Trade Among the East-African Countries, 1967

(thousands of U.S. dollars)

Country	Uganda	Kenya	Tanzania^a	Ethiopia	Somalia	Zambia	Rwanda	Burundi	Total Intra-African Trade
Uganda^b									
Exports	--	--	--	1	452	180	1,046	138	5,660
Imports	--	--	--	92	1	408	28	2	605
Balance	--	--	--	-91	+451	-228	+1,018	+136	+5,055
Kenya^b									
Exports	--		--	533	9	4,770	1,104	1,015	15,117
Imports	--		--	49	39	368	112	--	4,132
Balance	--		--	+484	-30	+4,402	+992	--	+10,985
Tanzania^ab									
Exports	--	--		94	531	17,167	69	1,523	22,384
Imports	--	--		11	77	571	--	36	1,280
Balance	--	--		+83	+454	+16,596	--	+1,487	+21,104
Ethiopia									
Exports	5	262	15		--	--	--	--	3,471
Imports		719	211		--	--	--	--	1,467
Balance		-455	-196		--	--	--	--	+2,004
Somalia^c									
Exports		633	100	4		--	--	--	3,471
Imports				1,346		--	--	--	
Balance				-1,342		--	--	--	
Zambia									
Exports	39	550	392	--	--		--	--	231,158
Imports	14	4,075	12,605	1	--		--	--	169,554
Balance		-3,525	-12,213	--	--		--	--	+61,604
Rwanda									
Exports	621	73	--	--	--	--		--	1,418
Imports	2,725	557	157	--	--	--		--	4,414
Balance	-2,104	-484	--	--	--	--		--	-2,996
Burundi									
Exports	157	--	13	--	--	--	--		--
Imports	355	395	1,085	--	--	--	--		2,510
Balance	-198	--	-1,072	--	--	--	--		--

a Excluding Zanzibar.
b Excluding interstate trade among Uganda, Tanzania, and Kenya.
c Figures for 1966.

Source: United Nations, Foreign Trade Statistics for Africa (E/CN.14/STAT/SER.A/14.)

finished structural parts, aluminium circles, aluminium utensils, metal containers, and footwear. Other trading partners are Sudan, U.A.R., Congo (Kinshasa), Malawi, Mauritius, Reunion, and Mozambique.

Uganda

Uganda is not a major exporter to the countries of East Africa outside the East African Community, where its main export items are few. Uganda exports mainly cottonseed oil, 90 percent of which went to Somalia; cement, which was exported exclusively to Rwanda; and coffee and tea, which were shipped to Somalia, Zanzibar, and Mauritius. Small quantities of wood products and cordage were exported to Somalia and hippopotamus teeth were exported to Zanzibar. Uganda's principal buyers remain its two East African neighbors.

Tanzania

In 1967, the major export items from Tanzania (excluding Zanzibar) to other countries in the subregion were cottonseed oil to Somalia; fish (salted and dried) to Zambia, salt to Burundi and Rwanda, coated iron sheets to Burundi, tea and coffee to Somalia, and animal fats mainly to Rwanda. Other African trading partners are Congo (Kinshasa), the U.A.R., and Sudan.

Zambia

In 1967, the commodity composition of Zambia's intra-African trade included live animals, hides and skins, oilseeds, pottery, finished structural parts, furniture, cement, paper manufactures, cereals, and ivory. With non-African countries, trade is mainly in zinc and copper (unwrought). Zambia's imports from other African countries include tea, rice, oilcakes, fish, vegetables, fishing nets, cordage, and toilet preparations. Until recently, many of Zambia's imports came from Southern Rhodesia and South Africa, but considerable efforts have been made to decrease reliance on Southern African neighbors. Other African trading partners are Mauritius, Mozambique, and Congo (Kinshasa).

Trade Within the East African Community

Trade among Kenya, Uganda, and Tanzania is very well developed and covers a wide range of goods. In fact, this group of countries is almost self-sufficient in requirements in certain categories of consumer goods, especially those produced within Africa. Therefore, trade with the rest of Africa is relatively smaller than trade among the member states. The bulk of trade is in manufactured goods of all kinds. Tanzania exports an equal amount of agricultural primary products and manufactures, while the other two countries export more manufactured goods than primary products. This suggests that industrial development is more advanced in Kenya and Uganda than in Tanzania. The trade among these countries by Standard International Trade Classification (SITC) groups is shown in Table 6.9, which indicates Kenya's predominance in its trade with the other two partner states.

There is a wide selection of foods produced, especially in Kenya which exports large quantities to its neighbors both inside and outside East Africa. Uganda still imports from third countries such items as powdered milk, rice, malt, sugar confectionery, chocolate, spices, margarine, and other food products. Tanzania imports similar items, including such products as maize flour, beans, and vegetables, while Kenya buys sugar and tea in large quantities from countries outside the area.

Import substitution in East Africa is almost complete, especially in such products as Portland cement, paper bags, corrugated iron sheets, finished structural parts, aluminium circles, and aluminium domestic utensils. Import substitution also is fairly advanced in the manufacture of bottles, clothing and footwear. With regard to such items as paints, insecticides, plastic articles, blankets, metal furniture, bars and rods, cotton, and other textiles and clothing, there are still large quantities of imports from overseas.

Three important features regarding the development of trade in East Africa are immediately brought to the forefront. First, between 1961 and 1967 Kenya had a trade surplus with Uganda and Tanzania. Second, Uganda had a trade surplus with Tanzania during the same period. Third, the trade deficit of Uganda and Tanzania with Kenya grew considerably during the period under review.

Kenya's exports to Uganda stood at $19.732 million in 1961 and grew to $41.426 million in 1965, an increase of about 137 percent, whereas Kenya's imports from Uganda rose from $14.426 million to $28.462 million, an increase of about 100 percent. During the same period, Kenya's exports to Tanzania rose from $24.923 million to $31.869 million, an increase of about 30 percent, while Kenya's imports from Tanzania rose from $5.163 million to $9.206 million, an increase of over 147 percent. Uganda's deficit balance with Kenya

TABLE 6.9

Trade Within the East African Community, 1967
(thousands of U.S. dollars)

Main SITC Items	From Kenya		From Uganda		From Tanzania	
	To Uganda	To Tanzania	To Kenya	To Tanzania	To Kenya	To Uganda
Food and live animals	9,366	7,854	8,624	873	2,397	563
Beverages and tobacco	991	2,511	3,239	697	798	28
Crude materials, inedible	1,179	543	946	187	1,176	159
Mineral fuels, lubricants, and related materials	7,367	4,693	1,554	19	465	--
Animal and vegetable oils and fats	204	218	2,310	308	941	257
Chemicals	6,608	3,567	1,657	190	311	19
Manufactured goods classified chiefly by material	8,344	9,251	9,467	4,155	2,103	792
Machinery and transport equipment	669	638	36	17	308	162
Miscellaneous manufactured articles	6,535	2,464	610	350	683	101
Commodities and transactions not classified according to kind	162	120	17	8	25	14
Total	41,426	31,869	28,462	6,807	9,206	2,097

Source: East African Customs and Excise Department, Annual Trade Report of Tanzania, Uganda and Kenya, 1967, Mombasa: Commissioner General of Customs and Excise.

rose from $5.306 million in 1961 to $12.964 million in 1965, an increase of about 160 percent; Tanzania's deficit with Kenya during the same period rose by 15 percent from $19.760 million to $22.666 million. There are more Tanzanian imports from Uganda than exports to Uganda. In 1961, Tanzania's exports to Uganda came to $1.092 million while its imports from Uganda came to $4.771 million. In 1965, the exports rose to $2.097 million and the imports rose by 50 percent to $6.807 million.

The composition of exports of the East African countries indicates that certain commodities are exported by all three countries. For instance, in 1965 Kenya exported margarine and shortening worth $403,000 to Uganda and worth $8,500 to Tanzania. During the same year, Uganda exported similar items worth $1.375 million to Kenya and worth $67,000 to Tanzania while Tanzania's exports of the same commodity to Kenya amounted to $89,000 and to Uganda amounted to $5,000. Another interesting point to note is that, contrary to the popular notion that Uganda and Tanzania serve merely as markets for Kenya's products, there is a wide exchange of goods among the three states; the only relevant point is that Kenya generally exports more to Uganda and Tanzania than it imports from them.

According to SITC classification, Kenya's largest exports in 1967 were food and live animals, followed by manufactured goods, mineral fuels, chemicals, and miscellaneous manufactured articles. The pattern is generally the same with regard to exports from Tanzania except for Uganda where beverages and tobacco were important. In 1965, exports of manufactured goods by Kenya to Uganda came to about 26 percent of Kenya's total exports to Uganda, while exports of food and live animals came to nearly 22 percent. The corresponding percentages for Kenya's exports to Tanzania were 21 and 19 respectively. Uganda's exports of manufactured goods to Kenya came to about 24 percent of Uganda's total exports to Kenya, while Tanzania's exports of manufactured goods to Kenya came to about 32 percent of its total exports to Kenya.

In 1965, Kenya's exports of meat and meat preparations to Uganda came to $585,000 and to Tanzania came to $426,000, Tanzania's exports of meat products to Kenya came to $355,000. Uganda did not export meat to its two neighbors. With regard to wheat and maslin, Kenya's exports to Uganda and Tanzania in 1965 came to $2.436 million and $2.349 million, respectively. There is a large volume of trade in cigarettes: in 1965, Kenya's exports to Uganda came to $1.265 million and to Tanzania came to $1.016 million. Also in 1965, Uganda's exports of cigarettes to Kenya came to $495,000 and to Tanzania came to $134,000; while Tanzania's exports of cigarettes to its neighbors were negligible, but Tanzania's exports of unmanufactured tobacco formed an important export item amounting to $1.145 million to Kenya and $655,000 to Uganda.

There was booming trade of cotton seed oil among the three countries. Uganda was the chief exporter in 1965, with exports to Kenya worth $2.727 million and exports to Tanzania worth $196,000. Second in importance was Tanzania, with exports of $1.013 million to Kenya and $129,000 to Uganda.

In 1965, Kenya's exports of soaps and detergents to Uganda came to $1.683 million and to Tanzania came to $1.489 million--a drop from $2.553 million in 1964, a fall of some 42 percent. Uganda was the only exporter of superphosphates. Its exports to Kenya increased from $288,000 in 1964 to $574,000 in 1965, an increase of 99 percent; Uganda's exports to Tanzania increased by over 256 percent from $109,000 to $389,000 during the same period. With regard to paper bags and boxes, Kenya was the principal exporter to both Uganda and Tanzania, though the latter also had small exports.

There is a growing trade in woven cotton fabrics among the three countries, and Uganda is the principal exporter. In 1965, Uganda's exports to Kenya came to $3.531 million and to Tanzania came to $3.192 million. Kenya and Tanzania also export cotton fabrics. Kenya was the most important exporter of clothing of all kinds, and in 1965 its exports to Uganda came to $3.8 million and to Tanzania came to $2.9 million. It is interesting to note that, although Uganda has a large textile industry, its exports to Kenya and Tanzania were very small in both 1964 and 1965. This could imply a large degree of self-sufficiency in this industry. Kenya was the largest exporter of footwear to Uganda and Tanzania. In 1965, Uganda imported some $1.7 million of footwear from Kenya while Tanzania imported about $1.943 million.

Tanzania exported about $487,000 of aluminium circles to Kenya in 1964; in 1965 the value of such exports rose to $1.299 million, an increase of over 200 percent.

INTRA-AFRICAN TRADE IN SOUTHERN AFRICA

There is considerable interchange of goods among the countries of Southern Africa; in this text, Southern Africa includes Malawi, Rhodesia, Mozambique, Angola, Namibia, Botswana, Lesotho, Swaziland, Madagascar (the Malagasy Republic), Mauritius, Reunion, and

TABLE 6.10

Trade Among the Countries of Southern Africa, 1967
(thousands of U.S. dollars)

Country	Malawi	Botswana	Lesotho	Swaziland	Madagascar	Mauritius	Angola	Mozambique	Southern Rhodesia	South Africa	Total Intra-African Trade
Malawi											
Exports	--	--	--	14	88	8	1	292	1,777	1,276	7,808
Imports	--	51	--	--	4	6	14	832	15,161	5,488	26,898
Balance	--	--	--	--	+84	+2	-13	-540	-13,384	-4,212	-19,090
Madagascar											
Exports	--	--	--	--		1,092	--	--	--	--	22,209
Imports	--	--	--	--		111	--	--	--	--	6,535
Balance	--	--	--	--		+981	--	--	--	--	+15,674
Mauritius											
Exports	1	--	--	--	166		--	103	--	--	696
Imports	5	86	--	--	1,501		3	49	--	6,412	11,552
Balance	-4	--	--	--	-1,335		--	+54	--	--	-10,856
Angola											
Exports	--	--	--	--	--	--		4,081	214	3,109	13,772
Imports	--	--	--	--	--	--		4,797	1,137	4,146	10,936
Balance	--	--	--	--	--	--		-716	-923	-1,037	+2,836
Mozambique											
Exports	757	--	--	--	1	--	4,896		3,818	16,447	28,364
Imports	64	--	--	--	--	--	4,387		4,458	22,433	32,778
Balance	+693	--	--	--	--	--	+509		-640	-5,986	-4,414

Sources: United Nations, Foreign Trade Statistics for Africa, E/CN.14/STAT/SER.A/14; United Nations, Foreign Trade Statistics for Africa, E/CN.14/STAT/SER.B/16.

the Republic of South Africa. Individual trade statistics for Botswana, Lesotho, and Swaziland are not readily available because these countries constitute a customs union with South Africa. For this reason, Table 6.10 does not include these countries. The available data show that most of the trade of the countries of Southern Africa is conducted with South Africa, followed by Southern Rhodesia, Mozambique, and Angola.

The Pattern of Trade Among the Countries of
Southern Africa

Malawi

In 1967, Malawi's imports from other African countries outside the subregion came mainly from South Africa and Southern Rhodesia; of Malawi's total imports from Africa of some $27 million, about $20 million, nearly 74 percent, came from these two countries. Malawi's other trading partners are Mozambique and to a lesser extent Madagascar.

In 1967, Malawi's exports to Kenya amounted to $500,000, Malawi's exports to Zambia represented $700,000 thousand, and Malawi had smaller exports to Tanzania. Malawi's exports to other countries in Africa were negligible. Malawi exports mainly tea to Kenya, Somalia, Uganda, and Tanzania; beans to Zambia, Kenya, and Zanzibar; fishing nets and cordage to Zambia and Tanzania; coffee to Tanzania and Kenya; tobacco to Madagascar; and mineral waters to Zambia. Malawi's African trade partners outside the subregion are the Sudan, Ivory Coast, Sierra Leone, Liberia, Cameroun, Congo (Kinshasa), and the countries of the UDEAC.

Mauritius

Mauritius trades mainly with Madagascar and Mozambique and to some extent with Botswana and Malawi. In 1967, Mauritius' total exports to all Africa amounted to $696,000, of which nearly 33 percent went to Madagascar and Mozambique. The main supplier for Mauritius is South Africa, which in 1967 accounted for over 54 percent of Mauritius' total imports from all Africa. Outside the Southern African area, Mauritius' other trading partners are Nigeria, Tanzania, Uganda, Kenya, Ethiopia, and Reunion.

Madagascar

Complete data for Madagascar's trade with its immediate neighbors are not available. However, it is known that Madagascar's trade
in Southern Africa is confined to Mauritius, Reunion, and the Comoro
Islands. In 1967, Madagascar exported $11 million worth of goods to
Reunion, which accounted for 49 percent of its total exports to all
Africa. There is also some trade with South Africa. Outside the area,
Madagascar trade, mainly with its OCAM partners. In 1967, Madagascar's exports to Senegal amounted to $4.684 million while its exports
to Ivory Coast equaled $1.426 million; together, these two countries
accounted for just over 27 percent of Madagascar's total exports to
all African countries. In 1967, Madagascar's largest imports from
Africa came from Senegal $2.139 million, Ivory Coast $91,000, and
Cameroun $901,000, which together accounted for nearly 50 percent
of Madagascar's total imports from all Africa.

FORMS OF AFRICAN TRADE
AND BILATERAL AGREEMENTS

In recent years, there has been a growing awareness in Africa
of the need to develop closer mutual trade links in order to promote
intra-African trade. Thus, in the late 1960's a number of African
countries made attempts to create and strengthen their economic
ties through negotiations for trade, customs, and other payments
agreements. There are now nearly 400 such agreements in force.
Although these trade agreements are limited due to the absence of
manufactures and the narrow base of industrial and agricultural
goods that can be exchanged, they have brought to the forefront the
need to develop trading activities through close consultation. Due to
lack of adequate statistics, the effect of these agreements on intra-
African trade cannot easily be assessed. Space does not permit an
examination of all these agreements, but a few examples of such
intra-African trade agreements are described below. [4]

Ivory Coast-Upper Volta

A trade agreement between the Ivory Coast and the Upper Volta
signed on February 19, 1966, stated that goods originating in the Ivory
Coast exported to Upper Volta would be subject to a 50 percent reduction of duties and taxes applicable to third countries in cases where
the similar goods were imported by the latter from countries duty-
free. Goods covered by the treaty included plastic footwear, metal

beds, ready-made clothing (except for hosiery), bicycles, confectionery, and cosmetics. Items included on the list were cyclometers, soap, and cola nuts. Paints and bottled beer were eliminated from the list. Matches would benefit from a 62 percent margin of protection until a new match factory in Upper Volta was put into operation. The agreement provided that, when goods from the Ivory Coast became competitive with similar goods produced in the Upper Volta, the margin of protection for Ivory Coast goods could be reduced to 30 percent. Goods originating in Upper Volta were to receive preferential treatment in Ivory Coast.

The agreement also contained certain other general provisions. The two governments agreed to consult when contemplating the granting of preferential tariff treatment to competitive products originating in third countries. The two governments also bound themselves to refrain from granting discriminatory preferences in favor of third country products similar to those covered by the agreement.

Quota provisions under the agreement provided for increasing the annual quota on motor vehicles assembled in the Ivory Coast and benefiting from a 50 percent margin of protection from 150 to 290 vehicles. The Ivory Coast agreed to import 500 tons of cotton fiber from Upper Volta annually. Instead of hides and skins, Ivory Coast agreed to import 40,000 pairs of men's leather footwear made of material originating in Upper Volta at a price not to exceed 1,000 francs (CFA) per pair upon arrival at Abidjan. Ivory Coast also agreed to import 2,000 tons of shelled groundnuts annually, either in natural form or as oil. In 1966, Ivory Coast agreed to buy 60,000 cattle, 120,000 goats and 1,200 tons of frozen meat from Upper Volta. Ivory Coast was committed to buy from Upper Volta the following vegetables and fruits: 150 tons of potatoes, 1,000 tons of onions, 3 tons of watermelons, 3 tons of strawberries, 1,000 tons of mangoes, 3 tons of lettuce, 5 tons of cabbage, and 5 tons of green beans.

Cameroun-United Arab Republic

A trade agreement between Cameroun and the U.A.R. was signed on August 19, 1966, replacing the previous agreement concluded in December 1961. Trade between the two countries, which was virtually nonexistent before 1961, had grown to half a billion francs (CFA) in 1966, and it was hoped that the volume of trade would continue to increase as a result of the new agreement. Under the terms of the agreement, Cameroun and the U.A.R. were committed to accord each other all facilities for export and import of commodities stipulated in the agreement, notably as regards the granting of import-export licenses in conformity with the regulations in force in each country. The agreement also provided for reciprocal most-favored-nation treatment and the organization of trade fairs and exhibitions in the two countries. At the time the treaty was signed, trade between the two countries consisted mainly of aluminium, coffee, and cocoa from Cameroun to the U.A.R., and and cement, rice, and sugar from the U. A. R. to Cameroun.

Central African Republic-Congo (Kinshasa)

Under a trade agreement concluded in 1966 between the Central African Republic and Congo (Kinshasa), the contracting parties undertook to grant each other the necessary facilities for trade in the lists of of commodities included in the annex to the agreement. List A consisted of exports from Congo (Kinshasa), including tea, cement and fiber-cement products, galvanized sheets, paints, varnishes, and siccatives, perfumery, footwear, plastic manufactures, margarine, refractory material, records, casks, bottles and cans, bicycle tires and tubes, copper wire, wood products, iron, and plastic tubes. List B consisted of exports from the Central African Republic and included pimento, wood, cotton, groundnuts, sesame, rubber, printed fabrics, hides and skins, household utensils, bricks, ceramics, industrial gas, wood products, tobacco, wax, honey, and cheese and other dairy products. The agreement provided that the two lists of products could be modified by a joint commission established for the purpose of examining any difficulties arising from the operation of the agreement. This commission also was responsible for submitting proposals for the expansion of trade between the two countries.

The contracting parties also undertook to grant each other import and export licenses for goods outside the two lists according to demand, in conformity with their respective legislations and taking account of previous commitments. The agreement provided for reciprocal most-favored-nation treatment with respect to customs duties and for equivalent taxes on exports and imports. However, the most-favored-nation clause did not apply to (1) preferences that were accorded to neighboring countries for the purpose of facilitating border traffic; (2) preferences that were derived from customs union or free trade area arrangements concluded or to be concluded; and (3) preferences resulting from special treatment granted to certain countries in the framework of foreign aid in goods and materials assistance in kind, foreign exchange, or credits granted to these countries.

PROBLEMS OF INTRA-AFRICAN TRADE

The basic problems of intra-African trade lie in the structure of the African economies. The high dependence on agriculture for export earnings and the absence of manufacturing industries have restricted the African countries' trade with the advanced countries. This has limited the extent to which the African countries can take advantage of market opportunities, even where a common market or customs union has been created. Therefore, the development of intra-African trade must be considered in terms of the establishment of industries for import substitution on a multinational scale. Chapter 5 indicated that the establishment of small and medium-scale industries was one way of transforming the structures of the African economies from subsistence to market economies. The countries should begin by making an inventory of existing domestic products and agree on a system of exchange for this group of products. For new industries, special agreements should be made for free market access to ensure that the products of new industries find an adequate market.

Several factors have been responsible for the slow rate of development of intra-African trade. In the first place, except for a few groups such as the East African Community and UDEAC, most of the trade groups identified earlier do not really constitute homogeneous economic units. The major problem is that, as in most developing countries, the trade pattern of the African countries is export-oriented. These countries export raw materials and other agricultural products to the former metropolitan countries and import most of their requirements for manufactured and capital goods. The main market for the UDEAC countries is France; Congo (Kinshasa), Rwanda, and Burundi trade mainly with Belgium; and the former British colonies trade mainly with the United Kingdom.

Traditionally there was very little trading among these countries. A decline in prices of primary commodities has resulted in a fall in export earnings for some African countries. Furthermore, the rise in import prices has caused substantial trade deficits. An attempt has been made to increase export earnings through increasing the volume of exports to the developed countries, almost at the expense of intra-African trade.

The second obstacle to intra-African trade is the difference in consumption habits in the various countries in Africa and the fact that most countries basically consume what they produce. Thus, there is very little complementarity in production and consumption patterns among the African countries. The diet of the countries on the coast is based on starchy root and tuber crops, but as one moves to the west and the north and approaches the savannah zone, the diet progressively changes from roots and tubers to corn and millet. In urban areas, the consumption of wheat products and rice has increased considerably. Because of this divergence, the food produced in each area either must be consumed locally or must be exported to the developed countries.

The third problem hindering the development of intra-African trade is the inadequacy of the transport pattern. Existing transport links were intended almost exclusively to serve overseas trade. In other words, the transport links were not oriented to facilitate contacts among the African countries but to link them with their overseas markets. Naturally, this kind of transport pattern does not encourage development of intra-African trade. Moreover, in a sparsely populated region such as Africa where different urban centers are separated by large semi-empty areas, moving goods from one place to another is very costly, especially for unprocessed food and other bulky agricultural products.

The fourth factor is that there is a virtual absence of complementarity among the commodities produced by the African countries. This is particularly more pronounced in the industrial and the agricultural sectors. It therefore follows that any attempts to increase the flow of trade among the African countries must aim not only toward devising measures for the removal of trade barriers but also toward increasing the production of consumer goods. Essentially, this must be a long-term objective, and one that can suitably be tackled within the framework for multinational cooperation. Unless there is a radical change in the existing production structures to reorient them toward intra-African trade, the development of intra-African trade will be one of the most difficult aspects of multinational economic cooperation. As noted earlier, trade among African countries has developed very slowly in the past, due not only to historical factors but also to the underdeveloped nature of the African economies. An increase in the flow of trade among these countries can be effected only by establishing manufacturing and processing industries. This means that tremendous resources must be spent on providing the means with which to conduct trade. It must be recognized that it will be difficult to break the present pattern of trade between the African states and the former metropolitan powers, but there is an urgent need to initiate such steps.

SOME METHODS OF TRADE LIBERALIZATION

It has been noted that, although there are a number of trade agreements between African states in operation, these have not contributed significantly to the expansion of intra-African trade. Nevertheless, the trade agreements constitute an attempt by the African countries to liberalize mutual trade as a means of enhancing their rates of economic development. In the negotiations for trade liberalization, countries might wish to consider adopting one of the methods discussed below.

The Across-the-Board Method

A group of countries might wish to enter negotiations to grant free access into their markets for products produced in the partner states that fall under an agreed list of industries to be accorded special treatment. In regard to industrial products of basic importance, there may be problems in liberalizing trade in these products without harming the individual national economies. One answer to this problem is for the countries to agree that basic industrial goods that are recognized as multinational for the purpose of granting special treatment should enjoy some kind of monopoly within the member states, at least for a given period of time. The countries also might agree that the negotiations be based on an agreed allocation of new industries in such a way as to lead to an equitable distribution of benefits.

The agreement might initially cover products of a limited group of industries and gradually be extended to include a wider variety of products. It also might be agreed that the distribution of such industries among the participating states be done in stages so that adequate compensation is provided through a system of transfers for the diversion of imports from cheaper sources to higher cost goods produced in the partner countries. This provision is especially relevant for the less industrialized partners because, unless some safeguards are built into such agreements, the least industrialized partners will in effect be subsidizing the industries of the more advanced partners. Where countries are not prepared to enter into definite commitments for trade liberalization, this approach would be preferred so that a start would be made toward the removal of trade barriers.

The package deal method, as it is sometimes called, raises a number of economic and political problems. On the economic side, the development of joint ventures raises the problem of the introduction of multinational planning embracing all vital industrial sectors. Even in countries where comprehensive planning has been adopted by central planning authorities, as in some countries of Eastern Europe, it has been difficult to effectively introduce regional planning for purposes of ensuring effective trade liberalization. In some developing regions of the world, such as Latin America, some governments have attempted to introduce techniques aimed at avoiding these problems. For example, the Central American governments adopted a method of allocating at least one multinational industry to each state initially, followed by the subsequent distribution of the remaining list of industries in turn for each country. Although initially this method appeared attractive and successful, in subsequent allocation rounds difficulties arose because the countries still maintained their freedom to select and establish any industries they liked.

On the political side, countries often find it difficult to accept any kind of blueprint for the allocation of basic industries among partner states because this would imply tying their hands in certain areas of vital importance. Countries would hesitate mainly because of uncertainty as to whether such allocation of industry would be in their best interests or would remove glaring imbalances in industrial development levels. Where establishing a multinational industry prima facie appears to jeopardize a national economic interest, the country would tend to hesitate to grant the products of the multinational industry free access to its market because of fear of disrupting economic life.

The Item-by-Item Method

The item-by-item method seems preferable where countries do not wish to commit their entire industrial development policies to a multinational set-up, and this method of trade liberalization appears to have a special appeal to some African governments. Under this approach, countries grant free access into their markets to items on an agreed list, with each item negotiated separately during a given period of time. It might be agreed to reduce or remove, at regular intervals, tariffs for each product selected for special treatment. The selection of items for which trade barriers would be eliminated might be done on a bilateral basis in the initial stages, although this need not be the case if a product is of interest to several countries. The list would be prepared after consultations by the interested parties and could be adjusted from time to time to include new items.

The advantage of this method is that, due to the limited number of products on which the African countries can commit themselves to trade liberalization, they might be prepared to initiate the process even on an ad hoc basis. This is especially true where a country depends on a few commodities for the major portion of its foreign exchange earnings; the country might wish to exclude such basic items from the negotiations unless special arrangements were made. Furthermore, in most African countries a producer seldom thinks of neighboring markets in allocating production resources but often has overseas consumers in mind. It therefore follows that opening up new prospects for a given product in neighboring states even on a limited basis might give rise to new trade relations and could start the process of liberalization, especially if the country could see the clear advantages of such a step.

In some African countries, it is thought that the item-by-item approach also might provide the required links between the countries. A chance of a better exchange of commodities even on a selective basis might lead to measures toward more comprehensive economic cooperation agreements. This method is important because countries are free to adopt independent policies in vital areas, providing sufficient safeguards to dispel any fears among the less developed partners that their economies would become dependent upon the more advanced partners. This method also appears very useful where countries might agree to apply selective tariff deductions to all partners based on the agreed list.

Where quantitative restrictions constitute the main obstacle to trade, the item-by-item approach would be particularly useful. Here, the countries might establish quotas for selective products over and above the global quotas from third parties and the partner countries would therefore grant import licenses for products from the partner states on the agreed list. In the initial steps, a basic quota might be agreed for each country but not necessarily uniform for all partner countries. The essential element is that the countries could undertake to abolish trade barriers on the selected commodities over a reasonable period of time within which the economically weaker states could establish their industries on a more competitive basis.

PRODUCT COVERAGE UNDER TRADE
LIBERALIZATION ARRANGEMENTS

The adoption of trade liberalization as an instrument for trade expansion implies three major objectives: (1) free circulation of goods produced by industries designated multinational, including new industries established specifically to serve the expanded market and industries already existing at the time of the negotiations that are capable

of converting to multinational status; (2) guaranteed free circulation
of agricultural products, whose status must be clearly defined within
the new multinational markets; (3) gradual elimination of all internal
barriers on products of existing industries that, although not of a
multinational character, are sufficiently large and make a sufficient
contribution toward production in individual countries to warrant
special treatment.

The New Multinational Industries

The creation of a wide market for the products of new industries
established specifically to serve a multinational market would require
that the African countries tacitly accept far-reaching commitments
affecting their domestic and foreign policies. Free access of the new
products to such a market is a necessary precondition for the establishment of the new industries. Negotiations about the creation of new
industries would tend to be less cumbersome and therefore would be
preferred by the African countries since they would not fundamentally
affect existing industries. The main problem that arises in the case
of new industries is that some participating states might fear that,
due to the more advanced development of the other states, they would
not get a fair share in the new investments. This is a genuine fear in
some African countries. In order to eliminate this fear, it would be
essential to provide for the distribution of new investment at the outset
or to provide special measures in favor of countries that are likely
to end up relatively worse off.

In the developing countries, most industries are heavily protected
against external competition. Therefore, it is necessary to give
adequate attention to the problems of adjustment within the new arrangement and to make such adjustments gradually rather than immediately.
What is really important is not the immediate removal of trade restrictions but rather the acceptance of the commitment to such an
objective over the long run. Instead of working for total abolition of
barriers, it might be essential to agree on a limited target in the
first stage and then work gradually toward complete abolition. If
effected over a reasonably long period of time, this process would
enable domestic industries to continue to enjoy some degree of protection while making the necessary adjustments in production capacities and techniques to face the new competition. The merging of
markets almost certainly will disturb the existing equilibrium in
industry and in labor supply, but after some time the equilibrium will
tend to settle at a higher level due to the operation of such factors as
the economies of scale. The flow of new investments would increase

resources available to both new and existing industries. Therefore,
adequate provision should be made to ensure that the industrial structure and the labor market are able to adjust themselves to the new
conditions. It will be essential to earmark some financial resources
to enable some industries to modernize or to convert existing production techniques to match those of the new industries.

Liberalization of Trade in Agricultural Products

The case for cooperation in agriculture was considered in Chapter 4. Although liberalization of trade in agricultural products is
presumed to be more difficult to achieve than liberalization in respect
of manufactured and other industrial goods, the African countries
could ill afford to exclude agriculture from the general program for
economic cooperation. In the EEC, attempts toward the adoption of a
common agricultural policy preceded the liberalization of trade in
agricultural products, while in EFTA agricultural products are not
liberalized. Although it is not possible in the African context to argue
the case for economies of scale in agricultural production as in industrial production, there is still a prima facie case for joint action.
Here, the argument would focus on specialization in agricultural production as dictated by climatic conditions. Furthermore, the African
countries could take advantage of liberalization of trade in agricultural products by substituting imports of foodstuffs and other agricultural products from Africa for imports from the developed countries.

Where specialization in agricultural production is possible--as
in the production of butter, cheese, meat and meat preparations, and
textile goods--countries might wish to consider granting these individual products free access into their markets as the basis for further
negotiations on the general plan for trade liberalization in agriculture.
The question of processed agricultural products acquires special significance where an industry could be established using the processed
commodities as raw materials. In the case of agricultural products
it would be difficult to envisage the adoption of the package deal method
in negotiations, but individual items could be considered separately
at each stage of negotiations.

The case for cooperation in the agricultural field also arises in
respect of attempts by the developing producer countries to obtain
access for their products into the markets of the developed countries
at more favorable terms. In this respect, the action of the producers
would not result in the expansion of intra-African agricultural trade
but would strengthen the African countries' bargaining position vis-
à-vis the developed countries.

The main obstacle to the liberalization of trade in agricultural products lies in the maintenance of price support policies, especially for staple foodstuffs. Quite often, governments resort to protection in order to insulate their markets from foreign competition. The removal of such protection without adequate safeguards may result in undesirable effects on the domestic economy. Moreover, since a large proportion of the population in developing Africa works in the agricultural sector, the removal of trade barriers would subject local products to severe competition, which might ultimately result in acute unemployment problems, especially if the displaced rural population cannot be absorbed by the industrial sector.

The rigidity in the agricultural structure is another obstacle to the introduction of liberalization policies in agricultural trade. For various reasons, some African countries do not wish to have any discussions leading toward cooperation in agriculture. Another special problem in this respect is that the African countries are tending to move toward self-sufficiency in food production, which, together with the differences in the consumption habits of the African people, would tend to limit the scope for liberalization to plantation crops that presently are grown for markets in the developed countries.

The Existing Industries

The question of existing industries calls for special treatment. The problem that arises is whether these industries should be completely excluded from trade liberalization arrangements or be singled out for special treatment. Where a country has already reached a fairly high level of industrialization, the exclusion of such industries from the new arrangements not only would be greeted by stiff opposition but also would prevent such industries from taking advantage of the new and expanded market possibilities. Furthermore, to exclude the products of existing industries would preserve the existing industrial structure, which would only perpetuate the inefficiency in such industries. This in turn would tend to affect the structure of the new industries, since if old industries continue to operate behind protective tariffs they could still continue to pay low wages while charging higher prices for their products.

Within this group are included the products of industries that, although not of multinational status, are sufficiently large to have a decisive impact upon domestic economies. These industries cannot be ignored in the multinational set-up because they constitute an important core of the industrial complex. It is argued here that, where such industries are capable of introducing innovations, they should be accorded limited access to the markets of the other partners. The countries could agree on a program designed to gradually reduce tariffs and to relax other trade restrictions on specified products or groups of products. These arrangements could be implemented outside the general plan for trade liberalization. In order to ensure effective coordination, the countries could agree on a target to be achieved over a given period of time, preferably in stages. The negotiations at each stage could be designed so that the mutual concessions granted ultimately would lead to complete liberalization of trade in the selected products or groups of products.

An important policy instrument in the negotiations for the elimination of tariffs and other trade restrictions is the adoption of procedures for harmonizing legislation to prevent such discriminatory practices as cartels and combines so as to ensure fair competition. Such an agreement would be difficult to achieve since normally countries would not be excepted to give specific commitments regarding such matters as support programs for less prosperous but promising business enterprises. In order to protect small business enterprises from severe competition from larger and more efficient production units, it would be essential for countries to negotiate a complementary agreement granting certain concessions to products of the smaller industries that fall within the category of industries subject to negotiations. This would be useful especially with regard to the least developed partner states. Within the framework for multinational cooperation, it might be useful to provide institutional machinery to control the application of the complementarity agreements.

GROUND RULES AND PROCEDURES FOR
TRADE LIBERALIZATION

Before the actual negotiations for trade liberalization begin, it is essential to examine the ground rules and procedures to be adopted. This is as important as the actual negotiations. It is essential that each participating state have a clear idea of what to demand and what to expect from such negotiations. Any element of misunderstanding in the procedures would eventually throw the agreements off-balance. It might be essential that such negotiations be conducted under the supervision of the United Nations Economic Commission for Africa, which would ensure that the ground rules are adhered to. However, for practical reasons such negotiations might be conducted bilaterally in the initial stages, especially if the participating states favor the item-by-item approach. However, there should be provisions for

other countries to participtae at a later stage if the product concerned
is of a sufficiently multinational character. Proposals for negotiations
have been suggested along the following lines: 5

1. In order to protect the infant industries, especially in the
economically weaker partner states, countries might apply quotas on
a list of goods imported into the partner states duty-free or at reduced
rates. There might be a specific provision that this approach apply
only to products originating in the partner countries. Any imports
over and above the quotas could be accorded most-favored-nation
treatment, but the more advanced partner states might not insist on
such treatment. For goods falling under this category, countries
might agree not to subsidize, either directly or indirectly, the exports
of such goods to partner states and not to permit unfair practices or
price undercutting by domestic producers to the detriment of the other
partner states. They also could refrain from imposing export levies
or any export restrictions on the agreed list of goods.

2. With regard to goods that are subject to tariff concessions
or trade liberalization, the countries might undertake not to impose
any new import taxes or other charges with the exception of charges
reciprocally applied on their goods in the other partner states. It
also would be essential for the countries to agree not to apply any
other restrictions or prohibitions except prohibitions imposed for such
noneconomic reasons as public security, health protection, or public
morality. If, after an agreement is reached, any member state feels
obliged to impose such restrictions, it should be obligated to inform
the other partner states, which may wish to abrogate the agreement
if an amicable solution cannot be found.

3. Since the exercise for trade liberalization is a fairly new one,
it might be necessary to include a time clause providing that the agreement should operate for a period of at least five years and then be reviewed. The stipulation of a time limit is essential to ensure that
partner states are safeguarded and is particularly advantageous for
the least developed partners which may subsequently wish to establish
new industries and could therefore institute a new set of negotiations
at the end of the period. It could also be agreed that, during the stipulated period, countries should not withdraw or modify unilaterally
the provisions of the agreement. However, in order not to restrict
unduly the actions of the partner states, the agreements might provide
that prior to the time for review the partners could consult among
themselves if a country wished to modify the agreement in its economic
interests. In such cases, the other partner states likely to be affected
might demand additional concessions or withdraw from the agreement.

Due to the strains imposed by the efforts to develop, most African countries might not wish, at this stage of development, to enter into definite commitments toward complete liberalization of much of their intra-African trade. The above procedures, although not in themselves conclusive, would provide the framework for beginning negotiations. One important factor that must be borne in mind is that, the more concrete the agreements toward liberalization, the better the chances for such agreements to survive. In some agreements, such as the East African Community, the time clause is considered an important provision. This gives ample time for the parties to assess the effect of such agreements on their economies and to propose necessary modifications. As in most agreements leading to multinational cooperation, what is required is the acceptance of the principle of negotiations by the parties concerned. The countries also must be prepared to take the measures necessary to ensure the success of the negotiations.

PROTECTION WITHIN A COMMON MARKET

In the process of trade liberalization among the African countries, it would be necessary to take certain measures to ensure that the economically weaker partner countries do not suffer as a result of the removal of their trade barriers with the economically stronger partners. Free trade arrangements between countries with different levels of development would deprive the less developed partner countries of the chance to protect their infant industries against competing industries from the more advanced partner countries. Consequently, such infant industries either would be wiped out of existence or would have to struggle for existence under uneconomic conditions. In extreme cases, less developed partner countries may not be able to set up new industries without special safeguards.

Furthermore, under integration the less advanced countries would also lose revenues as a result of the abolition of duties on goods from the more advanced partners. Where, as is the case in most African countries, revenue from import duties constitutes a high proportion of total revenue, the countries might resist any measures toward abolition of such duties. The trade diversion from third countries would result in further loss of revenue from duties. The goods from partner countries also may be more expensive than goods from third countries due to production conditions, which would mean that the weaker partner countries would pay higher prices for similar goods. Consequently, the balance of trade and payments position of these countries would be worsened. If this happened, integration would have aggravated the situation that it was intended to correct.

If trade liberalization under economic integration is accompanied by an agreement to establish a common external tariff, the problems of the least developed partner countries are more acute unless special measures are put into effect. A common external tariff would result in further trade diversion to more expensive sources of supply in the partner countries. To alleviate this problem, the weaker partner countries should be allowed to continue to protect their infant industries against the stronger partner states for an agreed period of time, depending upon the type of industry in question. This arrangement also could be extended to the establishment of new industries in the less advanced partner countries if such industries could not survive without some measure of protection. Another solution is the establishment of a fund that the weaker partner states could draw upon to compensate actual or future losses of revenue.

These above measures apply to imports of the least developed partner states. In the case of exports, problems also would arise in the establishment of industries by the less advanced partners. It would be necessary for the more advanced partner countries to give preferential treatment to goods produced in the less advanced partners. Assuming that free trade already exists among the partners, such preferences may take the form of quotas and other restrictions against goods from third countries. These preferential arrangements should be applied only over an agreed time period since if they are unduly prolonged the countries granting the preferences will begin to sustain loss from trade.

In the granting of preferential treatment, it may turn out that a weaker partner state, although having an adverse balance of trade with its partners, maintains constant favorable balance of trade with third countries. (For example, this was the position of Tanzania under the old common market arrangements involving Kenya, Uganda, and Tanzania.) If such a situation exists, the granting of preferences must be measured in relation to the relative loss sustained by any country under the new trade arrangements. Hence, the concept of balancing the new trade flows among the partner countries must be governed by the principle of reciprocal trade agreements to ensure that in the long run the more advanced partners are not placed in a less advantageous position vis-a-vis the weaker partners. However, the principle of reciprocity should only be insisted upon by more advanced partner countries where there is clear evidence that the less advanced partners gain undue advantage. In any case, the balancing of trade among partner countries under integration should not be employed as a statistical exercise but only when it will enhance balanced economic development of the area as a whole.

PROSPECTS FOR TRADE PROMOTION IN AFRICA

The problem of expansion of trade of the developing African countries is now receiving increasing attention both in Africa and in the United Nations. The expansion of trade and foreign exchange is regarded as a factor for accelerating the rate of economic advancement of the developing countries. Consequently, at a special meeting of the Executive Secretaries of the Regional Economic Commissions in January 1967, it was decided to establish a coordinated United Nations Export Promotion Program. This program aims at combining the knowledge, activities, and resources of all United Nations agencies connected with the field of trade promotion in order to ensure a proper response to the increasing requests from developing countries for assistance in this field. Recognizing the potential role that the Regional Economic Commission could play in export promotion matters and in view of their knowledge of local conditions, the meeting of the Executive Secretaries held at Geneva in July 1967 agreed that each Regional Economic Commission in the developing parts of the world should be a center of initiative for the United Nations Export Promotion Program. For this purpose, it was recommended that regional trade promotion centers be established in the Economic Commission for Africa (ECA), Economic Commission for Latin America (ECLA), and Economic Commission for Asia and the Far East (ECAFE), and that these centers be operated under the direction of the respective Executive Secretaries.

Under the United Nations Export Promotion Program, the Regional Economic Commission would undertake the following functions: (1) to assist member governments in their export promotion efforts to increase trade both among themselves and with countries outside the region; (2) to assist the governments in developing deliberate and concerted export policies in light of each Regional Economic Commission's intimate knowledge of conditions in its region; (3) to assist in formulating requests for advisory services, research, market surveys, and training; and (4) to assist in arranging for training within the given region. Proposals were put forward to establish a regional trade promotion center for Africa within ECA in order to further the objectives to the United Nations Export Promotion Program. The primary functions of the center would be to advise and give technical assistance to member states of ECA in the following areas: (1) all matters concerning the promotion of export trade, intra-African and overseas; (2) the simplification and standardization of trade documents; (3) the promotion and establishment of export-oriented industries; and (4) the training of personnel in actual trade promotion work. [6]

It was proposed that activities of the trade promotion center be expanded by stages to include advice and assistance in marketing and market surveys and in organizing trade exhibitions. The functions and activities proposed for each stage are to be undertaken in accordance with the demand from member states and the availability of funds and personnel. In meeting the requests of African countries in matters of trade promotion, the trade promotion center will seek the assistance and cooperation of the UNCTAD/GATT Trade Center, United Nations Development Program (UNDP), United Nations Industrial Development Organization (UNIDO), and other international organizations, particularly in training personnel and in obtaining technical and commercial information.

Some of the measures which are suggested in this text for the promotion of trade in Africa are as follows: (1) the organization and strengthening of national trade intelligence services, export promotion policies and techniques, activity by diplomatic and commercial representatives abroad, trade missions, planning of export production, government incentives for export growth, market research and marketing channels, training in export techniques, and the creation of such ancillary export services as export credit guarantee systems and credit insurance, standardization, pricing, packing and packaging, labeling, freight handling, and trade publications; (2) the simplification and standardization of trade documents, on which preliminary work has already been done; (3) the establishment of export-oriented industries and the encouragement and expansion of those already in existence, with special emphasis on increasing intra-African trade; (4) the establishment of industries to process local raw materials now exported as primary products; (5) the expansion and diversification of nontraditional exports of African countries, particularly semimanufactures; (6) the fostering of the African countries' overseas export trade by cooperation with existing multinational bodies established in Africa to promote the interests of producers and exporters of such primary products as cocoa, coffee, and groundnuts.

Within the African countries, the creation of fairs and exhibitions is another possibility for expansion of both trade and industry, especially small-scale industry. The special problems that prevent the African countries from mounting up useful trade fairs include the lack of appropriate institutional machinery in the African region to render advice and technical assistance to the African countries; the lack of trained personnel to manage fairs and exhibitions; and the lack of financial resources. Other problems in this respect include the lack of cooperation among international trade fairs and other organizations; the lack of proper foresight and planning in order to ensure that trade fairs achieve maximum results; and the problem of admission of African fairs to international fairs.

In order to promote trade expansion, it is necessary to create a permanent body of experts who would be available at any time to render advice and technical assistance and would conduct studies on the problems of creation of fairs and exhibitions in Africa. International organizations and international trade fairs interested in African fairs and exhibitions should cooperate in giving technical assistance to African fairs and exhibitions, and ways and means should be found to give maximum assistance to African countries wishing to create such fairs. Developed countries and international fairs should be asked to grant increased facilities for the creation of fairs and to enable the African countries to participate in international fairs, especially those organized in the developed countries.

The Union of International Fairs (UFI) has shown great interest in the trade promotion efforts through the creation of trade fairs and exhibitions in Africa. A number of existing fairs in Africa are not yet members of UFI, whose rules and regulations provide that in order to be eligible for membership a fair must have been in existence for at least five years. This requirement makes most African fairs ineligible for membership to UFI and provides no incentive for new fairs. More-over, the new fairs in Africa have difficulty obtaining assistance from UFI. Fairs in Africa urgently need to shift emphasis from general fairs to specialized fairs (such as small-scale industrial exhibitions) to serve the special needs of the African countries. In order to assist the African countries in the creation of fairs and exhibitions, a list of international fairs interested in African fairs should be compiled, indicating the fields in which a given fair is willing to offer technical assistance and training facilities to African countries. Such a list would enable the African countries to organize or modify the structure of their fairs according to the availability of resources.

At a seminar on technical cooperation between the union of inter-national fairs and the economic organizations of the African countries held in Algiers in June 1969, the recommendations discussed above were accepted. [7] The African representations asked UFI to consider providing free stands to African countries at international fairs in order to enable the participation of countries that are not able to meet the expenses. UFI also was asked to examine the possibility of granting preferential treatment to enable one fair to participate in another fair at reasonable outlay. This is particularly essential for the participation of African fairs in international fairs.

In order to facilitate the creation of fairs and exhibitions in Africa, the Algiers seminar recommended the establishment of a standing committee on fairs and exhibitions composed of representatives from the Economic Commission for Africa, the Organization of African Unity, and the Afro-Asian Organization for Economic Cooperation (AFRASEC). The purpose of the committee would be to study the problems facing African countries in the creation of trade fairs and exhibitions and to coordinate technical assistance to them. The committee also would be a focal point for African efforts and aspirations in this field. Furthermore, the committee would provide a link between African fairs and international fairs outside Africa. The establishment of such a committee has generally been accepted as one way to promote trade among the African countries.

CONCLUSIONS

To conclude these remarks, a few observations seem relevant. In the first place, there is very little trade among developing African countries and most of their trade is with the advanced countries. It therefore follows that in a majority of cases the African countries cannot take advantage of the trade creation effect arising from the creation of new trade opportunities. Furthermore, it is very difficult to determine which country should produce which goods. This problem may be acute where a number of countries possess the capacity to produce a given commodity.

In the second place, it must be stressed that tariff reduction or elimination presents special problems to countries with an adverse balance of trade. In the absence of special payment arrangements, the weaker countries may be forced to impose quota and exchange control restrictions in order to avoid worsening the balance of payments. A less developed country may upset its economic development process by opening up its market to goods from partner states. This was in fact the case in the East African Community; Tanzania suffered a setback in its efforts to industrialize as a result of opening its market to goods from Kenya, which was more advanced. In other parts of Africa, as in the Central African Customs and Economic Union, the liberalization of trade among the partner states without compensatory factors merely helped the more advanced partner countries to advance further.

For this reason, although the principle of trade liberalization is generally accepted, the African countries are not eager to eliminate their
customs duties.

A country is likely to gain more from trade liberalization if it
has a high initial level of tariffs and if its demand for goods produced
in the partner countries is perfectly elastic. This result is equally
true in developed and developing countries. It implies that under such
circumstances a country would be more responsive to the changes in
price structure brought about by the creation of a common market or a
customs union. Where a group of countries generally has low tariff
duties on goods produced within the area, the gain from trade creation
would be nominal. Most African countries have high tariff rates charged
on goods originating in other African countries, and the argument therefore is that trade liberalization would generally increase trade among
them. One of the main problems in this regard is that in most cases,
the demand for goods from other African countries is inelastic implying
that the creation of a common market or customs union may initially
not result in considerable increase in intra-African trade. The loss
to any country in a customs union or free trade area will be marginal
if its cost structure is similar or less than that of third country source
of supply. This is so because a change in prices in the third country,
unless very substantial, will not affect the demand of the partner countries from third sources of supply.

It also can be argued that, where the goods produced by a given
country and its potential partner states are initially similar, the country will gain more from membership in a customs union or common
market if there is a cost differential between its goods and those of its
partners and if its cost structure is lower. This argument holds particularly where the consumption of such goods rises rapidly as the level
of development rise. Furthermore, where the member countries of the
customs union or common market have different production structures
and consumption habits as compared with third countries, there is likely
to be gain in trade creation since the demand from third country will be
inelastic. With the possible exception of a few items, the demand for
consumer goods from third countries is perfectly elastic in most African
countries, which reduces the level of gains from trade creation within
the existing customs unions or common market arrangements unless
such goods can be produced within the African countries.

It follows that the mere liberalization of trade among the African
countries--without the adoption of common policies in relation to planning, fiscal and monetary policy, and currency and exchange control-

would fail to bring about the benefits of trade creation under present conditions. This is particularly pertinent because, although the principle of trade liberalization has been accepted, countries tend to fear the liberalization of trade through the removal of tariffs if it is not followed by other agreements for compensation for the loss of revenue from tariffs. Therefore, it seems that, unless a compensatory mechanism such as the transfer tax, is built into agreements for trade liberalization, proposals to free trade are bound to meet with resistance, especially from countries where tariff rates are high and where revenue from tariffs constitutes a high percentage of total revenue.

In light of African conditions, therefore, it seems that an immediate removal of tariffs is not possible, let alone acceptable. What is required is a gradual freeing of trade over a given period of time during which the weaker economies can bring their production and wage structures in line with the general production and wage structure prevailing in the common market or customs union.

NOTES

1. Economic Commission for Africa, Africa's Trade, Trends, Problems and Policies, E/CN.14/UNCTAD II/1, Chapter 1, pp. 1-32.

2. Ibid., p. 18.

3. See United Nations, Report of the Fourth Inter-regional Seminar on Development Planning, ST/TAO/SER.C/116, pp. 26-28.

4. See Economic Commission for Africa, Foreign Trade Newsletter, E/CN.14/STC/FTN/1-20.

5. See also Economic Commission for Africa, Trade Expansion in Eastern Africa, E/CN.14/EA/EC/2, pp. 64-66.

6. Economic Commission for Africa, Regional Trade Promotion Center within ECA, E/CN.14/434, p. 3.

7. See Union of International Fairs, Report of the First Seminar on Technical Cooperation of the Union of International Fairs and the Economic Organizations of African Countries (Algiers, June 1969).

7

**COOPERATION
IN
THE DEVELOPMENT
OF TRANSPORT
AND COMMUNICATIONS**

THE CASE FOR COOPERATION IN
TRANSPORT DEVELOPMENT

The case for cooperation in transport lies in the fact that in order to develop a country must be able to move factors of production to where they are needed. Bottlenecks that prevent a country from effectively deploying the factors of production will retard the general rate of economic development, as has been the case in most African countries. Therefore, one of the major prerequisites for economic cooperation in Africa is the development of adequate infrastructure, especially transport and communications. The problems of transport development in Africa have been acute even at the national level, and they will increase in any plan for multinational cooperation. Industrial development, agricultural development, and the expansion of intra-African trade have a direct bearing on the state of transport and communication facilities. In the strategy for multinational cooperation, priority should be given to the development of regional or subregional transport networks to link the existing transport systems of the various states. The choice of the form of transport to be given priority will depend upon the requirements under multinational cooperation, the existing conditions, and the requirements for future economic development.

The pattern of transport systems developed in Africa throughout the colonial era had many shortcomings. A quick glance at the transport network in any subregion shows that no deliberate effort was made to link up the different transport systems. During the scramble for Africa, the basis for claiming possession of a given territory was laid down at the Berlin Conference. It was agreed that the building of a railway line was to be regarded as ample evidence of effective occupancy of any territory in Africa.[1] Immediately thereafter, several railway lines were started by the various European powers; the main consideration was not development but symbolic possession of territory. In Africa, the settlers did not find it profitable or economic to build roads and railways linking the various territories; where these existed, they were built either for strategic reasons or as outlets for raw materials. Even within the territories, there were no roads or railways linking rural areas and urban centers. The transport system clearly was not built to serve economic development in the territories.

THE DEVELOPMENT OF ROAD TRANSPORT

In recent years, road transport systems have developed appreciably in most African states. There have been successful attempts to build all-weather roads, and road transport has increasingly played a vital role in the process of economic development. Its role will increase in the future since this form of transport is relatively cheaper to develop, especially for land-locked countries. But the greatest limitation is that the road systems in most African states were built with specific objectives, such as connecting a given piece of farmland with the railway line. For future development, a number of problems must be faced in order to ensure that the roads advance economic integration. Swamps, damp climatic conditions, and in some cases topography present considerable difficulties in road construction, which can be very costly in terms of initial capital outlay and maintenance. However, road transport development would become another major item in plans for economic cooperation.

The present pattern of road development leaves much to be desired. Road transport often has developed in keen competition with the railways. Because railways and road transport systems are owned by different companies, the roads either run parallel to the railway line or independently of it, which has served to retard economic development. Another major problem is that there are no good roads connecting most of the capital cities and large commercial centers in Africa. What is required is to coordinate the development of roads and railways at the multinational level in order to ensure effective complementarity.

The Existing Road System in Africa

North Africa

The Maghreb countries. These countries are connected by very good
tank roads. From Casablanca in Morocco, a road runs through Rabat
and then to Oujda, from whence it connects with Oran in Algeria.
Another road runs from Tindouf in southwest Morocco through Bechar
to Ain-Sefra in Algeria. Another road runs from Casablanca southward through Marrakech to Tessalit in Mali and is the only road
connection between Morocco and Mali. From Algeria, a road runs
southeast through Ghardaia, El-Golea, and In-Salah to Gara-Ekar on
the border with Niger. From Algiers, another road runs through
Annab to Tunis, while another road runs from Constantine to Gebes.
A road that runs from Tunis south through Gebes and then on to
Tripoli is the only road link between Tunisia and Libya.

The United Arab Republic. From Cairo, a road runs westward through
Alexandria then on to Benghazi in Libya; this is the only road link
between the U.A.R. and the Maghreb countries. Another road runs
southward from Cairo to the Aswan Dam. Another road from Cairo
runs along the Suez Canal to link with Port Sudan and is the only road
connecting the U.A.R. and the Sudan.

Sudan. From Khartoum, a road runs southward through Kosti and
Juba to Numule on the border with Uganda. From Kosti, a road runs
westward through El Obeid and El Fashir to El Geneina and then on
to Abéché; this is the Sudan's only road link with Chad. Another road
runs from Khartoum to Aba and then on to Isiro and Kisangani in
Congo (Kinshasa). The link between Sudan and Ethiopia runs through
Massala and then on to Asmara.

West Africa

Mauritania. Mauritania does not have many good roads. Its main
road runs from Nouakchott through Zouerate and Bir-Moghreni into
Morocco. From Nouakchott, another road runs south to Rosso and
then to Richard Toll in Senegal.

Mali. In the northwest, a road runs from Kayes to Tambacounda in

Senegal. From Bamako, a road runs south branching off at Bougouni
to Kankan in Guinea and another through Sikasso to Bobo-Dioulasso in
Upper Volta. Another main road runs from Gao to Niamey and from
Gao through Tessalit into South Algeria. The main road runs from
Bamako through Sikasso and then on to Feressedougou and Abidjan on
the coast. This is the main road outlet for Mali to the sea.

Senegal and Gambia. From Dakar, a road runs north to Nouakchott in
Mauritania and another runs southeast to Tambacounda and then on to
Mali. Another road that runs from Dakar through Kaolack then to
Bathurst in Gambia is the only road link between Gambia and Senegal.
From Kaolack, a road runs through to Bissau (Portuguese Guinea).

Guinea. From Conakry one road runs to Freetown in Sierra Leone
and a second road runs east through Kankan to Upper Volta. From
Kankan, a road runs south to Monrovia in Liberia and another branch
goes to Mau in Ivory Coast.

Liberia. One principal road runs from Monrovia through Gbarnga to
Mau in Ivory Coast and Freetown in Sierra Leone.

The Conseil d'Entente Countries. Two main trunk roads run from
Abidjan, one north through Yamoussoukro to Mau and on to Guinea
and the other to Sikasso and Bobo-Dioulasso in Upper Volta. Another
road runs eastward through Abengourou to Kumasi in Ghana. In Upper
Volta, a road runs from Ouagadougou through Po, then to Tamale in
North Ghana, and then on to Accra. Another road runs west through
Bobo-Dioulasso to connect with Ivory Coast and Mali. From Togo,
a road runs north through Sansanné-Mango and Dapango to Ouagadougou.
Another runs east along the coast to Cotonou. From Cotonou, a road
runs west to Accra in Ghana and another runs north through Kandi to
Niamey in Niger. A third trunk road runs east through Port Novo to
Lagos. From Niamey, a road runs south to Katsina in Nigeria. This
road is the main outlet to the sea and is important for Niger's trade.

Nigeria. Nigeria has good trunk roads linking Lagos and Port Harcourt
with the interior as well as with neighboring countries. From Lagos,
a road runs through Ibadan and Kaduna to Kano, where it branches off
to Katsina, then Niamey, and on to Ziner (Niger). A second road runs
from Port Harcourt through Onitsha, Enugu, Jos, and Ngala and on to
Fort Lamy in Chad; this is the principal outlet for merchandise from
Chad. From Enugu, a road runs south to Mamfé in Cameroun. Lagos
also is linked with Cotonou in Dahomey. Another road runs from Kano
to Zinder through Agadez in Niger to Tamanrasset in Algeria.

Central Africa

The Central African subregion particularly suffers from one problem of transport that has contributed greatly to the problems of trade development in the area. The major transport links are oriented to overseas trade and there are very few interstate links. Even within the UDEAC, transport links between member states must be greatly expanded to serve present and future trade.

Cameroun. There are three principal road links in Cameroun. The first runs east-west from Douala to Batouri; the second runs south-north from Ambam to Yaoundé, continuing to Bertocea and Nora; and the third runs from Douala to Ngaoundéré. Cameroun is connected with Gabon by one road that runs from Ebolowa through Oyem to Lambaréné, and with Central African Republic by a road that runs from Ngaoundéré through Bouar to Baugui. There are two direct road links with Congo (Brazzaville) and Chad.

Chad. Chad is connected with Central African Republic by a road that runs from Fort Lamy to Bangui, and with Nigeria by another road that runs from Fort Lamy to Sudan. Due to its low level of economic development, Chad has been unable to develop a better transport system.

The Central African Republic. The Central African Republic has a road link that runs from Bangui to Chad at Fort Lamy. From Bangui, another road links with Cameroun. Within the Central African Republic, there is a good road system. The Oubangui and Congo rivers provide a river transport link to the railhead at Brazzaville, from whence a railway line links with the coast at Pointe Noire. Congo (Kinshasa) is well linked with Central African Republic by roads to Kinsangani and by a river transport system to Kinshasa.

Congo (Brazzaville). Congo (Brazzaville) has a major road link that runs to Pointe Noire and another road that runs north to Ouesst. The Congo river and its tributary, the Oubangui, provide good waterways throughout the year connecting Brazzaville with Bangui in Central African Republic.

Gabon. Gabon has two major road connections with Cameroun and Congo (Brazzaville). From Libreville, a road runs south to Bifoam where it branches, with one branch running south to Pointe Noire and the other north to Yaoundé. Within Gabon, a good road network exists.

Congo (Kinshasa). In Congo (Kinshasa), there are three short road stretches. One runs from Matadi to Kinshasa and then on to Kenge. Another runs from Kolwezi to Lubumbashi and then on to N'dola in Zambia. The third road link runs from Kisangani to Bukanu in Rwanda and then on to Bujumbura in Burundi. Some seasonal road links exist with Central African Republic. The Congo river provides water transport links with Central African Republic.

Rwanda-Burundi. From Bujumbura, the principal road runs northward to Kigali and on to Kampala in Uganda. Another road runs south through Fizi to Albertville in Congo (Kinshasa). Another road runs northwest from Bujumbura to Bukavu. From Kigali, a road runs north through Ruhengeri and Goma to connect with Kisangani.

East and Southern Africa

Ethiopia. Ethiopia lacks good connecting roads with neighboring states. However, a road runs from Addis Ababa to Asmara and then on to Sudan. A second road runs from Addis Ababa through Dire Dawa on to Djibouti, from whence it connects with Somali. The third main road runs through Shashamane and Mega and then on to Moyale on the border with Kenya; this is the only road link between Ethiopia and the East African countries. There should be joint efforts by Ethiopia and Kenya to develop this route.

Somalia. As in Ethiopia, Somalia's main problem is the lack of good road links, especially with Kenya, its main African trading partner. A road runs from Mogadishu through Gelib and Kisimayo on the Garissa in Kenya. Another road runs north to Hergeisa and then on to Djibouti. From Hergeisa, a road runs through Harar to connect with Dire Dawa in Ethiopia.

The East African Community. A trunk road runs from Mombasa in Kenya through Nairobi to Kampala in Uganda, from whence it connects with Kigali in Rwanda; this is the main outlet for Uganda and Rwanda. From Nairobi, another main road runs through Arusha to Iringa, Morogoro, and Dar-es-Salaam. From Nairobi, a road runs north to Moyale and then on to Addis Ababa in Ethiopia. From Iringa in Tanzania, a road runs west through Nzega to Kibondo and then on to Bujumbura; this is an important link between Tanzania and Burundi. Tanzania's link with Zambia runs from Iringa through Mbeya and then on to Lusaka. This is Zambia's main outlet to the sea through the port of Dar-es-Salaam and has proved to be of extreme importance to Zambia in recent years.

Zambia-Malawi-Southern Rhodesia. These three countries developed good road links during federal days. From Lusaka, a road runs southward through Chirundu and then on to Salisbury; another runs from Lukasa through Livingstone (Victoria Falls) to Buluwayo and Salisbury. Another road from Lusaka runs east through Fort Jameson and then to Lilongwe and Blantyre in Malawi. There is another road which runs from Lusaka through the Copper Belt to Lubumbashi in Congo (Kinshasa). From Blantyre in Malawi, a road runs through Zomba, Fort Johnston, and Mandimba and on to the port of Mozambique. Another road from Blantyre runs south through Mlanje to Quilimane (also in Mozambique). These two roads are proving to be important road outlets to the Indian Ocean for Malawi's goods. A road link with Salisbury runs from Blantyre through Tete in Western Mozambique and on to Salisbury.

From Salisbury, roads radiate in all directions. A road from Salisbury to Botswana runs through Buluwayo and then on to Francistown and Gamerones. Another road from Salisbury runs south through Mesina and on to Pretoria in South Africa; this is the vital road link between Southern Rhodesia and South Africa. Another road from Salisbury runs through Umtali to Beira and is also an important outlet to the sea for Rhodesian goods.

South Africa. South Africa has developed very good all-weather roads. Its main link with neighboring countries is a road through Pretoria and then on to Mesina and Buluwayo in Southern Rhodesia. Another road runs from Pretoria to Mafeking and then on to Gaberones in Botswana. A trunk road from Cape Town connects South Africa with Windhoek in Namibia. South Africa also is linked with Lesotho, Swaziland, and Mozambique.

The Capacity of Road Transportation in Africa

Table 7. 1 shows the total number of vehicles for each African country in 1965, together with the density, i.e., the number of persons per vehicle. There were some 3.2 million motor vehicles in Africa in 1965, of which 2.3 million were passenger cars and the remainder were commercial vehicles. Africa as a whole accounted for less than 2 percent of all vehicles in circulation in the world in 1965; one vehicle was available for every 19 persons in the world as a whole, as against an average of 93 persons per vehicle in Africa. African roads were comparatively less crowded than roads in other parts of the world; there were fewer than 3 vehicles for every kilometer

Table 7. 1

Number of Motor Vehicles in Africa, 1965
(thousands of vehicles)

Country	Total Number of Vehicles	Commercial Vehicles	Passenger Cars	Persons per Motor Vehicle
North Africa				
Algeria	305.5	95.5	210.0	39
Morocco	229.5	65.1	164.4	58
Tunisia	83.4	32.2	51.2	44
Libya	63.0	20.7	42.3	26
U.A.R.	123.7	26.0	97.7	240
Sudan[a]	40.2	19.7	20.5	337
West Africa				
Mauritania	0.3	0.2	0.1	3,500
Mali	9.4	4.9	4.5	487
Senegal	46.2	18.1	28.1	76
Guinea	22.8	13.5	9.3	154
Gambia	3.8	1.8	2.0	87
Sierra Leone	13.1	4.3	8.8	175
Liberia	11.5	3.7	7.8	93
Ivory Coast	55.2	23.2	32.0	70
Upper Volta	9.0	4.6	4.2	540
Ghana	49.5	19.5	30.5	156
Togo	0.9	0.4	0.5	1,820
Dahomey	9.6	3.9	5.7	246
Niger	7.1	4.5	2.0	470
Nigeria	70.0	24.0	46.0	729
Central Africa				
Cameroun	39.2	21.9	17.3	133
Chad	8.1	4.8	3.3	408
Central African Republic	9.5	5.9	3.6	142
Congo (Brazzaville)	12.0	4.5	7.5	70
Gabon	9.0	5.8	3.2	51
Congo (Kinshasa)	75.4	32.9	42.5	208
Rwanda	4.7	1.9	2.8	662
Burundi	4.7	1.9	2.8	684
Equatorial Guinea	--	--	--	--
East and Southern Africa				
Ethiopia	32.8	8.9	23.9	690
Somalia	11.3	6.3	5.0	221
Uganda	36.2	5.9	30.3	208
Kenya	84.0	11.0	73.0	101
Tanzania[a]	43.1	10.0	33.1	244
Zambia	55.1	11.4	43.7	67
Malawi[a]	15.6	7.6	8.0	252
Botswana[b]	3.0	1.9	1.1	186
Lesotho[b]	4.9	2.0	2.9	171
Swaziland[b]	9.3	2.5	6.8	40
Madagascar	59.2	27.1	32.1	108
Mauritius	--	--	--	--
Southern Rhodesia[a]	118.0	23.3	94.7	36
South Africa	1,408.0	291.0	1,117.0	13

[a]Figures for 1964.
[b]Figures for 1966.

Source: ECA, A Survey of Economic Conditions in Africa, 1967, E/CN.14/409/Rev. 1.

234

of road as compared to more than 11 vehicles per kilometer through-out the world. The number of cars per kilometer of road ranged from under 1 in Central Africa to more than 4 in North Africa and Southern Africa. The total number of vehicles in developing Africa increased almost 22 percent, from 1.5 to 1.8 million between 1960 and 1963 and from 1.8 to 3.2 million between 1963 and 1965. (Data by type of road are given in Table 7. 2). Fourteen countries in Africa increased their expenditures on road construction between 1963 and 1966, with increases ranging from 4.9 to over 1,400 percent. The overall annual rate of increase in highway expenditures in Africa was about 17 percent between 1963 and 1966. Paved road length in-creased by an annual rate of 10 percent during the period, while total motor vehicle registrations increased at an annual rate of about 6 percent. On the whole, the highway network improved substantially during the period 1963-66.

Future Development of Roads

The future development program for road construction in Africa essentially consists of two major proposals. First, there should be improvement of existing interstate links, which should be upgraded into all-weather permanent roads. Such upgrading would immediately increase the usefulness of existing roads for economic cooperation. Second, the gaps in the road systems should be identified and programs initiated to fill these gaps through coordinated transport policy involving the states concerned. There are many such gaps in the transport systems, but only a few obvious ones will be mentioned here.

In Central Africa, several trunk roads should be improved as a matter of urgency if trade among the countries is to be expanded. Among these roads is the Kisangani-Bangui-Fort Lamy road. This road is the vital link between Chad and Congo (Kinshasa), which are members of the Union of Central African States. A second road needing improvement is the Brazzaville-Pointe Noire-Yaoundé-Fort Lamy road, which connects the countries of UDEAC. This road is vital for the proper flow of trade among these countries under the taxe unique. As a long-term project, the Fort Lamy-Khartoum road would link Central Africa with the Sudan. Chad and Libya may wish to study the possibility of a road link between Fort Lamy and Tripoli through Abéché, Zouar, and Sebha. The Bujumbura-Tabora-Dar-es-Salaam road, if improved, could prove useful in Tanzania's trade with Rwanda and Burundi. It would also be an alternative to the rail outlet to the sea.

Table 7. 2

Development of Roads in African Countries by Surface Type
(kilometers)

	Year	Total, All Types of Roads	All-Weather (permanent) Roads	Improved Roads	Unimproved Roads
North Africa					
Algeria	1968	48,654	32,917	--	15,727*
Morocco	1968	51,787	18,029	5,221	28,537
Tunisia	1968	16,727	7,411	4,070	5,246
Libya	1968	5,900	3,999	401	1,500
U.A.R.	1964	48,762	9,656	11,265	27,841
Sudan	1966	10,560	310	1,750	8,499
West Africa					
Mauritania	1966	5,904	29	975	4,900
Mali	1966	12,081	1,070	6,431	4,580
Guinea	1968	28,420	520	7,900	20,000
Senegal	1968	6,326	2,044	2,177	2,105
Gambia	1965	1,175	208	311	656
Sierra Leone	1968	6,727	478	2,548	3,701
Liberia	1968	7,585	489	5,486	1,610
Ivory Coast	1966	33,314	983	12,060	20,271
Upper Volta	1966	16,701	64	5,967	10,673
Ghana	1968	33,264	3,943	11,941	17,380
Togo	1960	4,862	206	1,500	3,156
Dahomey	1960	6,160	594	2,986	2,580
Niger	1960	7,213	195	3,083	3,935
Nigeria	1968	88,924	15,250	64,100	9,574
Central Africa					
Cameroun	1966	32,990	870	5,728	26,392
Chad	1966	11,840	971	--	10,869
Central African Republic	1966	18,225	87	4,749	13,389
Gabon	1965	5,850	84	4,566	1,200
Congo (Brazzaville)	1966	10,842	237	--	10,605*
Congo (Kinshasa)	latest	139,000	--	--	--
Rwanda	1964	7,200	1,465*	--	5,735
Burundi	1965	5,232	1,210*	--	4,022
Equatorial Guinea	--	--	--	--	--
East and Southern Africa					
Somalia	1966	13,059	600	3,510	8,949
Ethiopia	1968	23,000	1,766	4,600	16,634
Uganda	1967	24,164	1,278	14,624	8,262
Kenya	1968	42,292	3,025	7,081	32,186
Tanzania	1968	34,534	1,453	14,873	18,208
Zambia	1967	33,519	1,588	4,631	27,300
Malawi	1968	10,531	492	--	10,039
Botswana	1967	7,784	--	--	--
Lesotho	1965	4,000	895*	--	3,105
Swaziland	1968	2,570	200	1,250	1,120
Madagascar	1966	40,000	2,000	7,000	31,000
Mauritius	1966	1,326	1,048	--	278*
Angola	1967	71,633	3,500	--	68,133
Mozambique	1968	37,525	--	--	--
Namibia	1967	33,517	--	--	--
Southern Rhodesia	1965	73,000	5,760	29,940	37,300
South Africa	1965	330,000	32,205	158,795	136,000

*Includes improved roads.

Source: ECA, A Survey of Economic Conditions in Africa, 1969, E/CN.14/480.

In East Africa, the Nairobi-Garissa-Mogadishu road is imperative if trade between Somalia and the East African Community is to be improved. This is especially pressing in light of Somalia's application to join the East African Community. Another equally important road link is the Nairobi-Moyale-Addis Ababa road. Ethiopia currently is interested in the common market aspect of the East African Community, and this road link would be vital for the success of such arrangements. The development of these two roads must constitute part of the negotiations for the entry of Ethiopia and Somalia into the East African Community. Elsewhere in the area, the Kampala-Nimule-Juba-Khartoum road would also open up trade possibilities between Sudan and the U.A.R. on the one hand and the East African Community on the other.

In West Africa there may not appear to be an immediate need for the construction of new roads, but the program for road development could consist in improving existing road links, especially in Mali, Upper Volta, and Niger, which are land-locked. In this respect, the Bamako-Conakry road should be developed as an addition to the Bamako-Abidjan outlet. If improved, this road would shorten the distance to the sea for goods from Mali and would perhaps reduce transport costs. Another possible outlet for Mali is the Bamako-Dakar road, which if developed could increase Mali's access to the sea. In Niger, there is need to develop the Niamey-Ouagadougou road as an outlet for Niger in addition to the Niamey-Port Harcourt road link. This should increase the load capacity for goods from Niger to the sea and improve the contacts among the Conseil d'Entente countries. Niger and Algeria also may wish to study the possibility of developing a first-class road link between Niamey and Algiers through Zinder and Agadex in Niger to Tamanrasset, In-Salah, and El-Goléa in Algeria. In Mauritania, the Nouakchott road north to Tindouf is the only trade route between the West African coastal countries and the Maghreb, and consideration should be given to the development of this road in order to increase the flow of goods between these two areas.

THE DEVELOPMENT OF RAILWAY
TRANSPORT IN AFRICA

In the past, the development of railways was not motivated by the need to increase contact among the African countries. One of the main reasons for building a railway was to lay claim to possession

of a particular territory; the railway systems in most countries south
of the Sahara were started in this way. It therefore follows that, since
economic matters were not the major considerations at this stage, the
railway did not serve to advance economic progress in Africa.

In West Africa, there was great rivalry between the French and
the British. The French out-maneuvered the British, and British possessions in West Africa were in isolated areas along the coast with the
rest of the region under French rule. In East Africa, the British met
opposition from the Portuguese and the Germans, but after World War
I the Germans lost their possessions to the British. As a result of
rivalry among colonial powers in the region, some railway lines were
built for strategic reasons and ran from the coast to the interior. The
British contended that their railway construction was motivated by a
desire to stop the slave trade in East Africa. However, others argue
that the prime purpose was to be able to move troops from the coastal
settlements to the interior so as to halt the advancement of the other
powers. Some historians believe that German rule was spreading
rapidly in East Africa and that if the Germans were not halted all
British possessions in East and Central Africa would have been in
serious danger.[2] Therefore, a railway line was built from Mombasa
to Kampala to halt the advancement of the Germans from Tanganyika,
although the British later claimed that this railway was built for trade
purposes. In Malawi too, the British extended the railway line from
Beira up to Salima to halt the advance of the Germans from the north.

When the craze for acquisition of possessions had died out, the
main consideration in building railway lines shifted from strategic to
trade reasons. With the discovery of valuable primary products in
Africa, especially minerals and other raw materials, the entire policy
for railway construction changed and lines were built to transport
these materials to the coastal ports from whence they were shipped to
Europe. These policies contributed to the lack of coordinated economic
development within each state, reduced the volume of trade among
the various states, and caused economic development to be concentrated
within a few miles of the rail lines. Trade among the various states
cannot be developed unless there are effective means of transport
and communication. To overcome this difficulty, interstate railway
development projects should be carried out with close collaboration
among the African states.

Existing and Potential Railway Systems in Africa

An important aspect of the railway systems in the different
African countries is the absence of connections among them. With the

exception of a few areas, such as the countries in East and Southern
Africa, most of railways run from the coast to somewhere near the
country's borders; because the African countries belonged to different
colonial powers, it was not found expedient to connect the railway
lines.

East and Southern Africa

In East and Southern Africa, railway lines are fairly well
connected because much of this area, excepting Ethiopia and Somalia,
was under British rule. In Ethiopia, one railway line runs from the
port of Djibouti to Addis Ababa. Somalia has no railway line. In
East Africa, a railway line runs from Mombasa in Kenya through
Nairobi to Kampala in Uganda. Another line runs from Mombasa
through Moshi to Dar-es-Salaam, from whence a line runs to Tabora.
From Tabora, one branch runs north to Mwanza on Lake Victoria
and another branch runs west to Kigoma on Lake Tanganyika. This
line serves as one of the main outlets for goods from Congo (Kinshasa),
Rwanda, and Burundi. Zambia has two main rail links to the sea. One
runs through Salisbury in Southern Rhodesia to Beira in Mozambique.
The second line runs through Lubumbashi to connect with the Benguela
railway line and on to the port of Lobito in Angola. The third line now
under construction will link Lusaka and Dar-es-Salaam through Kapiri
Mposhi, Tuduma, and Mbeya. Malawi has one main line running from
Salima on Lake Malawi to Beira. A second line currently under
construction will link Metangula on the eastern shore of Lake Malawi,
through Vila Cabral, with the port of Mozambique on the Indian Ocean.
Southern Rhodesia is linked by rail with Zambia, Malawi, Mozambique,
Botswana, and Southern Africa. A railway line in Botswana links
Gaberones with Buluwayo and Salisbury in the north; from Gaberones,
the line runs south through Mafeking to Pretoria and another line runs
to Cape Town in South Africa.

Central Africa

The Central African countries have the least developed railway
systems in Africa. In Congo (Kinshasa), one line runs from the port
of Matadi to Kinshasa. Another line runs from Port Francqui to
Lubumbashi and then on to the Copper Belt in Zambia. In Congo
(Brazzaville), one railway line runs from Pointe Noire to Brazzaville
and another runs from Pointe Noire through Dolisie to Moanda.
Cameroun has a short line running from Douala to Yaoundé. Future
railway lines are envisaged on the Yaoundé-Bangui and the Yaoundé-
Fort Archambault stretches. Chad may find it advisable in future to
consider linking Fort Lamy with Khartoum by rail; this would form the
second transcontinental railway, running from Lagos in Nigeria to the

Port Sudan harbor. There are also projects for a rail line to run from Libreville to Belinga in Gabon.

West Africa

All the countries in West Africa have railway lines running from the coast to the interior. In Nigeria, one line from Port Harcourt joins the line from Lagos at Kaduna from whence it runs through Kano to Nguru in northeast Nigeria. From Zaria, another line runs through Gazau to Kaura Namoda, and there are projects for extension of this line to Sokoto from whence a link with Niamey in Niger would be vital for Niger's trade. From Kafanchan, a railway line runs through Bauchi to Maiduguri near the border between Nigeria and Chad. There are projects for extending this line to Fort Lamy, which would be essential for the development of Chad. Dahomey, Togo, and Ghana each have a railway line intended to serve local transport requirements, and these lines are of limited use in enhancing intra-African trade.

In the Ivory Coast, a railway line runs from Abidjan through Bobo-Dioulasso to Ouagadogou and is an important outlet for goods from Upper Volta. There are plans for a railway line from Abidjan to Man on the western frontier of Ivory Coast and Liberia. In Liberia, a line runs from Buchanan to Sanniguellie near the border with Ivory Coast and there are proposals for a connection between Sanniguellie and Man to increase contacts between the two countries. In Guinea, a line runs from Conakry to Kankan. Future plans for railway development should consider the extension of this line to Bamako, which would give Mali a second railway outlet to the sea in addition to the Bamako-Kayes-Dakar line linking Senegal and Mali. In Mauritania, a railway line runs along the border with Spanish Sahara from Port-Etienne to Zouerate.

North Africa

In North Africa, the Maghreb countries have good railway connections. A railway line runs from Safi in Morocco through Rabat to Tangiers. Another line runs from Rabat through Oran and Algiers to Tunis. From Constantine in Algeria, another line runs south to Touggourt and El Oued, and from Tunis a line runs to Tozeur. Libya is not connected by rail with the other countries of the Maghreb or with the U.A.R. In the U.A.R., a railway line runs from Salum on the border with Libya through Alexandria to Cairo. From Cairo, a line runs east to Gaza. A second line from Cairo runs south along the River Nile to Aswan, where it is connected by a series of barges with Wadi Halfa in Sudan. With the development of stronger economic

links between Sudan and the U.A.R., consideration should be given to
the possibility of joining Aswan and Wadi Halfa by rail.

Sudan has developed a good railway network. From Khartoum,
one line runs north to Wadi Halfa and a second line runs through Halya
to Port Sudan on the Red Sea. Halya also is connected with Sennar
in Central Sudan. The Halya-Sennar line could be connected with
Tesenai in Ethiopia and then Massawa and could enhance trade and
other economic relations between Sudan and Ethiopia. From Khartoum,
another line runs south through Sennar to Er Roseires, and there are
projects for a connection from Er Roseires to Juba. Future plans
should be carried out jointly by Sudan and Uganda, which might consider
linking Juba with Kampala through Nimule in Uganda. From Sennar,
a railway line runs west to Babanusa, from whence one branch runs
south to Wau, and west through Ed Da'ein to Nyala, and there are plans
to extend the line to El Geneina.

Table 7.3 shows the development of railway freight between 1960
and 1967, which was encouraging In 1965, the North and East African
subregions taken together accounted for over 80 percent of total rail
freight carried by African railways. In the East African subregion
in 1960-67, there was an overall gain of 19 percent although there
were declines in freight in Mauritius and Malawi. There was a large
increase in freight movements in the East African Community, Rhodesia, and Zambia. In West Africa, there was a considerable decline
in the volume of rail freight between 1960 and 1967. This also was
true of some North African countries especially Algeria, where the
heavy reduction in freight traffic reflected the general economic
difficulties of the immediate post-independence years. The volume
of freight traffic in Africa as a whole increased from 57,609 to 81,359
million tons per kilometer between 1960 and 1967. Passenger traffic
on African railways increased in almost all countries during the period
1960-67.

Problems of Railway Development in Africa

The coordination of railway construction by the African countries
will present serious problems. Other factors in addition to the limitations inherited from the past will influence the development of development of railway systems in Africa. The intensity of these factors will
vary from country to country, but by and large the same problems
are found in almost all the African countries. Some of these problems
are briefly outlined below.

TABLE 7.3

Volume of Freight and Passenger Traffic Carried by
Railways in Africa, 1960 and 1967

Country	Total Number of Vehicles[a]	Freight Traffic (in million tons per kilometer)		Passenger Traffic (in millions of passenger per kilometer)	
		1960	1967	1960	1967
North Africa					
Algeria	11,654	1,728	915	626	715
Morocco	7,197	1,757	2,534	477	408
Tunisia	7,845	--	--	--	--
Libya	248	--	--	--	--
U.A.R.	21,080	2,096	3,068	3,634	6,268
Sudan	6,051	1,608	2,162	--	--
West Africa					
Mauritania	885	--	4,876	--	--
Mali	502	122	116	61	66
Senegal	1,085	140	188	197	249
Guinea	435	20[b]	21	63	50
Sierra Leone	1,003	25[b]	25[d]	89[b]	89[b]
Ivory Coast	882[c]	215	325	220	479
Ghana	3,614	357	282	276	404
Togo	545	8	11	79	71
Dahomey	492	46	75	71	67
Nigeria	6,725	1,931	1,613	698	388
Central Africa					
Cameroun	982	122	200	90	140
Congo (Brazzaville)	1,672	209	396	62	128
Congo (Kinshasa)	8,537	1,725	1,848	544	457
East and Southern Africa					
Ethiopia	1,345	180	175	65	81
Kenya					
Uganda	12,345	2,925	3,844	4,242	4,000
Tanzania					
Zambia	2,377	6,726[d]	5,500[d]	--	--
Southern Rhodesia	11,791	--	--	--	--
Malawi	523	116	176	48	45
Madagascar	994	131	179	136	171
Angola	3,700	1,625	2,164	99	151
Mozambique	6,381	2,020	3,000	199	240
South Africa	154,546	30,883	46,875	--	--
Total, all Africa	277,185	57,609	81,359	12,129[e]	15,078[e]

[a]Includes locomotives and freight and passenger cars.
[b]Estimates.
[c]Includes figures for Upper Volta.
[d]Includes Zambia and Southern Rhodesia.
[e]Total excludes South Africa.

Source: Economic Commission for Africa. A Survey of Economic Conditions in Africa, 1969
(E/CN.14/480/Rev. 1) 1971.

Geographical Factors

One great obstacle to the development of railway systems in Africa is the difference in the topography in the various countries. The differences in rock formation also present great difficulties in the construction of railway lines in certain countries and will be a major problem in the construction of interstate lines. This factor also has made railway construction projects very expensive in the past, and it will be necessary for the countries in a given integrated region to pool their financial resources. In most cases, the construction of rail lines from the coastal belt to the interior involves the consideration of altitudes that vary from sea level to as high as 8,000 feet above sea level. Although such a situation apparently would not present problems in the highly advanced countries, it certainly is a big problem for the underdeveloped countries of Africa.

Limitations in Volume of Trade

The low level of trade among the African countries has itself been responsible for the lack of interest shown thus far in the development of interstate and trans-African railway networks. It is interesting to note that there is only one trans-African rail line, which starts from Beira on the Mozambique coast, runs through Salisbury (Southern Rhodesia) and Lusaka (Zambia) to Lubumbashi in Congo (Kinshasa), and joins the Banguela rail line to Lobito on Angola's Atlantic coastline. A study of this line reveals that it was not a deliberate plan but merely resulted from the necessity of shipping some of the minerals from Katanga and the Copper Belt via Beira in order to ease the situation at Lobito. No other line in Africa runs from coast to coast, and interstate rail links are very few.

The Technical Aspects of the Rail Systems

The specifications in the development of the rail systems in Africa have built-in disadvantages because the fact that the rail lines in various states are constructed in different gauges present problems for interstate connections and trans-Africa systems. Table 7.4 shows that in Southern Africa including Zambia the rail systems are in 1.067-meter gauge while the East African countries and Ethiopia have 1.000-meter gauge. In West Africa, the former British territories have the 1.067-meter gauge while the majority of the former French colonies have 1.000-meter gauge. The North African countries have the wider 1.435-meter gauge. Even within the British possessions, gauges are slightly different in certain cases. Unless

TABLE 7.4

Railway Systems in Africa, 1967

Country	Total Length in Kilometers	Type of Gauge			
		1,435-Meter	1,067-Meter	1,000-Meter	Less than 1,000-Meter
North Africa					
Algeria	4,241*	3,757	--	3,377	107
Morocco	2,082	2,051	--	31	--
Tunisia	2,461	480	--	1,981	--
Libya	174	--	--	--	174
U.A.R.	5,110	4,510	--	253	347
Sudan	4,752	--	4,752	--	--
West Africa					
Mauritania	650	650	--	--	--
Mali	640	--	640	--	--
Guinea	808	--	--	808	--
Senegal	1,032	--	--	1,032	--
Sierra Leone	500	—	--	--	500
Liberia	344	344	--	--	--
Ivory Coast) Upper Volta)	1,173	--	--	1,173	--
Ghana	948	--	948	--	--
Togo	442	--	--	442	--
Dahomey	579	--	--	579	--
Nigeria	3,505	--	3,505	--	--
Central Africa					
Cameroun	534	--	--	534	--
Congo (Brazzaville)	800	--	800	--	--
Congo (Kinshasa)	5,358	--	3,924	--	1,100
East and Southern Africa					
Ethiopia) Kenya) Uganda) Tanzania)	5,894	--	--	5,894	--
Zambia	1,099	--	1,099	--	--
Malawi	507	--	507	--	--
Swaziland	220	--	220	--	--
Madagascar	864	--	--	864	--
Southern Rhodesia	3,255	--	3,255	--	--
Angola	2,778	--	2,531	--	247
Mozambique	2,221	--	2,221	--	--
South Africa	22,059	--	21,353	--	706
Total, all Africa	75,842	11,792	45,115	15,302	3,487

*Including 1.450-meter and 1.055-meter gauges.

Source: ECA, A Survey of Economic Conditions in Africa, 1969, E/CN.14/480.

244

standardization is introduced, interstate rail lines will be very expensive ways of promoting economic development through transport coordination. If trains must be changed at border stations, which would mean unloading and reloading, the operations will be long, cumbersome, and expensive, which would greatly effect the price of rail transport.

In recent years, there has been little railway building in Africa and statistical data relating to rail transport in Africa are inadequate and must be interpreted with great caution. However, the growth of both passenger and freight traffic between 1960 and 1967 in most African countries indicates the increasing role of railway transportation in the development of Africa. This in itself should provide the a priori case for coordination of the railway development policies of the African countries. An example of cooperation in the development of railway transport is the Zambia-Tanzania rail link, which is discussed below.

The Zambia-Tanzania Rail Link

One of the best examples of cooperation in development of railway transport in recent times is the construction of the Zambia-Tanzania rail link connecting Lusaka and Dar-es-Salaam. Its construction was inaugurated in October 1970 by the presidents of Zambia and Tanzánia. The rail line is to be built jointly by the two states, with Chinese aid. It will cover a total distance of some 1,859 kilometers using the 1.067-meter gauge. The haulage tonnage will be about 1,300 tons per train throughout the whole line, and the line's capacity is estimated at 3.5 million tons per year in each direction, or a total of 7 million tons.

The plans for the rail line were started as early as 1947 by what were then called Northern Rhodesia and Tanzania. In 1952, the preliminary engineering reports were completed by the East African Railways and Harbors Department and other agencies. These reports indicated that the project was both feasible and economically sound. The World Bank also made a survey, but its report rejected the proposal as economically unsound. Added impetus for making the final decision to build this rail line was given by Southern Rhodesia's unilateral declaration of independence and the subsequent difficulties that Zambia faced in its efforts to maintain its external links especially with regard to imports as a result of the blockade imposed by the Southern Rhodesian government.

In September 1967, the governments of Zambia, Tanzania, and China signed the first agreement, under which the Peoples Republic of China undertook to carry out detailed surveys for the design and construction of the line. These surveys were completed during the first half of 1970. Following the surveys, the Chinese government granted an interest-free loan of 2,865 million shillings ($409 million) to the governments of Zambia and Tanzania for the construction of the rail line. There will also be a school at Mpika in Zambia to train Zambian nationals to run the Zambian portion of the railway when it is completed. It is estimated that construction will be completed by 1976.

THE DEVELOPMENT OF MARITIME
TRANSPORT IN AFRICA

There are two main arguments for the development of maritime shipping in Africa. First, because freight rates contribute to the final prices of African exports and imports, the African countries must adopt measures to ensure that freight rates are reasonably low and competitive. Second, ships carry the bulk of African primary commodity exports and any measures for the improvement of maritime transport would greatly enhance the development of African exports to the developed countries. Even within the African continent, shipping is playing an increasingly important role in economic development. In recent years, the African countries have taken a greater interest in the development of their own shipping companies to facilitate their external trade.

Maritime Shipping

The development of maritime transport is extremely important to African countries because of the openness of their economies and the fact that a very high proportion of total trade is conducted with overseas countries by means of sea transport. The importance of maritime transport may be noted by the fact that from 1960 to 1968 the total volume of freight loaded and unloaded at African ports increased from 135.838 million metric tons to 388.237 million metric tons, an increase of over 185 percent. Table 7.5 shows that there was considerable increase in freight in Libya during this period, which was largely due to the increase in exports of petroleum in bulk. In Nigeria, freight decreased considerably in 1968 due to the civil war.

Much of the increase in world cargo shipping in recent years has consisted of commodities carried in bulk, which constitute an

TABLE 7.5

Maritime Freight Traffic (Total Goods Loaded and Unloaded
in Africa), 1960, 1965, and 1968
(thousands of metric tons)

Country	1960	1965	1968
North Africa			
Algeria	21,562	24,800	46,740
Morocco	12,806	14,556	16,284
Tunisia	5,239	7,583	8,076
Libya	911	60,135	127,872
U.A.R.	11,767	17,116	10,920
Sudan	1,618	2,346	2,522
West Africa			
Mauritania	51	6,148	7,749
Senegal	3,159	3,456	4,068
Guinea	2,099	2,015	1,410
Sierra Leone	2,313	3,178	3,733
Liberia	3,498	15,805*	19,590*
Ivory Coast	1,909	8,870	3,156
Ghana	3,989	5,207	4,579
Togo	134	986	1,722
Gambia	101	146	160*
Dahomey	305	322	445
Nigeria	6,343	19,395	5,004
Central Africa			
Cameroun	973	1,164	1,736
Congo (Brazzaville)	767	2,208	2,512
Equatorial Guinea	387	435	432*
Gabon	1,697	2,170	5,094
Congo (Kinshasa)	1,342	1,064	1,279
East and Southern Africa			
Ethiopia	478	745	1,129*
Somalia	351	574	500
Kenya	2,677	4,414	5,196
Tanzania	1,510	1,676	3,240
Madagascar	685	875	1,393
Mauritius	836	1,257	1,363
Angola	2,559	3,053	5,874
Mozambique	6,609	9,752	14,196
South Africa	12,838	21,754	21,327*
Total, all Africa	135,838	287,754	388,237

*Estimates.

Sources: United Nations, Statistical Yearbook, 1968; ECA, A Survey of
Economic Conditions in Africa, 1969, E/CN.14/480.

important element of African exports. The African share of total
world exports rose in volume terms from 5.9 percent in 1960 to 9.9
percent in 1965. This is partly due to the African countries' efforts
to increase exports of primary commodities following independence,
but it primarily results from the spectacular increase in petroleum
exports. The share of petroleum, by volume, of total African exports
rose to 62 percent in 1965.

In recent years, progress has been made in the development of
national shipping lines. In Morocco, a state company, with a gross
registered tonnage of 39,310, the Compagnie Marocaine de Navigation,
is one of the 13 companies registered in the·country. A good start has
been made in several other African countries. Ethiopia has 3 ships
with a gross registered tonnage of 32,000; the Sudan has 4 ships with
a gross registered tonnage of 20,000; the Malagasy Republic has 7
ships with a gross registered tonnage of 19,000; Tunisia has 8 ships
with a gross registered tonnage of 17,000; and Algeria has 4 ships
with a gross registered tonnage of 15,000.

As a means of ensuring more economical and efficient utilization
of maritime shipping facilities, it is essential that groups of African
countries should establish their own joint shipping lines which should
eventually be integrated where possible so as to achieve the advantages
of large-scale operations. The need for joint action in the development
of maritime transportation was recognized by the formation of a joint
shipping line among Kenya, Tanzania, Uganda, and Zambia near the
end of 1966. Apart from the advantages of lower freight rates, cooperative efforts also could deal with the problems of financing expansion
and training personnel that are currently among the main difficulties
confronting African shipping companies. Joint shipping lines would be
particularly important for the land-locked countries by reducing transportation charges for both import and export trade.

The need for owning a multinational shipping line has been sharply
felt in recent years by the countries in Eastern Africa. Between 1963
and 1966, freight rates on these routes increased from 15 to 30 percent.
More recently, the most significant freight rate changes effecting these
countries have been those resulting from the Arab-Israeli war and
the consequent closing of the Suez Canal. Since the East African
countries have no control over the fixing of these rates, they introduced
a surcharge of 15 percent on shipments between Europe and East
Africa that use the route around Africa which has raised the price
structures of these countries.

Inland Waterways

Africa does not have ample scope for the development of inland waterways on a very large scale. Except for the few lakes, mostly in East and Central Africa, the inland waters of Africa have very little potential for development of river transport systems due to the fact that almost all the big rivers, except the Niger and the Benue, have falls and rapids near their estuaries. This has made it impossible for ocean-going craft to go far into the interior. However, the Congo River is navigable in certain stretches and could be exploited jointly by Congo (Kinshasa) and Congo (Brazzaville). The Niger and the Benue have very great potential as inland waterways, and Nigeria already has made considerable progress in utilizing river transport to enhance economic development. Chad and Niger could greatly benefit from joint exploitation of the Niger/Benue river transport system with the Nigeria. The Senegal River also could be developed for inland waterways, and the Nile also has good potential for the Sudan and the U.A.R.

The other problem with regard to river transport is that in the past it was developed in direct competition with either roads or railways, which has tended to reduce the usefulness of river transport in projects of economic development. There is urgent need to coordinate both coastal and inland waterways with the roads and railways. But, as stated earlier, due to Africa's rugged terrain, which results in rivers forming cataracts, rapids, and falls toward their estuaries, Africa lacks sizable inland water transport. In any case, there are only a few important river systems in Africa--the Congo, the Niger, the Nile, the Senegal, and the Zambezi,--and except for limited stretches most of these rivers are useless for navigation.

Africa therefore, cannot, develop inland waterways on a large scale as a means of enhancing economic progress. It appears that greater reliance must be placed on the development of roads and railways. However, on the basis of available data, the following river transport systems could be considered to the general advantage of the states concerned:

1. On the Zambezi, river transport could be developed to serve Zambia, Rhodesia, Malawi, Mozambique, and possibly Botswana.

2. On the Nile, river transport that has been developed to serve Egypt and the Sudan and possibly could be expanded in the future to serve Ethiopia and Uganda.

3. On the Congo, a river transport system could be developed to serve Congo (Kinshasa), Congo (Brazzaville), Rwanda, Burundi, and possibly the Central African Republic.

4. The Niger River is already being developed to serve Nigeria, Dahomey, Niger, Upper Volta, Mali, Guinea, and Chad, but considerable work has yet to be undertaken to make the river an important link for trade among these countries.

5. On the Volta, transport could be developed to serve Ghana, Upper Volta, Dahomey, and Togo.

6. The Senegal is being developed by the countries of the OERS. Future plans should concentrate not only in transport development but also in joint irrigation and fisheries projects.

In addition to water transport, these rivers have very high potential for the development of hydroelectric projects that could increase power supply. They also could provide tremendous irrigation facilities.

The development of inland transport on a coordinated scale also can be envisaged among the countries that surround the lakes. For example, Lake Tanganyika forms a natural boundary for Zambia, Tanzania, and Congo (Kinshasa). It should be possible to develop a fairly large lake transport network among these three states. Lake Mweru forms a boundary for Zambia and Congo (Kinshasa) and in the future should provide transport facilities between the two countries. Further north, Lake Victoria forms a boundary for Kenya, Uganda, Rwanda, Burundi, and Tanzania. It should be possible to develop ferry services across the lake to link up with the road and railway systems. In fact, the lake was used to provide an outlet for copper from the Congo during colonial days.* Lake Malawi forms a boundary for Tanzania, Malawi, and Mozambique and could be developed to serve as links among these countries. (It was at one time considered feasible to use Lake Malawi to carry exports and imports from Zambia to the port of

---

*Recently, ECA has made intensive studies of the potential for the development of inland transport systems to serve a number of countries in the East African subregion. There are indications that the development of these lakes could greatly speed up the achievement of economic integration in the area.

Mozambique as a result of Rhodesia's unilateral declaration of independence.) Another use to which these lakes could be put is the
development of large-scale fishing industry. Rather than each country
trying to set up a small individual fishing industry, a larger one could
be developed, with one fish-canning factory situated at a convenient
jointly selected site to serve the group of countries surrounding each
of these lakes.

Ports and Harbors

Ports and harbors play a vital role in the economic development
of the African continent. The basic problem with ports in Africa is
that they are inadequate to meet trade growing as a result of the accelerated rate of economic development, and this problem is bound to be
more acute when the states are integrated. For instance, it is amazing
to note that much of East and Southern Africa depends upon a few large
ports: Djibouti, Mombasa, Dar-es-Salaam, Lourenço Marques, and
Beira. West and North Africa have good harbor facilities. The facilities offered at these ports, although excellent, are much too small.
The plan for economic integration will consist of joint development of
these ports in order to provide ample facilities for the land-locked
countries of Africa.

The development of ports is a vital key to the development of
the countries of the interior. The coastal countries no longer can
afford to ignore the transport problems of the land-locked countries
because on the development of the interior depends the survival and
the strength of African unity. Previously, the land-locked countries
had to pay high dock dues and wharfage, which had the effect of increasing prices of both imports and exports. The possibility of developing
new ports and harbors could be jointly explored by the integrated
states including the land-locked countries so as to increase the facilities for handling the larger traffic that would result from economic
integration, and the states would be well advised to look at this problem
with increasing interest. The countries with coastlines must learn to
recognize the problems of the land-locked countries.

Unlike other continents, Africa lacks good sites for ports and
harbors. In fact, apart from Lagos, Accra, Cape Town, Port Said,
and Dar-es-Salaam, most African parts are exposed to the sea, which
reduces their usefulness. Therefore, any plan for development of new
ports and harbors will be very costly. This calls for a united effort
among the African states so that these costs can be shared on an agreed
basis, thereby reducing the individual burden of each state. Whatever

the form of cooperation established in this respect, there is genuine
and urgent need to give the development of maritime shipping priority
in the plans for economic integration, especially if the land-locked
countries are to be assured of port facilities for the increasing imports
and exports that will result from economic integration.

THE DEVELOPMENT OF AIR TRANSPORT
IN AFRICA

There was rapid expansion in the development of air transport
over the 1960's. In 1960, only eleven countries in developing Africa
operated national airlines. In 1965, there were sixteen additional
national airlines bringing the total to twenty-seven, and by 1968 the
number had risen to thirty-four. Both domestic and national routes
have increased.

During colonial days, air transport was so little developed that
a person traveling from, for example, Abidjan to Lusaka first had to
fly to Paris and then to Rome, Cairo, Nairobi, (sometimes Salisbury),
and Lusaka. Similarly, a person traveling to Algeria from Madagascar,
had to go via Paris. The problem of integration of airlines is difficult
due to the fact that some African airlines are operated almost entirely
by private enterprise and were developed independently. This has
resulted in competition which greatly reduces the airlines' usefulness in advancing economic development.

The development of air traffic, both passenger and cargo, also
has been remarkable. As indicated in Table 7.6, total passenger
traffic grew from 4,771 to 6,627.4 million passenger kilometers
between 1965 and 1968, and the average annual rate of growth was
14.8 percent. The annual rate of growth in freight traffic was 19.7
percent. Developing Africa accounted for only 1.6 percent of the total
passenger traffic carried in the world in 1968, which emphasizes the
need for greater efforts in the development of air transport.

The growth in air traffic was most rapid in East and Southern
Africa between 1965 and 1968; passenger traffic grew by 15.6 percent
while cargo increased by more than 26 percent. In Central Africa,
total air traffic grew by some 12 percent. There were somewhat
modest rates of growth in West and North Africa, 6 percent and 9
percent respectively. East African Airways contributed to over half
of the total air traffic in East and Southern Africa in 1968. South
African Airways also has developed very rapidly in recent years.

TABLE 7. 6

Development of Air Traffic
in Africa, 1965 and 1968

Country	Passengers (million passengers per kilometer)		Cargo and mail (million tons per kilometer)		Total Weight, Including Passengers (million tons per kilometer)	
	1965	1968	1965	1968	1965	1968
North Africa						
Algeria	236.3	317.9	2.6	3.2	21.5	31.4
Morocco	213.3	335.4	4.5	4.2	24.4	34.5
Tunisia	110.3	179.1	1.6	2.0	11.3	17.7
Libya	30.5	183.8	0.5	1.4	3.1	17.2
U.A.R.	594.0	580.9	7.0	8.0	61.6	61.6
Sudan	110.9	99.6	2.3	2.2	12.3	10.6
West Africa						
Mauritania	61.2	64.5	3.1	5.0	8.5	10.7
Mali	48.3	37.5	2.0	3.1	6.9	6.4
Senegal	54.4	61.8	3.1	5.0	7.9	10.5
Sierra Leone	25.9	24.1	0.2	0.8	2.9	2.9
Liberia	2.4	5.8	0.0	0.0	0.2	0.5
Guinea	9.1	14.0	0.1	0.1	0.8	1.3
Ivory Coast	51.8	61.0	3.1	5.1	7.8	10.5
Upper Volta	48.8	55.7	3.1	5.0	7.4	9.9
Togo	0.5	55.9	0.0	5.0	0.0	10.0
Dahomey	48.8	55.7	3.0	5.0	7.4	9.9
Ghana	149.7	126.3	4.6	6.7	17.7	16.5
Niger	48.8	61.9	3.0	5.0	7.4	10.5
Nigeria	202.7	132.8	5.8	5.4	24.1	17.4
Central Africa						
Cameroun	78.5	76.1	3.2	5.2	10.3	10.9
Chad	48.8	64.3	3.0	5.4	7.4	11.2
Central African Republic	48.8	57.0	3.0	5.0	7.4	10.1
Gabon	59.7	75.4	3.2	5.1	8.5	11.9
Congo (Brazzaville)	62.1	62.5	3.2	5.1	8.8	10.7
Congo (Kinshasa)	282.0	455.4	11.6	14.7	37.3	55.5
East and Southern Africa						
Ethiopia	233.2	303.4	9.6	18.1	30.4	45.2
Somalia	6.5	8.4	0.1	0.1	0.7	0.8
Kenya	117.4	235.8	3.2	8.9	13.3	29.1
Uganda	117.4	235.8	3.2	8.9	13.3	29.1
Tanzania	117.4	235.8	3.2	8.9	13.3	29.1
Zambia	71.3	74.6	0.9	0.9	6.9	7.6
Malawi	15.8	13.4	0.2	0.4	1.5	2.4
Madagascar	145.1	208.4	5.8	7.4	18.3	25.6
Southern Rhodesia	71.3	66.0	0.9	0.9	6.9	6.3
South Africa	1,159.8	1,858.5	34.9	47.4	137.0	208.6
Total, all Africa	4,771.0	6,627.4	142.0	218.4	565.0	802.4

Source: International Civil Aviation Organization (ICAO), Digest of Statistiques, No. 135, 1960-1967, and Addenda and Corrigenda No. 3, (February 1969).

Some Examples of Cooperation in Air Transport

There is increasing recognition in African countries of the fact that the development of adequate means of transport and communications is of vital importance to the success of economic cooperation in Africa. But, due to political and other factors, efforts toward coordination of air transport have achieved only modest results and few groups of African countries have attempted to combine their efforts in this field. Some examples of cooperation are examined below.

The Association of African Airlines

The Association of African Airlines (AAFRA) was established by Ghana Airways, United Arab Airlines, East African Airways, Tunis-Air, Zambia Airways, Ethiopian Airlines, Air Maroc and Air Afrique. AAFRA's aims are to encourage air traffic in Africa; to study means of speeding up the development of air transport on the African continent; to improve airport facilities; and to provide regular and economic passenger transport. AAFRA has set up an executive committee to study the ways of achieving these objectives.

The African Civil Aviation Commission

The African Civil Aviation Commission (AFCAC) was established at a meeting held in Addis Ababa in January 1969.* The AFCAC Constitution came into force provisionally on January 17, 1969, pending ratification by at least twenty of the states represented at the meeting. The objectives laid down in the AFCAC Constitution are: (1) to provide civil aviation authorities in the member states with a framework for discussing and planning all the required measures of coordination and cooperation in all matters relating to civil aviation activities and (2) to promote coordination, better utilization, and orderly development of African air transport systems. AFCAC will establish a secretariat for organizing studies and meetings and

---

*The following independent states were represented: Algeria, Burundi, Cameroun, Congo (Kinshasa), Ethiopia, Gabon, Ivory Coast, Kenya, Liberia, Libya, Malawi, Mauritania, Morocco, Niger, Nigeria, Congo (Brazzaville), Rwanda, Senegal, Sierra Leone, Sudan, Swaziland, Togo, Tunisia, United Arab Republic, Tanzania, Upper Volta, Zambia, Chad, Malagasy Republic, and Uganda.

maintaining records. In the initial stages, the secretariat facilities and studies for AFCAC will be provided by the International
Civil Aviation Organization.

Air Afrique

Air Afrique has twelve members; Cameroun, Central African
Republic, Chad, Congo (Brazzaville), Dahomey, Gabon, Ivory Coast,
Mauritania, Niger, Senegal, Togo, and Upper Volta. Cameroun withdrew
her membership in 1971. Air Afrique was established in 1961 to operate
a joint regional air service for all its members except the Malagasy
Republic. Each of the original eleven participating ex-French African
states contributed 6 percent of the capital, a total of 66 percent. The
remainder of the equity capital, 34 percent, is held by the French
airline Union des Transports Aériens (UTA). Air Afrique provides
service within West and Equatorial Africa as well as to Europe. Since
1964, Air Afrique has also leased blocks of space for its passengers
on Pan American flights between New York and Douala. Air Afrique
presently serves 23 countries and has its headquarters in Abidjan,
Ivory Coast.

Problems of Air Transport

One of the main problems facing the African national airlines
is that of providing larger and more modern aircraft to meet competitive standards; plans to deal with this problem are currently being
implemented. On the other hand, solutions have not yet been found for
the problem of providing adequate and satisfactory service among the
African states. The increase in the number of African national airlines
naturally will increase competition on international routes, and this
problem is already being felt in Africa. Therefore, further expansion
of air transport must be viewed within the framework for multinational
economic cooperation.

In the scheme of integration, it may be necessary for national
governments to have effective control of the airways and if necessary
to enforce coordination of the airlines on a subregional basis.
Government controlled corporations are an answer to the problems
related to future expansion of air transportation. For example, in the
East African subregion integration in the early stages will consist in
coordination of the services currently offered by the Zambia Airways,
East African Airways, Ethiopian Airlines, and other smaller airlines
to make their services complementary rather than competitive.

Such coordination need not jeopardize the existing operations of any airline. Similar approaches should be used in Central, West, and North Africa.

In the long run, the plan for integration of air transport should seek to provide direct flights connecting the East, North, Central, and West African capitals. The absurdity of having to pass through Paris to go from North Africa to West Africa should not be left uncorrected for a long time, even in the absence of economic integration. In this respect, priority should be given to the development of air links between the British and French African states. Most large cities have or are developing excellent international airports with modern facilities, and this will go a long way to enhance the development of air transport.

Air transport is becoming an increasingly important factor of African economic development. Compared to road and rail, the initial capital outlays for establishing an air transport network are relatively low, and the greater flexibility inherent in an air network makes possible access to areas that could be reached by surface transport only at great cost. If well coordinated, air transport can contribute effectively to the integration of national and multinational markets. Thus, raising the level of development of air transport would reduce transportation costs and enhance economic development. These factors strengthen the case for cooperation in the development of air transport in Africa.

THE DEVELOPMENT OF PIPELINES

The development of pipelines is a form of transportation that is becoming increasingly useful in both the developing and the developed countries. In Africa, pipelines are used largely for transporting crude petroleum, such petroleum products as refined oil, and natural gas; therefore, they are a specialized form of transportation. The difficulty in the development of rail and road transport in Africa caused by geographical and climate factors makes pipelines particularly suitable in countries where the distance from the ports is great and the risk involved in transportation of oil is more hazardous. In 1966, the longest pipeline networks were in Algeria and Libya (see Table 7. 7).

In East Africa, the pipeline constructed between Dar-es-Salaam and the Copper Belt area in Zambia considerably eased the petroleum situation in Zambia caused by the unilateral declaration of independence in Southern Rhodesia. A pipeline from Beira in Mozambique to Umtali in Rhodesia was forced to close as a consequence of the sanction

TABLE 7.7

Development of Pipelines in Africa, 1966
(kilometers)

Country	Crude Petroleum	Petroleum Products	Natural Gas	Gathering	Total
North Africa					
Algeria	2,205	295	505	850	3,855
Morocco	120	--	13	--	--
Tunisia	545	--	--	--	133
Libya	2,018	--	--	142	2,160
U.A.R.	--	508	--	--	508
West Africa					
Nigeria	362	--	50	50	462
Central Africa					
Gabon	70	--	--	70	140
Congo (Kinshasa)	--	709	--	--	709
East and Southern Africa					
Tanzania	(1,000	--	--	--	1,000
Zambia	(	--	--	--	
Angola	110	--	--	--	110
Mozambique	300	--	--	--	300
Southern Rhodesia	--	--	--	--	--
South Africa	410	750	--	--	1,160
Total, all Africa	7,140	2,262	568	1,112	11,082

Source: ECA, A Survey of Economic Conditions in Africa, 1967, E/CN.14/409/Rev.1.

257

imposed on Southern Rhodesia. It is believed that plans for a pipeline connecting Mombasa and Lake Victoria are under consideration. The UNDP has undertaken to finance a feasibility study of a proposal to construct a pipeline under the Mediterranean from Algeria to Europe.

Pipelines would provide ample opportunity for cooperation by several countries because many pipelines cross national boundaries. For example, the oil pipeline between the Copper Belt and Dar-es-Salaam was developed through cooperation by Zambia and Tanzania. There should be new efforts to investigate the feasibility of joint development of pipelines, especially between the coastal and land-locked countries.

THE ROLE OF COMMUNICATIONS
IN ECONOMIC DEVELOPMENT

The availability of adequate means of communication between nations is an important feature of economic development. The ability to transmit information quickly and accurately encourages efficiency in modern enterprises and government administration. Therefore, the role of communications in any plan for economic cooperation acquires special significance. The present difficulties in economic cooperation arise largely out of lack of knowledge in most African countries of economic policies, social behavior patterns, and consumption habits and consumer preferences in the other African countries.

In the past, the internal communication systems in some states were fairly developed but the inter-African communication systems are far from adequate. The problem is that during the colonial era links were maintained between the colonial territories and the metropolitan powers but there were inadequate interterritorial communications. At one time, the pattern of communications was such that to send a telegram or telephone message from one African state to a neighboring state it was necessary to call through London, Paris or Brussels. This bottleneck in the development of communications was quickly realized by some African countries, and in recent years a number of African states including Ghana, Kenya, Tanzania, Zambia, Ethiopia, and the Maghreb countries have decided to open up new telephone and telex links with their neighbors.

Adequate statistical material is not available to indicate the extent of growth of communication facilities in Africa. However, from the scanty data available, there is indication that in 1966 there were 2.5 million telephones in Africa, with an average of 100 persons

per telephone; this represented less than 2 percent of the telephones
in operation in the world. The distribution of telephones is concentrated
in a few countries. Five countries--the U.A.R., Algeria, Morocco,
Southern Rhodesia, and South Africa--accounted for nearly 75 percent
of the total telephones in use in Africa in 1966. Data on postal services
indicate that the number of post offices in developing Africa increased
by some 74 percent between 1961 and 1965.[3]

Development in other fields of communications also was significant.
Between 1964 and 1966, the total number of radio transmitters in
Africa grew from 390 to 446, an increase of about 14 percent. The
number of television transmitters grew from 99 to 134 over the same
period, an increase of nearly 34 percent. In 1966, there were over
1.1 million television sets in Africa; of these, the East and Southern
African countries accounted for nearly 54 percent and North Africa
accounted for about 36 percent. The substantial increase in the number
of radio and television transmitters installed in the African countries
in recent years demonstrates the increased importance attached to
the development of adequate communications facilities to serve economic
development.

There is also a growing interest in the establishment of links
with countries outside Africa. For example, at the meeting of the
International Telecommunications Union Regional Plan Committee for
Africa in Addis Ababa in 1967, several African countries--U.A.R.
Sudan, Ethiopia, Zambia, Congo (Kinshasa), Nigeria, Cameroun, Ivory
Coast, Senegal, Morocco, and Tunisia--expressed interest in the
establishment of earth satellite tracking stations that could be used as
means of communications. There are suggestions that the INTELSAT
II C relay satellite that was launched in the United States in March
1967 and is rotating along the orbit passing through the equator could
provide communications for all of Africa, the Middle East, some
parts of Europe, South America, and the eastern part of North America.
In recent years, Kenya has actively considered plans for a satellite
receiving station. Possibilities for the development of these earth
satellite stations on a multinational basis should be explored.

The problem of communications in economic integration will
consist in developing new links connecting the capitals of the states
in the integrated area. This is of utmost importance and will go a
long way to enhance better understanding among the African people.
Here too, the problem is common concern because an individual state
can achieve little without the cooperation of the other states.

What could be done in order to integrate the interstate links within a given area is, through mutual agreement, to choose a center where large telex, telegram, radio, and telephone systems could be installed. All the states within the subregion should be connected through the center for all outside communications. This project should be run jointly by all the states within the subregion. The advantages of this plan include not only improved communication systems within the area and with the outside world but also increased employment opportunities. This plan would reduce the cost of establishing the communications network by using large scale and would also greatly reduce the number of hours required to place a phone call to the major cities of the world. It also would reduce the operations costs and charges for trunk calls.

PROSPECTS FOR COOPERATION IN DEVELOPMENT OF TRANSPORT

The magnitude of the problems of transport and communications development outlined in the preceding sections leave no room for doubt as to the urgent need for the adoption of concrete steps for the development of transport and communications on a joint basis. Although priorities in investments differ from country to country, there should be adequate provision for development of the transport sector in national development plans. Indeed, the problems of the development of industry, agriculture, and intra-African trade would be eased through increased ability of the African countries to move goods and services efficiently across national boundaries. The question of the enlargement of the national market presupposes the development of adequate means of transport and communications joining the various African states.

The African countries have found it difficult to raise loans to finance transport development projects. The construction of roads and railways generally is regarded as part of the development of social infrastructure and therefore private capital has tended to shy away from such projects. This implies that the burden of providing adequate means of transport and communications lies with the governments. This factor makes it imperative for the African states to come together to plan the development of roads and railways to connect them. Even if one individual state had access to adequate funds to develop its internal transport system, this would be of little use to development of intra-African trade without the corresponding development of transport in the adjoining states.

The coordination of transport systems is of vital importance and will have to be carried out on a subregional or multinational basis.

Countries with common boundaries within an integrated area could work jointly on transport projects to establish sound subregional networks. Subsequently, an all-African survey should be conducted to determine where transcontinental roads, railways, and waterways could be developed. Coordinated research studies should be undertaken to assess the feasibility of such transcontinental links. Another logical step toward transport coordination in Africa would be the unification of maritime, road, railway, and air traffic legislation and the standardization of fares and freight charges, taking into account not only the needs of the individual states but also the subregional and all-Africa requirements. Even before such plans are put into effect, the African countries might wish to cooperate in establishing railway training schools. Studies also should be undertaken on the problem of achieving the required technical standardization among the different rail gauges.

It is clear that there is room for coordination of transport development in Africa. For example, land-locked countries--such as Zambia, Uganda, Southern Rhodesia, Malawi, Botswana, Lesotho, and Swaziland in East and Southern Africa; Rwanda, Burundi, Central African Republic, and Chad in Central Africa; and Niger, Upper Volta, and Mali in West Africa--would benefit considerably from any plans for transport coordination involving adjoining states that have a coastline and ports. This has ceased to be a novel idea and is a very serious consideration on which much of the future economic progress of the land-locked states will depend. These countries should be assured of adequate port and harbor facilities as well as transit rights within the coastal countries. Such facilities often are more easily negotiated where countries have similar economic objectives. Such plans would be very advantageous for the states with coastlines because of the increased revenues that they would derive from such development.

The present networks of transport and communications greatly hinder the development of intra-African trade and thus severely limit the development of industry and the widening of domestic markets. In the past, the transport systems have resulted in distortion of the price and cost structure not only between coastal and interior countries but also between primary commodities and manufactured goods. The price differential between two points in Africa often is great. Because imported manufactures often are lighter than raw materials the past transport pattern resulted in higher transport charges for exports than for imports. The result has been that African industries have lagged behind those of the advanced countries and even those of other developing regions.

Therefore, the coordination of transport and communications in

Africa offers another field in which economic cooperation can be fostered. Areas of common interest should be sought in order to harmonize transport policies governing the development of road, rail, water, and air transport on an integrated basis. It was noted earlier that in the past the construction of roads and railways in Africa was either export-oriented or for strategic reasons and not primarily for the purpose of economic development. Now that the aim of the African states is to increase the rate of economic development, greater cooperation in matters of transport is of vital importance. Furthermore, the need for closer relationship among the African states especially in the field of trade and development and the importance of consultation on matters of common interest underline the urgency of integrating the transport and communications systems. By integrating the transport systems into multinational networks based on uniform policies and rates, great strides can be achieved not only in the transport field but also in the economic, political, and social advancement of the African countries.

NOTES

1. Lord Hailey, An African Survey (Oxford: Oxford University Press, 1967), p. 1537.

2. Ibid., pp. 1556-73.

3. Economic Commission for Africa, A Survey of Economic Conditions in Africa, 1967, E/CN.14/409/Rev. 1.

PART

III

ONE DECADE
OF
MULTINATIONAL
COOPERATION
IN AFRICA

8

**A REVIEW
OF THE MAJOR
MULTISECTORAL
ECONOMIC GROUPINGS
IN AFRICA**

THE DRIVE TOWARD ECONOMIC COOPERATION

The turning point in the economic cooperation efforts of the African countries occurred around 1960 when a number of African countries gained their independence. The main spur to cooperation has been the realization that, based on its individual national market alone, a single African country's efforts to develop would not overcome the problems of poverty, ignorance, and disease. Individual resource endowment is too limited to permit the application of technology on a wide range of industrial activities. As a result, groups of African countries found it advisable at the time of independence to continue the economic links created during the colonial period or to create new ones. Thus, most of the economic groupings now found in Africa are based on the economic links and institutions developed in the past. Membership in these groupings is limited to countries that were administered by the same colonial power.

Multinational economic cooperation in Africa has taken many forms and the African countries have made numerous attempts to form economic groupings, although few of these groupings can really be described as successful. The main objective of African economic groupings has been to achieve balanced economic development not only in the individual states but also in the multinational grouping as a whole. During the 1960's, the African states showed their willingness to coordinate their efforts toward accelerating the rate of economic development in Africa within the framework for multinational cooperation discussed in Chapters 1 and 2.

Three major factors have been responsible for the emergence of these economic groupings: (1) the African countries see economic cooperation as a means of consolidating their political independence and thereby strengthening their overall position vis-à-vis that of the developed countries, especially the former metropolitan powers; (2) economic cooperation is regarded as the means for preserving the economic and other links that existed during the colonial period; and (3) economic cooperation is regarded as the means for solving the problems of economic development on the African continent. The interplay of these three forces has resulted in the creation of economic associations unique to the African region. Although most of these associations are largely politically oriented, they also adopt economic cooperation (or integration) as a major objective. A central feature common to most of the existing economic groupings in Africa is that the establishment of a common market is regarded as a primary policy objective under economic cooperation.

The attainment of political unity in Africa has been one of the objectives of some African states, but in the immediate or foreseeable future the attainment of such unity presents formidable problems. The differences in political background, level of development, and social and cultural outlook mean that a new formula or a common denominator for unity must be found. In other words, the problem was not that of reaching agreement as to the need for unity but that of finding methods for achieving it. It was soon discovered that economic development through cooperation was a positive method of consolidating the sovereignty of the independent African states. Therefore toward the close of the 1950's, the African states became aware of the urgent need to foster economic cooperation among themselves and actively took measures toward achieving it.

COOPERATION IN EAST AND SOUTHERN AFRICA*

The history of economic cooperation in East and Southern Africa dates back to the early twentieth century. There are currently two main economic groupings in this area: (1) the East African Community, made up of Uganda, Kenya, and Tanzania, and (2) what is generally called the Southern African Customs Union, made up of South Africa, Botswana, Lesotho, and Swaziland. Some smaller economic associations

---

*For the purposes of this text, East and Southern Africa includes Kenya, Uganda, Tanzania, Ethiopia, Somalia, Zambia, Malawi, Southern Rhodesia, Mozambique, Angola, Namibia, Botswana, Lesotho, Swaziland, South Africa, Madagascar, Mauritius, and Reunion.

also exist in the area, and these will be briefly examined.

The East African Community

The origins of the East African Community (whose members are Kenya, Uganda, and Tanzania) were discussed in Chapter 1. The evolution of the common market arrangements among the three countries was not governed by any specific agreement giving rise to legal obligations but grew up over time. Industrial development was left to be governed by market forces and investment opportunity. As a result, some economic imbalance developed, not only in trade but also in the rate of industrialization. Kenya derived considerable economic advantages from association at the expense of the other two countries.

The attainment of independence by the East African countries changed the concept of economic cooperation in East Africa. The new political institutions that emerged necessitated a reexamination of the basis for the economic relations among the three countries. Therefore, as soon as Tanzania gained its independence, an attempt was made to transform the existing system of interterritorial cooperation in a formal federation.

By 1964, it had become obvious that a conscious and balanced program was essential in order to redistribute the benefits of cooperation more equitably. Some difficulties had developed in the periodic negotiations, and although the three governments had a long-standing tradition of cooperation, the institutional arrangements among them constituted a barrier to the continuation of economic cooperation and joint development. Due to political differences, the attempt toward federation did not succeed, but in April 1964 the governments signed the Kampala Agreement, which was designed to redress the imbalance of trade and industrial development among the three countries.

The main principles of the Kampala Agreement were as follows: (1) immediate action within certain interterritorially connected firms to increase production in Tanzania and Uganda which were served by Kenyan industries; (2) agreement as to the immediate allocation of certain major industries; (3) the application of a system of quotas and suspended quotas whereby exports from surplus countries would be progressively reduced and local production increased in the deficit countries; (4) increased sales from a country in deficit to a country in surplus; and (5) an early agreement in the East African Common Market on a system of inducements and allocations of industry in order to secure the equitable distribution of industrial development among the three countries.[1]

In order to effect the required balance in the allocation of industries, the three countries agreed to institute the following measures: (1) Tanzania was given exclusive right to manufacture and assemble landrovers, but no country was given a monopoly for the manufacture and assembly of trucks; (2) Tanzania was given exclusive rights in radio assembly and manufacture, but reasonable arrangements were to be made to safeguard the interest of existing assembly firms, provided that they purchased from Tanzania those parts manufactured in Tanzania; (3) Tanzania also had exclusive rights in the manufacture of motor vehicle tires and tubes; (4) Uganda was given sole rights in the manufacture of bicycles, and assembly firms were obligated to buy from Uganda those parts that were manufactured in Uganda; (5) Uganda also was given exclusive rights for the manufacture of nitrogenous fertilizers; (6) Kenya was given exclusive rights in the manufacture of electric light bulbs and could apply for scheduling of neon and fluorescent tubes if necessary.

The Kampala Agreement, carefully thought out as it might have been, however, failed to solve the problem of balancing industrial development due to three major problems. The first major problem was the lack of concrete agreement with regard to industrialization programs, largely because the list of industries enumerated in the preceding paragraph proved to be vital interest to all three countries and because the absence of any effective machinery for coordination of development planning in effect meant that each country was at liberty to institute any project without necessarily consulting the other partners. The absence of an effective supranational institution to ensure that the agreements were carried out was another obstacle. These difficulties and the absence of effective institutional reorganization within each of the partner states to accommodate economic cooperation rendered the Kampala Agreement ineffective as an instrument for strengthening economic ties among the East African countries.

The second major problem in the implementation of the Kampala Agreement was that the allocation of major industries among the members of the East African Common Market covered such industries as vehicle assembly and manufacture, bicycle manufacture, electric light bulbs manufacture, radio assembly and manufacture, nitrogeneous fertilizer production, and vehicle tires and tube production. These industries were not at that time in the process of being established in the countries to which they were allocated. It therefore followed that this part of the agreement could contribute neither to a reduction in trade imbalance among the three countries nor to a more equitable sharing of such benefits of industrialization and as growth of national income and level of employment.

The third major problem was the absence of joint planning

machinery to harmonize the development policies of the three countries. The growing importance of individual national development planning in the East African countries resulted in the formulation of plans on the basis of national interests and aspirations without joint consultations. Consequently, each country could develop a large area of economic interest outside the framework of the agreement. This in itself was a factor that diminished the importance of the East African Common Market. For these reasons, it was found expedient to establish a new basis for economic cooperation, and the negotiations toward this objective ultimately resulted in the creation of the East African Community.

The present Treaty for East African Cooperation was signed in June 1967 by Uganda, Tanzania, and Kenya and came into operation in December 1967. Although the East African Community may be regarded as an attempt to preserve through treaty obligations the old de facto common market arrangements, it differs fundamentally in that it established for the first time a legal framework for cooperation in all fields of development. The new treaty goes beyond preserving the old common market arrangements by providing for possible coordination of industrial development and general development policies.

The Objectives of the East African Community

The aim of the treaty is "to strengthen and regulate the industrial, commercial and other relations of the partner States to the end that there shall be accelerated harmonious and balanced development and sustained expansion of economic activities the benefits of which shall be equitably distributed."[2] The countries also agreed to ensure: (1) the establishment and maintenance, subject to certain exceptions, of a common customs tariff and a common excise tariff; (2) the abolition, generally, of restrictions on trade between partner states; (3) the inauguration, in the long term, of a common agricultural policy; (4) the establishment of an East African Development Bank in accordance with the charter contained in Annex VI of the treaty; (5) the retention of freedom of current account payments between partner states and of freedom of capital account payments necessary to further the aims of the East African Community; (6) the harmonization required for the proper functioning of the common market and the monetary policies of the partner states and, in particular, consultations in case of a disequilibrium in the balance of payments of any partner state; (7) the operation of services common to the partner states; (8) the coordination of economic planning; (9) the coordination of transport policy; (10) the approximation of commercial laws of the partner states; and (11) such other activities calculated to further the aims of the East African Community as the partner states may from time to time decide to undertake in common.

The renovations introduced in the new treaty distinguished it from the earlier arrangements for cooperation in East Africa. For the purposes of this text, only a few of these features will be discussed in detail--the transfer tax, the East African Development Bank, and decentralization of the headquarters of the various institutions, and the question of new members in the East African Community.

Common Market Arrangements

In order to give effect to the common market arrangements, the three countries agreed that there would be no internal tariff or customs duty on the goods originating in any state that are transferred to another member state. (The free trade arrangements exclude certain agricultural goods as listed in Annex III to the treaty.) The goods granted duty-free treatment must be wholly produced within the partner states or, if imported raw materials are used in the production of such goods, the value of such materials should not exceed 70 percent of the ex-factory value of the finished goods. The countries also agreed to remove all quotas and quantitative restrictions on goods originating within the member states. However, there is, restricted movement of arms and ammunition; gold, silver, precious and semiprecious stones; and such goods as may endanger public health and security.

The treaty contains an escape clause providing that a country in balance of payments difficulties may, taking into account its overall economic position, impose such restrictions as may be necessary to overcome the balance of payments problems. However, these would, be regarded as temporary measures.

As regards trade relationships with third countries, the East African Community established and maintains a common excise tariff in respect of excisable goods manufactured, processed, or produced outside the partner states. In principle, this provision may be exempted in special cases, such as when a country wishes to collect additional revenue, provided that the country has prior consultations with the other partner states.

Money and Currency

From 1919 to 1966, the three East African countries had a common currency administered by the East African Currency Board. This arrangement was similar to the West African and the Central African Currency Boards developed under British administration. The East African Currency Board was responsible for issue of notes and coins and for maintaining the joint reserves of the three countries.

Local currency was required to be backed by 100 percent reserves held in sterling securities. However, in practice the Currency Board had some degree of autonomy in financial matters, permitting the necessary flexibility in monetary policies. In 1960, it became necessary to increase the degree of flexibility especially in dealing with deficit financing problems of the constituent governments, and as a result powers for a fiduciary issue were granted to the Currency Board.

With the coming of independence, there was an obvious need for the countries to have direct access to financial resources for purposes of economic development. Thus, although the need for monetary cooperation still was felt by the three states, it was agreed that each country would have the right to establish its own central bank with independent powers of issue. In 1966, the common currency that had existed for 47 years was replaced by national currencies. Under the new monetary arrangements in East Africa, currencies of the three countries are to be exchanged at par value, i.e., without exchange commission, but in case of money transfers between states the respective central banks have discretion to impose such charges as may be necessary to cover the cost of such transfers.

Other arrangements in the monetary field include provisions for freedom of movement of capital and other financial resources. In order to ensure equilibrium in the overall balances of payments of the member states, they are to endeavor to harmonize their monetary policies to facilitate the smooth working of the common market arrangements. In order to achieve effective harmonization, it is provided that the governors of the three central banks shall meet at least four times each year for consultation and review of their monetary and balance of payments policies.

The Transfer Tax

An innovation in the Treaty for East African Cooperation is the introduction of the transfer tax, which is regarded as a measure for the promotion of new industries in those partner states that are less developed industrially so as to restore industrial balance among the member countries. Article 20 of the treaty defines a transfer tax as a charge imposed by one partner state upon manufactured goods transferred from another partner state where the state imposing such tax produces such goods in a certain quantity or value. A country that has a deficit in total trade in manufactured goods with the other partner states may impose taxes upon transfer of goods originating within the other partner countries. The tax may be imposed on the manufactured goods with a value not exceeding the amount of the trade deficit.

In order to safeguard against possible abuse, there is a proviso that a country can only impose the transfer tax if it produces goods similar to those being taxed or there is reasonable expectation that the manufacture of such goods will commence within a period of three months following the imposition of the tax. Conditions regarding the size of the industry also must be fulfilled: within the ensuing year, the industry must have a capacity to produce a quantity of goods equivalent to not less than 15 percent of the goods of that particular kind consumed within the period of twelve months immediately preceding the imposition of the tax within that partner state or goods of that particular kind with an ex-factory value of not less than 2 million shillings ($285,714).

The rate of the transfer tax is left to the country imposing it, but the tax is not to exceed 50 percent of the ad valorem duty imposed by the state on similar goods imported from third countries. Alternatively, if the duty is specific, the tax is not to exceed the equivalent ad valorem duty from outside the area. If, on the other hand, the same goods are admitted duty-free from third countries, no tax may be imposed on similar goods from the partner countries.

The duration of the transfer tax is eight years after the date on which it was first imposed. In other words, each tax shall expire at the end of eight years unless it is revoked sooner. Every transfer tax, whatever its duration, shall automatically cease to operate fifteen years after the date of coming into force of the East African Treaty for Cooperation unless revoked earlier. This provision is interesting because, whereas similar infant industry protective tariffs normally have no specific period of duration, the Treaty for East African Cooperation implies that after fifteen years each of the partner states will have developed its industries sufficiently to withstand free and perfect competition from similar industries in the other partner states.

Any transfer tax may be revoked if the imposing country fails to establish a similar industry within three months of the date the tax is imposed or if after the period of one year the industry's output fails to reach the required minimum. It also is provided that a partner state imposing a transfer tax may not directly or indirectly subsidize the transfer of any manufactured goods that are subject to such taxes so as to sell such goods in its territory at prices lower than those charged for similar goods in the other states, after taking into account transportation and other handling charges.

Decentralization of Functions and
Location of Headquarters

As previously mentioned, the development of institutions for joint action under the old arrangements tended to concentrate in Nairobi. In the new treaty, this anomaly was redressed by a deliberate distribution of functions. It was agreed (1) that the headquarters of the East African Community, including the Tribunal and the Central Secretariat, would be situated at Arusha in Tanzania and that the headquarters of the East African Harbors Corporation would be situated in Dar-es-Salaam, Tanzania; (2) that the headquarters of the East African Development Bank and the East African Posts and Telecommunications Corporations would be situated in Kampala, Uganda; and (3) that the headquarters of the East African Railways Corporation and the East African Airways Corporation would be situated in Nairobi, Kenya (Article 87 of the treaty). Thus, each partner state had at least two headquarters on its territory.

The East African Development Bank

The problems of industrialization acquired special significance in the new treaty. Industrial development was seen as one of the most effective measures for enhancing the rate of economic development of the partner states individually and collectively. In order to ensure the harmonization of industrial development, the countries decided to establish the East African Development Bank. The bank's objectives include providing financial and technical assistance toward the promotion of industrial development to the partner states. In this respect, priority is to be given to industrialization programs in the less industrially developed partner states. It is also the objective of the East African Development Bank to ensure that, in initiating the plans for industrial development, the projects are designed in such a way as to promote complementarity in the industrial field.

The East African Development Bank started off with a capital of 400 million Eastern African shillings ($48 million) of account, equally subscribed by the three partner states. The bank provides finances to any agencies or enterprises within the East African Community by granting direct loans, by participating in direct loans financed with funds it raises in the capital or money markets, or by investing its own funds in the equity capital of an institution or enterprise. It may also guarantee loans made by any other institution for the purposes of industrial development in East Africa.

New Membership in the East
African Community

Soon after the coming into force of the Treaty for East African Cooperation, several adjoining countries expressed their intentions to join or to be associated with the East African Community. The provision relating to new membership in the East African Community states that "the partner States may together negotiate with any foreign country with a view to the association of that country with the Community or its participation in any of the activities of the Community or Corporations" (Article 93 of the treaty). On the basis of this article, several countries in East Africa, including Zambia, Somalia, Ethiopia, Burundi, Rwanda, and Swaziland, have submitted applications or made known their desire to join the East African Community. The main problem in this respect is that, in the absence of any precedents, neither the applicant countries nor the existing members of the East African Community really know what form the negotiations for new membership should take. Some countries are interested in the common market or trade aspects while others are interested only in the development of transport and communications. Some applicant countries are interested in full membership while others are interested in "associate" membership. There are also some fears that enlarging the East African Community would reduce the benefits currently enjoyed by the existing members. The terms and conditions for joining in respect of each applicant country have not yet been worked out. This must essentially be a long-term exercise. Nevertheless, there is a clear indication that the countries in East Africa take the question of cooperation quite seriously.

Problems of Implementation

The establishment of new institutions as laid out in the treaty has gone quite smoothly and most of these institutions are already fully operational. However, difficulties have arisen in the implementation of the provisions relating to the transfer tax. Due to differences in the interpretation of the various clauses, a number of cases have had to be referred to the Common Market Tribunal for settlement. It will not be possible to fully assess the treaty's impact on the development of the three economies until it has been in effect for a longer time. Some of the problems encountered in the implementation of the treaty thus far are outlined below.

The first major problem facing the East African Community is the absence of pronouncement on how the development plans of the constituent states are to be coordinated. Chapter 5 indicated that this was an essential condition for the development of industrial projects. There is mention of the need for consultation in matters relating to planning but, although an Economic Consultative and Planning Council was established, it was given no specific mandate to tackle the question of joint planning. Therefore, as long as the main policy decisions affecting industrialization are left to the individual states, difficulties will arise as to how to implement the joint industrial development projects even when they are fully supported by all three partner states.

The second major problem of the East African Community has been experienced in the attempts to implement the provisions relating to the allocation of industries. A large proportion of the industries in East Africa are of equal interest to all the East African countries; therefore, problems often arise because, due to the lack of proper machinery for coordination of the national development plans, these industries are subject to national rather than multinational policies. In the absence of machinery for coordination of national development plans, important economic decisions must necessarily be taken at the national level, thereby defeating the principle of economic cooperation. Although the treaty provides for consultations in development planning, more often than not the countries have acted on their own. The Economic Consultative and Planning Council has met only a few times to decide matters relating to the coordination of development efforts, and it has no powers to take up the question of implementation of the individual national development plans. The development of joint institutions in East Africa often has been taken for granted, but it must be stressed here that there is urgent need, in order to introduce the necessary dynamism for accelerated economic growth, to change the traditional form of economic cooperation that existed during the de facto common market period.

The third major problem relates to the question of the elimination of customs duties and the application of transfer tax arrangements. Doubts have been expressed by some applicant countries as to whether appropriate safeguards would be built into the agreement to ensure compensation for any possible losses of revenue from import duties.[3] It has been argued that the East African countries, like all developing African countries, depend heavily on indirect taxes, not only as protective measures for their import-substituting industries but also as the major source of government revenue. In the countries of the East African Community, revenue from customs and excise together account for nearly 35 percent of total revenue. It is believed that the degree of dependence is much higher in most of the applicant countries. Therefore, the question of import taxes in any system of economic cooperation features prominently in determining the applications to the East African Community.

In the political field, the change of government leadership in Uganda in the early part of 1971, caused serious problems in the working of the East African Community. The East African Authority, which is composed of the three heads of state, cannot meet since Tanzania refused to recognize the new Government. At the technical level, some country representatives in the institutions of the Community have been refused permission to take up their appointments at headquarters situated in Tanzania or Uganda. These can only be regarded as teething problems of the Community but they are nonetheless obstacles in the implementation of current cooperation projects of this organization.

The point to stress in this regard is that the advantages of economic cooperation would not weigh heavily in presence of indirect taxes hindering the freedom of movement of capital-skilled personnel, and labor force among countries, even though these taxes are supposed to raise finances at the national level to enhance economic progress. At the same time, it would be unrealistic to expect countries to move swiftly from heavy dependence on indirect taxes to free trade. This implies that countries cannot be expected to free trade unconditionally for purposes of enhancing the negotiations for membership in the East African Community. Therefore, it would seem necessary to have this question carefully examined by both the applicant countries and the current partner states. The applicant countries may have to be provided with adequate compensatory arrangements for the loss of revenue before import duties can be eliminated or reduced, especially since the East African Community as a whole is more industrialized than the adjoining states.

The Southern African Customs Union

The cooperation between South Africa (including Namibia) and the three former High Commission Territories of Botswana, Lesotho, and Swaziland is not confined to customs arrangements but extends to such fields of economic activity as trade, economic development, and the control of the movement of such factors of production as labor and capital. The customs union is supported by a de facto common market and currency union of Southern Africa, Botswana, Lesotho, and Swaziland. There are also arrangements in the field of development of transport and other social infrastructure.

The Southern African Customs Union originated during the early
days of colonial occupation; the initial move to create a free trade area
was made in 1889. At that time, there was a kind of understanding between Britain and South Africa that the former High Commission Territories would eventually be fully integrated with South Africa. In the
1909 act which created the Union of South Africa, there were provisions
for the incorporation of the three territories. Subsequently, with the
introduction of apartheid policies in South Africa, a political merger with
the three territories became impossible. After 1960, the United Kingdom began to take the necessary steps to prepare the territories for full
independence. This meant that future economic association between
South Africa and the former High Commission Territories would be
governed by the wishes of the free independent sovereign states. At
the time of independence, the question of relations with Southern Africa
was raised. The geographical location of the three states and their
heavy economic dependence on South Africa logically meant that it
was to their advantage to maintain the economic links with Southern
Africa that had existed for so long.

The formal arrangements for the creation of a customs union
by Southern Africa, Bechuanaland, Basutoland, and Swaziland were
completed when an agreement was signed at Potchefstroom in June,
1910.[4] The agreement provided (1) that Southern Africa and the territories should maintain a common external tariff; (2) that there should
be a free trade area providing for unrestricted movement of goods and
other services among the member countries; (3) that the revenue collected at any point of entry into the customs union from third countries
should be collected and distributed in an equitable manner to the three
territories. The distribution of the customs revenue was based on the
average import of each of the territories during the three-year period
1906-08 (see Chapter 10). In 1968, the amount paid to the three countries was a little more than 6,000,000 Rand ($8.4 million). In terms
of administrative arrangements, this allocation was regarded as sound.
In addition to saving the three territories from the burden of duty collection, it also prevented smuggling across national frontiers, which
was quite substantial before the creation of the customs union.

The countries also cooperate in monetary matters. There is a
currency union whereby notes and coins are freely transferrable among
member countries, and the Rand is the legal tender in all these countries. Moreover, all member countries are in the sterling area.
There is also free movement of capital and other financial resources
among them.

In the field of transport and communications, the countries
operate joint services. All postal services, such as telegraph,

telephone, telex, and mail, between these countries and the rest of the world operate through South Africa. In the field of civil aviation, Southern African Airways provides the required international links and there are small domestic air services linking the capital with remote areas within each country.

In 1969, after a series of negotiations between South Africa and the three other states, a new customs union was created replacing the 1910 arrangements, which had become obsolete. The new arrangements provide for the establishment of a Consolidated Revenue Fund derived from customs, excise, and sales tax. The new sharing of the revenues will be based on a number of calculations including the value of South African goods entering each country and the value of imports from third countries. Although the total amount of revenue for distribution remains the same, there is indication that the three former High Commission Territories will derive greater benefits under the new agreement than under the old arrangements.

In addition to these adjustments, the three former British territories, particularly Botswana, have sought a new monetary arrangement in which they will have (1) a direct say in control and other fiscal policies that have the effect of protecting the Rand and boosting the economy of the member countries (2) a share in the interest accruing on securities held by the South African Reserve Bank, which would increase the reserves of the three countries; (3) the right to raise capital within the customs union through government bonds and treasury bills, which would increase the power of the three countries to raise finances for economic development. These arrangements are based on the desire of the three former British territories to have more control over the mechanism for the adoption of monetary and other economic policies.

Other Systems of Cooperation in
East and Southern Africa

In addition to the East African Community and the Southern African Customs Union, there are other small economic associations in East and Southern Africa that are both useful and effective in their limited but concrete objectives. In East Africa, the East African Cargo Handling Company operates outside the Treaty for East African Cooperation and is responsible for shipping and forwarding arrangements of Kenya, Tanzania, and Uganda. There is also the East African Shipping Line, which is owned in equal shares by Kenya, Uganda, Tanzania, and Zambia. The Zambia-Tanzania Road Services and the

Zambia-Tanzania Railway Link are designed to operate joint services in the respective fields.

In Southern Africa, a Testing Resource and Training Center has been established by Malawi, Botswana, Lesotho, and Swaziland. It operates in collaboration with the University of Lesotho and Swaziland in development of aptitude and selection tests designed to help fill the requirements for manpower in the four countries. A plan for telecommunications linking Botswana, Zambia, and South Africa has been in operation for some time. A survey has been completed for the development of a road link between Zambia and Botswana with the aid of finances from the United States Agency for International Development (USAID).

In the off-shore islands of Madagascar, Mauritius, Reunion, and Comoro, new areas for cooperation are being explored, including a proposed joint oil refinery to be constructed in Reunion to serve that island as well as Mauritius and the Comoro Islands and a proposed chemical fertilizer plant to be built in Mauritius to serve that country as well as Madagascar and Reunion. These small beginnings provide the necessary economic and social links among the member states toward wider cooperation.

COOPERATION IN CENTRAL AFRICA

In Central Africa, three economic cooperation patterns can be distinguished: (1) the UDEAC countries; (2) Congo (Kinshasa) and Chad; and (3) Congo (Kinshasa), Rwanda, and Burundi. There is considerable trade within each of these groups but trade between these groups is limited except in the case of Chad, which trades with the UDEAC countries.

The Central African Customs and Economic Union

The Central African Customs and Economic Union (UDEAC) evolved from the pre-independence links created by the French administration beginning early in the twentieth century. It now consists of four countries; Central African Republic, Congo (Brazzaville), Gabon, and Cameroun.* A union was established at the time of independence

---

*Chad and Central African Republic, which were among the

to replace the economic and other links that existed under the colonial administration. Originally, the Equatorial Customs Union (UDE) was founded in June 1959 by Chad, Gabon, Congo (Brazzaville), and Central African Republic. The UDEAC Treaty was signed in December 1964 after a series of contacts and consultations involving Chad, Gabon, Congo (Brazzaville), Central African Republic, and Cameroun. The UDEAC countries aim at the gradual establishment of a Central African common market through the expansion of small national markets by removing obstacles to trade among between them; the adoption of a procedure for the equitable sharing of industrialization projects; and the coordination of programs for development of the various economic sectors.

The main features of the UDEAC arrangements for economic cooperation are (1) a common market providing for complete freedom in the movement of goods, services, capital, and labor among the constituent states; (2) an agreement regarding the adoption of a common external tariff against third countries; (3) a special system for the distribution of production tax (taxe unique) among the member states; and (4) a system of financial compensation by the more industrialized countries to the less advanced partner states for the loss of customs revenue as a result of the adoption of a common external tariff.

Common Market Arrangements

A common market among the UDEAC countries is to be achieved through the adoption of special measures to allow for free movement of factors of production including labor and capital. The countries are guided by the firm conviction that the expansion of the small individual markets through the removal of all trade restrictions would enhance their rate of development. It is provided that products originating in one member country when moved to other member states shall be exempt from all import and export duties and charges. In order to safeguard the development of industries that are not ready to face competition, any member state may introduce quantitative restrictions on goods originating from third countries.

In order to support the arrangements for the adoption of a common

---

original members of the UDEAC, withdrew membership in April 1968 and, together with Congo (Kinshasa), formed the Union of Central African States (UEAC). Later in the year, the Central African Republic rejoined the UDEAC.

external tariff, the countries agreed (1) to adopt a common customs
and fiscal import tariff against third countries and (2) to prohibit
all duties and charges on import and export trade among the member
states. There is also a common fiscal charge on imports and a common turnover tax. The member countries have complete freedom as
regards the levying of export duties and charges, but it is provided
that there should be consultations in order to ensure some uniformity
in the application of the export charges. The treaty also provides for
the establishment of joint customs offices, whose functions include the
collection of export duties and the distribution of customs proceeds to
the exporting country. This arrangement was intended to ease the
situation of the land-locked countries, whose position could not be
adequately safeguarded by ordinary transit arrangements.

Common Solidarity Fund

Since the adoption of a common external tariff could have resulted
in the loss of customs revenue to the inland countries, the UDEAC
countries created a common fund with the objective of adequately compensating through appropriate measures for the special position of the
economically weaker partner states. The fund is financed by the ap-
propriation of revenue proceeds from all the duties and taxes levied
on imports from third countries and collected by the joint customs
offices. The proceeds are then distributed in agreed proportions to
the member states (see Chapter 10).

Taxe Unique

The need for balancing economic development among the member
states also was recognized. It was recognized that, where disparities
in the levels of development existed, it was necessary to ensure that
the common market arrangements would not aggravate the situation.
Hence, the countries introduced the taxe unique, a single tax applicable
to all products manufactured within any of the member states whose
market extends or is likely to extend to the other member states. The
tax excludes duties and charges on imports of raw materials and essential products used in industry for manufacturing consumption goods
for trade and all internal charges on raw materials and essential
products used in manufacturing industry. The tax is levied by the
exporting country and the proceeds are paid to the country consuming
that particular product in proportion to its consumption. In this way,
the member countries are compensated for the loss of equivalent duty
on similar products that would have been collected if the product had
been imported from third countries.

Industrial Harmonization

In line with the general desire to balance industrial development, the UDEAC agreed on a special system of industrial classification under which there are five categories of industries (1) industries mainly devoted to exports outside UDEAC; (2) industries affecting the market of a single state for which no economic, fiscal, or customs advantages are requested from other member states (in other words, industries whose establishment would not be likely to affect similar industries in other partner states); (3) industries that, although affecting the market of only one state, are likely to compete with existing industry in other partner states (this list also includes industries envisaged for establishment in the development plans or programs of the other member states); (4) industrial projects whose market is limited to two member states where harmonization can be sought between these two member states; and (5) industrial projects affecting the markets of more than two member states, for which harmonization is sought within the UDEAC.

It is provided that industries falling in categories 1 and 2 can be established within any member state without reference to UDEAC provided that the industries in category 2 do not extend their markets beyond national boundaries. As regards the establishment of industries in category 4, any two member states wishing to establish such industries are required jointly to notify the General Secretariat of their plans. No member country may establish industries in categories 3 and 5, without prior notification and approval of the other UDEAC members. It is further provided that any decisions regarding the establishment of industries in category 5 shall be governed by the raw materials situation; the volume of investment already made in the various states in such industries and the comparison of advantages granted by each state to its partners; and the desirability for compensating the less economically advanced member states.

Some Problems of Implementation

UDEAC has made great progress toward the establishment of a common market, and a number of institutions are now fully operational. Although the infrastructure, especially transport and communications, is not yet adequate to serve the expanded institutions, there are concrete steps to ensure the success of UDEAC. However, some problems have arisen within the UDEAC, reflected in both the economic and the political relations among the member states. These problems are largely historical. It will be recalled that UDEAC evolved from former

French Equatorial Africa. At the time of independence, the countries hastily signed agreements to preserve the economic and other links that existed during the colonial days without much thought about the implications of such agreements. As time went on, it was discovered that these agreements, or at least their implementation, raised serious practical problems because independence brought about nationhood and the desire to preserve the power of self-determination, which did not exist under colonial administration.

Thus, on the economic side the question of the implementation of the treaty, especially with regard to the collection and distribution of import revenues, raised practical problems whose solution has not yet been devised. The lack of adequate and reliable data on import tariffs and export duties made it difficult to determine total revenue collections. Inevitably, the distribution of such revenue was arbitrary. Furthermore, in view of the different interpretations of the aims for which the taxe unique was instituted, its calculation presented problems and therefore it was difficult to find a logical basis for taking joint decisions.

In other fields of economic activity, the questions of industrial harmonization, the protection of new industries, and the equalization of revenue and customs receipts have not yet been fully tackled. The treaty provided that the member states would consult on matters relating to development planning and the regulation of foreign and domestic investments, but in practice these provisions have not been followed. Although the UDEAC is a homogeneous economic unit, trade among member states generally has remained minimal compared with external trade, and intra-UDEAC trade consists mainly of such consumption goods as meat, cereals, beverages, and tobacco. The trade pattern of the countries individually as well as collectively is still oriented toward the exports of raw materials to the European countries, especially the EEC.

On the political side, the withdrawal of Chad and the Central African Republic from the UDEAC in the beginning of 1968 disturbed the mechanism for economic cooperation that had been set in motion. The major reasons for withdrawal were clearly political, resulting from disagreements and rivalry between some of the member states, but the apparent lack of economic benefits derived by the land-locked countries, such as Chad and the Central African Republic, were cited as reasons why these states found it necessary to withdraw. It must also be pointed out that the failure to establish effective supranational institutional machinery for taking joint decisions has inhibited moves toward more advanced levels of economic cooperation, and this has become largely a political matter.

Toward the end of 1968, the Central African Republic rejoined the UDEAC. Chad, although remaining in the Union of Central African States, pledged full cooperation with the UDEAC. These developments contributed to the creation of an uncertain political and economic atmosphere not conducive to cooperation among the UDEAC states. In recent years, however, there have been new measures aimed at strengthening the economic relations among the UDEAC countries.

The Union of Central African States

The problems of the development of closer economic links between the Congo (Kinshasa) and the UDEAC were raised on a number of occasions. It was argued that the expansion of the UDEAC market would increase industrial opportunities and thus would enhance the economic development of the area as a whole. Although this principle is generally accepted, the political situation in the area does not appear to be ready to permit the level of cooperation that would really contribute to the area's economic development. However, in April 1968, the Union of Central African States (UEAC) was established by a protocol signed in Bangui by Congo (Kinshasa), the Central African Republic, and Chad. As noted previously, Central African Republic left UEAC and rejoined UDEAC at the end of 1968. UEAC now consists of Congo (Kinshasa) and Chad.

> The High Contracting parties [states the UEAC protocol] hereby decide to establish a common market of the Central African States. To that end they hereby agree to coordinate their industrialization policies, their development plans, and their transportation and telecommunication policies in order to promote balanced development and the diversification of the economies of the member States of the Union within a framework designed to make it possible to expand trade between the States and to improve the living conditions of the people.[5]

In order to facilitate the common market arrangements as stipulated in the protocol, the UEAC states agreed (1) to adopt a joint import tariff or customs and excise charges against third parties and to abolish all import and export duties among the member states; (2) to eliminate all obstacles to free movement of persons, services, and capital among member states; (3) to adopt a joint economic policy to ensure steady and balanced economic expansion, economic stability, and a rapid rise in the standard of living in the member states by coordinating domestic taxation policies, development plans, and industrial development; (4) to coordinate the development of transport and communications among the member states; (5) to set up a compensation and investment fund; (6) to introduce a consumption tax designed to encourage the consumption of goods originating in the member states; (7) to devise appropriate steps to increase trade among the member states; and (8) to set up an investment bank to facilitate economic expansion in UEAC by creating new resources.

The Conference of Heads of State, which is the supreme organ of the Union, has as its function the approval of the budget and the direction and coordination of the policy of the member states in the fields of trade, customs, transport and communications, education, culture, health, science and technology, defense and security, and general economic policy. This organ is assisted by the Council of Ministers of Foreign Affairs, whose task is to direct the day-to-day functioning of UEAC affairs.

Although it is too early to venture an opinion as to whether UEAC will develop into a strong economic entity, doubt has often been expressed as to the economic benefits to be derived from the association. Trade within the UEAC constitutes an insignificant proportion of both the intra-African trade and the total external trade of the member states. Transport and communications connecting them are far from adequate to serve the implementation of the objectives stipulated in the protocol. The levels of development in the partner states indicate great disparities in both income per capita and industrialization. In light of these observations, it would seem that UEAC would have difficulty developing into a viable economic unit to serve as an instrument for economic development of the member countries. Despite the apparent lack of economic advantages, the countries have shown a strong desire to continue, and as development proceeds some new avenues for cooperation may emerge.

Other Systems of Cooperation in Central Africa

In addition to ÙDEAC and UEAC, there are numerous other examples of cooperation in Central Africa, largely at the sectoral or even project level. These small groupings provide the necessary leverage toward more comprehensive forms of economic cooperation.

In recent years, negotiations have been held by Congo (Kinshasa), Rwanda, and Burundi aimed at reviving the old economic links created during the colonial period and hastily broken up at the time of independence. The three countries have established a joint commission to promote coordinated economic, technical, social, and judicial action.

They also have signed the International Transit Routes (TIR) Convention of road transport. There are indications that this new association may prove economically beneficial to Rwanda and Burundi in their development efforts.

Regarding cooperation in the monetary field, the Central Bank of the States of Equatorial Africa and Cameroun (BCEAEC) has existed in Central Africa for a long time. Its members are the UDEAC countries and Chad. The countries also established a monetary union that coordinates the monetary policies of the member states and is the means for integration of their fiscal, banking, monetary, and exchange control regulations. It also facilitates economic transactions among the member countries through its services as a clearing house.

In other economic fields, there exists cooperation between Cameroun and Chad in customs, commerce, and economic development aspects. These aspects give positive indication of the strong conviction of the need to build and maintain economic ties between the two countries. There is also a joint commission for the development of the resources of the Logone River, and there is agreement on a plan to extend the railway system in Cameroun to Chad. By increasing Chad's access to the sea, such a plan would promote faster development in the country.

COOPERATION IN WEST AFRICA

There are many economic groupings in West Africa, ranging from the more elaborate groupings, such as the Organization of the Senegal River States and the Conseil de l'Entente, to the rather limited groupings, such as the West African Examination Council. In all, there are over fourteen such groupings but in this section only a few will be examined in detail.

The Conseil de l'Entente

The original idea behind the creation of the Conseil de l'Entente (Council of Understanding) was not to develop comprehensive plans for economic cooperation but merely to strengthen the solidarity of the member states through mutual loan guarantees. This organization was set up in 1959 by four countries; Dahomey, Ivory Coast, Niger, and Upper Volta. Togo joined the Conseil de l'Entente in 1966. The countries agreed to establish a Solidarity Fund whose purpose was to guarantee the loans that any member state contracted with external sources.

The establishment of the Solidarity Fund was prompted by the general feeling that, in order to enhance economic development, countries should have access to adequate financial resources. The creation of the Solidarity Fund ensured that the development efforts of the member countries would be facilitated through their ability to raise needed loans, and it was particularly welcomed by the less economically prosperous partner states.

The Mutual Aid and Loan Guarantee Fund

The desire to make a more positive contribution to economic development called for a reorganization, and in June 1966 the Conseil de l'Entente adopted a convention establishing the Mutual Aid and Loan Guarantee Fund (Fonds d'Entraide et de Garantie des Emprunts), re- placing the Solidarity Fund. The object of this fund is to provide maxi- mum security to foreign capital investments, to coordinate and harmo- nize the efforts of the member states with a view to assuring acceler- ated and homogeneous economic growth, and to extend to the financial field the political solidarity of the member states through the creation of a multilateral guarantee organism.

The Mutual Aid and Loan Guarantee Fund will guarantee any foreign loans for payment of principal and interest and will reimburse any foreign creditors in the case of inability by any enterprise to honor its obligations. However, preference is being given to the development of multinational projects. In other words, the Conseil de l'Entente is steadily moving from somewhat limited objectives to a wider form of economic cooperation.

The Mutual Aid and Loan Guarantee Fund was seen as a supplement to the guarantees already given to the foreign investors through the cus- tomary liberalization of investment laws and regulations. This fund may be used to back loans granted to governments, public authorities, semi- public bodies, or private enterprises with head offices in one of the member states. Such loans must be for industrial, agricultural, or commercial projects that are proved to be economically sound and would help to strengthen the economic infrastructure of the member states. The fund is maintained through annual payments by the member states, whose amounts are determined every five years; subventions and gifts from any source; profit earnings from the operations of the fund; and income from investments. Projects submitted for loan guar- antee must be supported by detalied studies of technical, economic, and financial requirements.

In 1966, Niger submitted an application for the backing of the Mutual Aid and Loan Guarantee Fund in the construction of a railway line from Parakou to Dosso in Niger, covering a distance of 500 kilometers at a total cost of 11,000 million francs (CFA). By June 1967, the fund had already made surveys covering several main areas of activities envisaged in the agreement; the promotion of tourism; the production, processing, and marketing of meat; the exploitation of limestone deposits in Dahomey and Togo; the development of the Banfora Falls for hydroelectricity; the extension of the Dori-Tera-Niamey railway line; the stabilization of cereal stocks; and bicycle tire marketing. In all, these surveys would involve a sum of 182.7 million francs (CFA). Financial guarantee involved considerations of the sum of 173.5 million francs (CFA), and future projects for which backing would be sought were valued at 708.5 million francs (CFA). In September 1967, the fund approved a guarantee of a loan of 80 million francs (CFA) granted to the Ouagadougou Chamber of Commerce by the Central Bank of West Africa (BCEAO) and a loan of 81 million francs (CFA) to Niger for drilling and providing equipment for wells near Lake Chad.

The Managing Committee of the Mutual Aid and Loan Guarantee Fund approved two projects presented by Upper Volta: (1) a loan for the purchase of agricultural and works equipment used by the army's engineering division for the improvement of roads and certain agricultural schemes and (2) a loan for the development of infrastructure in Ouagadougou aimed at improving the city's industrial and commercial areas. Measures are underway to implement these projects.

The activities of the Mutual Aid and Loan Guarantee Fund are not confined to the guaranteeing of loans. There is now a definite move to enhance cooperation in other areas. To this end, in January 1968 the Conseil de l'Entente decided on the following measures: (1) that the member states agree to operate their tourist facilities in common; (2) that an Industrial Information Advisory Center be set up to work out sector-by-sector plans for cooperation of industries; (3) that the Administrative Secretary of the Mutual Aid and Loan Guarantee Fund pursue studies on the extension of the Abidjan-Niger railway. Studies also have been carried out on the possibility of improving roads connecting member states and coordinating national highway development programs.

The Conseil de l'Entente is one of the most active organizations in West Africa; it has demonstrated that it is forward-looking and has the means to implement its joint decisions. The member states have agreed to set up several institutional arrangements to cover the various aspects of development within the member countries. They also have established a Regional Commission on Industrialization whose

responsiblity is to study the coordination of industrial development. In other fields, studies have been carried out showing possible
areas of joint action in (1) the coordination of cement manufacturing
in the five countries; (2) a project for a tire and inner tube factory
for bicycles and motorcycles in Upper Volta; (3) manufacture of petroleum products for the Conseil de l'Entente in the Ivory Coast; and (4)
a regional center for maritime training in Abidjan. The countries
also have established an Inter-Cattle Meat Bureau in Ouagadougou to
coordinate statistics and other data on cattle trade and to harmonize
policies, financing, customs, and commercial legislation on meat.

In 1970, as a means of stepping up the production of meat, the
countries of the Conseil de l'Entente agreed to establish a common
meat market (Communauté Economique du Bétail et de la Viande).
There also were agreements aided at fostering cooperation in trade,
industry, customs services, income tax, transport, and telecommunications. The member countries also decided to create an Entente
School for Training Mechanics and Heavy Machinery Operators at Lommé
in Togo; to create a Fisherman's Training Center at Abidjan in Ivory
Coast; to expand the Industrial Training Center at Abidjan to serve
all the member countries; and to establish a printing textile and a group
of nut oil works in Dahomey. The Mutual Aid and Loan Guarantee
Fund backed loans for the establishment of an agro-industrial complex
for the utilization of kenaf, a fiber plant for making bags and cordage,
in Dahomey, for the improvement of industrial and commercial infrastructure, and for the purchase of agricultural and public works equipment for road and agricultural development in Upper Volta.

The prospects for future expansion of the Conseil de l'Entente
include possible membership of Ghana. Proposals also are sometimes
put forward for the exploration of possibilities of cooperation of the
Conseil de l'Entente with Nigeria and Liberia.

Economic Community of West Africa

The West African Economic Community, which was created by a
protocol signed in May 1970, evolved from the West African Customs
Union (UDEAO) which was established in 1959. The UDEAO was created
to preserve the links which were established under the former Federation of French West Africa, on similar lines to the former French
Equatorial Africa. Before the break-up of the federation, the entire
area constituted a single territory for customs and other administrative
purposes. But, as was stated in Chapter 1, internal autonomy was
not granted to the area as a whole but to individual states, which proved
prejudicial to these small economies. By 1959, it was found inevitable

to reestablish the economic relations joining the countries, and the UDEAO was therefore created by Dahomey, Ivory Coast, Mali, Mauritania, Niger, Senegal, Togo, and Upper Volta. The countries were primarily concerned with the need to liberalize their mutual trade as a measure for enhancing the area's rate of development.

Its convention provided for (1) free circulation of goods and the abolition of duties between member states and (2) common external duties on imports from third countries and the distribution of such duties among the member states in an equitable manner. The convention also provided for the distribution of duties under the refund system, which provided that import duties collected at the port of entry into the UDEAO would be distributed to the member states in agreed proportions based on the volume of imports by each member state. Most of the inland countries gradually established customs duties within UDEAO. Although the convention provided that natural products originating within the member states be admitted freely in the UDEAO, mounting restrictions, such as indirect taxes and development policies, prevented the full application of this agreement. It subsequently became clear that there was need to review the charter.

As a result, a new treaty reorganizing the UDEAO was signed in 1966 by the member states. The charter of the new UDEAO provided (1) for the adoption of a common external tariff comprising a minimum tariff and a general tariff, with no tariff concessions below the established minimum tariff to be granted to third countries; (2) that products originating within the UDEAO and coming into the member states would be subject to a fiscal tax, the total amount of which would not exceed 50 percent of the overall rate of duty paid on similar goods originating from third countries;* (3) that there would be free circulation of goods within the UDEAO, but in order to correct any possible imbalances in its economy a member state could impose quantitative restrictions, subject to immediate notification to the Council of Ministers of UDEAO; and (4) that goods originating from third countries and transferred from one member state to another would be subject to import duties applicable to such third country.

---

*The convention also stipulated that, although member states are free to establish any industry, such industry should not be to the detriment of existing industries in the other member countries. If a competitive industry is set up in any of the member states, the Council of Ministers may be required to raise fiscal duties in respect to such industry to 70 percent of the aggregate rate.

However, the new arrangements adopted in 1966 did not bring about any substantial changes in the volume of trade among the member states, nor were they sufficient to offset the fears generally associated with the problems of the administration of the customs union agreement. One aspect of this factor was the lack of clearly defined objectives in the the convention and the absence of adequate institutional machinery to implement and follow up the agreement. There was urgent need to define the methods for the collection and administration of the customs agreements and to draft a convention for the transportation of goods between member states, especially with regard to transit arrangements.

Despite the efforts to revitalize the UDEAO in 1966, this organization has remained largely dormant. The major problem arose with respect to the implementation of the agreements regarding the distribution of import duties under the refund system. Like the UDEAO, grouping experienced great difficulties in collection of import duties and the equitable distribution of the revenue. The inland countries failed to gain the benefits for which this system was established, and gradually most of the land-locked states were obliged to impose customs duties on products from other member states, especially the coastal countries. The system of the refund of duties worked only for a few countries. The charter provided that natural products originating within member states would be admitted freely throughout UDEAO. However, due to the absence of benefits from the agreement, the countries gradually mounted trade restrictions and other indirect taxes that, together with the lack of coordination of national development policies, prevented the full application of the provisions of the charter.

In May 1970, the member states of the UDEAO met to consider the reorganization of the grouping to provide a more effective arrangement for (1) the joint development of the area, especially the improvement of transport and communications; (2) the acceleration of industrial development so as to achieve a balance in the development of the member states; and (3) the promotion of trade in domestically produced industrial and agricultural goods. The countries decided to create an Economic Community of West Africa to replace the West African Customs Union created in 1969. A new treaty embodying the proposed reorganization is being drawn up, and membership in the organization will be open to other West African countries that wish to join.

The Organization of the Senegal River States

The countries of the Senegal River Basin have had social and cultural ties for a long time. When independence came to these

countries, the need for joint development of the basin was seen as
the only logical step for accelerating the rate of development. There
was a need for joint development to provide power and to improve
the navigation of the river for purposes of industrial and agricultural
development. Thus, in 1963 the Inter-State Committee of the Senegal
River States was created by Mali, Guinea, Senegal, and Mauritania.
The heads of state pledged to ensure the economic, social, and cultural
integration of the member states; to promote understanding and solidarity; and to harmonize their activities in the political field. The member
countries also aspired to harmonize their development plans and to encourage cooperation in industrial development.

The statute agreement signed in March 1968 defines the purpose
of the Organization of Senegal River States (OERS) as follows:

> The Governments of member States solemnly undertake
> to apply suitable joint solutions to the problems arising
> out of the current systems of trade, education, movement
> of goods and establishment of persons in member States
> . . . undertake to facilitate inter-State payments with a
> view to expanding trade between members and to coordi-
> nate and adapt their educational systems with a view to
> standardizing instructions, programs and recruitment
> levels and establishing equivalence between certificates
> granted by teaching establishments of member States of
> the regional sub-group.

The initial plan of action was to conduct studies on (1) the cartography and hydrological and geological conditions of the upper
reaches of the Senegal River in order to determine the possibility
of building a reservoir; (2) the navigation problems along the river
and the development of the St. Louis and Kayes port facilities; (3)
agricultural problems relating to soil erosion, crop development, and
livestock farming; and (4) industrial development and mineral prospecting in the area. The first studies of the hydroagricultural projects
involved a sum of 1,135 million francs (CFA), of which 928 million
francs (CFA) was provided by the United Nations Development Program
and the remainder by the OERS member states.

As a means of facilitating the study of the navigation and port
services of the Senegal River, a fiber glass houseboat costing about
$10 million was purchased in 1969. At the meeting of the Council of
Ministers held in March 1970, recommendations were adopted for (1)
the creation of an office to coordinate the development of railways in
Guinea, Mali, and Senegal; (2) the creation of a unified code governing
the merchant marines of the four member states; (3) the classification

of roads in the member countries into four categories for purposes of joint action--interstate, national, regional, and local; and (4) the study of the possibilities for the creation of an organization for coastal and river traffic and a common navigational company to handle foreign trade of the member states.

An agreement for cooperation by the OERS states allocated various economic activities among the countries; Guinea would concentrate on the development of paper industries; Senegal would develop petrochemical industries; and Mali and Mauritania would develop iron and steel industries. The industries were presumed to be of a multi-national character to supply the requirements of the member states. There was also a complementary list of industries that allotted the manufacture of rubber tires to Guinea; nitrogen products to Mali; copper to Mauritania; and pharmaceutical products to Senegal. The output of these industries also was to be sufficient to satisfy the markets of all four member states.

Other joint multinational projects in the OERS include recommendations for the harmonization of statistical methods relating to customs legislation and documentation. There are also proposals for the organization of interstate trade fairs and the adoption of multinational trade agreements. In the field of communications, joint action would include the establishment of a postal and telecommunications training center and the coordination of telex services. In the agricultural field, activities would include the eradication of cattle diseases and the construction of a dam at Manatali in Mali for the irrigation of an estimated 200,000 hectares of land.

Other Systems of Cooperation in West Africa

The idea of a larger West African economic grouping comprising both the anglophone and francophone African states was vigorously advocated by the Economic Commission for Africa during most of the 1960's, but it was not until early 1968 that the African countries took initiative toward this objective. In April 1968 the West African Regional Group was created by Guinea, Liberia, Mali, Mauritania, Senegal, Upper Volta, Gambia, Ghana, and Nigeria. The establishment of this group was largely the result of active consultations initiated by the President Mouktar ould Daddah of Mauritania and the late President Tubman of Liberia in an effort to establish links between the OERS and other West African states.

The countries sought to coordinate their economic development activities. The aim of the West African Regional Group was to take immediate steps to achieve cooperation in the fields of agriculture, industry, communications, transport, energy, health, education, research, and cultural exchanges. The group also sought to harmonize the activities of member states for peaceful and rapid development of their respective countries, and to create a West African common market.

The protocol establishing the West African Regional Group set up several institutions to facilitate smooth functioning. The Conference of Heads of State and Government was to be the supreme body of the group; the Council of Ministers would be responsible for directing the day-to-day functions; an Executive Secretariat would conduct studies in all aspects of economic cooperation and make recommendations to the Council of Ministers; and subsidiary bodies would be created as they became necessary.

In addition to the more sophisticated economic groupings described above, there are in West Africa several other smaller economic groupings, sometimes consisting of two or three countries. There are also bilateral trade agreements between pairs of countries including Ghana and Guinea, Mali and Upper Volta, Mali and Ivory Coast, and Senegal and Gambia. The multinational projects include a clinker-based cement plant costing 250 million francs (CFA), established jointly by Dahomey and Togo, and financed largely by private foreign investors. One form of cooperation involves an arrangement under which Ghana is to sell power from the Volta hydroelectric plant to Togo and Dahomey. In the field of transportation development, Nigeria Airways and Ghana Airways agreed to pool jointly the West African route and to have joint deployment of equipment and staff.

COOPERATION IN NORTH AFRICA

In terms of cooperation, the North African countries have an advantage over most areas in Africa in that the majority of the people have a common background and speak a common language. They also have had trade and other social contacts for a very long time. The entire area had a population of 76.3 million in 1966, and its gross domestic product (at 1960 market prices) was $13.4 billion. This constitutes a viable market for the establishment of large-scale manufacturing industries. However, cooperation has not been achieved on a subregional basis. There are two groupings in the area, one made up of the Maghreb countries and another by Egypt, the Sudan, and Libya.

The Maghreb Permanent Consultative Committee

The Maghreb is a closely-knit economic area comprising Algeria, Morocco, Tunisia, and Libya. In contrast to other areas formerly administered by France, there were no serious efforts by the French to create joint institutions in the Maghreb during the colonial era. One reason was that, due to the proximity of France, there were fewer problems of administration; also, Libya was not under French rule.

The first initiative toward cooperation undertaken by the countries of the Maghreb was the meeting held at the expert level early in 1964 in Tangier, at the invitation of the ECA. Following the recommendation of the expert meeting, a Conference of Maghreb Ministers for Economy was held in Tunis on September 29, 1964. The Maghreb governments and heads of state became acutely aware of the need for building a viable economic group as a means of stepping up the rate of progress. Therefore, the ministers agreed to establish a special relationship in economic cooperation and trade by setting up the Maghreb Permanent Consultative Committee (CPCM), and a protocol agreement was signed governing a preferential arrangement for trade exchanges and for initiating the harmonization of trade policies.

In the early stages of their efforts, the Maghreb countries adopted a sector-by-sector approach. Later, they agreed to replace this system by a general framework for cooperation. A general transitional plan covering all the Maghreb countries over a five-year period was prepared, including the following features: (1) the preparation of a list of industries whose products would be assured free access to the markets of the member countries; (2) the easing of foreign exchange between member states in order to stimulate trade among them; (3) the harmonization of customs tariffs against third countries; (4) a plan to increase trade in agricultural products; (5) the creation of a Maghreb bank to finance common projects; and (6) the establishment of an appropriate mechanism for multilateral payments.

Implementation of Joint Projects

As a means of facilitating cooperation in the various economic sectors, the Maghreb countries have set up several committees and specialized agencies to conduct studies and to make recommendations for cooperation in various fields. The Committee on Post Office and Telecommunications Coordination is responsible for matters regarding the linking up of telecommunication facilities, especially the Tunis-Algiers, Algiers-Casablanca, and Rabat-Tripoli lines. Progress in this aspect has already been made. The Committee on Tourism

MAP 8.1

Multinational Economic Organizations in Africa
As of January 1, 1971

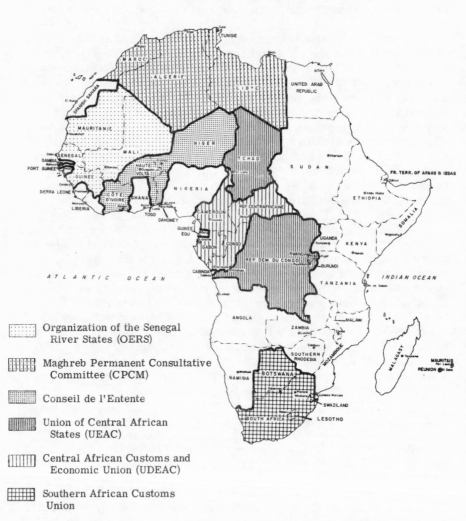

::::: Organization of the Senegal
      River States (OERS)

▦▦▦ Maghreb Permanent Consultative
      Committee (CPCM)

▥▥▥ Conseil de l'Entente

▨▨▨ Union of Central African
      States (UEAC)

▥▥▥ Central African Customs and
      Economic Union (UDEAC)

▦▦▦ Southern African Customs
      Union

MAP 8.2

Multinational Economic Organizations in Africa
As of January 1, 1971

MAP 8.3

Multinational Economic Organizations in Africa
As of January 1, 1971

Conference of East and
Central African States

West African Rice Development
Association (WARDA)

conducted studies for the establishment of a Maghreb Institute for
Training in Hotel and Tourist Trade Affairs, which has been established
and is also responsible for the coordination of advertising and the
organization of the Maghreb tourist festivals. The Esparto Grass
Agency was set up to commercialize the production of esparto grass
(a kind of grass used in the manufacture of cordage, bags and, paper)
on the basis of annual export quotas and to coordinate the activities
of all producers in the Maghreb. The Industrial Studies Center (ISC)
was set up with the assistance of the United Nations Development
Program to promote the coordinated industrialization of the Maghreb;
to conduct research and studies in the field of industry of interest to
two or more Maghreb countries; and to study the possibilities for the
coordination of national development plans. In 1968 the program of
the ISC included studies concerning the desalination of sea water,
chemical fertilizers production, the manufacture of pharmaceutical
goods, the development of esparto grass, and the advancement of
training of skilled labor. Several committees have been created each
to deal with special aspects in transport development, such as road,
railways, air, and marine.

The Maghreb Permanent Consultative Committee has made considerable efforts to advance cooperation among the member countries.
Attempts also were made to find effective ways of ensuring coordinated
action at all levels of economic activity and more particularly in the
field of trade expansion among them. For the past two years, however,
the political problems in the area, and in particular, the deterioration
of the relationship between Libya and Morocco has considerably reduced
chances for cooperation between the two countries. In fact, Libya and
not attended a number of important Maghreb consultative meetings on
economic cooperation. In practice, the Maghreb now virtually consists
only of Morocco, Algeria, and Tunisia. Libya is now cooperating with
Egypt and the Sudan, and in 1971, a federation between Libya, Egypt,
and Syria was created in which the Sudan has expressed its intention
to enter in 1972.

Other Areas of Cooperation Within
the Maghreb

Much of the progress toward economic cooperation in the CPCM
has consisted of individual projects in a specific field involving at least
two countries. These single projects have nonetheless encouraged
the spirit of cooperation and are proving vital for the strengthening of
the wider framework for cooperation in the Maghreb. These efforts
include the Treaty of Brotherhood, Good Neighborliness and Cooperation between Algeria and Tunisia, which provides, inter alia, for the

strengthening of economic ties through economic cooperation by the
member countries. The Algerian-Tunisian Transport Commission
was established to adopt conventions on public transport for travelers,
the international transportation of goods by roads, the prevention of
customs subventions, and joint control of frontiers.

A bilateral agreement also exists between Algeria and Libya,
which established joint commissions for economic, cultural, scientific,
and technical cooperation and agreed to establish joint companies to
develop the petroleum industry including producing, processing, marketing, transportation, and coordination of policies affecting this industry.
Algeria, Libya, the U.A.R., and Iraq agreed to cooperate and coordinate
the oil activities of their individual national oil companies. There is
an agreement by Algeria, Libya, and Iraq to establish a joint fund for
support and assistance in the development of the petroleum industry
and to formulate joint projects in industry and maritime transport.

Algeria and Tunisia have adopted cooperation agreements in
development including the goals of increasing trade between the two
countries, establishing transit through Tunisia of petroleum from
Algeria, coordinating petroleum policy, and creating an Algerian-
Tunisian Chamber of Commerce to enhance cooperation through the
financing of industry and trade.

Future areas of cooperation include an agreement between
Tunisia and Libya to cooperate in the production of fertilizers and
sulfuric acid. Under this agreement, Tunisia will specialize in the
phosphate industry and Libya in the ammonia industry. A joint industrial organization has been proposed to produce sulfuric acid, cement,
and natural gypsum in Tunisia. The two countries also will cooperate
in agriculture, technical assistance, and human resources development.
The effect of the recent political upheavals in North Africa on these
agreements cannot be readily assessed.

Some countries of the Maghreb have established cooperation
with countries outside the Maghreb. Libya has ratified an economic
cooperation agreement and a technical cooperation agreement concluded
by Libya, Sudan, and the U.A.R.

Economic cooperation involving some Maghreb countries and
Mauritania has increased since the past two to three years, and Mauritania attends the meetings of the CPCM as an observer. A joint commission for Algerian-Mauritanian cooperation was created to promote
economic, cultural, scientific, and technical cooperation. This commission has made far-reaching proposals including the construction

of a road and the establishment of an air service link between Tindouf in Algeria and Mauritania. There are also cooperation arrangements in higher education. A shipping shuttle service operated by a Mauritanian shipping company has been established between Casablanca in Morocco and Nouakchott in Mauritania.

Cooperation Involving Libya, the U.A.R., and Sudan

In recent years, there have been efforts to foster cooperation of Libya, U.A.R., and Sudan. The driving force is political motivation, but these countries have pledged to develop jointly certain aspects of economic activity in order to enhance their rates of economic advancement. The agreement establishing economic cooperation provides for the creation of sectoral committees to be responsible for the joint development of the various sectors, especially air, road, and maritime transportation, and also to seek ways of harmonizing economic development in the area.

Sudan and the U.A.R. have had cooperation arrangements for many years. In the past, the economic relations included mainly bilateral and trade agreements. There was also a customs agreement under which goods originating in either of the two countries were accorded preferential treatment when moved from one to the other. There was also cooperation in the development of human resources and manpower training.

In 1969, an agreement for economic cooperation by the two countries was signed, with the goal of providing a comprehensive framework for wider forms of economic cooperation. A joint project was established for reducing water wastage in the upper reaches of the Nile; scientific and technical cooperation in agriculture; the establishment of a joint permanent committee of experts on cotton growing; and the development of artesian wells. There is also cooperation in transport development, including navigation on the Nile River; a joint transport company to develop transportation on Lake Nasser, and a joint road project to develop the road link from Aswan to Omdurman.

One of the main problems which this group of countries will encounter if they wish to institute comprehensive schemes for cooperation is the lack of adequate transport facilities. As was pointed out in Chapter 7, there are hardly any good links between Libya and Sudan or U.A.R. In the future, programs for joint development should consider the development of transport and communication as having great priority, especially with regard to the development of the Tripoli-Benghazi-Alexandria-Cairo highway.

OTHER SYSTEMS OF COOPERATION IN AFRICA

There exist in Africa other systems of cooperation that do not follow the subregional patterns described in Chapter 2. Most of these economic groupings have wide membership--members of the Afro-Malagasy Common Organization, for example, range all the way from Mauritius in Southern Africa to Senegal in West Africa. Some of the groupings aspire to cooperate in limited fields of economic activity while others aim at joint development of all sectors of the economy. Some prominent economic groupings in this category are examined in detail below.

The Afro-Malagasy Common Organization

The Afro-Malagasy Common Organization (OCAM) was established in 1966 with fourteen member countries of former French West and Central Africa. The member countries are Cameroun, Central African Republic, Congo (Brazzaville), Ivory Coast, Dahomey, Gabon, Upper Volta, Congo (Kinshasa), Niger, Togo, Rwanda, Senegal, Chad, Madagascar, and Mauritius which joined the organization in 1969. The OCAM has evolved from a series of other institutions for cooperation. In 1960, the need to reestablish the old economic links was realized and a conference held in Abidjan of the heads of states of eleven countries agreed to set up an organization for economic and political cooperation. Subsequently, at a meeting held in Brazzaville, a group commonly called the Brazzaville Group was established by Cameroun, Central African Republic, Congo (Brazzaville), Ivory Coast, Dahomey, Gabon, Upper Volta, Mauritania, Niger, Senegal, Chad, and Madagascar. This organization was primarily concerned with political matters, and its objective was to foster peace, noninterference in the internal affairs of the member states, and economic and cultural cooperation. However, the countries recognized the need for strong economic links and in September 1961, they signed a treaty establishing the Afro-Malagasy Organization for Economic Cooperation (OAMCE).

At about the same time, another organization, the Afro-Malagasy Union (UAM) came into existence. Its purpose was to achieve economic cooperation among its members in matters relating to foreign policy in order to strengthen solidarity. The countries also aspired to guarantee their collective security and to maintain peace in Africa,

Madagascar, and the rest of the world. UAM had three specialized subsidiary organs to deal with technical aspects: (1) the Afro-Malagasy Organization for Economic Cooperation (OAMCE) referred to above, to deal with matters relating to economic cooperation and development; (2) the Afro-Malagasy Defense Union (UAMD), to deal with matters of defence and security; and (3) the Afro-Malagasy Postal and Telecommunications Union (UAMPT), responsible for postal and telecommunications services within the member states. In 1962, an additional organization, the Afro-Malagasy Office for Industrial Property (OAMPI), was established to take charge of matters relating to industry especially with regard to applications for patents, trade marks, and industrial designs.

In March 1964, problems resulting from the apparent proliferation of organizations in the group were felt; the OAMCE and the UAM were consequently dissolved and replaced by a single institution called the Afro-Malagasy Economic Cooperation Union (UAMCE), whose aim was to strengthen cooperation and solidarity among the African and Malagasy states as a means of enhancing their political, economic, social, technical, and cultural development. There were still difficulties in defining concrete objectives that would be sufficiently flexible to serve the aspirations of the individual member states and still maintain the identity of the group. Subsequently, at the meeting of heads of state held at Nouakchott in February 1965, the member states agreed that the UAMCE should be dissolved and replaced by the OCAM, whose charter was signed in Tananarive in June 1966; however, Mauritania, one of the founder members of the Brazzaville Group, resigned.

The Aims and Objectives of the OCAM

Like most of the existing economic groupings in Africa, the OCAM aims at economic development through cooperation in all major fields of economic activity. The objectives of the OCAM are, inter alia, to strengthen the solidarity and close cooperation among member states in order to raise their people's standard of living and to achieve a progressive harmonization of economic policies and coordination of development plans. The areas of cooperation include: (1) in the field of production and industrialization, the question of credit, fiscal policy, investment codes, and development funds; (2) in the field of domestic and foreign trade, problems of price and markets, customs tariffs, trade policy, and intra-African trade; (3) in the monetary field, establishment of a common monetary policy toward third countries; and (4) in the international field, developing relationships with regional and international economic organization. (Articles 1, 2, and 3 of the charter).

Implementation of Joint Programs

The OCAM has a wide membership with complex and often con-
flicting objectives in their economic development policies; some OCAM
members also belong to the OERS, the Conseil de l'Entente, the UDEAC,
the UEAC, and the Conference of East and Central African States. It
therefore becomes difficult to envisage multinational projects that are
not the subject of an agreement in any of the other organizations and
in which most OCAM member states can participate directly. However,
in recent years there have been serious attempts to define a wide range
of potential projects including harmonization of planning policies. There
also have been recommendations with the goal of achieving uniformity
in sanitary legislation, joint savings plans and credit facilities, and
harmonization of customs and commercial regulations.

As a means of enhancing economic cooperation, the OCAM has
set up a number of other subsidiary organizations which, although
essentially autonomous, are nonetheless the offsprings of the parent
organization. These are the UAMPT and the OAMPI, which were incorporated from the previous institution; the Inter-State School of
Rural Engineering, whose function is to train engineers in agricultural
and scientific techniques for economic development; the Institute of
Veterinary Sciences and Medicine at Dakar, whose function is to prepare for the adaptation of teaching in animal husbandry within the member states; and the Organization for the Development of African Tourism, (ODTA) which is responsible for the development of tourism in
the OCAM countries. Other major achievements of the OCAM are the
OCAM sugar and meat agreements.

The OCAM Sugar Agreement

Sugar is one of the commodities that have been subject to overproduction and low prices in recent years. These two factors were
felt within the OCAM, especially by the principal sugar producers.
Accordingly, some concerted action was necessary to maintain prices
and to avoid wasteful competition. In 1966, the OCAM countries established an Executive Council under the Afro-Malagasy Sugar Agreement.
The main object of the agreement is the coordination of trading arrangements by the sugar producing and sugar importing countries within the
OCAM, including the establishment of prices, the control of imports
and exports, and quota systems.

The sugar agreement also provides for the standardization of
sugar prices to ensure stable and reasonable prices to the producers
while at the same time protecting consumer interests. The OCAM

sugar price is fixed by the Executive Council every year independently of world prices, this procedure was introduced to ensure the profitability of the sugar industry. Imports of sugar from nonmembers are subject to an import levy to bring their prices in line with the OCAM price level. Membership in the sugar agreement is open to both producers and consumers. The sugar agreement is of particular importance to Madagascar, which has an annual surplus of sugar in the region of 75,000 tons; to Congo (Brazzaville), another major producer; and to Mauritius since its economy entirely depends upon the proceeds from sugar exports.

At its sixth session, the OCAM Executive Council recommended reduction of the tax paid to the producing countries--the most important of which are Madagascar and Congo (Brazzaville)--from 8,500 francs (CFA) to 4,500 francs (CFA) per ton during the 1969 crop season. The total production of sugar within the OCAM was estimated at about 260,000 tons in 1970, while the consumption of the importing countries within the OCAM was about 150,000 tons. Therefore, there was surplus of some 110,000 tons. In January 1970, the Executive Council recommended new measures for stabilizing sugar prices and the EEC agreed to grant an advance of about $1.2 million toward instituting an Equalization Fund.

Some further changes were introduced in the sugar agreement in 1970. It was agreed that the member states would buy 80 percent of their sugar from within the OCAM as against 70 percent under the previous arrangements. The question of quotas between the main producers, which dragged on from 1966-70, also was finally settled. Madagascar had maintained that, since consumption in Congo (Brazzaville) was only 3,000 tons as against 40,000 tons in Madagascar, the quota should reflect consumption levels rather than production levels, since otherwise Congo (Brazzaville) actually received a higher quota. This proposal was accepted by the OCAM states. Another innovation in the sugar agreement was the removal of the stabilization tax under which a tax was paid on imports of sugar from sources outside the OCAM, with proceeds from the taxes subsequently paid to the sugar exporters. The stabilization tax had presented problems in the implementation of the sugar agreement.

A number of problems that in recent years have caused some concern about the effective working of the OCAM involve both economic and political considerations. On the economic side, one problem has been that of sheer numbers. Although nearly all the OCAM countries were once under French administration, they have widely varying economic interests and therefore OCAM cannot be described as a

homogeneous economic unit. The countries also have found it difficult
to implement their economic agreements, especially with regard to the
development of joint industrial projects.

On the political side, the sharp differences between Congo (Kinshasa) and Congo (Brazzaville) have been a major setback for cooperation. In this instance, politics clearly acted as a block against economic
cooperation efforts. This fact has been recognized and consequently
in recent years a series of talks were held in an attempt to normalize
the relations of Congo (Kinshasa) and Congo (Brazzaville) in the fields
of economic, cultural, and telecommunications development. The ferry
services across the River Congo were resumed but diplomatic relations
are still strained.

The Lake Chad Basin Commission

The Lake Chad Basin Commission is one of the few economic
groupings in Africa to include both English- and French-speaking
African states. In 1964, the countries near Lake Chad--Cameroun,
Chad, Niger, and Nigeria--decided to establish an organization responsible for the joint utilization of the resources of the Lake Chad Basin
and its waters for economic development. Thus, in the same year the
countries signed the Convention and Statute Relating to the Development
of the Chad Basin, which is the principal instrument for regulating joint
programs in the development of the area. The four countries agreed
to work together closely for the social and economic development of the
Chad Basin. Priority was given to the determination of the basin's
total water resources and to the program for development of agriculture,
livestock, and fisheries in the area. The countries also agreed to find
means of coordinating transport development and to unite their efforts
against the tsetse fly.

Aims and Objectives

The aims and objectives of the Lake Chad Basin Commission as
laid out in Article IX of the statute annexed to its convention are: (1)
to prepare general regulations for the proper implementation of the
convention; (2) to collect, evaluate, and disseminate information on
the proposals made by the member states and to recommend joint
projects and research programs in the Lake Chad Basin; (3) to maintain close contacts among the member states so as to ensure the most
efficient use of the water of the Lake Chad Basin. It is also the intention of the member states to formulate proposals to encourage economic
cooperation in other fields.

Execution and Implementation of
Joint Programs

Much progress has been made in the joint implementation of the
common projects within the Lake Chad Basin Commission. In the development of natural resources, a study of the total water resources of
the area was conducted, providing the technical data required for future
development at a cost of $479,998 financed by the United Nations Devel-
opment Program. An electric model of water resources development
was erected by UNESCO and is said to be the first of its kind in Africa.
Another study project costing over $3.2 million was started in 1967 to
evaluate the surface and subterranean water resources of the basin,
including proposals for joint action in development of the water resources. There also were studies of animal husbandry, including the
eradication of bovine diseases, and studies of methods of increasing
the total tonnage of fish from the Lake Chad Basin waters through improvement in fishing equipment, processing, and marketing.

In the field of mineral resources development, a survey of the
water and fisheries resources of the area has been completed with
the assistance of the United Nations Development Programs and
the Economic Commission for Africa is believed to be interested
in this project. There are also projects in the transport field,
including a study of the transport and communications links within
the Lake Chad Basin area. A report on telecommunications links was
completed, and a road feasibility study was commissioned to provide
the basis for joint action in the development of road transport links in
the area. There are also surveys of the navigability of the waterways
of Lake Chad and the rivers flowing into it. Some rules and regulations
were prepared governing the movement of persons, fishermen, fishing
equipment, and products around the lake, including common rules for
the preservation of wildlife.

The Conference of East and Central African States

The political situation in Southern Africa and the problem of
refugees, especially in the countries bordering on the minority white
regimes resulted in the creation of the Conference of East and Central
African states. The following independent African states are members:
Ethiopia, Sudan, Kenya, Uganda, Tanzania, Congo (Kinshasa), Central
African Republic, Congo (Brazzaville), Burundi, Zambia, Chad, Somalia, and Malawi. This is a quasi-political organization with a strong
economic bias. It has evolved from a series of summit meetings of
the heads of state and government; the organization has no treaty,
charter, or convention to govern its operations.

In the early stages, some member states were principally concerned with matters of security, the problem of refugees, the question
of decolonization, and assistance to freedom fighters in Southern Africa.
At that time, an idea emerged that an organization of free independent
African states stretching from the Indian Ocean to the Atlantic Ocean
would form an effective front against the racist regimes in Southern
Africa. There were no specific agreements relating to these problems,
but the countries sought to coordinate their positions and support for
the liberation movements through periodical discussions and consultations. The group also was seen as a way of affording an opportunity
for amicable settlement of disputes between neighboring states, thereby
contributing to peace and security in Africa and strengthening and stabilizing African unity.

Subsequently, the member states showed growing interest in
economic cooperation as a means of strengthening their relations.
At the summit meeting of the heads of state and government held in
Kampala in 1967, decisions were made affecting economic cooperation,
including recommendations for the coordination of national development
plans and steps to avoid the duplication of projects in order to promote
cooperation within the group. In the field of the development of transport and communications, especially road, rail, and water transport,
it was decided that the countries would coordinate their policies in
order to provide a sound infrastructure for the economic development
of the area.

Implementation of Joint Plans

In the absence of a treaty to govern operations or a permanent
secretariat to implement and follow up joint programs, it is rather
difficult to assess the progress of the Conference of East and Central
African States in the economic field. In order to encourage joint development of various sectors, the member states decided at an April
1969 conference held in Lusaka to set up five sectoral committees to
deal with agriculture, industry and energy, transport and communications, trade and tourism, and human resources. Several countries
agreed to host meetings of the sectoral committees. Zambia was
responsible for the Committee on Industry and Energy; Sudan for the
Committee on Agriculture; Ethiopia for the Committee on Transport
and Communications; Uganda for the Committee on Human Resources;
and Central African Republic for the Committee on Trade and Tourism.
These countries were to serve as secretariats for the respective committees and as venue for meetings. A general secretariat also was
set up on a rotating basis, with the country playing host to the current
summit meeting usually designated as general secretariat unitl further
notice.

At the summit conference of the heads of state and government held in Khartoum in January 1970, the countries resolved to strengthen economic cooperation efforts in the various sectors. In the field of agriculture, it was decided to establish an Agricultural Research Consultative Committee to deal with cooperation within existing and future multinational research projects, to conduct training programs for manpower research, and to maintain regular exchange of information on agricultural research within the member states. There also were recommendations relating to the establishment of an Advisory Committee on Forestry Development to deal with research problems related to forestry development and a Committee on Fisheries to deal with research problems related to fisheries resources.

In the field of industry and energy, the 1970 conference recommended that studies be carried out on the financing of multinational industrial projects and on the question of rationalization of sources of supply of industrial equipment. A number of intergovernmental working parties on the utilization of energy were set up by groups of two or more countries within the organization to examine possibilities for joint exploitation of energy resources. As regards transport and communications, the 1970 conference recommended a study of enhancing trade among them. The development of railway links, in particular the link between Chad and Sudan, was another aspect of cooperation that was given priority at the 1970 conference.

Other recommendations included the promotion of trade among the member states, with special measures to be taken for the landlocked countries. In this regard, the 1970 conference urged countries that had not done so to sign the International Convention on Transit in Land-Locked Countries. In the field of human resources development, the conference decided to establish a working group to study factors affecting labor productivity in member states. It also recommended the joint utilization of industrial training facilities; the coordination of agricultural education and training; and the establishment of a special committee on language training as a means of improving communications among the member states.

It is still too early to assess the group's effectiveness in fostering economic cooperation, especially as it lacks an institutional framework. Moreover, the absence of any treaty obligations raises serious doubts as to how a group of this magnitude can effectively cooperate. Nonetheless, the member states seem determined to go ahead with their efforts toward cooperation. The only common factor among them is that, except for one or two countries, there is general accord on the political situation, especially in Southern Africa, and hence a favorable political atmosphere exists for fostering economic cooperation.

Problems could arise because the member states belong to different economic groups. For instance, Kenya, Uganda, and Tanzania belong to the East African Community and Zambia, Ethiopia, Somalia, and Burundi are interested in membership in the East African Community; Central African Republic and Congo (Brazzaville) belong to the Central African Customs and Economic Union; Chad is a member of the Union of Central African States; Congo (Kinshasa), Congo (Brazzaville), Central African Republic, and Chad are members of the Afro-Malagasy Common Organization; Sudan is interested in closer economic cooperation with Libya and the U.A.R.; and Malawi maintains trade and economic links with South Africa, Rhodesia, and Portugal. Although in the short run these associations may not present practical problems, the proliferation of membership in several organizations could result in duplication of efforts and hence a wasting of resources. Therefore, it would appear that at some stage the member states will have to take far-reaching decisions regarding economic cooperation, especially in the implementation of multinational projects in the event of conflict of interests between the Conference of East and Central African states and other existing economic groupings.

The African Development Bank

The efforts to promote joint development projects among the African countries gave rise to the need to provide adequate financial and technical assistance to these countries to sustain their development programs. Therefore, it was necessary to establish a truly African financial institution that would channel resources toward the realization of joint programs. Hence, agreement establishing the African Development Bank (ADB) was signed in August 1963 under the guidance of the Economic Commission for Africa, and ADB was inaugurated in November 1964. Membership in ADB is open to any country that has the status of an independent state within the African continent and its islands. Present members are Algeria, Botswana, Burundi, Cameroun, Chad, Congo (Brazzaville), Congo (Kinshasa), Dahomey, Ethiopia, Ghana, Guinea, Ivory Coast, Kenya, Liberia, Malawi, Mali, Mauritania, Morocco, Niger, Nigeria, Rwanda, Senegal, Sierra Leone, Somalia, Sudan, Swaziland, Tanzania, Togo, Tunisia, Uganda, U.A.R., Upper Volta, and Zambia.

The creation of the ADB was a concrete step by the African countries to strengthen their solidarity by means of economic cooperation and a sign of their recognition of the importance of coordinating national plans for economic and social development with a view to promoting the harmonious economic growth of Africa as a whole and the expansion of foreign trade, in particular intra-African trade.

Aims and Objectives

The main objective of the ADB is to contribute to the economic development and social progress of its members individually and jointly. It is also the aim of ADB (1) to use the resources at its disposal for the financing of investment projects and programs relating to the economic and social development of its members, giving special priority to projects or programs that by their nature or scope concern several members and to projects or programs designed to make the economies of ADB's members increasingly complementary, and to bring about an orderly expansion of the foreign trade of members; (2) to mobilize and increase resources for the financing of investment projects and programs contributing to the development of Africa; (3) to promote investments of public and private capital in Africa in projects or programs designed to contribute to the economic development or social progress of ADB's members; and (4) to provide such technical assistance as may be needed in Africa for the study, preparation, financing, and execution of development projects.

Resources and Operations

The ADB started off with an authorized capital stock of $250 million divided into 25,000 shares of a par value of $10,000 per share. Each member state was required initially to subscribe an equal number of paid-up and callable shares. The ADB was authorized by its statutes to create a special fund to supplement the capital stock. The ADB carries out its operation (1) by making direct loans or participating in direct loans out of funds from its subscribed capital, its reserves, or its undistributed profits; (2) by providing direct loans or participating in direct loans out of funds borrowed from other sources; (3) by investing funds in the equity capital of any undertaking or financial institution; and (4) by giving guarantees on loans made by other organizations to any of the member states.

The ADB made tremendous progress in the mobilization of external resources, and by the end of 1966 it had some $40 million compared with its total paid-up capital of $107.5 million. The international agencies have shown special interest in providing financial support for the ADB. In 1969, the total gross income earned on the ordinary capital resources amounted to nearly $5.6 million and the ADB's net income stood at $3.5 million.

Implementation of Objectives

In recent years, the ADB has been active in supporting or financing projects within the African countries.[6] In 1969, for instance, the ADB approved four projects amounting to $8 million in the member countries. These included urban water supply and sewerage plans in Uganda, which cost about $300,000. The ADB also participated in the equity capital of the East African Development Bank to the value of $1 million and extended a line of credit up to $2 million. Under its technical assistance program, the ADB granted $35,000 to the East African Development Bank to meet the salaries of its staff and recruitment for a period of three years.

In July 1969, a loan of just over $1.3 million was granted to Liberia for the installation of a 15-megawatt gas turbine in Monrovia. The loan was to be repayable over a period of fifteen years. Another loan of $1.5 million was granted to Sierra Leone for the development of the Guma Valley water supply plan, which is intended to increase the water supply in Freetown. Malawi obtained a loan of $3 million for a number of projects for the supply and distribution of electricity in various parts of the country. These projects included 165 miles of 66-kilovolt transmission line from the Nkula hydroplant to Lilongwe; 26 miles of 66-kilovolt transmission line from Tedzani to Blantyre; and various other extension plans around the urban areas.

In 1970, loans were approved for financing several other projects in the African countries. A loan of $2.8 million was granted to Morocco for the construction of transmission lines, substations, and high voltage lines from Jerada to the towns on the Atlantic coast. A loan was given to the National Development Bank of Mali for participation in the share of capital of the Mali Textile Industry (Industrie Textile du Mali). Pan-African Paper Mills (East Africa), Ltd., obtained a loan of over $1.4 million for the establishment of a kraft pulp and paper mill in Kenya.

Future Development Projects

The ADB is considering a number of multinational projects in its future work program and priorities. These include the establishment of a regional and subregional insurance and reinsurance business; the creation of a multinational private investment company; an African energy survey; a study of the possibilities for economic cooperation between Ghana and the Conseil de l'Entente countries; the development of a limestone deposit in Togo for the production of clinker and cement for the West African subregion; the reconstruction of three airports in Nigeria; the construction of the Hargeisa-Berbera road in Somalia; the Yarkofji irrigation plan in Nigeria; the drainage and sewerage plan for Fort Lamy in Chad; a fishing complex in Congo (Brazzaville); the improvement of the Bukoba-Kyaba road in Tanzania; and an agricultural development plan in Zambia that will include the development

of a large-scale commercial farm, the establishment of a national
seed company, and a settlement plan to accomodate 275 families in
the southern part of the country.

THE STRENGTHENING OF EXISTING
ECONOMIC GROUPINGS

An examination of the list of intergovernmental economic groupings
in Africa in the Appendix clearly indicates that there is a problem of
proliferation of economic associations. There are well over sixty economic groupings in Africa, and the main difficulty is that some countries
belong to six or more economic groupings. Whether this is in the best
interests of those countries is difficult to know. In fact, the situation
in terms of manpower and financial resources in most of these countries
is such that they cannot afford to divert these resources from national
to multinational projects. There is, therefore, a prima facie case for
introducing some rationalization in the number of economic organizations in Africa if they are to serve their purpose as instruments for
enhancing economic development of the African countries.

In the quest for effective means to ensure progress toward multinational economic cooperation in Africa, the question of strengthening
or expanding the existing economic groupings, both in terms of economic
objectives as well as membership, becomes an important issue within
the general strategy for economic development. In the past, the majority of African countries have had vague ideas as to what they wish to
achieve by cooperating with other countries. As a result, a number of
the existing groupings were established without a clear notion about
their economic implications. In certain cases, these groupings were
established almost entirely for political reasons, and due to lack of a
sound economic base a majority of these groupings are now of historical
interest rather than of practical value toward economic development.
It is suggested that the African countries seriously consider the possibilities discussed below with regard to future economic groupings.[7]
These proposals are based primarily on economic considerations, some
of which were discussed earlier in this study.

In North Africa, the economic basis for a strong economic grouping already exists and the Maghreb grouping has shown potential for
further development. Although trade among the Maghreb countries
still constitutes a small percentage of their total trade, it has become
increasingly important in recent years. There is a considerable flow
of trade between the Sudan and the U.A.R., but neither of these countries
has much trade with the Maghreb. A greater degree of cooperation

between the Maghreb on the one hand and the U.A.R. and the Sudan on the other would increase economic opportunities for all. The suggestion here is that, rather than create new economic groupings in North Africa, the countries consider expanding the Maghreb to form a stronger economic unit through accession by those countries presently outside it.

In West Africa, the Organization of the Senegal River States is a strong and growing economic grouping. It is suggested that Gambia, Liberia, and Sierra Leone consider joining the OERS. Their membership could result in great advantages to these states through the expansion of the market. For historical reasons, there have been limited economic contacts between some of the countries in the area. But times have changed and there is a need to foster closer ties.

In Mid-West Africa, the Conseil de l'Entente has in recent years been one of the most active economic groupings in Africa. There are signs that the member countries take seriously the question of economic cooperation as a means of enhancing development. In recent years, they have taken concrete measures to expand the areas of common activity, especially in economic development. Given adequate support, this grouping could easily develop into a strong economic entity. It is therefore suggested that Nigeria and Ghana explore the possibility of membership in this organization. Ghana has in fact shown interest in the Conseil de l'Entente, and this interest should be given all possible encouragement. Although Ghana and Nigeria are separated from the Conseil de l'Entente countries by linguistic and other historical factors, the addition of Ghana and Nigeria to this grouping would make it a viable economic unit.

In Central Africa, it is suggested that the Central African Customs and Economic Union be strengthened and that adjoining countries, especially Equatorial Guinea and Chad, consider possibilities for closer economic cooperation with the UDEAC. Congo (Kinshasa) also might consider joining the UDEAC. The UDEAC already forms a strong economic entity, and the addition of two or more states to its membership would be a step in the right direction.

In East Africa, the East African Community has in recent years been reorganized and could easily be developed into a natural nucleus for further economic cooperation. The accession to membership in the East African Community by Zambia, Ethiopia, Somalia, and possibly Burundi and Rwanda would increase the group's economic viability and widen opportunities in trade and industrial development. Since the basis for trade and other economic relations between these countries and the East African Community already exists, it is suggested that negotiations for membership be given greater attention than in the past. If it is difficult to work out more elaborate arrangements, the adjoining states should start by cooperating in such single projects as the Zambia-Tanzania rail link. Such small operations increase the chances for wider cooperation.

In Southern Africa, the geographical location of the independent African states in relation to South Africa is noteworthy. Based on trade and other economic relations, especially in recent years, Malawi, Botswana, Lesotho, Swaziland, Madagascar, and Mauritius could constitute an economic unit that, although not homogeneous under present conditions, nevertheless could develop into some limited form of economic cooperation. In a long-term view, the inclusion of Southern Rhodesia, Angola, Mozambique, Namibia, South Africa, and Reunion in economic cooperation schemes could be seen to contribute to the economic viability of such a grouping and would widen industrial opportunities. The form of cooperation that might be feasible would be at the project level, involving such fields as transport and communications, currency and exchange control, movement of labor, and trade. By special agreements, certain industries could be developed at the multinational level to serve two or more countries.

In the final analysis, it may be that a country or group of countries cannot properly fit within any of the existing economic groupings, due to geographical location or other considerations. Such countries as Rwanda, Burundi, Sudan, Mauritius, Madagascar, Congo (Kinshasa), and Malawi immediately come to mind as examples of countries which, for one reason or another, may not be able to participate directly in some multinational projects because they cannot fit within one economic grouping. Such countries should be given the opportunity to initially participate in the activities of any grouping through bilateral agreements with adjoining states. Subsequently, a more comprehensive scheme could be worked out for more direct participation in a group of their choice. Unfortunately, some of the countries cited above are not only land-locked but also the least developed among the developing African countries. Their development problems therefore are more acute and require urgent action. These are the countries that would tend to benefit most from cooperation. In such cases where the land-locked countries do not belong to the existing groupings the member states should consider special bilateral economic agreements covering the fields in which cooperation would bring about mutual advantages. In addition, these groupings should be prepared to invite nonmembers to their meetings as observers.

In essence, then, the African countries should consider rationalizing the number and form of economic groupings. Based on purely economic considerations, it is difficult to see how some of the small countries that constantly experience shortages of manpower and other resources can effectively belong to more than one economic grouping. At some stage, therefore, it might be advisable for each and every African state to make a bold decision to join one (or at the most two) economic grouping and, having done so, to decide to set aside adequate resources for ensuring the success of the economic grouping so that maximum benefits are derived. If economic cooperation is not regarded as a game of chance, common sense would demand that the African states seriously consider the problems resulting from the proliferation of economic groupings.

HOW MUCH COOPERATION HAS BEEN
ACHIEVED IN AFRICA?

The question that is often asked about economic cooperation in Africa is whether there really is cooperation among the African countries. Or, put in a different way, how much cooperation has been achieved in Africa. These are not easy questions to answer and, although an attempt to provide answers will be made in Chapter 12, it is essential to emphasize two important issues that were raised earlier. The first is that economic cooperation should be viewed as a means of enhancing the economic development of the African countries, whether this takes the form of a single project or involves wider areas of cooperation, as is envisaged in the East African Community, the UDEAC, or the Maghreb. To the extent that these economic groupings, large or small, are achieving their objectives, it cannot be disputed that economic cooperation is successful. The second point is that the extent to which the countries consider cooperation essential and are willing to bind themselves by means of treaties, charters, and conventions represents a major step toward joint economic development. It is therefore erroneous and unrealistic to judge the success of any economic grouping in the light of other associations, even in the same area, since two groupings cannot be identical in form, content, and objectives.

From the discussion in earlier sections of this chapter, three major categories of cooperation can be distinguished, although the lines of demarcation are not precise. The first type of cooperation has consisted of efforts to set up single multinational enterprises and institutions, such as joint airlines, shipping lines, and research institutions. The OERS, OCAM, and Lake Chad Basin Commission fall under this category of cooperation. Their agreements did not originally involve the coordination of economic policies but merely provide for joint action in a specified field. The multinational banks, such as the

central banks in West and Central Africa, although they have close
bearing on the domestic and foreign trade of the member countries,
are not in themselves designed to be instruments for devising or effecting policies for economic integration and development.

The second type of cooperation has consisted of efforts to group
countries into customs unions or free trade areas in which the members
grant each other preferential tariff treatment and ensure free movement
of goods and services. The UDEAO, and many intergovernmental organizations in Africa are examples of this kind of cooperation.

The third type of economic cooperation that has been tried in the
African region has consisted of efforts by some countries to achieve
concerted planning in a wide range of economic activities. The Maghreb
countries of North Africa, for instance, were initially concerned with
joint selective planning and development of defined areas of activities,
but in recent years the group has developed to a more advanced stage
of cooperation. The East African Community, although essentially a
common market, gave greater emphasis to questions of joint development planning and harmonization of industrial policies for balancing
development among the member states.

In looking at development in Africa in the field of economic cooperation, the picture that emerges is one of groups of African countries
constantly coming together in customs unions and other economic associations that, although basically politically oriented, consider economic
development through economic cooperation as a goal. The main concern
of the African states in the early stages was to consolidate their newly
won independence and to prevent further exploitation by external vested
interests. Therefore, the emphasis was on political unity with economic
development as a means of consolidating independence. Now there has
been shift in emphasis from political unity to economic integration.

One of the main problems that confront the African states is that
the type of economic cooperation envisaged means that, for instance,
countries agree to talk about the desirability of building a road, rail
line, or multipurpose hydroelectric project but normally make no firm
commitments and do not give any autonomous or semi-autonomous
agency the green light to proceed with the implementation of the project.[8]
Furthermore, if and when the plans are initiated machinery is not
usually developed for implementing decisions or for follow-up. The
question of financing the projects is left to the individual countries.
When, after four to five years, the countries decide to take stock of
progress made on their joint decisions, they often are dismayed to
discover that their efforts were in vain. What is required is to define

each project under integration very clearly, to assess the financial and manpower requirements, and to provide the necessary institutional machinery for financing the project's implementation as well as follow-up. If this procedure were followed, it would be easy to find out why a plan failed and thus learn what mistakes to avoid in subsequent plans.

In organizational terms, considerable problems have been caused by differences in the patterns of social, political, and economic development in the African countries. As a result of differences in external influences and the intensity of social contacts between Africans and their former rulers, the social outlook of the African people tends to differ from country to country and sometimes even from tribe to tribe. This has created invisible barriers between the peoples of Africa, and strong will power, patience, and greater understanding will be necessary to break these barriers.

Differences in the political, economic and social policy objectives of the metropolitan countries, resulted in differences in the development of the political institutions in Africa. On the attainment of independence, no attempt was made to introduce major changes in the political machinery even though the government changed hands. The effect of this fact on cooperation is that government representatives in the multinational groupings find it difficult to make decisions without ratification by their national parliaments. Sometimes the economic situation has changed by the time ratification is obtained. On the economic side, differences in levels of economic development, the determination of basic national economic requirements have and the development priorities have been reflected in the attitude of the African leaders and their people to questions of economic cooperation.

In regard to structural aspects, the problem of economic cooperation lies in the institutional framework for economic development. The undeveloped nature of a country's institutions is in itself an obstacle to further efforts to develop and tends to limit the country's ability to reap benefits from cooperation. Thus, a country remains economically underdeveloped because it is underdeveloped. Unfortunately, this is exactly the situation in which the African countries find themselves today. Due to the countries' small size, resources necessary for development are few; there is a chronic and acute shortage of skilled manpower; industries operate at excess capacity due to lack of demand as a result of the narrowness of domestic markets; imports rise as does the import bill while export earnings remain constant or decline; and foreign aid constantly is reduced by the advanced countries and unemployment continues to rise. All these problems, which exist because a country is poor, point to the need for coordinated effort. The degree of intensity of these problems differs from state to state, as does the level of economic performance. As a result, certain countries tend to benefit more from economic cooperation than others. This factor has made it difficult for some countries to accept wholeheartedly the idea of economic cooperation, and it is the problem facing most of the intergovernmental organizations.

On the practical side, the intergovernmental economic groupings have experienced considerable difficulty in their attempts to create institutional machinery for cooperation that is capable of making decisions binding on the member states and implementing and following such decisions. With the possible exception of the East African Community and the Maghreb countries, most of these economic groupings have not yet created a strong multinational organ for cooperation. Even within the East African Community, most of the existing institutional arrangements were incorporated from the past and the creation of new ones has not proved easy.

The other problem confronting the intergovernmental groupings relates to the question of distribution of benefits under multinational cooperation, especially with regard to the land-locked and the least developed countries. No ideal formula has yet been devised for the equitable distribution of benefits, especially the sharing of import revenues in the customs unions and common markets. This problem has been tackled on an ad hoc basis, with the result that countries are never quite certain as to how they can assess such gains vis-à-vis possible disadvantages. There is always the genuine fear that the smaller countries may end up perpetually dependent on the more advanced partners in a multinational set-up.

In order that these multinational economic groupings realize their programs, it is essential that the member states reexamine their objectives and consider whether their present treaties or charters really reflect their individual aspirations and also serve multinational cooperation. This is important because the conflict between national and multinational interests has been a strong factor in slowing down the development of economic cooperation. For instance, it is necessary to determine whether the internal economic policies of these groups--such as customs and industrial legislation, currency and exchange control, and fiscal and other indirect taxes--really are oriented toward economic cooperation. If the answer to this question is negative, it is suggested that a serious review of these policies should be the first step toward ensuring that joint decisions meet development requirements. Moreover, the countries must consider whether they really have taken adequate measures, at both the national and multinational level, to sustain the efforts toward cooperation. Within the same context, the next question that the states should consider seriously is whether their political policies help or hinder the efforts toward economic cooperation. If the answer is that political policies are a hindrance, as indeed it might be in most African countries, then steps must be taken to change the situation.

NOTES

1. See the American Association of International Law, International Legal Materials, Vol. III, No. 6 (September 1964), pp. 1106-15.

2. East African Common Services Organization, Treaty for East African Cooperation (Nairobi, June 1967) Article 2, pp. 2-3.

3. See Ethiopian Herald, Sunday, March 29, 1970.

4. For full details see the Customs Agreement-Union of South Africa-Territories of Basutoland, Swaziland and the Bechuanaland Protectorate (Potchefstroom, 1910), contained in British High Commissioner's Notice 65 of 1910.

5. See Article 2 of the Charter of the Union of Central African States in the American Society of International Law, International Legal Material Vol VII No. 4, July 1968, p. 735.

6. For full details, see African Development Bank, Report of the Board of Governors, Abidjan (Ivory Coast) 1967 to 1969.

7. See also Economic Commission for Africa, Report of the Second Meeting of the Executive Committee, E/CN.14/462, pp. 50-51.

8. Economic Commission for Africa, Report of the Sub-regional Meeting on Economic Cooperation in East Africa, E/CN.14/346, Annex VII, p. 3.

9

SOME
POLITICAL
ASPECTS
OF ECONOMIC
COOPERATION
IN AFRICA

THE ROLE OF POLITICS IN ECONOMIC DEVELOPMENT

In discussing the problems of economic development in Africa, it is customary for economists to argue that politics lies outside the scope of economic theory. It is argued that politics is a very delicate issue in Africa and therefore economists should not try to discuss its implications on economic development. Although this may be so, it merely implies that one is looking at the development problems from one limited aspect and that the analysis therefore cannot present a true picture of the situation.

In this text, it is not intended to bring out political discussions, which indeed belong elsewhere; what is intended is to examine those aspects of political institutions that directly influence economic decisions, especially in regard to economic cooperation. It is argued here that it is imperative for economists to understand the political aspects of economic development because economic development policies can be made to really reflect the thinking of the African leaders only through a clear conception of politics. In much the same way, politicians should have a fair understanding of economic principles so that their development policies are economically realistic.

Even during the colonial period, political considerations influenced the development of social and economic institutions in the African territories. The development of such institutions was geared to strengthening political structures in the metropolitan countries. In reviewing economic progress, it can be noted that throughout the 1960's politics played a decisive role in determining the course of economic development in post-independence Africa. The effects of politics

321

on economic cooperation have been so great that it is essential to examine briefly how economic cooperation is directly or indirectly related to political harmony among the African states.

The political differences between the various African states, the differences in their foreign policies as dictated by their affiliations with extra-African organizations, the questions of national sovereignty manifested in the desire to safeguard the power of self-determination and territorial integrity, and the attitudes of the African people to the question of economic development in general, all contributed toward slowing down the tempo of development in Africa and often frustrated efforts to create suitable institutional machinery for economic cooperation. Where political differences existed, no amount of economic reasoning appealed to the African leaders.

Although the concept of cooperation at the multinational level has been accepted by the countries in Africa as the most effective strategy for economic development, these countries have not yet accepted the idea of a supranational body with sufficient mandate to make decisions that are binding on the member countries with regard to joint economic development of the subregions. A supranational body appears contrary to the power of self-determination and national sovereignty to which the African countries attach the greatest importance, and any institution that tends to encroach upon such sovereign powers, even in the field of economic development, is generally unacceptable. Under these circumstances, at best only very loose forms of association have been or can be created in Africa and the question of fragmentation of the continent remains unsolved. It should be pointed out that, although economic cooperation would be enhanced by the existence of an effective multinational institutional machinery, there are organizations such as the Conference of East and Central African States, the Customs Agreement between Botswana, Lesotho, Swaziland, South Africa, and the Niger River Basin Commission, which have not created any elaborate machinery for cooperation. In fact, the idea of some binding legal machinery upon them frightens some African countries. Hence, if three or four countries agree to cooperate without the need for any machinery, they should be encouraged.

The political instability and the tendency for further subdivision of the African continent, as witnessed in recent years, have created considerable uncertainty. Although some African states genuinely wish to see multinational cooperation established, the political instability in neighboring states causes them to adopt a very cautious approach or reserved attitude toward economic cooperation. Enthusiasm is to a considerable extent limited by this uncertainty. Closely related to this problem is the lack of sustained adherence by the African states to decisions concerning the establishment of subregional machinery for cooperation, which has been influenced by a multiplicity of causes. Whatever the reasons for this phenomenon, there must be a strong political will for economic cooperation to be a success. This is important because the decision-making machinery in the African states lies in the hands of the political leaders even with regard to purely economic matters. The African countries must demonstrate their willingness to yield to a multinational body a certain degree of decision-making in matters relating to economic development. Furthermore, they must be prepared to take appropriate measures to ensure that the decisions taken by the organ they have created are fully supported, both morally and materially. Unless this approach is fully accepted, the institutional arrangements that have been or are being created will be no more than economic debating clubs.

Previously in Africa, politics has played a decidely negative role in economic development. Vital industries, infrastructure, and other economic factors contributing to development have been established in isolation. This is not because the African countries failed to recognize the need for cooperation but because political considerations dictated the vital economic decisions. There is an enormous quantity of information on the possibilities for cooperation by the African countries, especially within the secretariats of the United Nations, such as the Economic Commission for Africa. Therefore, the lack of decision on the part of the African states is not due to lack of information but, rather to lack of political will and the power to take and support decisions toward economic cooperation. It must be remembered that economic development largely depends upon the attitudes of the leaders who are in a position to take concrete decisions. Since under present conditions in Africa politics plays a major role in influencing economic decisions, it is essential that the African countries be prepared to take appropriate policy measures, at both the national and multinational levels, to support and sustain efforts toward economic cooperation. In addition, the principle of a multinational organ-- entrusted with the general economic policies and oriented specifically toward multinational cooperation--must be unequivocally accepted by the African countries. In short, the African countries must now earnestly begin to take measures to enable politics to play a positive role toward economic development. This is a problem for which only the African countries themselves can find an acceptable solution.

TOWARD THE UNION OF AFRICAN STATES

Chapter 1 pointed out that the original concept of economic co-operation in Africa envisaged as ideal for enhancing the rate of economic development in Africa a system of cooperation in which all independent African states could participate. Some African leaders thought at one time that the form of unity required was a single strong continental government with a single parliament, a single navy, a single air force, and a single army. Some African leaders firmly believed that the ideal form of African unity would be the establishment of one political organization that would give full expression to all ethnic groups and yet maintain the individual aspirations of the countries.[1] This approach presupposed the existence of one leader at the apex of the continental government.

There was the general belief that by establishing a strong con-tinental government the African countries would be in a position to influence the development of their own institutions. It was further believed that any piecemeal approach to the question of African unity was bound to be susceptible to the intrigues and machinations of external vested interests and thus would fail to achieve the desired objectives. The charter in Article 2 Section I of the UAS provided that "the Union of African States shall be regarded as the nucleus of the United States of Africa."[2]

Perhaps the principle behind the establishment of the UAS was a genuine desire to achieve unity in Africa more rapidly as a means of solving the pressing problems of the African people, but the approach was not accepted by all the African leaders. For one thing, this con-cept of unity assumed that the African countries would readily agree to the idea of one leader in Africa. It also overlooked the fact that many African leaders wanted a more gradual approach. Even among the founders of the UAS, there were some misgivings as to whether it was realistic to expect all the African states to join UAS. Some countries wished to see the development of small groupings as steps toward the establishment of one African government. However, other African leaders interpreted this move as an attempt by some leaders to gain political control of the whole of Africa. To them this was no more than an attempt to introduce neocolonialism or to reintroduce imperialism. In fact, many African leaders made no attempt at all to hide their feelings against any move that might be interpreted as tending to revive imperialism.* To most of them, imperialism was imperialism no matter who practiced it. In fact, the fear of imperialism contributed to slowing down the momentum toward African/Unity that developed during the early days of Pan-Africanism.

The African leaders now seem to prefer the development of small economic or even quasi-political groupings that will later develop into larger unions and perhaps lead to all-African unity. This idea has been the most popular approach to unity in Africa in establishing economic communities through economic integration within the various areas of Africa. These small economic communities will serve as springboards for the development of greater cooperation embracing political consider-ations. It is now recognized that political unity would be neither feasi-ble nor realistic under present conditions in Africa and that there is no common foundation upon which to build such unity. Although the ob-jectives of all the African states are identical in most aspects, it is rightly felt that, due to internal differences in governmental and political machinery and to differences in historical background, it would be very difficult to envisage a political union within the foreseeable future, even on a subregional scale. In fact, rather than move toward political unity, in recent years the African states have seemed to be moving further away from it.

For this reason, many leaders now think that economic cooperation offers a solution to development problems in Africa. Under economic cooperation, the countries need not give up national sovereignty and would be able to unite forces while preserving their individual political aspirations. The idea is that, after the economic foundations are firmly established, it will be possible to work for a political union from a common and concrete foundation.

---

*This resentment was clearly voiced by the leader of the Nigerian delegation to the Second Conference of Independent African States held in Addis Ababa in June 1960 when he said ". . . if anybody makes the mistake of feeling that he is a Messiah who has got a mission to lead Africa, then the whole purpose of Pan-Africanism will, I fear, be defeated."

THE ORGANIZATION OF AFRICAN UNITY

The aspirations of the African people to foster unity was mani-
fested through the establishment of the Organization of African Unity
(OAU) in May 1963. Membership in the OAU is open to any country in
Africa that has the status of an independent state. The 41 independent
African states belonging to OAU are Algeria, Botswana, Burundi,
Cameroun, Central African Republic, Chad, Congo (Brazzaville), Congo
(Kinshasa), Dahomey, Equatorial Guinea, Ethiopia, Gabon, Gambia,
Ghana, Guinea, Ivory Coast, Kenya, Lesotho, Liberia, Libya, Malagasy
Republic, Malawi, Mali, Mauritania, Mauritius, Morocco, Niger,
Nigeria, Rwanda, Senegal, Sierra Leone, Somalia, Sudan, Swaziland,
Tanzania, Togo, Tunisia, Uganda, U.A.R., Upper Volta, and Zambia.

The relationship between politics and economics is clearly seen
in the objectives and functioning of OAU. Although OAU is basically a
political organization, the member states have recognized the necessity
of ensuring economic development in Africa, including the expansion of
trade through the elimination of obstacles to intra-African exchanges;
the joint utilization of natural resources and the river basins; the coordination of transport and communications; and the creation of joint
research projects in industry and human resources in order to stimulate
the expansion of trade and economic growth. These measures are also
seen as measures for consolidating the independence of the African
states.

Aims and Objectives

In the economic field, the aims of the OAU include the following:
(1) to promote unity and solidarity of the African states; (2) to coordinate
and intensify cooperation and efforts to achieve a better life for the
peoples of Africa; (3) to defend the sovereignty, territorial integrity,
and independence of members; (4) to eradicate all forms of colonialism
from Africa; and (5) to promote international cooperation, with due
regard for the Charter of the United Nations and the Universal Declaration of Human Rights.[3]

In order to achieve these objectives, the member states agreed to
coordinate their general policies, especially to achieve: (1) political
and diplomatic cooperation; (2) economic cooperation, including transport and communications; (3) educational and cultural cooperation;
(4) health, sanitation, and nutritional cooperation; (5) scientific and
technical cooperation; and (6) cooperation for defense and security.

Institutions

The Assembly of Heads of State and Government is the supreme organ of OAU. It discusses matters of common concern to Africa with a view to coordinating and harmonizing the general policies of the OAU countries. It has the power to review the structure, functions, and activities of other OAU organs and any specialized agencies created in accordance with the charter.

The Council of Ministers is responsible to the Assembly in all matters. It is entrusted with the responsibility of preparing Assembly conferences and implementing Assembly decisions and resolutions including the coordination of African cooperation efforts. The General Secretariat is responsible for the day-to-day administration of the OAU. The Commission for Mediation, Conciliation and Arbitration has the function of settling all disputes among the member states by peaceful means and without external influence. The specialized commissions of the OAU include the Economic and Social Commission, the Educational and Cultural Commission, the Health, Sanitation and Nutritional Commission, the Defense Commission, and the Scientific, Technical and Research Commission. In the political field, there are OAU committees to deal with the various aspects of decolonization and liberation movements in Africa. The OAU was created essentially as a political organization, but in recent years the need to enhance economic development of the African countries has acquired special importance. The OAU now places great emphasis on economic cooperation as a major objective.

The summit meeting of the heads of state and government of the OAU member countries is held once every year to discuss and coordinate action, not only in political matters but also in economic development. Any economic issue that affects a group of African countries must be discussed by the OAU Council of Ministers, whose recommedations are passed to the Assembly for final action. In practice, this means that no economic policies can be implemented within the OAU at any level without approval by the Assembly, which underlines the strong relationship between politics and economics in Africa.

THE MAIN POLITICAL OBSTACLES
TO COOPERATION IN AFRICA

Major political obstacles to effective cooperation among the Africa countries have continued to exist after the creation of the OAU.

As an aftermath of the colonial division of Africa, there are now two blocs: the French-speaking states and the English-speaking states. The French-speaking African states cover virtually all of West Africa and a substantial portion of Equatorial Africa and have very strong links with Paris and the EEC. The English-speaking countries lean heavily on Britain and the Commonwealth.

The eighteen African states associated with the EEC and the EEC have signed the Yaounde Convention setting up a free trade area between the EEC and each of the eighteen states. The convention imposed certain obligations in regard to customs duties and quantitative restrictions. The associated states are obligated to accord equal treatment to products originating from the EEC and to gradually eliminate customs duties and charges with the effect of customs duties levied on imports from the EEC. All associated states now apply the same import tariff and protective and revenue duties to the EEC countries, without discrimination. The original Yaounde Convention provided that any preferential treatment accorded by the eighteen states to third countries also must be accorded to the EEC and, although the convention did not prevent any of the eighteen states from joining other free trade arrangements in practice the application of this provision was an obstacle to economic groupings in Africa, especially with African states not associated with the EEC. However, under the new Yaounde Convention signed in July 1969, this obstacle has apparently been removed by the provision that the Associated African States are not prevented from establishing customs agreements or free trade zones among themselves or other African countries with a comparable level of development.

The former British territories, now members of the British Commonwealth of Nations, face a similar problem although somewhat different in degree. Under the Commonwealth system, the member states accord one another preferential treatment on goods originating within the Commonwealth. Any preferential treatment accorded to third countries must automatically be granted to Commonwealth members. There is no specific provision relating to economic association with nonmember countries. However, any major concessions resulting from a common market or free trade area arrangement would be subject to negotiation within the Commonwealth.

Although in principle neither the EEC nor the Commonwealth opposes the formation of subgroupings in Africa for purposes of trade and economic cooperation, the application of various "catch" clauses in the agreements for association effectively prevents the African states from entering into meaningful association with other African states outside the EEC or the Commonwealth, as the case may be.

This situation also has been important in perpetuating differences between the two main language groups in Africa. It will be noted that the treaties establishing these European economic groupings call for reciprocity in certain matters, such as customs duties and import restrictions on certain goods and products. Therefore, in entering into bilateral agreements some African countries cannot offer certain favorable terms to other African countries without extending them to the members of the EEC or Commonwealth. Thus, in order to reduce import duties on products of another African country, it may be necessary to offer the same terms to a highly industrialized European country. The net effect would be to enable goods of the industrialized country to be sold in the African country at much cheaper prices to the detriment of industry in the African country and also to the detriment of intra-African trade. But, just as the EEC and the Commonwealth were not formed purely for purposes of economic cooperation, their relationships with the African countries are governed more by political than economic considerations.

Some political observers have argued that it would be dangerous to hide the fact that the association of African states with the EEC was a political action behind the technicality of economic relationship. Although it is a fact that the African countries could not develop rapidly without assistance from the European countries, it must be understood that political motives were equally important in the establishment of close links between the EEC and the overseas Associated States.[4] Whereas some African states have attempted to break off any ties that remind them of colonial days, other states firmly believe that their economic and political survival will be safeguarded by some form of association with Western Europe.

THE EFFECTS OF FOREIGN POLICY
ON ECONOMIC COOPERATION

Throughout the 1960's, the foreign policies of the African countries have influenced the rate of economic development. The most important aspect of the foreign policies of African states is the interpretation of the doctrine of nonalignment as the basis for external relations. This has had tremendous impact on the rate of economic development because the transition between colonial administration and the establishment of full national services in the independent African states presented some problems in the form of a political vacuum. In an attempt to fill up this vacuum, the African countries have sought to express their feelings through the creation of new political concepts and new value judgements.

This development is manifest in the fact that, to the African states, neither the capitalist form of economic development, nor communism, nor socialism (as the term is used in the socialist countries of Eastern Europe) was entirely acceptable or suitable under African conditions. In an attempt to overcome this problem, the African countries coined a new terminology--African socialism--which has gained popularity in the independent African states. The introduction of African socialism was really an attempt by the African people to revive and preserve the African social moral and spiritual values that were destroyed or restrained under colonial rule.

Virtually all the African states have, in principle, advocated nonalignment as the basis of foreign policy. Nonalignment has been described in different ways at different times, but the basic idea is the same--the desire to break off any ties that exist with the former colonial rulers and a desire to manage affairs without interference from outside. Unfortunately, except in a few cases, as a result of economic conditions and external pressures, the majority of African countries have become more attached to a particular ideological bloc.[5]

The idea behind nonalignment as a policy governing a country's external relations was to prevent the African states from associating themselves with any political bloc, East or West. This was essential if the independence was to have any political meaning. However, differences in interpretation and usage of nonalignment have caused some states to lean a little more to the West or to the East.[6] As a result of this conceptual difference, there is wide divergence in the approaches to economic development and cooperation of the various African states. This has greatly reduced the scope for concord on certain important issues. Even at the OAU, there has been difficuly in reaching certain agreements and above all in carrying them out. On the economic side, these differences are now becoming very evident. In matters of economic cooperation, for instance, some countries have been strong advocates of closer economic cooperation; others have been rather lukewarm; and still others have been indifferent, although they have at one time or another openly declared their solemn intentions to work toward cooperation in areas of common interest. The problem of nonalignment has been exacerbated by the dependence of the new African nations upon foreign aid for a great portion of their capital requirements for development. Since only a few African countries, especially those endowed with rich mineral resources, are in a position to raise capital from domestic sources, there is a growing awareness that foreign aid is becoming less and less sufficient to sustain even present levels of development.[7] Moreover, the African countries are not in a position to direct foreign aid toward the development of their priority projects since the donor

countries often specify the areas in which they want the aid utilized.
In most cases, foreign aid has failed to generate the rate of economic
progress necessary to provide an economic breakthrough in the African
economies.

The most important aspect of aid from the former metropolitan
powers is that it has never been truly disinterested. Apart from the
financial and economic strings usually attached to such aid, it has often
been given as a measure to combat "communism" in Africa. At times,
African states have clearly indicated that if aid was not forthcoming
from the West, they would naturally turn to the East. The countries
of the West know very well that the East would not hesitate to establish
or strengthen contacts with the African states whenever a chance occurs.
Recently, it has become increasingly evident that aid from the West is
taking the same pattern, coming not in a steady flow but in spurts in
response to particular political situations. Therefore, the African
states have never been sure at any time that the finances required to
build a road, railway, or dam would be available from the West, which
makes it extremely difficult for the developing African countries to
effectively plan their development. As a result, most African development plans are very vague as to how resources to finance the plan will
be obtained.

Closely associated with foreign policy is the concept of self-
reliance, which has recently developed in Africa as an expression of
a country's desire to develop through the full exploitation of its own
domestic resources. Some countries consider this approach a total
rejection of foreign aid, while others feel that a country should depend
primarily upon its own resources for economic development and resort
to foreign aid only if its own resources are inadequate to meet economic
development requirements. The differences in interpretation of the
concept of foreign aid arise because some African countries accept
aid as the main source of development finance while other countries
see aid as a supplement to domestic resources.

In this regard, it is encouraging to note that aid from international
organizations is becoming a vital element of economic development in
Africa. The International Bank for Reconstruction and Development
(World Bank) and its affiliated organizations, such as the International
Finance Corporation and the International Development Association,
have shown greater interest in Africa in the late 1960's. The International Monetary Fund also has helped some African countries to solve
balance of payments difficulties. The Economic Commission for Africa,
the United Nations Development Program, and the Special Fund--all of
which are organs of the United Nations--are stepping up technical

assistance to Africa and have greatly helped the acceleration of economic development. The bilateral agencies have assisted the African governments in conducting studies and in the financing certain projects, such as roads, railways, and inland transport. It is expected that these international organizations will step up their aid to Africa when economic cooperation is finally established.

Although aid should never be taken as an obsolute substitute for domestic resources, by and large aid has met the current development requirements. Many African countries are not sure of the type and quantity of aid they require. The problem therefore is not the inadequacy of aid in Africa but the lack of coordination among the aid recipients on the one hand and the donors on the other.

The lack of coordination among the aid donors should be emphasized. The donors have very little knowledge of the basic problems of the recipient countries and sometimes turn down a request for aid if they do not understand why such aid is required, even though it may be in the interests of the recipient country. The aid donors also have tended to work in competition with each other. A recipient country may be visited by two different teams of experts from different countries who conduct surveys which would have best been carried out jointly. The coordination of the activities of the donors is needed in order to assist the African states to direct such aid toward the promotion of plans that will help strengthen ties within Africa. If two, three, or four donor countries are approached for aid in different fields by the same country or by a few countries within the same subregion, it would be advantageous to all concerned to administer the aid jointly in order to ensure effective distribution. To this end, it might be necessary to form an international organization to be known as the African Aid Consortium and to be run by ECA where all organizations and agencies interested in the development of Africa would be represented and could discuss how aid could best be given and utilized. In the initial stages, it might be necessary for all the donor countries, together with the international organizations and in close consultation with the ECA, to jointly send experts to all the African countries to study aid requirements and to regularize the mode for requesting aid. After the aid that is actually available in each field has been determined, a program or schedule of priorities in plans for economic integration could be prepared. Since more and more aid will be required under economic cooperation, the need for the consortium will become imperative. Here again, the need for joint state control is of vital importance insofar as the recipient countries are concerned.

But differences in political outlook are not always externally based. When the Pan-African movement began, colonial policies were bitterly

attacked on the ground that Africans were not different by any natural
standards but had been divided by artificial boundaries created to suit
the convenience of the imperialists. The aim of Pan-Africanism was
to secure unity among all the peoples of Africa. On attainment of independence, however, the same artificial boundaries established by the
colonial powers came to be accepted as de' facto divisions between
African nations, and there is no indication that people of Africa are in
any mood to change this order. The "colonial" frontiers now formed
the national boundaries dividing the free independent states of Africa
and have become the basis for claims for national sovereignty. When
the struggle for independence gained momentum, a new phenomenon
developed in the relationships among the African peoples: They began
to resent the direct participation of Africans from other countries in
internal politiacal matters.

With independence, the problem assumed a new dimension. In
some African countries there are now four categories of "foreign"
Africans. The first category is made up of people who migrated to
work on mines and plantations. At the time independence was granted,
these people decided to stay and establish new permanent homes. There
is now growing demand from local laborers to have such individuals
deported because migrant labor means additional competition for employment.

The second category is that of educated young men who left their
countries either because they were dissatisfied, because of better
employment elsewhere, or to seek adventure. Since such individuals
often are highly educated and have experience, they frequently are
absorbed in good and responsible jobs within the civil service and in
private enterprise. All goes well so long as local people do not believe
that they can fill the same posts. But as soon as local people believe
that their chances of promotion are in jeopardy, trouble begins and the
"alien Africans" get fired or forced to resign and leave the country.

The third category of immigrant Africans is made up of refugees
from countries still under colonial rule. Apparently, such individuals
do not present employment problems, partly because they are concerned
primarily with the independence movements in their own countries and
have no time to seek jobs and partly because they do not necessarily
have high skills. Furthermore, such organizations as the International
Red Cross and the United Nations High Commission for Refugees provide for livelihood.

Apparently, the three categories of immigrant Africans described
above do not cause much friction among African states, at least not
openly. It is actually the fourth category--refugees fleeing from their

own independent governments either as a result of military takeovers or for other political "crimes" and other offenses--that presents the greatest problems by far to the African leaders under whose roof they seek refuge. There is always a conflict of attitudes because, although on humanitarian grounds such individuals cannot be deported, there is the desire to maintain friendly relations with other governments and to abstain from interfering with the internal politics of other states.

The African governments also passed elaborated immigration laws that prevent or make it difficult for labor or skilled African personnel to move from one country to another. Whereas under colonial rule individuals could, for instance, move freely between Rwanda and Burundi or Ghana and Nigeria, it is now difficult to do so, despite the fact that African leaders have stated publicly that the artificial boundaries created by the imperialists divide brother against brother. In fact, one is inclined to ask whether, after attaining independence, the African states are moving toward unity and closer cooperation or away from it.

THE HARMONIZATION OF ECONOMIC AND POLITICAL ELEMENTS IN ECONOMIC COOPERATION

There is now a general awareness that economic cooperation requires the development of a harmonious relationship between economic and political policies both at the national and multinational level. It is not a matter of accident that some of the most forward-looking economic groupings inside and outside Africa such as the UDEAC and the Conseil de l'Entente are built on a superstructure of political understanding and tolerance among member states. It has sometimes been argued that, given a sound joint economic project in which a group of countries can readily see economic advantages, such countries may consider joint exploitation of the project regardless of whether political harmony exists among them. However, experience suggests that, except in times of war or other national disasters, such situations are rare. Others argue that, given political understanding among several countries, joint economic projects can always be created to foster joint economic development. These issues are open to discussion.

What should be stressed is that, in order to encourage economic cooperation among the African countries as a means of accelerating the rate of economic development, there should be a radical change in the role of politics to ensure that it makes a positive contribution to economic development. Differences are not difficult to find in any economic grouping, but what is essential in Africa is not the discovery of such

differences but rather the search for common areas of interest and the
development of such common areas for the purpose of joint economic
advancement.

The outstanding political differences between Guinea and Senegal
in the OERS, Uganda and Tanzania in the East African Community,
Congo (Kinshasa) and Congo (Brazzaville) in the OCAM, and Morocco
and Libya in the Maghreb, and the political instability within a number
of African countries have considerably slowed down the progress
toward economic cooperation in Africa. Some formula ought to be found
to enable joint economic cooperation projects affecting these countries
to continue even if the political relations are temporarily strained.
This would be a test of real African statesmanship.

There is a growing movement toward interdependence among the
African countries and this is a healthy development which ought to be
given encouragement. The strengthening of this interdependence through
lessening political tensions in Africa constitutes an important element
in the economic development of these countries. After a period of trial
and error in the 1960's, it should be recognized that a new political
outlook, especially in relation to economic development, is desirable
to ensure the success of the joint development efforts throughout Africa.

NOTES

1. The view that it was possible to establish one all-Africa
organization in which cooperation could be achieved while at the same
time the aspirations of the individual African states were satisfied was
clearly summarized in Ghana Today (a biweekly review published by
the Ghana High Commission in London) on June 27, 1961, by a Ghanian
leader's statement: "I mean [the establishment of] an African Continental Government-- a single continent which would develop a feeling of one
community among the people of Africa. . . ."

2. Charter of the Union of African States (Accra, July 1961).

3. Organization of African Unity, Charter of the Organization of
African Unity (Addis Ababa, 1965), pp. 7-8.

4. See, for example, the Afrika Instituut, Relations Between the
African States and Madagascar and the EEC (The Hague, 1962), p. 12.
"We may even say that the political motives in the wider sense have
assumed greater importance, since it is probable that if the EEC member countries had decided not to maintain their special relations with

Africa a vacuum would have been created that other powers would have tried to fill with perhaps less experience and less disinterest."

5. See, for example, Julius K. Nyerere, Non-Alignment in the 1970's. Government Printer, Dar-es-Salam, April 1970. In Opening the Preparatory Meeting of the Non-Aligned Countries in Dar-es-Salaam in April 1970, Mr. Nyerere summed up the concept of nonalignment when he said, "We are all short of capital, and many of us are short also of the expertise which is just as vital to development. It is in these facts that lies the real threat to our independence. For in seeking to overcome our poverty we each inevitably run the risk of being sucked into the orbit of one or other of the Great Powers."

6. Some countries in Africa advocated what was called "positive neutralism and nonalignment," while others thought of nonalignment as the disassociation of a country from any power bloc. Nonalignment also was thought of as the right of any nation "to establish the type of government in desires, to freely choose its economic and social system and its way of line--in short, to act in accordance with its own guiding spirit unhampered by any pressure from outside." (Report of the Conference of Non-Aligned Nations, Belgrade, 1961.) Still other countries believed in what was called "discretionary nonalignment," which implied that a country could exercise its right to associate itself with any power at any time if it was in the country's interests, to do so. The main conclusion to draw is that, as a result of these different interpretations, there are also differences in the economic policies of the African countries. Moreover, whatever the policy of a government, economic expediency compels the developing African countries to rely on one of the big powers for assistance.

7. For instance, in 1967, total aid from the European Development Fund of the EEC amounted to $800 million, British aid to Africa came to about $373 million, United States assistance was $329 million, the aid commitments of the Centrally Planned Economies Communist bloc amounted to $428 million, and the aid from the IBRD and the IDA together came to about $75 million. Much of this aid was in social infrastructure, such as schools, hospitals, roads, ports, and harbors. For further details, see Paul Streeten, Aid to Africa, E/CN. 14/WP. 1/30-OAU TRAD/ 29; written for the Economic Commission for Africa.

10

THE DISTRIBUTION
OF BENEFITS
UNDER
MULTINATIONAL
COOPERATION

THE CONCEPT OF EQUITABLE
DISTRIBUTION OF BENEFITS

The equitable distribution of benefits presupposes that countries participating in a joint plan derive benefits from it in accordance with the amount of capital and other resources they invest in it. However, in economic cooperation the problem of equitable distribution of benefits is much more complex than the establishment of a mathematical proportion based on capital contributed.

The benefits under multinational cooperation include many items that are not readily quantifiable. For instance, in a multinational industrial project the benefits that can accrue to the participating countries include increased employment opportunities, economies of scale that result in lower prices of the finished product, market opportunities that which not have been available at the national level, and the possibility of developing other industries to take advantage of the multinational industry. Although some of these advantages can be readily assessed, others come about as development gathers momentum.

Therefore, problems of distribution of benefits arise, in any plan, whether related to economic or social development, where the interests transcend national boundaries. In plans for multinational economic cooperation, the distribution of benefits has constituted a major problem, largely because the establishment of a free trade area, common market, or customs union implies that the member countries will derive greater benefits as a matter of course. Countries will be prepared to consider the establishment of such common institutions if there are assurances that benefits will be shared equitably and that each participating country will gain distinct advantages.

337

If three countries are planning to develop jointly three industries and one industry is allocated to each country, in mathematical terms there has been a fair allocation of the multinational industries. However, the question that would arise is whether the advantages to be generated by these industries will be the same for each of the three countries. One industry may be labor-intensive and therefore employ more people while another may be capital-intensive. The profit margin also may differ since the final products are not identical. Hence, the advantages from cooperation cannot be equal. Moreover, because of their level of economic development and managerial skills some countries have the capability to take advantage of the new opportunities created as a result of economic cooperation. Such countries may establish subsidiary industries or reallocate resources. Clearly, a country that can adequately exploit such new possibilities will gain more from cooperation than countries that are not able to take advantage of the expanded market.

Most African countries consider economic cooperation or integration as though it were a basket of readily interchangeable commodities that, through some arithmetic formula are distributed among the member countries. However, economic integration is much more complicated. It envisages the establishment of a whole complex of industries and auxiliary services over a wide area involving many countries, with allocation of industries to be agreed upon before any industries are actually established. The main consideration is that the widening of the national markets under economic integration open up greater opportunities for industrialization through specialization and better utilization of the resources of the participating countries.

There is no hard and fast rule as to how the benefits under cooperation can be distributed, and the problem varies from one sector of the economy to another. For instance, in the trade aspect of cooperation the development of a free trade area involving a number of countries with different levels of economic development or the establishment of a customs union involving coastal and inland countries demands careful assessment of the advantages and compensatory arrangements for the less developed partners or the inland countries. In industrialization programs, the allocation of industries between the more advanced and the less advanced partners calls for careful balancing of the industrial structure; otherwise, the more industrialized partners will industrialize further while the least industrialized countries become less industrialized because new industries tend to be attracted to areas that are already industrialized and have developed auxiliary services.

However, the question of the equitable distribution of benefits does not arise only where there are less advanced and more advanced partners. Even where the levels of development appear fairly even, greater concern is caused by fears that a partner state may get a larger share of the advantages or that a country may be placed at a disadvantage in a vital sector of the economy. However, it should be understood that every country is likely to be at a disadvantage in one sector or another of the economy, regardless of whatever built-in safeguards the system includes. At the same time, every country is likely to derive greater advantages from establishing certain large-scale industries under integration than from establishing such industries based entirely on a limited domestic market. The main guiding principle here is that of striking a balance between the losses and the anticipated gains. After all, starting from a given level of economic development and assuming other things remain the same, the gain of one country must necessarily mean the loss of another country (or other countries) in the integrated area. It is through the process of development that some of the disadvantages that might be experienced in the initial stages of economic cooperation can be compensated by employment and wider markets.

The other factor in the distribution of benefits under integration is that each country usually views and interprets the principle of equitable distribution in light of its own experience and expectations. Hence, it must be expected that a clash of interest sometimes will develop. The main consideration that persuades a country to accept joint responsibility for the development of projects jointly with other countries is the expectation of what benefits the country will derive from such projects. This presents great problems since, if a scheme appears prima facie to be less advantageous to a given country, it may not be attractive for such a country to cooperate with the others. In weighing their economic interests under any project of cooperation, a less advanced country might find it useful to examine whether the income generated under the integrated industries would lead to greater employment within its own boundaries or to greater sales of its products to the more advanced partners. In the same way, the more advanced countries should take into consideration the advantages resulting from the wider market created under integration and the opportunities for a greater degree of specialization. In this regard, joint projects should be considered not only in terms of short- or medium- term benefits but also in terms of benefits over the long run.

It might be useful if the economic planners under economic

integration placed less emphasis on what their individual countries
might gain under economic integration in the short run and more emphasis on the development of a large area that definitely would create
new opportunities in the long run. Although this approach is generally
difficult to accept especially when the newly independent African states
have pledged to advance domestic development, it might be useful to
consider certain joint projects even if some countries may not derive
immediate gains. In the dynamic concept of economic integration, it
can be assumed that the results and benefits of economic integration
can be reassessed after the integrated industries have been given
sufficient time to develop. Therefore, in seeking to balance the benefits of economic integration it is necessary to bear in mind that integration is not intended to distribute benefits that exist from the outset
but, rather, to help create new industries that should help the African
countries to solve balance of payments and trade problems that, in
the absence of integration, would have deteriorated. Another factor
should be the recognition that cooperation will enable the countries to
attain a greater degree of economic interdependence not only insofar
as trade is concerned but in the entire field of economic growth.
Furthermore, through the adoption of a development strategy that embraces a wide range of economic activity, economic integration will
enable the attainment of a wider range of opportunities for economic
growth and greater flexibility in the choice of industrial development
projects than can be envisaged by any single country.

SOME BENEFIT-SHARING ARRANGEMENTS
IN AFRICA

Although a formula has not yet been devised for the distribution
of benefits in multinational projects, some ad hoc arrangements have
been tried with varying degrees of success. Most of the existing
arrangements relate to the distribution of revenue from import and
other charges within existing customs unions. Some data on how these
systems operate are given below.

The East African Community

The East African Community has created the Distributable Pool
Fund for the purpose of sharing out revenue among member states.
The fund is maintained through (1) the payment of a sum equal to 20
percent of the income tax collected by the East African Tax Department on gains or profits of companies engaged in manufacturing or
finance business and (2) the payment of a sum equal to 3 percent of

the amount of customs duty and excise duty collected by the East African Customs and Excise Department on the basis of declarations on the final destination of imports from third countries. The cost of collection is deducted from the total sum collected and paid into a General Fund for meeting certain expenses of the East African Community.

The balance of the revenue remaining in the Distributable Pool Fund after deduction of the cost of collection is distributed to the member states in equal shares. Where a country is entitled to impose a transfer tax, such tax is collected by the East African Customs and Excise Department and paid directly to that country, less the cost of collection, which is also paid into the General Fund. In 1968, $1.4 million was paid to Tanzania and $280,000 to Uganda, in transfer tax. This was an indication that new industries had been established in the two countries under the provisions of the treaty.

The allocation of the various sources of revenue in the East African Community is shown in Table 10.1. The total revenue collected and accrued to the account of the member states increased appreciably between 1966 and 1969.

The Central African Customs and Economic Union

The need for an effective way to distribute proceeds from the import duties was felt by the countries of the UDEAC even during the colonial days. The land-locked countries had to be assured that losses in import duties by virtue of the customs arrangements were fully compensated through a system of reallocation of customs revenues. Under the UDEAC Treaty, a sum of 20 percent is appropriated from import and excise duties and paid to a Common Solidarity Fund. The balance of the duties, after deduction of the cost of collection and other administrative charges, is paid directly into the budget of the state in whose territory such goods are finally consumed on the basis of the evidence shown by the declaration forms for delivery of the goods.

A major purpose of the Common Solidarity Fund is to compensate for any losses that may result from any possible errors in the final calculations of the import revenue. Article 38 of the UDEAC Treaty states:

> In a spirit of solidarity, and to take into account of any errors in indicating the State of consumption and of advantages deriving from transit activities, in particular for coastal States, a percentage of import duties and charges

TABLE 10.1

Allocation of Revenues in the East African Community
(thousands of U.S. dollars)

	Import Duty			Excise Duty			Income Tax		
	1966/67	1967/68	1968/69	1966/67	1967/68	1968/69	1966/67	1967/68	1968/69
Kenya	53,289	54,631	60,295	22,761	28,440	32,116	48,524	61,824	69,110
Tanzania	46,878	48,569	51,736	17,419	20,261	22,968	21,440	27,238	35,725
Uganda	34,644	33,972	36,260	17,780	20,395	19,301	14,456	18,903	19,110
Distribut-able Pool	8,450	7,412	9,909	3,696	3,752	5,415	7,386	4,374	2,013
Total	143,211	144,584	158,200	61,656	72,848	79,800	91,806	112,339	125,958

Source: East African Statistical Department, Economic and Statistical Review, No. 35 (June 1970), p. 90

levied by the common customs office of the five States,
shall be paid into a Common Solidarity Fund.

One other main purpose of the Common Solidarity Fund is to adequately compensate the land-locked countries and the economically
weaker partner states for the losses derived from the transit arrangements with the coastal countries.

Under the Equatorial Customs Union (UDE), the predecessor of
UDEAC, the total revenues from import and excise duties were distributed on a percentage basis. Gabon received about 22 percent; the
Central African Republic 20 percent; Congo (Brazzaville) 28 percent;
and Chad 30 percent. Since 1960, when the Common Solidarity Fund
was created, the percentages have been fixed as follows: Chad 62 percent; Central African Republic 35 percent; Congo (Brazzaville) 3 percent; and Gabon less than 1 percent (these percentages have been
rounded off for purposes of presentation). Chad received the highest share from the Common Solidarity Fund to compensate its level
of development vis-à-vis the other partner states and for its land-
locked position. Gabon, the most advanced among the four countries,
received only a small fraction of 1 percent of the Common Solidarity
Fund.

Since 1966, the UDEAC has adopted new provisions dividing its
customs tariff into four categories: (1) the import duty (droit fiscal d'
entree), (2) the customs duty (droit de douane), (3) the common import
turnover tax (taxe commune sur le chiffre d'affaires a l'importation),
and (4) the complementary import tax (taxe complementaire sur l'im
portation). The last one of these taxes may be imposed in addition to
the other three charges and varies from country to country depending
upon the difficulties that a country may experience in adopting a common
tariff or in balancing its national budget. The allocation of the total
proceeds in the Common Solidarity Fund remains the same as under
the old formula.

The Southern African Customs Union

The benefit-sharing arrangements under the Customs Union
Agreement between Swaziland, Botswana, Lesotho, and South Africa
date back to 1910, when this was signed to provide for the creation of
a free trade area comprising the four countries. Under this agreement, the distribution of tax revenue among the member countries was
made according to an agreed formula and the ratios were as shown in

TABLE 10.2

Distribution of Tax Revenue Under the Customs
Agreement Between the Governments of
Swaziland, Botswana, Lesotho, and
South Africa

Country	Percentage Share 1910-64	Percentage Share Since 1964
Lesotho (Basutoland)	0.88575	0.47093
Botswana (Bechuanaland)	0.27622	0.30971
Swaziland	0.14900	0.53033
Total	1.31097	1.31097

Table 10.2. The three High Commission Territories together received about 1.31 percent of the total revenues collected in the customs union area, and the balance went to South Africa.

In 1964, new sharing ratios as shown in Table 10.2, were introduced. In the new arrangement, though the total share paid by South Africa to the former High Commission Territories remained the same, Swaziland, which had previously received a smaller share, became the principal beneficiary. The new arrangement did not remove the provision that no tariff barriers were to be imposed on goods produced in South Africa when transferred into any of the three territories. The provision was unsatisfactory because it militated against the establishment of new industries in the three territories.

A new customs agreement was signed between Swaziland, Botswana, Lesotho and South Africa in 1969 and came into force in March 1970, replacing the 1910 agreement. The new agreement introduced a more complicated but perhaps more effective formula for distribution of revenue from customs duties. The percentage shares accruing to Swaziland, Botswana, and Lesotho are calculated as follows:

The cost-insurance-freight value at border of goods from all sources imported during the financial year into the area of each party, plus the value of excisable and sales duty goods produced and consumed in such area during such year, plus the excise and sales duties paid thereon during such year shall be expressed as a percentage of the cost-insurance-freight value of the goods imported during the financial year into the customs union area, plus the customs and sales duties paid thereon during such year, plus the value of excisable and sales duty goods produced and consumed during such year in the common customs area, plus the excise and sales duties paid thereon during such year The amount calculated by the application to the common revenue pool of the percentage so obtained, enhanced by multiplying factor of 1.42, shall represent the share of the three countries in respect of that financial year.

The share accruing to each of the three countries can be expressed in mathematical equation as shown below:

$$R_i = \frac{1.42 \ (R_t) \ (M_i + V_i + D_i)}{M_t + C_t + V_t + D_t} \times 100$$

$$= \frac{1.42 \ (C_t + D_t) \ (M_i + V_i + D_i)}{M_t + C_t + V_t + D_t} \times 100$$

Where R_t = $C_t + D_t$

M_t = total c.i.f. value of imports into the customs union area

M_i = imports c.i.f. value into each of the three countries

C_t = total customs and sales duties on total imports into the customs union area

V_t = value of excise and sales duty goods produced and consumed in the customs union area

V_i = value of excise and sales duty goods produced and consumed in each of the three countries

D_t = excise and sales duty paid on goods produced and consumed in the customs union area

D_i = excise and sales duty paid on goods produced and consumed in each of the three countries

R_t = Customs revenue pool of the area

R_i = share of revenue accruing to each of the three countries.

One of the main features of the new agreement is that South Africa cannot now impose duties without consulting the three other partner countries. Moreover, the countries can now impose a special duty on goods from the partner states to protect their new industries against competition from the more established industries in the customs union area This provision gives the three former High Commission Territories greater opportunity to establish new industries.

The payment by South Africa to the three countries in the new agreement was backdated to April 1969 and certain provisions laid down for the distribution of revenue in 1971 and 1972. In the financial year 1970, Swaziland received 7.1 million Rand, Lesotho 5.0 million Rand and Botswana 4.1 million Rand.

Transit Arrangements for Land-locked Countries

One form of benefit-sharing arrangements is the granting of transit facilities by the coastal to the inland countries.* The benefits take the form of special discount rates granted on the cost of trans-shipment of goods through the railways of the coastal countries. The main advantage for the inland countries is the opportunity to have access to port and harbor facilities. At the same time, the discount rates reduce export costs, thereby making the products of the inland countries more competitive on the world markets. For the coastal countries, the benefits take the form of increased revenues resulting from increased traffic over railways and increased employment both on the railways and at the ports. A few types of transit concessions are briefly summarized below.

Special Transit Tariffs

Nearly all land-locked countries enjoy special tariff rates for transporting their exports and imports through the railways and posts of the coastal countries. In some instances, these special rates are applicable to total trade, but in other cases the exports are granted more favorable discount rates. Examples of this kind of arrangement

---

*The following are the land-locked countries in Africa: Mali, Upper Volta, Niger, Chad, Central African Republic, Rwanda, Burundi, Uganda, Zambia, Malawi, Southern Rhodesia, Botswana, Lesotho, and Swaziland.

are goods from Chad and Central African Republic that pass through
Congo (Brazzaville); goods from Rwanda and Burundi that pass through
Uganda, Kenya, and Tanzania; and goods from Upper Volta that pass
through Ivory Coast.

Permanent Rebates

In certain cases, a land-locked country may agree with a coastal
country to transport all or a certain percentage of its merchandise via
a particular rail line. Since by such an agreement the land-locked
country would be precluded from using other modes of transportation,
the coastal country usually grants especially low transit charges.
This kind of arrangement usually operates over a very long period
of time. Since these arrangements are more or less permanent, the
inland countries have an assurance that the discount rates will not
fluctuate over a relatively short period. Such arrangements are
found in the rail transport of export crops from Upper Volta through
Ivory Coast; Joint Dahomey-Niger Organization for Railways and
Transport the organization commune Dahomey-Niger des Chemins de
Fers et des Transports (OCDN) between Dahomey and Niger, under
which the latter receives special permanent discount rates for its
exports; Chad and the Central African Republic export cotton and Chad
imports petroleum through Pointe Noire in Congo (Brazzaville).

Direct Government Subsidy

A country may grant special subsidies aimed at supporting the
exports from a land-locked country in return for an undertaking that
the other party would use the rail or port facilities of the coastal
country. This usually applies to specific crops, for example: donations
granted to Upper Volta for the export of "Karite," shea-butter made
from shea tree through Ivory Coast and donations granted to groundnut exports from Niger when transported through Dahomey.

Direct Through-Rate Concessions

There is a special arrangement between Uganda and Kenya where-
whereby shipments from Uganda are charged a special low rate when
transported nonstop to the port of Mombasa. These concessions
reduce export costs and stimulate exports.

Special Long Distance Rates

In certain instances when goods are transported over very long
distances, a country may grant special rates to assist exports of
particular goods. This was the case for Nigeria on the one hand and

Niger and Chad on the other when goods were trans-shipped through
the Nigerian Railways. The effect of this arrangement was to reduce
export costs for Niger and Chad.

SOME PROBLEMS OF BENEFIT-SHARING

It has been discovered that, although some of the distinct benefit-
sharing arrangements in Africa have indeed been useful in meeting the
special needs for which they were instituted, there are still large areas
in economic cooperation where no generally accepted formula has been
devised for equitable distribution of economic advantages. In such areas
as trade, industry, and agriculture, only ad hoc arrangements at best
can be made. This text does not claim to be able to supply such a formula. However, what is attempted is to highlight some of the problems
encountered with the hope that, once the magnitude of the problem is
clearly appreciated by the African countries, some measures may be
developed for a fair allocation of benefits from cooperation.

The major problem encountered in attempts to lay down principles
for the equitable distribution of benefits under multinational economic
cooperation has stemmed from differences in levels of economic development in general and industrial development in particular. As was
noted previously, a country will consider a plan for multinational cooperation only under a system of comparative advantages. A country's
advantages from the plan usually are weighed against the comparative
levels of industrialization in the other partner states; this is true
regardless of whether the cooperation involves isolated projects or
a comprehensive scheme for multinational development.

The African economies, although largely dependent upon agriculture, have differed greatly in their rates of progress throughout the
colonial period and after. These differences can be analyzed from two
aspects--the national aspect and the international aspect. With regard
to the national aspect, differences in the rates and levels of economic
development within countries exist between the urban and the rural
sectors. These differences relate to income, employment opportunities, labor productivity, social and health facilities, education, and
transport and communications. The urban population enjoys a better
standard of living than the rural population. Moreover, the urban or
industrial sector usually grows at a faster rate than the agricultural
sector, thereby increasing the imbalance in development between the
two sectors. With the coming of independence, this problem is essentially a domestic one for the national planners to solve and therefore
would not pose a formidable obstacle to economic integration, although
to some extent multinational economic decisions will be governed by

internal economic conditions. The urban-rural problem is relevant to economic cooperation insofar as any multinational agreement would help to generate income in the rural areas.

With regard to the international aspect, differences in levels of economic development exist between the various countries of Africa. This is relevant to economic cooperation because these differences greatly influence the decisions and willingness of the African governments to pursue common policies in matters of planning and economic development. These differences have arisen as a result of many factors influencing the course of development from the beginning of the colonial era up to the present day. A few of the most important causes for differences in levels of development are discussed below.

Causes of the Differences in Levels of Development

The first cause of differences in levels of development can be traced to colonial policies. It was noted earlier that the different colonial powers adopted different policies not only in politics but also in economic development. Hence, the development of a particular territory depended largely upon the aims of the colonial power in that territory. Only as much of economic development as was absolutely necessary was allowed. The colonial powers were principally concerned with strengthening the metropolitan economies. Therefore, there was no comprehensive planning in the modern sense. What the metropolitan powers did have were isolated capital investment programs related to a given project such as a highway, a rail line extension, or a small hydroelectric project. These plans were basically related to the need for raw materials in the metropolitan powers and were not to the overall development requirements of the African countries.

In the British possessions, development of the colonies as a conscious policy was observable after World War I when the Colonial Development Act of 1929 was passed. This act was governed by the need to combat the growing unemployment and excess capacity in the British economy following the war. Public works projects were initiated in the British territories as a means of stimulating the demand for capital goods and equipment manufactured in Britain. The 1929 act was followed by the Colonial Development and Welfare Acts of 1940 and 1945, which were deliberate measures to stimulate economic activities in the colonies to cushion the British economy during the slump following the Great Depression of the interwar period.

The Belgians started rather late in their efforts to initiate economic development projects in their possessions in Africa. The most noticeable plan was a capital development plan launched in 1948 to cover the ten-year period 1950-59. This was merely a public expenditure program in the development of certain projects dictated by the requirements for raw materials in metropolitan Belgium. As such, it could not justifiably be termed a development plan.

In the French African possessions efforts were made at initiating some planning in 1921. These plans were directed at increasing the supply of raw materials to France. After World War II, a number of short-term plans were initiated, such as the plan for 1947-51. An example of a deliberate project planning was the establishment of the Niger Office, whose primary aim was to increase the production of rice and cotton in the Niger River Basin.

The second major cause of differences in the levels of economic development resulted from the differences in the time when the national development plans were initiated. Most countries embarked upon deliberate planning for economic development after 1960. In all cases, development planning started soon after independence or immediately preceding it. The gestation periods of the different projects under the national development plans vary, and the various projects influence the economies at different times. The resulting incomes generated within the countries differ, making the differences between the various countries even more pronounced. If the plans are started at the same time within a group of African countries, after a given period the disparities in income levels would begin to diminish since differences in the gestation period would tend to be eliminated. This is the reason why the coordination of national development plans becomes an important aspect of economic integration in Africa, so as to ensure uniformity of purpose and to ensure that the states start from a common base using similar assumptions, value judgements, planning techniques.

The allocation of capital investment in national development plans also varies from country to country. For instance, it will be noted that, during the plan period 1960-64, in Morocco 28 percent of the total government capital expenditure was allocated to industry, 32 percent to agriculture, and 15 percent to infrastructure; in Senegal 4 percent was allocated to industry, 26 percent to agriculture, and 58 percent to infrastructure; and in Ghana only 8 percent to infrastructure. The priority ratings of government investment in the various African countries differ considerably. This difference is reflected in national incomes since the gestation period is not the same for all industries even if they are started at the same time. Furthermore, the gestation period in agriculture usually is shorter than for some industries, so that if a country places more emphasis on agriculture than on industry, the resulting income from investment may be generated much earlier than if the same amount of capital were invested in, for example, the building of a dam or a rail line. In Ghana, Ethiopia, and Cameroun great importance seems to be attached to the development of infrastructure, while in Tanzania, Ivory Coast, Morocco, and Uganda agricultural development figures prominently. Other African countries have no clear priority pattern.

The gross domestic product per capita for developing Africa in 1966 ranged from $990 to $46. Libya had the highest per capita GDP, followed by Gabon, Liberia, Zambia, and Ivory Coast. Only two countries in Africa had a GDP of over $400, while nine countries earned GDP of between $200 and $300. Some fifteen countries had per capita GDP of between $100 and $200, while seventeen countries were below $100. Burundi, Upper Volta, Rwanda, and Malawi has per capita GDP below $50.[1] Thus, disparity in income distribution is tremendous, and the land-locked countries also seem to be the least developed. With regard to rates of growth of per capita GDP, some thirteen countries representing about 22 percent of the population of developing Africa registered a negative rate of growth; six countries representing 17.4 percent of the total African population had 0-0.9; nine countries representing 33.1 percent of the population had 1.0-1.9 percent; five countries representing 12.6 percent of the population had 2.0-2.9 percent; five countries or 12.3 percent of the population had 3.0-3.9 percent; and only four countries representing 2.6 percent of the total population of developing Africa had over 5.0 percent. It therefore follows that 28 of 41 developing African countries had a low rate of growth of per capita GDP. Moreover, more than 72 percent of the population of developing Africa lives in areas that can accurately be described as least developed.

As regards GDP by industrial origin, in the North African subregion; agriculture contributed 50.7 percent in Sudan, 28.2 percent in Morocco and 26.9 percent in the U.A.R.; mining 55.4 percent in Libya, 23.7 percent in Algeria; and manufacturing industry 20.3 percent in the U.A.R., 17.1 percent in Tunisia, 13.6 percent in Morocco, and only 2.8 percent in Libya. Therefore, the disparity in the levels of manufacturing industry is quite pronounced in the North African subregion. In West Africa, the contribution of manufacturing industry to GDP is generally very low except for Senegal, Ivory Coast, and Upper Volta, with 13.6 percent, 11.8 percent, and 10.0 percent respectively, In the Central African countries, agriculture plays a significant role in GDP, ranging from 28 to 56 percent of the GDP. Mining is important only in Gabon, contributing to over 22 percent of the GDP. Manufacturing industry is important in Congo (Kinshasa),

contributing 20.9 percent of the GDP; Cameroun 13.6 percent, and Congo
(Brazzaville) 12.1 percent. In the East African subregion, agriculture
also plays a very important role. Except for Zambia, where agriculture
contributes only 9.5 percent to GDP, the countries have high dependence
on agriculture, ranging from 24.0 percent in Mauritius to 63.7 percent
in Malawi. The only country where mining is vital is Zambia with 37.2
percent of GDP in 1966, while manufacturing industry was important
in Mauritius, 18.0 percent; Kenya 13.1 percent; Uganda 9.4 percent;
Zambia 9.0 percent; and Malawi 8.8 percent. Manufacturing industry
was lowest in Madagascar with 4.6 percent.

Problems Arising from Differences in Levels
of Development

The preceding paragraphs show that the rates of economic development in Africa differ considerably from country to country and that
the African countries, although basically agricultural, show differences
in their reliance on agriculture or industry. These disparities will
present a number of problems in the quest for economic integration.
First, because some countries depend more on agriculture than on
industry while others depend more on mining than on agriculture,
their priority schedules will naturally be different. Although in the
long run all African countries are seeking to industrialize, in the
short run the development of agriculture will have more appeal to
some countries than to others. This will raise difficulties for the
planners in the allocation of industries to the various countries within
a given subregion and between subregions.

Second, it should be accepted that because some countries are
more industrialized* than others they are better placed to develop new
industries since they already have developed some external economies
such as the availability of by-product, better financial institutions,
and better transport facilities. Such countries will tend to benefit
more than the less industrialized states in any plan for economic integration. Furthermore, because the countries that have sizable industries usually are endowed with minerals, certain industries would
tend to be attracted to such countries if economic considerations alone
are taken into account. This is because industries that use heavy or

---

*The term "industrialized" is used here very loosely for purposes
of exposition and not necessarily in the same sense as in the advanced
countries.

bulky raw materials must be located near the source of supply of such materials, which implies that countries that already have some industries would tend to become more industrialized in comparison with the relatively less industrialized. In other words, the rich countries will tend to become richer while the poor countries will tend to become poorer. Unless some deliberate measures are taken to ensure that countries that are less endowed with rich minerals are compensated by other factors the disparity in income levels, productivity, and standards of living not only will continue to exist under economic integration but would tend to grow.

Third, because of differences in factor endowments, availability of financial resources, and productivity of labor and capital, some countries will be able to implement their shares of the economic integration plans earlier, while some less favored countries may be unable to carry out their allotted portions. If this were to happen there would be disparity in the accrual of benefits under economic integration, which would tend to make further agreements more difficult. It is easier for two countries with more or less the same income level and productive capacity to come together than for a rich country to unite with a poorer one. This is ironic, since the poorer countries need most to come together with the stronger countries so as to gain experience and the advantages of already established cooperation institutions.

SPECIAL MEASURES IN FAVOR OF THE LEAST DEVELOPED PARTNER STATES

It is a truism to say that the rates of growth of the African economies in terms of population, GDP, infrastructure, and external trade differ very widely even within the same economic grouping. Nonetheless, these differences have been responsible for difficulties in finding solutions to the general problems of economic development. In economic integration, it is necessary to recognize that measures should be adopted specifically to enable the least developed partner states to effectively play a role in the newly created multinational communities.

The main consideration in respect of the least developed partners in a multinational set-up is the need to raise their levels of economic performance in order to bridge or narrow the economic development gap between the partners. In order to increase investment, effective measures should be adopted to mobilize domestic savings in these countries in order to accelerate the rate of economic development. Furthermore, there is need to expand export earnings in order to raise the level of capital formation. Within the multinational strategy for economic development, the areas that require urgent action during the United Nations Second Development Decade have been identified by the United Nations Agencies. These include: (1) detailed studies of the various strategic sectors of development in order to identify the most serious bottlenecks; (2) preparation of adequate sectoral and multisectoral measures to eliminate bottlenecks in fields where the priority needs of the least developed countries have been identified; (3) mobilization of international financial assistance for the implementation of these measures, including special measures to improve the capacity of the least developed countries to absorb financial assistance; and (4) concentration on areas of special interest to the least developed countries in the design of technical assistance programs and projects. [2]

In a plan for multinational cooperation, the international community, especially the developed countries, ought to accept firm commitments on a limited number of specific measures to ensure that all developing countries meet certain minimum criteria for development. A close examination of the development needs of the least developed countries and countries at the earliest stages of development will reveal that the most effective course of action would center on measures in the development of manpower, transport, trade and economic cooperation, natural resources, research and innovation, industry, and agriculture. The current thought in Africa seems to be that the application of science and technology on a large scale in the development of the countries is the key factor to economic development. The rate and direction of development and the benefits that accrue to the local population depend upon how a country's resources are exploited and who exploits them. Therefore, an effective policy requires a series of special measures, superimposed on the general measures to be taken in the proposed integration plans, directed at increasing the rate of economic growth and parallel social progress in the least developed countries. These would include institutional, technical, social, and economic measures taken both at the national and the international level.

The question of the equitable distribution of the benefits of economic cooperation is of special importance to the least developed partners, which must be given assurances that the new economic associations will not make them perpetually dependent upon the more prosperous partners. The least developed countries require some guarantees, through the creation of special incentives, enabling them to balance the advantages against any possible disadvantages, especially in the short run. In order to prescribe appropriate measures, the United Nations Conference on Trade and Development (UNCTAD) has set out some criteria for identifying the least developed among

developing countries. These criteria were meant to be applied in
international measures to be taken within the general global strategy
for trade development. However, the same criteria can be modified
to suit the conditions within the African context in the plans for multinational cooperation.

In order to identify the least developed countries, UNCTAD used
such factors as the level of market-oriented activities in the economy;
the level of economic infrastructure; the level of social development;
and the nature of the country's economic relations with the rest of
the world. Within this framework, four broad criteria for determining
the least developed countries have been suggested: (1) the proportion
of total GDP originating in the manufacturing sector (or the percentage
of the labor force engaged in manufacturing activities) as a measure
of the level of market-oriented activities in the economy; (2) per
capita energy, cement, or steel consumption levels, as indicative of
the level of economic infrastructure; (3) the level of literacy or the
number, per thousand, of doctors, university graduates, or technical
school graduates, as a measure of social development; and (4) the
proportion of manufactures (including semimanufactures) in total
exports or the degree of export diversification, as indicative of the
vulnerability of an economy in relation to the rest of the world. In
this context, the ratio of exports to GDP could also be taken into
account as a supplementary indicator. [3]

On the basis of these and other criteria, the United Nations has
designated several countries among the developing nations as "least
developed" countries requiring special action to supplement national
efforts to raise the living standard. Most of these countries had a
per capita GDP of less than $100, in 1966, a literacy rate of 20 per-
cent or less, and a share of manufacturing industries in GDP of 10
percent or less. Nineteen of these least developed countries are in
Africa, including Botswana, Burundi, Central African Republic, Chad,
Dahomey, Ethiopia, Gambia, Guinea, Lesotho, Malawi, Mali, Niger,
Rwanda, Somalia, Sudan, Tanzania, Togo, Uganda, and Upper Volta.
For this group of countries, the adoption of special measures would
mark the difference between economic stagnation and prosperity in
the 1970's. In other words, unless appropriate and effective measures
are taken within the multinational structure to supplement the individual efforts, these countries will remain underdeveloped for a
long time. The developed countries not only should take note of this
situation but also should feel obligated to contribute more effectively
to the development of the least developed countries.

These criteria for identifying the least developed countries can
only give a rough estimation of a country's level of development

<u>vis-à-vis</u> the remaining countries within a multinational set-up, and therefore they cannot be regarded as satisfactory. Due to lack of adequate statistical data, problems would always arise as to whether a country has the right to claim special treatment on the ground of being least developed. A practical measure suggested by UNCTAD is to rank all the countries for which data is available according to the level of their per capita GDP. It could then be agreed that countries falling below a given level of per capita GDP would be regarded as least developed for purposes of introducing special measures. It could be established that a country could qualify as least developed and be granted special treatment if it met all the criteria outlined above or if it qualified on the basis of per capita GDP plus any one of the above criteria. The problem of this approach is that it has a measure of arbitrariness, which could lead to some difficulties, especially in respect of countries just below or above a given dividing level; it would be unreasonable to treat a country that lies just above a given level less favorably than another country that lies just below it.

In order to overcome these practical problems, an alternative approach is suggested here, the sector-by-sector identification approach. Instead of attempting to draw a list of countries on the basis of the development criteria alone, some modification could be introduced to meet each particular case. For this purpose, the least developed countries could be identified on the sector-by-sector basis instead of the overall criteria. Under this approach, each particular economic activity could be considered on its own merits. For instance, it could be agreed that intercountry trade balances be regarded as a basis for determining measures to be taken in the field of trade, that the level and concentration of manufacturing industry be a criteria for deciding the allocation of new industries, and so on. In this way, a country that may be regarded as least developed in the field of trade and would thus qualify for special measures in the development of trade might not be least developed in other sectors of economic activity. By a process of elimination and adjustment, a system of equitable distribution of benefits under multinational economic cooperation could be devised.

This approach seems particularly attractive for the African countries because of the difficulty in the application of the general criteria. It is to be noted that some African countries that have comparatively large aggregate GDP due to population factors have very low per capita GDP. In the same way, some countries that have lower aggregate GDP enjoy a higher per capita GDP due to lower population density. The proportion of dependence on primary commodities for foreign exchange earnings also differs from country to country. It therefore follows that certain international measures would tend to affect some countries more than others. As a result, comprehensive studies are required before attempts can be made to lay down some generally acceptable criteria for identification of the least developed partners under economic integration.

Three main problems will confront the least developed partners in any plan for integration; the degree of intensity of these problems wil will depend upon the kind of multinational agreements entered into and the specific fields in which multinational or subregional action is sought. The first problem relates to lack or limitation of the competitive ability of the least developed partners vis-à-vis the more advanced partners. This is particularly true with respect to the ability to expand trade under the trade liberalization arrangements, especially if a common external tariff is established. When the least developed partners increase their tariffs or erect new ones against third parties, the effect will be to increase the cost of economic development since the resultant trade diversion will mean that the less developed countries buy from sources in the partner countries that are more expensive than sources in third countries.

In order to expand the export capacity of the least developed partners, it would be necessary for the more advanced partners to grant preferential treatment to the less advanced ones with regard to agricultural and industrial products that the least developed partners can produce but that are not produced at all or are produced in insufficient quantities in the more advanced partner states. Although the system of preferences would be difficult to achieve over a short period, it would work to great advantage if considered over a long period. Over and above any such preferences, arrangements for trade reciprocity could be made to ensure a reasonable balance in the trade flows resulting from trade diversion. In the African context, as a result of the disparity in the levels of manufacturing ability and the limitation on the number of items covered under any reciprocity arrangements the resistance on reciprocity by either party may not be necessarily endure or be conducive to trade expansion within any given economic grouping. In other words, the more advanced partners could assist the less developed partner states by not insisting on the application of the item-by-item trade liberalization process as this would greatly limit the scope for negotiation on the part of the less developed States.

The second major problem facing the least developed partner states is the inability to raise sufficient financial resources for economic development. This is true even in cases of national development efforts. The limitation on the ability to raise funds places an impediment on the least developed partners by leaving them unable to take advantage of the new industrial opportunities created under economic integration. The granting of tax and other fiscal incentives could assist the least developed partners to ensure that they are able to attract industries. Here, the more advanced partner states could agree, for a given period of time, not to demand comparable incentives that would eliminate the advantages enjoyed by the least developed partner states. It might also be useful if the partner states agreed to establish a joint multinational financial institution through which the aid-giving agencies could operate.* This would ensure that the least developed partner states would obtain needed finances without being forced to offer unduly favorable terms to the donor countries. In Africa, the African Development Bank is capable of handling such specialized functions. The African Development Bank should be given the necessary mandate to obtain loans through the the international agencies for financing plans under economic integration.

The third problem that the least developed partner states would face under economic integration is the inability to attract technical and manpower resources. It is a truism to say that managerial and technical skill will often be attracted to the more advanced partner countries that have more complex and sophisticated industries. If there is free movement of personnel within an integrated area, the flow of such resources to the more advanced partners could be serious. Here, incentives could be used to prevent any serious imbalances in human resources allocation. Another interesting factor is that, through the natural psychological and sociological resistance for an average person to emigrate to certain areas at certain levels of development, it is sometimes impossible to control the movement of skilled personnel. This does not pose any problem insofar as internal technical and manpower resources are concerned, but with regard to attracting external resources the least developed partner states may be forced to offer extremely favorable conditions that over the long run, would cause a serious drain resources. Hence, a common recruitment and human resource allocation agency should be established, giving priority and special treatment to the requirements of the least developed partner states.

Measures to be adopted in favor of the least developed partners

---

*Some of the multinational economic groupings in Africa that have not established joint institutions for directing foreign reserves and investments should seriously consider the creation of a development institution like the East African Development Bank. In establishing policies for economic cooperation, countries should be able to direct investments and ensure a fair distribution of capital and technology, especially to the least developed partner states. A development bank could be used effectively as an instrument for balancing the gains from cooperation.

under economic cooperation may be viewed within two broad policy objectives: (1) that there is urgent need to introduce appropriate strategy to reduce the economic gap between the partner states and (2) that economic incentives should be given to the least developed partners in order to raise the general levels of economic activity in these countries, and thereby raise the standard of living. The measures suggested below may be taken into consideration in reaching agreements toward economic cooperation. [4]

Trade and Commercial Policy

In devising measures for the reduction or elimination of trade barriers, special consideration should be given guaranteeing free access into the markets of the more advanced partners to the goods, especially manufactures and semimanufactures, of the least developed partners. The question of access could be linked to special preferential treatment granted to third countries. In this context, measures such as the following could be taken: (1) the least developed partners might be given a period of grace, such as 3 to 5 years, in which to maintain certain tariffs against their partners in order to protect infant industries, on the explicit understanding that this temporary measure would be withdrawn unconditionally at the end of the agreed period; (2) the more advanced partners could agree to give preferential treatment to imports from the least developed partners for a given period during which time the latter could develop their competitive ability; (3) the least developed partners could be exempted temporarily from raising their internal tariffs to the level of the common external tariff; (4) consideration could be given to the possibility of granting fiscal incentives over a relatively longer period to industries established in the least developed partner countries and specifically geared toward export to the other partner states; (5) the partner states could establish an arrangement similar to the transfer tax or financial compensation by the more advanced partner countries to the least developed partner states for the loss of revenue that might result from shifting the source of supply from cheaper third countries to more expensive partner states (this could take the form of pro rata transfer of customs revenue or some lump-sum payments agreed on beforehand but subject to review after a given period) and (6) a financial institution could be set up at the subregional or multinational level with the main function of financing projects to maintain the economic balance between the partner states, giving priority to the least developed partner states— for example, credit facilities could be provided for the import of capital and industrial goods by the least developed partner states from the more advanced ones.

Multinational Commodity Agreements

Certain products that already are subject to international agreements--such as coffee, cocoa, and other primary products--could be subject to special treatment within a multinational cooperation group. It could be agreed that any country already enjoying preferential treatment in third countries in respect of its products should be allowed to maintain such position by waiving the condition for reciprocity to the more advanced partners. This is particularly important where a single commodity contributes a major portion of export earnings.

Preferential Treatment for
Manufactured Goods from Partner States

In order to ensure balanced development of the countries under multinational cooperation, it might be essential for the more advanced partner states to consider granting preferential treatment to the manufactured and semimanufactured goods from the least developed countries, especially where such goods directly compete with similar goods from third countries.

Technical and Financial Assistance

The more advanced partner states might consider granting technical and financial assistance to the least developed partner states in the implementation of joint projects. Quite often, the least developed countries are unable to fully exploit their resources, both human and physical, due largely to lack of finance and technical know-how. It is known that some African countries do have surplus trained and skilled manpower that could be diverted to assist other states within multinational cooperation. Hitherto, most African countries have depended upon the developed countries, especially the former metropolitan powers, for most of their requirements for technical and managerial skills as well as financial needs. Within the concept of self-reliance, the more advanced partner states should explore ways and means of assisting the least developed partner countries fulfill their requirements for these resources.

GENERAL PROPOSALS
FOR BENEFIT-SHARING ARRANGEMENTS

Before proposals can be made regarding possible arrangements that the African countries might wish to consider adopting for sharing the benefits from the various plans, certain observations must be stated as a premise for further action. These remarks are necessary in order to provide a proper perspective for the arrangements for joint development of certain projects. In the past, failure to understand some of these factors led to a misconception of economic cooperation and hence to an unrealistic expectation of gains from such cooperation.

Although trade liberalization is a logical step toward development, the African countries, in general, would not gain substantially from a regime of free trade because the level of intra-African trade is very low. Moreover, in the absence of cooperation, the trade situation could not be improved because of the narrow demand base for most manufactures within the African countries, which severely hinders the development of large-scale manufacturing industries. The smallness of the African economies also means that for each country the advantages of scale resulting from coordination of economic activities would be substantial, especially given the present scarcity of capital resources required for the establishment of large-scale industries. The limitation in the domestic economies, the need to diversify present productive capacity to encourage future development, and the general low levels of demand in Africa as a whole indicate that there are enormous advantages in economic cooperation. Differences in the levels of income give great scope for raising welfare by money and other capital transfers among the integrated countries.

It follows nonetheless that, insofar as economies of scale are important in manufacturing and other industries any economic association that involves pooling of markets and factors of production is advantageous, especially in the case of the least developed countries. Moreover, economies of scale resulting from cooperation are very important in sectors where there are common views on the political expediency of such projects and where geographical factors facilitate common public services.

Since integration implies free movement of factors of production, especially labor, capital, and technical know-how, under laissez-faire economic cooperation would aggravate the disparities in standards of living in the partner states, especially where the disparity was initially great. In such cases, the least developed partner states should insist on the adoption of certain safeguards, such as deliberate allocation of financial resources and investments to the more back-ward areas. They might also insist that certain development projects be encouraged in the least development partner states through the granting of economic incentives to foreign investors, and that the cost of such incentives be borne largely by the more advanced partner states. In certain cases, member countries might also agree not to grant licenses to certain industries unless they are established in the least developed partner countries.

The benefits from cooperation would be reinforced if arrange-ments were made for the transfer of certain financial resources to the least developed partner countries for the promotion of specific projects. To ensure that such financial resources are used in the projects for which they are intended, they should be channeled through a development bank such as the East African Development Bank. One guiding principle in this kind of exercise is that those partner states in the multinational economic grouping that have comparative ad-vantages in the production of a given item sold in the markets of other partner states will gain relatively less from free trade if such a product can sell equally to third countries. Similarly, where a country develops a secondary industry in which other partner states have greater advantages in skilled manpower, technology, transport facili-ties, and general location of the industry in relation to the integrated market as a whole, the country will gain relatively less from free trade. Nevertheless, where any form of cooperation provides for coordination of development planning, it is possible to envisage a general spread of secondary industries among the states through a deliberate plan for specialization, in which case all parties would be in a better position than in the absence of cooperation.

It should be stressed that the success of an economic grouping depends upon whether the participating states believe that the advan-tages are comparable and equitably spread. In this respect, it could be argued that in the African experience the most successful and stable economic unions are those involving small economies com-prising a few countries with somewhat similar political and economic objectives. Moreover, groups of countries whose strength and develop-ment depend largely upon exports of primary products to the advanced countries do not seem to present a strong prospect for integration, since advantages to be derived from the creation of a larger market cannot be exploited to the fullest.

As was stated previously, the African countries tend to think of economic integration as a situation where advantages exist from the outset and are readily distinguishable. Quite often, the African countries have thought that a country does not stand to gain from a multinational arrangement unless it is allocated at least some of the multinational industries. The importance of industries seems to have been overexaggerated in determing the gains or losses under economic cooperation. What is forgotten is the fact that, if certain industries are allotted to land-locked countries, such industries must be served by a road or railway from the coastal countries and be supported by adequate port and harbor facilities. Thus, the port and harbor facilities must be expanded while the road or rail services are improved. The country in which the port is situated or where the road or rail line passes does not normally consider these improvements and the increase in employment opportunities as benefits from cooperation, but they do represent real gains.

Therefore, it should be understood that in any multinational grouping the gains from cooperation cannot always be measured in terms of allocation of industries. Other unquantifiable advantages resulting from such aspects as ancillary services should be taken into account. In fact, in a static situation all countries in a multinational grouping cannot expect to maximize their gains from cooperation. It is the dynamic aspects of integration that call for special consideration, since when the economies move to a higher level of equilibrium countries will be able to increase their relative advantages. It might also be argued that some existing industries would benefit from the widening of markets, even though initially they were established for domestic markets.

Thus, the question of sharing of benefits should be given careful thought by the African countries wishing to participate in a multinational grouping. Where short-term benefits do not seem great, it should be understood that the resultant prospects for future economic development could be greater than the initial advantages. In such cases, existing, as well as future, enterprises should study the possibilities for large-scale industrial development to take advantage of possibilities for the expansion of both domestic and multinational markets resulting from closer coordination of economic development efforts. It should be stressed that the advantages of cooperation should be determined in comparison with the level of development a country could reach in the absence of cooperation.

In the final analysis, the gains from economic cooperation would be determined by the ability of each member state to take advantage of the new opportunities created as a result of the integration of the national markets. A country that takes adequate measures to explore the new efforts in development within the multinational market would tend to gain more from cooperation than a country that, for whatever reason, is unable to do so. Moreover, the individual member states should take appropriate measures at the national level to sustain their contributions to economic cooperation.

The preceding paragraphs have discussed at length the benefits derived from industrial development for the simple reason that most African countries view economic cooperation in terms of the industries they can establish if they cooperate with other countries. But this is not the whole picture. In an integrated area, not all countries will be in a position to establish large-scale industries even if such industries were allocated to them for technical and other reasons. But this does not mean that a country may not reap benefits from cooperation in other fields. For instance, the ability to sell goods in the other partner states where previously this was not possible represents a definite gain from cooperation. In the field of agriculture, the establishment of joint research facilities and the introduction of new techniques in production of such crops as rice in West Africa, sugar in the OCAM countries, and meat in the countries of the Conseil de l'Entente strengthens the positions of the individual member countries both in the production and marketing of these commodities. In the field of transportation, a land-locked country's ability to negotiate favorable transit arrangements with a coastal country for its exports and imports is an advantage under economic cooperation. Therefore, in determining the gains from cooperation a country should ask itself whether it would indeed be able to attain a fast rate of development of given sectors or of the entire economy in the absence of cooperation.

NOTES

1. Economic Commission for Africa, Economic Conditions in Africa in Recent Years, E/CN/.14/435, p. 4.

2. Economic Commission for Africa, Special Measures in Favor of the Least Developed among the Developing Countries, E/CN.14/WP.1/21; OAU/TRAD/20, p. 4.

3. United Nations Conference on Trade and Development, Special Measures to be Taken in Favor of the Least Developed Among the Developing Countries, TD/17/Supp.1, pp. 7-13.

4. See also, United Nations Conference on Trade and Development, <u>Trade Expansion and Economic Integration Among Developing Countries</u>, TD/B/85/Rev.1, pp. 102-3.

**TOWARD
DEFINING
A STRATEGY
FOR COOPERATION
IN THE 1970'S**

THE ELEMENTS OF A STRATEGY
FOR DEVELOPMENT

In the search for a strategy for economic development through cooperation, some pertinent questions should be answered: What is it that the countries wish to achieve through economic cooperation? How will such cooperation be achieved? What effect will cooperation have on the national economies, in terms of increased employment, industrial output, trade expansion, and agricultural development? If adequate answers are not found, it should be presumed that a strategy does not exist or that such a strategy is ill-conceived. An effective strategy would contain a general statement of the objectives of a given economic grouping, how such objectives are to be achieved, and what the countries expect in terms of the impact on the individual national economies as well as the group as a whole. The essential factor to bear in mind is that countries should not seek cooperation for its own sake but as a means of enhancing economic development.

However, on a continent where both the overall economic situation and the individual economic parameters are rapidly changing over a relatively short period, it becomes difficult to prescribe any realistic strategy for multinational economic cooperation. Even in regard to simple economic development projects, policy suggestions have tended to vary widely from time to time. In Africa today, as a result of various changes in political, social, and economic factors, a number of combinations are feasible in any plan for economic cooperation covering trade, industry, agriculture, and transport development. These combinations were discussed in detail in Chapter 2.

Since the concept of economic cooperation is now universally accepted, what is required is to agree on some concrete projects for putting cooperation into action. The main problem of cooperation in Africa has been, and will continue to be, the creation of ideal multinational institutional machinery capable of meeting the requirements for economic development at both the national and multinational level.

The problem of creating an ideal institutional machinery for cooperation is very closely linked with the question of national sovereignty (see Chapter 9). It is also related to the willingness of the African countries to give up some of their power of decision in economic matters. A strategy that does not demand much autonomy from the member states would appeal more to the African nations. Where sharp conflicts exist between a multinational strategy and national development plans, efforts should be made to reconcile the two sets of priorities in order to achieve harmonious development.

DEVELOPMENT PLANNING FOR MULTINATIONAL COOPERATION

Planning for development, whether on a national or multinational basis, is a necessity for enhancing the economic development of the developing countries. In recent years, the need for planning has acquired special significance in the wake of technological advances in the developed countries that tend to widen the economic gap between developed and developing countries and also due to the enormous amounts of investment, capital equipment, and technical know-how required for development.

Economic development is, by its nature, a slow process, but the problem that now confronts the African countries is how to develop and develop fast. Therefore, development planning must take into account the need for fast structural and technological change. The colonial pattern of development, under which the territories produced raw materials in exchange for manufactured goods from the metropolitan powers, must be changed. The traditional--and sometimes primitive--methods of production must be replaced by more advanced and up-to-date techniques. Industrial development necessitates a change in social values and the traditional pattern of life, and such changes must be introduced in such a way as to suit the requirements for both national and multinational development. In multinational planning, certain institutions and procedures, that were developed within individual countries must be changed to fit in with the new order; this change becomes an important factor in economic development.

In order to ensure effective multinational cooperation, the African countries also should endeavor to ensure the coordination of research, technical, and social skills and the standardization of statistical data. In the African experience, the concept of planning is a fairly new one--serious economic planning in the modern sense of the word was adopted in most African countries only after the attainment of independence--and many problems arise in the attempts to work out an acceptable formula for harmonization of the national development plans. Even within the individual countries, the problem of balancing development in the various sectors of the economy, especially between rural and urban areas, remains largely unsolved. Therefore, problems of planning arise at both the national and multinational level.

Multinational cooperation among the African states would be an effective measure for ensuring coordinated development planning in Africa. Since economic cooperation (or integration) is not an end in itself but a means to an end, its significance must be weighed against the background for social reforms and political stability and the overall requirements for economic development. The enlargement of the domestic markets through cooperation must be accompanied by the fulfillment of certain conditions, so as to derive the desired benefits. Therefore, a set of conditions, some of which are outlined below, must be met in order that multinational cooperation achieve its objectives (see Chapter 1).[1] It is not necessary that all these conditions be fulfilled at once by all the countries; partial fulfillment may, under certain conditions, provide a sound base for cooperation.

One of the main objectives of multinational planning should be to attain the harmonization of economic development policies. Treaties for multinational cooperation in Africa give some kind of legal framework for implementation of the various plans. However, the harmonization of economic policies often cannot be included in a treaty, and therefore the coordination of economic policies must be made through institutions capable of making necessary adjustments in the domestic policies of the individual countries within the framework of cooperation. Within a multinational structure involving countries with different economic policies, the problems of cooperation would be tackled through a system of adjustments of economic policies. In order to enhance the process of cooperation in the various fields, it is necessary to harmonize certain policies, especially tax laws and regulations, currency and exchange control, industrial legislation, and where possible, customs and tariff policies. Measures should be instituted to adopt common policies (or some adjustments toward common policies) in the development of trade and in the fiscal and monetary fields. A joint policy for the coordination of such policies would ensure the required freedom in the movement of goods, services, and other factors of production necessary to support the establishment of multinational industries.

There is also need to take measures aimed at harmonizing the national development plans. Multinational planning is an essential element of economic cooperation. Hitherto, the African countries have made planning decisions without due regard to the need for action coordinated with neighboring states, even though this was clearly a logical step to follow. Cooperation cannot succeed unless the countries are made to realize the need for joint action. It is essential that future development plans be adjusted within the framework for cooperation, and therefore an institution for joint planning composed of national planners should be established to work out concrete proposals for joint planning in Africa. The main functions of such institution would be to identify multinational projects in which coordinated planning is required, to conduct feasibility studies and to devise appropriate mechanism for the financing of multinational industrial projects.

With the recognition that national plans have been launched at different time periods and with varying objectives, the harmonization of these plans could take any of the following three alternatives:

1. The existing national plans of member countries of a given economic grouping should be carefully examined to determine areas of similarity on which joint action should be encouraged. Where objectives differ widely from country to country, reasons for such differences would be noted, and if possible, reconciliation measures should be instituted.

2. Within a group of countries with different plan periods, an agreement could be reached that no new plans should be initiated until the countries have reviewed them together so as to bring about harmonization in the plan periods. In the interim period between the end of any plan and the time joint planning is instituted, countries could adopt interim development plans to ensure that the development process in these countries is not unduly impeded.

3. In rare cases, countries may agree to terminate immediately their present plans and launch new ones at the same time to ensure coordination. This can be attained only at a level of cooperation approximating a political federation. If countries are not willing to

commit themselves to the coordination of their plans, they should at least accept the principle of consultations on planning policies.

In the process of economic integration, it must be recognized that though external aid is an important element, the development of the less developed countries depends largely on the efforts and enthusiasm of their own people: their determination to improve the rate of progress and their willingness to adjust their economic and social structure in order to facilitate the process of industrial development and the development of transport and agriculture. At the national level, the power of decision-making and the determination of development priorities is clearly established, and the national development planning agencies or departments have clear mandates to proceed according to certain clearly laid-out objectives. The problem becomes more complex when one envisages multinational planning for development. In planning for coordinated development, one deals with several countries and different policies and priorities. It is therefore difficult to establish a multinational set of priorities that unites national and multinational priorities; the degree of complexity cannot be overemphasized.

In this regard several questions must be answered: Who will be responsible for taking the joint planning decisions? If a supragovernmental institution is to be responsible for such decisions, how many of the vital decisions will be left to the national planning agencies? What would be the nature of the decisions taken within a multinational set-up, and once such decisions are taken how are they to be implemented? Would this supragovernmental machinery be empowered to enforce its decisions on the national governments? If so, how can decisions taken within the multinational set-up be adjusted to serve the aspirations of the member states while at the same time serving higher objectives and eliminating any conflicts of interests or, in other words, what mechanism would be necessary to adjust possible conflicts of economic interests between the national governments on the one hand and the multinational authorities on the other? Practical answers to these problems are not readily available and, even assuming that some of these problems were solved, what assurance can the member states have that the financial resources required for the implementation of the multinational programs will be available?

Problems in multinational planning in Africa also arise due to the fact that in recent years planning has come to be identified with the political thinking of the leaders in power and, since in most African countries the national governments have acquired control over the key industries the determination of planning priorities may be governed not only by economic considerations but also by political motivations.

The politicians have not yet accepted the idea of a supranational body with powers sufficient to make decisions that would be binding upon member states. Clearly, in order for any plan for multinational cooperation to be successful, the African countries must be ready to take unequivocal decisions to make cooperation a success.

The next question in multinational economic cooperation relates to the direction of private investment into the desired sectors, which is essential in multinational planning. In Africa, the major portion of investments is still controlled by private investors, directed from overseas, whose interests are not necessarily identical to those of the African countries. This being so, it is often difficult to devise a way of ensuring that capital and other resources are available for multinational projects. In the past, the international financial institutions do not appear to have been eager to finance infrastructural projects-- such as the development of roads and railways--which are necessary for multinational cooperation in Africa. Although by and large the situation has greatly improved in recent years, the problem of financing multinational projects is still acute.

A STRATEGY FOR COORDINATION OF INDUSTRIAL DEVELOPMENT

The basic constraint to the development of industries in the African countries is the limited size of the domestic markets. Moreover, the structure of the industries acts as a limitation to further expansion (see Chapter 5). Most African industries are oriented toward the processing of primary products for export to developed countries.

The main characteristics of these industries are: high unit costs, which means that most industries are operating below optimum; high excess capacity in most industries, which reflects the smallness of the domestic markets and the lack of coordination of industrial development program by the African countries; high capital cost components in the productive units; very limited utilization of by-products and other waste materials for subsidiary industries; and the almost total ownership of vital industries by foreign enterprise.* Furthermore, in African

----

*Several African countries have attempted to overcome this problem by partial ownership or nationalization of certain key industries. It is emphasized here that in a multinational set-up effective

industries production has been concentrated on perishable goods,
dairy products, beverages, and tobacco. Most durable consumer and
capital goods are wholly imported; cooperation will be essential in
this field.

In the strategy for industrial cooperation, it is essential that
immediate steps be taken to initiate consultations on the establishment
of multinational industries. Other measures should include the standardization of products and production techniques to ensure inter-
changeability of production components within specified industries;
the harmonization of investment laws and regulations; the creation
of industrial fairs and exhibitions, especially in small-scale industries;
the joint exploration of industrial opportunities in both mining and
manufacturing sectors; and the establishment of industrial research
institutes at the subregional level to ensure proper standardization
and exchange of technical and managerial skills as well as industrial
technology. These measures can best be carried out within the ambit
of international organizations, especially EAC, which along with other
United Nations agencies sponsored the establishment of the Institute
for Economic Development and Planning (IDEP) in Dakar, Senegal.
The main objectives of IDEP are to train officials from African countries engaged in economic development and planning, to conduct research in this field, and to provide advisory services to African governments. The African countries should make full use of the training
facilities of this institution.

Cooperation in industry could also include agreements on:

1. Ventures in which the enterprise in one country is essentially
a subcontractor supplying certain components in a production process.
The main enterprise would provide the subcontractor with technical
designs, technical know-how, and perhaps long-term credit facilities.

2. Jointly operated undertakings with one enterprise providing
long-term credits. The deliveries against such credit could comprise
industrial equipment and other capital goods required in the construction of plants, and the repayment of credit would be made from output.

3. Joint ownership under which one country would provide factory premises, raw materials, and manpower while another country

---

control of ownership of the major areas of industrial development is
an essential element for effective cooperation.

(or countries) would provide capital, technical know-how, and marketing facilities.[2]

Another way in which countries could cooperate in industrial
development is in providing industrial finance. Under such arrangements, an industrial financing institution, taking the form of a multinational industrial development corporation, could be set up within
each economic grouping specifically for financing multinational projects. In the initial stages, the national industrial development corporations could contribute to the capital and development fund of the
corporation through subsidies or grants from member states. This
multinational corporation could seek membership in other international
organizations such as the International Monetary Fund and the International Bank for Reconstruction and Development and should be given
powers to raise funds in the world money markets. Other private
governmental or quasi-governmental financial institutions could be
encouraged to cooperate with the multinational industrial development
corporation.

The efforts toward the coordination of industrial development in
Africa should include the following measures:

1. The multinational economic groupings should establish a
comprehensive list of industrial projects that could be developed jointly.
A number of projects on the list should be identified, and detailed
analysis of such projects be made to suggest how joint development
can be effected. A joint industrial promotion board should be set up
for this purpose, all member states should be equally represented on
this board, and each state should fully subscribe to its policies.

2. A deliberate effort should be made to develop small-scale
industries, and the countries should encourage trade in the products
of the small-scale industries identified in Chapter 5. Multinational
industrial finance corporations that may be established to provide
finances for large-scale projects should establish units to deal specifically with the promotion and financing of small-scale industries.

3. International financial institutions should be more forward-
looking in their policies on lending to economic groupings in Africa
that wish to set up multinational industries. Assistance to these
groupings should include not only provision of finances but also the
identification, selection, and evaluation of joint projects. These institutions should also be more willing to provide finances for technical
personnel to train local manpower in project identification techniques

and the formulation of proper requests for financial assistance, including the evaluation of the impact of foreign aid on economic development.

4. Governments within the multinational economic groupings should consider ways in which they can play a part, especially in the control and direction of investment into projects that would promote the economic development of the group.

A STRATEGY FOR JOINT AGRICULTURAL DEVELOPMENT

Agricultural development could provide the solution for the economic problems of a large number of countries in Africa for a long time to come. As was pointed out earlier, some 70 to 85 percent of the total population in Africa is engaged in agricultural activities. Moreover, agricultural exports in some countries constitute as much as 99 percent of total exports. Therefore, it would be unrealistic to envisage economic cooperation in Africa without cooperation in agriculture merely because there is little or no complementarity in this sector.

In the initial stages of cooperation, efforts could be directed toward promotion of such crops as wheat, rice, millet, sorghum, oilseeds, forestry products, meat and meat products, poultry, fish, rubber, sisal, cotton, and sugar. Consultative agricultural committees at the technical level could be established for each of these crops, with the task of studying the production, distribution, marketing, and control of pesticides and diseases. A multinational agricultural research and training institute could be set up to study and disseminate information and new production techniques. Special attention also could be given to the need to transform subsistence farming to modern farming in order to raise the rural population's standard of living. These are areas in which joint action seems logical.

The problem of food should be given special consideration. A committee on food could be set up within each economic grouping to study the food situation and the transfer of food from the surplus to the famine-stricken areas, not only between member states but also with countries outside the grouping. This is a field in which cooperation could bring rapid and tangible results. At a much more advanced stage, cooperation in agriculture could take the form of the establishment of processing and manufacturing industries for agricultural

commodities and raw materials that thus far have been largely exported
to the developed countries.

Other measures in the field of agricultural cooperation could include subregional or multinational irrigation schemes, especially in
semi-arid areas served by rivers. In this respect, countries along
the Nile, Niger, Senegal, Zambezi, and Congo rivers are well placed
to achieve effective cooperation. The establishment of chemical fertilizer plants and agricultural equipment assembly and maintenance
plants is another field in which cooperation is not only feasible but also
necessary. In the field of pest and insect control, great strides have
been made in such areas as locust control. Cooperative efforts in this
area should be intensified. Tsetse control is another area in which
cooperation can be achieved.

The strategy in the development of agriculture could be summarized as follows:

1. Joint research facilities in regard to new seed crops, brands,
and species should be stepped up to increase productivity in agricultural
crops. Extensive and intensive soil analysis should be made to discover
areas where new crops can be introduced on the African continent.

2. Joint measures should be taken at the multinational level to
provide means for the transformation of the rural areas from subsistence to modern farming. One such way is to introduce new concepts
in the land-tenure systems within the multinational groupings. New
multinational agricultural training institutions should be created to
provide the member countries with the necessary personnel and technical and financial support to enable this transformation to be achieved
effectively.

3. In order to increase agricultural production, multinational
organs should be set up to provide fertilizers, insecticides, machinery,
and agricultural implements to the peasant farmers. Along with these
measures, multinational grain marketing boards should be established
to provide facilities for marketing and distribution of agricultural produce and to ensure fair prices to the farmers, especially in the rural
areas.

TRADE PROMOTION AND EXPANSION AS A STRATEGY FOR DEVELOPMENT

It was established in Chapter 6 that trade constitutes one of the
most important elements in the economic development of the African

countries. The heavy dependence on trade for the major part of foreign exchange earnings and the large increases in the volume of imports, especially in recent years, make necessary the adoption of effective cooperation measures. Since it is obvious that the individual markets are too small to permit large-scale production and since the exports of African manufactures into the developed countries cannot be increased to any appreciable extent, the African countries must turn to the development of intra-African trade as the only possible alternative.

Broadly speaking, measures in the field of trade should consist of granting preferential treatment and easing of trade restrictions generally on products from partner states. Agreement should be reached on a list of commodities on which negotiations for trade liberalization should be started immediately. Even if the countries do not consider it necessary to establish free trade, there should at least be acceptance of trade liberalization as a long-term objective. Those countries experiencing balance of trade problems with partner states should be given special treatment to remove such imbalances. This could consist of transfer payments within specified limits. Trade negotiation conferences should be initiated for each multinational grouping to set the process in motion.

There are two broad aspects of the trade development strategy: (1) measures that must be taken at the international level by all the developing countries of the world toward the betterment of their overall position in relation to the developed countries and (2) measures to increase intra-African trade. Measures at the international level can be summed up as follows:

1. International commodity agreements in respect of primary commodities, especially those that now are facing stiffer competition from synthetics and are subject to high tariff duties in the advanced countries. The African countries, together with the rest of the developing world, should increase pressure on the developed countries to provide more favorable conditions of access for the primary commodities.

2. In respect of manufactures and semimanufactures, international agreements should be concluded by the developed and the developing countries whereby the developed countries agree to increase their imports of such products from African and other developing countries. The developed countries should be made to realize that the problems of world trade expansion and development equally affect them as well as the developing countries, and that any measures to improve the economic conditions of the developing countries will also result in increased prosperity in the developed nations.

Measures to increase intra-African trade should include the following:

1. New and more comprehensive trade agreements should be initiated by the African countries, and an inventory of the production patterns should be made including the type of products within the African countries in order to discover new commodities that can be included in the trade agreements. International organizations should be asked to give assistance in this regard.

2. A special system of preferences should be developed among the African countries whereby manufactured products originating in one African country would be accorded special preference in other African countries regardless of whether or not the countries belong to the same economic grouping. This would increase the movement of manufactured goods among the African countries. In line with the measures suggested in Chapter 6, multinational intra-African commodity agreements should be concluded for those primary commodities that are used as raw materials for industries in the African countries.

3. The existing trade and bilateral agreements among the African countries should be reviewed and revitalized to include a wider range of commodities. The countries should endeavor to adopt uniform trade and commercial legislation to ensure a smooth flow of goods and services. There should be regular conferences of traders and chamber of commerce officials to examine the customs and excise regulations in order to identify areas that hinder the development of intra-African trade. There also should be regular trade fairs and exhibitions primarily aimed at making the African countries aware of products manufactured in other African states.

A STRATEGY FOR DEVELOPMENT OF TRANSPORT AND COMMUNICATIONS

A serious bottleneck exists in the development efforts of the African countries as a result of the lack of adequate infrastructure, especially transport and communications. The existing transport systems are insufficient to sustain the development efforts even within the existing economic groupings because there are virtually no interstate connections as a result of past transportation policies, which were oriented toward the expansion of trade in raw materials with the countries of Europe.

An essential feature of the strategy for economic cooperation should be deliberate efforts to link up existing transport systems.

The first task in this respect is to identify the missing links. ECA has already done considerable work in this field. The major work would initially consist in the standardization of transport documentation, code rates, freight charges, and railway carriages and gauges. On the administration side of transport development, permanent transport and communications committees should be established within the multinational grouping, with subcommittees on road, railway, inland, maritime, and air transport. These subcommittees should have the task of the coordination of existing facilities as well as future development. In the field of communications, the African Postal Union (APU) should be strengthened and measures should be taken to establish telephone and telex centers at strategic locations to serve as points of contact with the rest of the world.

In the 1970's, the role of transport and communications in the economic development of Africa will increasingly become important as the countries move to more advanced stages of economic cooperation. The objective of the strategy for transport development should be the integration of the small national markets into more viable economic units. The policy for transport development should include some of the following measures:

1. There should be a more detailed evaluation of the existing transport systems to determine their capacities and their major defects in enhancing economic cooperation and to suggest measures for improvement.

2. Detailed studies of the different means of transportation should be jointly undertaken to determine which means are suitable for which kinds of merchandise. These studies would essentially influence decisions on priorities for the development of transportation.

3. Before any new road or railway systems are initiated on a multinational scale, the gaps between the African countries should be identified and connected to create transcontinental networks.

4. A joint railway training school should be established within each multinational economic grouping for countries with a rail line, to train railway personnel in modern techniques of management, supervision, and maintenance, including the manufacture of spare parts.

5. Special measures should immediately be instituted toward improvement of transit arrangements affecting the land-locked countries. The African countries should give priority to cooperation between the coastal and land-locked countries. This could take the form of reduction in freight charges, wharfage, and other handling charges.

Greater facilities and improved storage conditions at the ports and harbors also constitute an area in which such cooperation could be enhanced.

DEFINITION OF REALISTIC GROWTH TARGETS

In drawing up a strategy for economic cooperation in Africa, adequate consideration must be given to projects that are of interest to a group of countries. At the international level, the need for a development strategy has been recognized in the United Nations and its agencies. To this end, the United Nations General Assembly, by Resolution No. 2626 (XXV) of November 1970, adopted an "International Development Strategy for the Second United Nations Development Decade."[3] This strategy stresses that international cooperation for development is an essential element of efforts toward development. Economic and social progress should be the joint responsibility of the entire international community. However, the primary responsibility for the economic development of the developing countries lies with the countries themselves. The United Nations strategy lays out well-defined targets that are necessary for accelerating the rate of development in the 1970's (see Chapter 1). The strategy also emphasizes measures that must be taken at the national level to ensure that the international measures became effective.

At the African level, the Economic Commission for Africa has drawn up a strategy for economic development of the African region in the 1970's.[4] This broadly based strategy is intended to give a unified approach to the problems of development in Africa in line with the United Nations international strategy. The ECA strategy recognizes that the plurality in the characteristics of the African economies strengthens the case for integration in order to provide an adequate base to sustain development efforts in Africa. ECA also has proposed specific measures that it proposes to undertake to help the African countries realize their development targets. In order to enable the African countries to reap the full benefits of international assistance, ECA suggested that, for the new approach to the solution of development problems in the 1970's, the international organizations including ECA should coordinate their aid policies especially in manpower deployment in order to present a unified assistance program to the African countries.

In light of past experience and the present levels of development within the existing multinational economic groupings, it would appear

that a more realistic strategy for development should consider cooperation at the sectoral level, where opportunities for cooperation
are more readily identifiable. In certain cases, it might be more realistic to aim at joint development of individual projects within a given
economic grouping. Although multisectoral cooperation should be regarded as the most effective instrument for economic growth, attainment of multisectoral cooperation will be less demanding on the resources of the African countries when they move to higher levels of
development. Moreover, the small beginnings of cooperation in Africa
have already proved to be more effective in fostering joint action by
the African states. An essential element of such joint strategy should
be the joint mobilization of domestic and foreign resources for multinational projects. The harmonization of the national development
plans should also constitute an integral part of the development strategy for the 1970's.

NOTES

1. See also United Nations, Department of Economic and Social
Affairs: Multinational Planning, Economic Integration and Cooperation:
The African Experience, ISDP.5/A/R.3, pp. 42-47, prepared and pre-
sented by Webster Mutharika to the United Nations Fifth Inter-Regional
Seminar on Development Planning (Bangkok, September 1969) on behalf
of the secretariat of the Economic Commission for Africa.

2. See United Nations Conference on Trade and Development:
Trade Expansion and Economic Integration among Developing Countries, TD/B/85/Rev.1, p. 75.

3. See United Nations, International Development Strategy for
the Second United Nations Development Decade, A/RES/2626/(XXV),
(New York, November 1970).

4. See Economic Commission for Africa, Africa's Strategy for
Development in the 1970's, E/CN.14/493/Rev.3 (February 1971).

12

ONE DECADE OF ECONOMIC COOPERATION

In order to advance the rate of economic development in Africa, it is essential that the African countries have access to adequate capital resources, trained and skilled manpower, large-scale application of scientific and technical know-how, and wider markets. This presupposes a large degree of interdependence among the African countries, resulting in the integration of the small domestic markets into more viable economic units permitting the economic utilization of the factors of production. This, in effect, is the very essence of multinational economic cooperation in Africa.

The drive toward closer cooperation among the African countries has been motivated by three major factors. First, in order to avoid wasting the meager resources of the African countries through the establishment of industries of uneconomic size, it is necessary to establish multinational industries in which several countries participate. This would necessitate the coordination of activities in the fields of trade, industry, transport, natural resources, and manpower training. Second, if the African countries wish to develop and expand their exports of manufactures to the developed countries, it is essential to set up industries that are competitive both with industries in the developed countries and with industries in the developing countries of Asia and Latin America. This can be achieved only through economic cooperation. Third, in order to expand external trade the African countries will have to take concrete measures for increasing intra-African trade. The mounting trade and tariff restrictions in the developed countries and the high rate of advancement in science and technology have resulted in a steady decrease in the imports of primary commodities from the African countries. It therefore follows that, if trade must continue to sustain economic development in the African countries, the policy action should consist of efforts to develop and expand intra-African trade.

In drawing up a program of action for the future, the main consideration is not how much economic cooperation has been achieved in Africa but, rather, the contribution that cooperation has made toward the economic development of the African countries or toward their awareness of the need for joint action in order to accelerate the rate of development. Therefore, economic cooperation must be viewed in comparison to the level of development each individual African state would have achieved in the absence of cooperation. The case for joint action in all fields of economic development acquires greater significance in the development efforts in the 1970's because of the general recognition among the developing countries of the world that additional efforts must be undertaken by groups of countries in order to reduce the gaps in the level of development between the developing and the developed countries.

In order to accelerate the rate of growth of the African economies, special measures should be taken for joint development of industries manufacturing consumption goods; there should be an increase in agricultural production through the transformation of the rural sectors from subsistence to modern economy; and the African countries should take deliberate policies to develop adequate means of transport and communications and to promote intra-African trade. The African countries can no longer afford to continue to depend upon the markets of the developed countries to sustain their development efforts; they must take appropriate steps toward self-reliance. This will entail the adoption of bold and even radical economic reforms and a reorientation of the African people toward new value concepts in the development of political, social, cultural, and economic institutions.

Although economic cooperation has gained ground in Africa, there are still doubts in some African countries as to whether such cooperation is flexible enough to meet their individual aspirations. In order to ensure that economic cooperation serves as an instrument for development, it is essential that the countries constituting an economic grouping know exactly what they seek to gain by cooperation with others and how they will achieve the joint objectives. In the initial stages, it might be more advantageous for the countries to concentrate on the development of single multinational projects rather than a whole range of multinational economic activities. This is particularly important where there are wide divergences in the levels of economic development of the member countries, since in such cases the least developed partner countries may not be readily willing to commit their entire economic development policies. After deciding on a form of cooperation, it is essential that the participating countries give consideration to the creation of adequate and effective institutional machinery for joint action that not only will reflect the wishes of the member states but also will be respected by them.

Integrated economic development has taken place in most African countries at the national level and in specific sectors. Thus far, there has not been effective coordinated development of major sectors by any group of countries. For instance, agriculture, which is the backbone of economic development in Africa, is still undeveloped and countries continue to concentrate on the development and expansion of raw materials for exports to the developed countries.

Since the establishment of multinational industries requiring a wider market would entail the acceptance of far-reaching commitments by any group of countries, it is essential that separate measures be adopted for the new as well as the existing industries. Access to adequate markets is a necessary precondition for the establishment of new industries. Therefore, it is necessary that provisions be made for adjustments in the production structures of the countries so as to avoid serious disturbances in the structures of both industry and labor supply. The merging of the national markets will nonetheless disturb the general levels of equilibrium within the countries, but a new higher level of equilibrium will be achieved representing advantages from economies of scale. With regard to existing industries, special treatment should be accorded to industries that, although not basically multinational, have reached a level of production that would permit innovations enabling the products to enjoy advantages from the expanded market. Some limited protection should be accorded to infant industries in the least developed partner states to enable such industries to stand on their feet. Once this has been achieved, the protection should be withdrawn unconditionally. This is an essential incentive for countries to consider committing their industrial policies to cooperation, especially for the less privileged member states.

In the development of industries, problems often have arisen as to how to allocate certain vital industries to different countries within a group for joint development and market exploitation. Even in economic groupings where the process of integration is fairly advanced--such as the East African Community, the UDEAC, or the Maghreb group--the adoption of a program for joint industrial development still presents formidable problems. However, there is a general recognition that

joint industrialization is an effective strategy for the economic development of Africa. The main obstacles to industrial development are the
lack of effective consultation regarding investment policies and the
inadequacy of measures for harmonization of national development
plans. In evolving a policy for industrialization, the countries would
derive additional benefits if efforts were made to develop complementary
industries even where the countries' industrial development policies
were not harmonized. Such measures would gradually lead to the
diversification of industries within the economic groupings.

An important aspect of economic cooperation in Africa is the
development of intra-African trade. There is now a general awareness
that during the 1970's export earnings in most African countries will
become less and less sufficient to cover the import bill, which would
adversely affect development efforts. Although international measures
are being undertaken through UNCTAD and GATT, at best these
can only help to maintain existing economic development levels in
the African countries. What is required is the adoption of adequate
policies for deliberate development and expansion of trade among the
African countries themselves. To this end, both industrial and agricultural production in the African countries should be transformed from
the traditional pattern to a more diversified structure, especially
through the modernization of agricultural production and the establishment of multinational manufacturing industries.

The existing economic groupings in Africa have demonstrated
the determination of the African countries to cooperate in order to
raise their standards of living. During the 1960's the momentum
toward cooperation slowed down somewhat due to several problems,
including political and economic considerations. On the political side,
differences in political approach to economic development and in
external relations presented formidable obstacles to cooperation
efforts in some parts of Africa. There is now urgent need to adjust
the political policies of the African countries so that politics will play
a more positive role in the economic development of Africa. On the
economic side, the differences in the level of economic development
in member countries in a given economic grouping also caused serious
problems, especially in regard to the sharing of benefits from cooperation. The main problem in this respect is that no effective formula
has yet been devised for ensuring equitable distribution of benefits.
Some benefit-sharing plans have been tried with a certain degree of
success, but they related only to small specific aspects of cooperation.
In such major aspects of economic development as industry and
agriculture, difficulties still arise in regard to the establishment of
a system for distribution of benefits.

In adopting measures for enhancing economic cooperation in the 1970's, the African countries should consider preparing a clearly defined strategy for joint development of the major economic sectors (see Chapter 11 for some suggestions for such a strategy). It is not essential that the entire economy be brought under one general strategy, but the countries should know what they want to achieve and how they seek to achieve it. The main consideration is that, where countries would derive distinct advantages from economic cooperation, every effort should be made to achieve cooperation. Initially, a group of countries might find it to their advantage to cooperate in areas where there are likely to be minimal differences of approach and then work toward more complicated institutions for cooperation. In deciding upon new strategies for the 1970's, countries belonging to the existing economic groupings should consider opening their doors to adjoining nonmember countries and allowing them to participate in limited aspects of cooperation. Ideally, the first step would be to invite the nonmembers to attend meetings as observers. Gradually, a system would be found to permit these countries to participate more directly in areas of cooperation where there is sufficient interest by the group members and the nonmember countries.

FUTURE PROSPECTS FOR COOPERATION IN AFRICA

Economic cooperation as a means for stepping up the rate of economic development in Africa constitutes the most effective strategy for solving the problems of development. Throughout the world, both the developed and developing countries are now moving toward a greater degree of interdependence. The case for cooperation has acquired special significance because joint action would mitigate the constraints to development caused by the limitations in the size of the domestic markets. The main conclusion to be drawn from experience in Africa is that economic cooperation, whether at a limited or advanced level, still holds the key to economic development of Africa, at both national and multinational levels. The prospects for economic cooperation and integration in Africa are quite bright so long as the African countries adopt appropriate measures to exploit these opportunities. In view of the limited prospects for expansion of exports to the markets of developed countries, cooperation among the developing African countries will be an effective instrument for expanding trade, especially in manufactured goods; for achieving the required diversification in agricultural production; and for putting the necessary process of import substitution on a more rational basis. Now that they are convinced of the need to integrate their economic structures,

the African countries should explore opportunities to accelerate
economic growth through the full exploitation of economies of scale
resulting from joint ventures and the sharing of markets and resources.
Although it must be stressed that economic integration is not a panacea
for redressing the basic evils of underdevelopment, it can be argued
that the establishment of a multinational framework conducive to a
more effective allocation and utilization of resources would be an
important ingredient of the development strategy for the 1970's.

During the 1960's there were encouraging measures for groups
of African countries with broadly comparable levels of economic
development to foster close trade and other economic cooperation
relations. In the developing African countries, the increased interest
in the advantages of specialization for orderly economic expansion
has generated a marked movement toward exploration of the possibilities for expansion of intra-African trade. This is seen as a way
of reducing the African countries' economic dependence on the advanced
nations. The important outcome of this recognition has been the
creation of the various multinational economic groupings and the
efforts toward the establishment of common market arrangements
among the various groups of countries through the coordination of
commercial policies.

Concerted action by groups of developing African countries to
foster joint economic development and to facilitate multinational
planning has not been confined to the expansion of foreign trade.
Multinational cooperation has been sought in such projects as the
joint development of river basins falling within more than one country,
the joint development of port and other transport facilities, and concerted action in the development of selected agricultural commodities.
The need for cooperation in the financial field has led to the establishment of such regional development banks as the African Development Bank. There are also effective monetary arrangements within
some of the economic associations. Moreover, regional development
institutes in Africa, such as the Institute for Development Planning
(IDEP), have recently been established in order to provide centers
for training government officials in planning methods and for conducting research and dissemination of information. There are now
indications of a growing awareness of the need for greater cooperation
in the planning of new industries. In the economically weaker countries
where the size of the domestic market is too small to permit efficient
levels of plant operation, proposals for multinational planning for
cooperation have special significance.

In the formulation of national development plans, especially in
the initial phase of economic development, countries often are able--

with sufficient accuracy and without the use of refined analytical tools--
to identify development programs and priorities that could be singled
out for specific action. However, as the process of growth gathers
momentum, such priorities usually become less obvious and more
complex. The major difficulty in this respect arises in project analysis
and formulation and the lack of overall coordination among the major
sectors within the economic groupings. The lack of adequate and
accurate knowledge about technical skills and other resources and
the absence of basic statistical data concerning main features of the
economy also present serious obstacles to realistic appraisal of
development problems. This, in turn, affects priority ratings both
within the individual countries and among nations. Since it takes considerable time and resources to build up adequate statistical facilities,
it is important that the African countries jointly take systematic steps
to improve statistical and other economic data needed in the process
of planning for multinational cooperation.

The incorporation of foreign trade into national economic plans
has presented difficult problems in the African countries. Important
questions relating to market conditions for primary commodities,
access of primary commodities into the developed countries, and
possibilities for absorption of imports of manufactured and semimanufactured commodities from other developing African countries
have been the subject of vigorous discussions in recent years. It is
suggested that the problems of trade and development be viewed together, at both the national and multinational levels. The African countries
should formulate their plans and policies so as to take full advantage
of increased market possibilities resulting from cooperation. The
development of intra-African trade demands sustained action through
national plans and through programs for investment and deployment
of technical skills in a wide range of productive activities. Therefore,
the African states should endeavor to evolve measures and policies
to ensure an increased intra-African flow of goods and services in
the context of multinational economic cooperation.

It is sometimes argued that plan harmonization at the multinational level could be conceived of as either a necessary complement
or an alternative to arrangements for regional trade liberalization.
As an alternative to the free trade approach, the plan harmonization
approach seems to assume special importance in the African countries
where, although the national planning machinery has been effectively
established, there is still no harmonization of plans among countries,
even within the same grouping. This situation results from the fact
that, in view of the lack of complementarity in the production structures
of the developing African countries, it is generally held that a liberalization of trade will not lead to a considerable increase in intra-

African trade without the adoption of much more far-reaching measures. Even in areas where groups of countries chose the trade liberalization approach as a step toward economic cooperation, as in Latin
America, trade liberalization failed to generate the necessary upward
thrust in economic growth. In such cases, harmonization of industrial
development programs within the framework of a free trade area or a
common market would result in considerable trade expansion and
growth. However, in general the liberalization of intra-African trade
may present development problems since a large portion of national
income is derived from exports. A reduction of trade barriers even
on a limited scale may have long-term effects on the production structures of certain countries through an inevitable adjustment process,
but it must still be argued that a planned system for joint industrial
development coupled with an effective policy for trade liberalization
would be a desirable method of attaining a higher rate of development.
However, experience in Africa has shown that an attempt to harmonize
national development plans very likely would encounter great difficulties owing to differences in basic approaches to development planning.
It therefore follows that, provided care is taken to ensure the necessary
structural changes in the development process, the free trade approach
to economic integration, taken in accord with other development policies, constitutes an integral part of the general strategy for development, especially in the short run; however, as a long-term objective
countries should aim at harmonizing their development plans.

Planning for multinational economic cooperation can succeed
only when gains from integration are equitably distributed among
participating nations. To achieve economic development that is equitably spread among the various countries, it is argued that, where possible, countries should envisage more than one project or sector
within the framework for multinational strategy. However, there is
a growing feeling in the African countries that at the present time
the most effective approach to integration on the continent is through
integration at the project level. In some multinational organizations,
the coordination of sectoral production programs at the project level
is regarded as the central instrument for achieving economic integration. In other words, the African countries seem to prefer the
project-by-project approach to cooperation (or cooperation on a commodity basis), examples of which include the West African Rice Development Association, and the OCAM sugar agreement.

Despite the general acceptance of economic cooperation as an
effective strategy for development in Africa, thus far the progress
toward cooperation in the operational sense has been rather slow in
some of the economic groupings. A major practical problem was

encountered in attempts to create institutional cooperation machinery capable of taking joint decisions that would be binding upon the member states. There also were problems in ensuring that the joint decisions were implemented. In most of the African cooperation groupings, the lack of political decisions to back multinational efforts and the lack of sustained adherence to such decisions slowed down the movement toward cooperation and in some instances limited the advantages derived from cooperation.

It is suggested that, where possible, political decisions should be based on economic realism, especially where such decisions have direct impact on economic development. It is further suggested that, if cooperation is to serve as a catalyst for economic development, the international agencies should be urged to give more positive assistance to these joint ventures and to pay special attention to action-oriented studies. The African countries now require a list of carefully selected multinational projects, indicating investment requirements, cost structures, employment opportunities, and phasing-in time. The project analysis also should include proposals for action that may be undertaken by the international agencies; action to be taken jointly by the group of countries; and action to be taken at the national level in order to lend support to the multinational action. There is every reason to expect that a strategy for cooperation prepared on the basis of com-prehensive studies would help inspire the courage to take appropriate decisions in joint programs that is now lacking in the national leader-ship of most African countries, and that such a strategy for cooperation would enable the dream of cooperation to be transformed into reality. The first steps toward cooperation have now been taken; what is re-quired is to strengthen the foundations for cooperation. It must be recognized that the process toward joint development in Africa will essentially be slow but, based on past experience, cooperation will gather momentum in the 1970's.

APPENDIX:
LIST
OF MULTINATIONAL
ECONOMIC ORGANIZATIONS
IN AFRICA
AS OF SEPTEMBER 1, 1971

LIST OF MULTINATIONAL AND
INTERGOVERNMENTAL ORGANIZATIONS
IN AFRICA
(As of September 1, 1971)

1. GENERAL ECONOMIC, POLITICAL AND SEMIPOLITICAL GROUP-INGS

Economic Commission for Africa (ECA)
Commission Economique pour l'Afrique

Date established: April, 1958

Headquarters: Addis Ababa (Ethiopia), Africa Hall, P.O. Box 3001

Membership: Algeria, Botswana, Burundi, Cameroun, Central African Republic, Chad, Congo (Brazzaville), Congo (Kinshasa), Dahomey, Egypt, Equatorial Guinea, Ethiopia, Gabon, Gambia, Ghana, Guinea, Ivory Coast, Kenya, Lesotho, Liberia, Libya, Madagascar, Malawi, Mali, Mauritania, Mauritius, Morocco, Niger, Nigeria, Rwanda, Senegal, Sierra Leone, Somalia, Sudan, Swaziland, Tanzania, Togo, Tunisia, Uganda, Upper Volta, Zambia.

Observations: South Africa is a member of the ECA but has been suspended from attending its meetings; all other countries in Africa that are still under colonial rule are members of the ECA and the powers controlling them such as Spain, France and United Kingdom, are associate members. The ECA, like all other Regional Commissions in Asia, Latin America, and Europe, come under the Economic and Social Council of the United Nations. It has four subregional offices in Tangiers (Morocco), Niamey (Niger), Kinshasa (Congo), and Lusaka (Zambia).

Organization of African Unity (OAU)
Organization de l'Unite Africaine

Date established: May, 1963

Headquarters: Addis Ababa (Ethiopia), African Unity House,
                       P.O. Box 3243

Membership: Algeria, Botswana, Burundi, Cameroun, Central
                       African Republic, Chad, Congo (Brazzaville), Congo
                       (Kinshasa), Dahomey, Egypt, Equatorial Guinea,
                       Ethiopia, Gabon, Gambia, Ghana, Guinea, Ivory
                       Coast, Kenya, Lesotho, Liberia, Libya, Madagascar,
                       Malawi, Mali, Mauritania, Mauritius, Morocco,
                       Niger, Nigeria, Rwanda, Senegal, Sierra Leone,
                       Somalia, Sudan, Swaziland, Tanzania, Togo, Tunisia,
                       Uganda, Upper Volta, Zambia.

Observations: Although the OAU is basically a political organiza-
                       tion, it has adopted economic development of Afri-
                       ca, as one of its principal objectives. It has
                       regional offices in Dar-es-Salaam (Tanzania),
                       Lagos (Nigeria), and a third one is planned to be
                       opened in Conakry (Guinea).

East African Community (EAC)

Date established: December, 1967

Headquarters: Arusha (Tanzania), P.O.Box 1001

Membership: Kenya, Tanzania, Uganda

Observations: The EAC evolved from the earlier economic
                       associations such as the East African Common
                       Market, the East African Common Services
                       Organization (EACSO), and the East African High
                       Commission. Some neighboring countries such
                       as Ethiopia, Somalia, Rwanda, Burundi, Zambia,
                       Botswana and Lesotho, have applied for member-
                       ship or have expressed their interest in the EAC.

Lake Chad Basin Commission
Commission du Bassin du Lac Tchad

Date established: May, 1964

Headquarters: Fort Lamy (Chad), P.O.Box 727

Membership: Cameroun, Chad, Niger, Nigeria.

Federation of Arab Republics

Date established: April, 1971

Headquarters: Not established

Membership: Egypt, Libya, Syria.

Observations: Sudan has indicated its desire to join the feder-
                        ation.

League of Arab States

Date established: March, 1945

Headquarters: Cairo (Egypt), Midan El Tahrir

Membership: Algeria, Iraq, Jordan, Kuwait, Lebanon, Libya
                        Morocco, Saudi Arabia, Egypt, Sudan, Syria,
                        Tunisia, Yemen, South Yemen.

Observations: The League of Arab States has an Economic
                        Council responsible for promoting economic
                        cooperation among the member countries.

Central African Customs and Economic Union
Union Douanière et Economique de l' Afrique Centrale (UDEAC)

Date established: December, 1964

Headquarters: Bangui (Central African Republic), B.P. 969

Membership: Cameroun, Central African Republic, Congo
                        (Brazzaville), Gabon.

Observations: The UDEAC replaced the Equatorial Customs
                        Union (Union Douanière Equatoriale) which
                        was created in 1959. In the beginning of 1968,
                        Chad and Central African Republic announced
                        their intentions to withdraw from membership
                        in the UDEAC but later in the same year,
                        Central African Republic decided to remain in
                        the grouping: Chad's withdrawal became effec-
                        tive on January 1, 1969, but she still maintains
                        close economic contacts with the UDEAC.

Organization of the Senegal River States
Organization des Etats Riverains du Sénégal (OERS)

Date established: March, 1968

Headquarters: Dakar (Senegal), 5, Place de l' Independence

Membership: Guinea, Mali, Mauritania, Senegal

Observations: The OERS replaced the Inter-State Committee
                     of the Senegal River (Comité Inter-Etats des
                     Riverains du Fleuve Sénégal) which was created
                     in 1962. Gambia is an associate member of the
                     OERS.

Conference of East and Central African States

Date established: Economic cooperation activities started in 1967.

Headquarters: Rotating headquarters.

Membership: Burundi, Central African Republic, Chad, Congo,
                     (Brazzaville), Congo (Kinshasa), Ethiopia, Kenya,
                     Malawi, Rwanda, Somalia, Sudan, Tanzania,
                     Uganda, Zambia.

Observations: This grouping is not governed by a treaty or
                     convention, but operates through mutual under-
                     standing. It has no fixed secretariat and the
                     venue (host country) for the Summit Conference
                     of the Heads of State and Government acts as
                     the headquarters until the next meeting.

Senegambia Permanent Committee

Date established: 1967

Headquarters: Bathurst (Gambia), 4, Marina Street

Membership: Gambia, Senegal

Observations: This organization was created following the
                     recommendation of the United Nations to
                     examine the question of creation of common
                     customs arrangements between the two countries

to combat the incidence of large scale smuggling
across the frontiers; considerations also have
been taken for the establishment of a federation.

Union of Central African States
Union des Etats de l'Afrique Centrale (UEAC)

Date established: February, 1968

Headquarters: Fort Lamy (Chad)

Membership: Chad, Congo (Kinshasa)

Observations: Central African Republic which was one of the
                        founder members of the UEAC withdrew from
                        membership in December, 1968.

Economic Community of West Africa
Communauté Economique de l'Afrique de l'Ouest (CEAO)

Date established: May, 1970

Headquarters: Ouagadougou (Upper Volta), B.P. 28

Membership: Dahomey, Ivory Coast, Mali, Mauritania, Niger,
                        Senegal, Upper Volta.

Observations: The CEAO was established to replace the West
                        African customs Union (UDEAO) which was
                        created in June, 1959 to preserve the customs
                        arrangements which existed during the French
                        administration. The new organization has
                        adopted wider economic objectives than mere
                        customs agreements.

Maghreb Permanent Consultative Committee
Comité Permanent Consultaif du Maghreb (CPCM)

Date established: October, 1964

Headquarters: Tunis (Tunisia), 47, Avenue Habib Bourguiba

Membership: Algeria, Morocco, Tunisia.

Observations: Libya has withdrawn from membership in the
                        CPCM.

Economic Community of West Africa

Date established:　　Articles of Association were signed in May, 1967

Headquarters:　　Not established

Membership:　　Dahomey, Gambia, Ghana, Guinea, Ivory Coast, Liberia, Mali, Mauritania, Niger, Nigeria, Senegal, Sierra Leone, Togo, Upper Volta.

Observations:　　This grouping was created under the auspices of the ECA to promote economic cooperation on a subregional scale. No treaty has been signed. It is distinct from CEAO.

West African Regional Group

Date established:　　April, 1968

Headquarters:　　Not established; provisionally Monrovia (Liberia)

Membership:　　Gambia, Ghana, Guinea, Liberia, Mali, Mauritania, Nigeria, Senegal, Upper Volta.

Observations:　　This grouping decided to adopt the Articles of Association of the ECA-sponsored Economic Community of West Africa created in 1967 to constitute an integral part of its proposed treaty.

Economic Community of Eastern Africa

Date established:　　Terms of Association were signed in May, 1966

Headquarters:　　Not established; provisionally ECA secretariat.

Membership:　　Burundi, Botswana, Ethiopia, Kenya, Lesotho, Madagascar, Malawi, Mauritius, Rwanda, Somalia, Swaziland, Tanzania, Uganda, Zambia.

Observations:　　This grouping was created under the auspices of the ECA to promote economic cooperation on a subregional scale. No treaty has been signed. It is distinct from the East African Community.

Council of Understanding

Date established:	May, 1959
Headquarters:	Abidjan (Ivory Coast), B.P. 1878
Membership:	Dahomey, Ivory Coast, Niger, Togo, Upper Volta.
Observations:	Togo joined the Council of Understanding in 1966. In order to promote economic cooperation among the member countries, the grouping sponsored the creation of two specialized institutions: The Mutual Aid and Loan Guarantee Fund (Fonds d'Entraide et de Garantie des Emprunts) and the Entente Livestock and Meat Community (Communauté Economique du Bétail et de la Viande).

Afro-Malagasy Common Organization
Organization Commune Africaine, Malgache et Mauricienne (OCAM)

Date established:	June, 1966
Headquarters:	Yaoundé (Cameroun), B.P. 437
Membership:	Cameroun, Central African Republic, Chad, Congo (Brazzaville), Congo (Kinshasa), Dahomey, Gabon, Ivory Coast, Madagascar, Mauritius, Niger, Rwanda, Senegal, Togo, Upper Volta.
Observations:	Mauritania, which was one of the founder members of the Brazzaville Group from which the OCAM was created, is not a member but participates in the activities of some of the specialized agencies of this organization. Mauritius joined the OCAM in 1969.

Authority for the Development of the Liptako-Gourma Region
Autorité de Développement de la Région du Liptako-Gourma

Date established:	June, 1971
Headquarters:	Ouagadougou (Upper Volta)

Membership: Mali, Niger, Upper Volta

Observations: The activities of this organization are currently
                      limited to the development of the Liptako-Gourma
                      area which is common to the three countries.

Joint Organization for Economic Cooperation in Central Africa
Organisation Commune pour la Coopération Economique en
Afrique Centrale (OCCEAC)

Date established: Not formally established

Headquarters: Not established

Membership: Burundi, Congo (Kinshasa), Rwanda

Observations: The creation of the OCCEAC was recommended
                      at a meeting of Ministers of Foreign Affairs
                      of the three countries held in 1969. These
                      countries constituted a free trade and monetary
                      area during the Belgian administration.

II AGRICULTURAL RESEARCH AND DEVELOPMENT ORGANIZATIONS

Inter-African Coffe Organization
Organisation Inter-Africaine du Café

Date established: December, 1960

Headquarters: Paris (France), 24, Rue Madeleine-Michelis

Membership: Burundi, Cameroun, Central African Republic,
                      Congo (Brazzaville), Congo (Kinshasa), Dahomey,
                      Ethiopia, Ivory Coast, Madagascar, Nigeria,
                      Rwanda, Sierra Leone, Tanzania, Togo, Uganda,
                      Upper Volta, Gabon.

Observations: Kenya withdrew membership from this organ-
                      ization in 1969. Since 1971, all other coffee
                      producers, such as Guinea, Equatorial Guinea,
                      Kenya, Liberia, and Ghana will be permitted
                      to attend and participate in the meetings of
                      the group.

African Peanut (Groundnut) Council (APC)
Conseil Africain de l'Arachide

Date established: June, 1964

Headquarters: Lagos (Nigeria), P.O. Box 3025

Membership: Congo (Kinshasa), Gambia, Mali, Niger, Nigeria,
                        Senegal, Sudan.

Observations: This organization is being expanded to include
                        the production and marketing of other oilseeds
                        in Africa requiring international action.

Cocoa Producers Alliance (CPA)
Alliance des Producteurs de Cacao

Date established: 1962

Headquarters: Lagos (Nigeria)

Membership: Cameroun, Ghana, Ivory Coast, Nigeria, Togo,
                        Brazil.

Afro-Malagasy Coffe Organization
Organization Africaine et Malgache du Café (OAMCAF)

Date established: 1960

Headquarters: Paris (France), 150, Avenue Champs Elysées

Membership: Cameroun, Central Africa Republic, Congo
                        (Brazzaville), Dahomey, Gabon, Ivory Coast,
                        Madagascar, Togo.

Maghreb Esparto Bureau
Comptoir Maghrébin de l'Alfa (COMALFA)

Date established: 1965

Headquarters: Algiers (Algeria)

Membership: Algeria, Morocco, Tunisia

Observations: Libya withdrew from membership in this organ-
                  ization reportedly because of a substantial decline
                  in its production of esparto. This grouping was
                  created under the auspices of the CPCM.

Afro-Malagasy Sugar Agreement
Accord Africain et Malagache sur le Sucre

Date established: June, 1966

Headquarters: Fort Lamy (Chad), P.O.Box 763

Membership: All OCAM member countries except Senegal

Observations: Senegal withdrew from membership in this
                      organization in 1970.

International Organization for African Migratory Locust Control
Organisation Internationale contre le Criquet Migrateur Africain
(OICMA)

Date established: May, 1962

Headquarters: Bamako (Mali), P.O.Box 136

Membership: Cameroun, Central African Republic, Congo
                      (Brazzaville), Congo (Kinshasa), Dahomey,
                      Chad, Gambia, Ghana, Ivory Coast, Kenya,
                      Mali, Mauritania, Niger, Nigeria, Senegal,
                      Sierra Leone, Sudan, Tanzania, Togo, Uganda,
                      Upper Volta, Zambia.

Observations: The OICMA replaced the convention on locust
                      control signed in May, 1952 between United
                      Kingdom, France, and Belgium.

Economic Community for Livestock and Meat
Communauté Economique du Bétail et de la Viande

Date established: May, 1970

Headquarters: Ouagadougou (Upper Volta)

Membership: Dahomey, Ivory Coast, Niger, Togo, Upper
                      Volta.

Observations: This organization was created under the aus-
                         pices of the Mutual Aid and Loan Guarantee
                         Fund of the Conseil de l'Entente.

West African Rice Development Association (WARDA)
Association pour le Dévelopment de la Riziculture en Afrique de l'Ouest

Date established: 1970

Headquarters: Monrovia (Liberia)

Membership: Dahomey, Gambia, Ghana, Guinea, Ivory Coast,
                         Liberia, Mali, Mauritania, Niger, Nigeria,
                         Senegal, Sierra Leone, Togo, Upper Volta.

Observations: The FAO is responsible for running the assoc-
                         iation pending the creation of its own permanent
                         secretariat arrangements.

African Society for the Development of Millet and Sorghum Based
Food Industry

Date established: January, 1971

Headquarters: Niamey, (Niger)

Membership: Cameroun, Mali, Mauritania, Niger, Senegal,
                         Sudan, Upper Volta.

Association for the Advancement of Agricultural Sciences in Africa
   (AAASA)
Association pour l'Avancement en Afrique des Sciences de l'Agricul-
ture

Date established: 1969

Headquarters: Addis Ababa (Ethiopia)

Membership: 253 members from 34 countries all over the
                         world.

Observations: Membership to this association is open to any
                         person engaged in agricultural research,
                         teaching and extension education.

Desert Locust Control Organization for Eastern Africa (DLCOEA)

Date established: August, 1962

Headquarters: Asmara (Ethiopia), P.O.Box 231

Membership: Ethiopia, France (on behalf of its territory, Djibouti), Kenya, Somalia, Sudan, Tanzania, Uganda.

Observations: The DLCOEA was established under the initiative of the FAO and works closely with it. There are plans to move the headquarters to Addis Ababa.

III TRANSPORT, COMMUNICATIONS, AND TOURIST
     ORGANIZATIONS:

Niger River Basin Commission
Commission du Fleuve Niger

Date established: November, 1964

Headquarters: Niamey (Niger), Maison de l'Afrique

Membership: Cameroun, Chad, Dahomey, Guinea, Ivory Coast, Mali, Niger, Nigeria, Upper Volta.

East African Joint Shipping Line

Date established: 1965

Headquarters: Dar-es-Salaam (Tanzania)

Membership: Kenya, Tanzania, Uganda, Zambia.

Observations: This organization operates independently of the East African Community institutions.

Joint Dahomey-Niger Organization for Railways and Transport
Organization Commune Dahomey-Niger des Chemis de Fer et des
    Transports (OCDN)

Date established: 1959

Headquarters: Cotonou (Dahomey), P.O. Box 16

Membership: Dahomey, Niger.

Society for Hotel and Tourism Development in West Africa
Société de Dévelopment Hôtelieur et Touristique de l'Afrique de l' Ouest
  (HOTAFRIC)

Date established: 1969

Headquarters: Abidjan (Ivory Coast)

Membership: Cameroun, Central African Republic, Chad,
                             Dahomey, Gabon, Ivory Coast, Mauritania,
                             Niger, Senegal, Togo, Upper Volta.

Air Afrique

Date established: 1961

Headquarters: Abidjan (Ivory Coast), P.O. Box 21017

Membership: Congo (Brazzaville), Chad, Dahomey, Ivory
                             Coast, Gabon, Mauritania, Niger, Senegal,
                             Togo, Upper Volta.

Observations: 34 percent of equity shares are held by the
                             Union des Transports Aériens (UTA), a French
                             seminational company. Cameroun and Central
                             African Republic withdrew from membership
                             in this organization in 1971.

African Postal Union (APU)

Date established: December, 1961

Headquarters: Cairo (Egypt).

Membership: Algeria, Egypt, Ghana, Guinea, Mali, Morocco.

Afro-Malagasy Postal and Telecommunications Union
Union Africaine et Malgache des Postes et Télécommunications
  (UAMPT)

Date established: September, 1961

Headquarters: Brazzaville (Congo), P.O. Box 44

Membership: Cameroun, Central African Republic, Chad, Congo
                       (Brazzaville), Dahomey, Gabon, Ivory Coast,
                       Madagascar, Mauritania, Niger, Rwanda, Senegal,
                       Togo, Upper Volta.

Observations: The UAMPT is a specialized institution of the
                       OCAM.

Organization for the Development of Tourism in Africa
Organization pour le Développment du Tourisme en Afrique (ODTA)

Date established: 1961

Headquarters: Yaoundé (Cameroun)

Membership: Cameroun, Central African Republic, Chad,
                       Congo,(Brazzaville), Dahomey, Gabon, Ivory
                       Coast, Mali, Mauritania, Niger, Senegal, Togo,
                       Upper Volta.

Observations: The ODTA replaced the Inter-State Bureau for
                       Tourism in Africa (Office Inter-Etats du
                       Tourisme Africaine (OIETA) which was created
                       in 1961, and is a specialized institution of the
                       OCAM.

Union of National Radio and Televisions in Africa
Union des Radiodiffusions et Télévisions Nationales d'Afrique (URTNA)

Date established: September, 1962

Headquarters: Dakar (Senegal), IOI, Rue Carnot, P.O. Box 3237

Membership: Algeria, Cameroun, Chad, Congo,(Brazzaville),
                       Congo (Kinshasa), Dahomey, Ghana, Guinea,
                       Ivory Coast, Libya, Mali, Mauritania, Morocco,
                       Niger, Nigeria, Egypt, Senegal, Sierra Leone,
                       Tanzania, Togo, Tunisia, Upper Volta, Zambia.

Union of African News Agencies

Date established: 1963

Headquarters: Algiers (Algeria)

Membership: All national news agencies established in Africa
                       that are members or associate members of
                       UNESCO.

Agency for Air Safety in Africa and Madagascar
Agence pour la Sécurité de la Navigation Aérienne en Afrique et
   Malgache (ASECNA)

Date established: December, 1959

Headquarters: Saint Louis (Senegal)

Membership: Cameroun, Central African Republic, Chad,
                       Congo,(Brazzaville), Dahomey, Gabon, Ivory
                       Coast, Madagascar, Mali, Mauritania, Niger,
                       Senegal, Togo, Upper Volta.

Association of African Airlines

Date established: 1968

Headquarters: Nairobi (Kenya)

Membership: Air Afrique, Ghana Airways, Air Maroc, East
                       African Airways, Ethiopian Airlines, Tunis-
                       Air, United Arab Airlines, Zambia Airways.

Observations: This organization was established through ECA
                       initiatives and works in close collaboration with
                       the ECA, the OAU, the African Civil Aviation
                       Commission and the International Air Transport
                       Association (IATA).

African Civil Aviation Commission

Date established: 1969

Headquarters: International Civil Aviation Commission (ICAO)
                       Regional Office, Dakar, Senegal.

Membership: Algeria, Burundi, Cameroun, Chad, Congo
                       (Brazzaville), Congo (Kinshasa), Egypt,

Ethiopia, Gabon, Ivory Coast, Kenya, Liberia,
Libya, Madagascar, Malawi, Mauritania,
Morocco, Niger, Nigeria, Rwanda, Senegal,
Sierra Leone, Sudan, Swaziland, Tanzania,
Togo, Tunisia, Uganda, Upper Volta, Zambia.

Observations: This organization was created under ECA
auspices.

Zambia-Tanzania Road Services Organization (ZAMTAN)

Date established: 1966

Headquarters: Dar-es-Salaam (Tanzania)

Membership: Tanzania, Zambia

Observations: This association operates outside the East
African Community.

Agreement establishing the Zambia-Tanzania Rail Link

Date established: October, 1970

Headquarters: Dar-es-Salaam (Tanzania)

Membership: Tanzania, Zambia.

Observations: This agreement operates outside the East
African Community.

Transsaharan Liaison Committee
Comité de la Liaison Transsaharienne

Date established: May, 1964

Headquarters: Algiers (Algeria), 135, Rue Didouche Mourade.

Membership: Algeria, Mali, Niger, Tunisia;

Observations: This organization was established at the
initiative of the ECA.

Trans-African Highway Coordination Committee
Comité de Coordination de la Route Transafricaine

Date established: June, 1971

Headquarters: ECA, P.O. Box 3001, Addis Ababa (Ethiopia)

Membership: Cameroun, Central African Republic, Congo
                       (Kinshasa), Kenya, Nigeria, Uganda.

Observations: This committee was established to coordinate
                       the development of the trans-African Highway
                       running from Mombasa (Kenya) through Uganda,
                       Congo (Kinshasa), Central African Republic,
                       Cameroun, and end up in Lagos (Nigeria)

IV. INDUSTRIAL DEVELOPMENT AND RESEARCH ORGANIZATIONS

African and Malagasy Bureau for Industrial Property
Office Africain et Malgache de la Propriete Industrielle (OAMPI)

Date established: September, 1962

Headquarters: Yaounde (Cameroun), B. P. 887

Membership: Cameroun, Central African Republic, Chad,
                       Congo (Brazzaville), Dahomey, Gabon, Ivory
                       Coast, Madagascar, Mauritania, Niger, Senegal,
                       Togo, Upper Volta.

Observations: The OAMPI is a specialized institution created
                       through the initiatives of the OCAM

Inter-African Committee for Hydraulic Research
Comité Inter-Africain d'Etudes Hydrauliques (CIEH)

Date established: 1960

Headquarters: Ouagadougou (Upper Volta), B. P. 369

Membership: Congo (Brazzaville), Chad, Dahomey, Gabon,
                       Ivory Coast, Madagascar, Mali, Mauritania,
                       Niger, Senegal, Togo, Upper Volta.

Observations: The CIEH works closely with the ECA.

Maghreb Industrial Studies Center (ISC)
Centre Maghrébin d'Etudes Industrielles

Date established: 1967

Headquarters: Tangiers (Morocco)

Membership: Algeria, Morocco, Tunisia

Observations: The ISC is a specialized institution of the CPCM
                        and was created with the assistance of the UNDP.

Industrial Development Center for Arab States (IDCAS)

Date established: May, 1968

Headquarters: Cairo (Egypt), I, Shihab Street, P.O. Box 1297

Membership: Algeria, Libya, Morocco, Egypt, Sudan, Iraq,
                        Jordan, Lebanon, Saudi Arabia, Yemen, Kuwait,
                        Tunisia, South Yemen, Syria.

Observations: The IDCAS was established under the auspices
                        of the League of Arab States. It has five asso-
                        ciate members from the Persian Gulf countries.

V. HUMAN RESOURCES DEVELOPMENT

West African Examination Council

Date established: 1952

Headquarters: Accra (Ghana), 7th Avenue Extension, P.O. Box
                        917

Membership: Gambia, Ghana, Nigeria, Sierra Leone

Observations: Liberia is an associate member.

Institute for Economic Development and Planning
Institut pour le Développement Economique et la Planification (IDEP)

Date established: March, 1962

Headquarters: Dakar (Senegal), P.O. Box 3186

Membership: All independent African countries except
                        Equatorial Guinea, Lesotho, and Swaziland.

African Training and Research Center in Administration
Centre Africain de Formation et de Recherche Administrative
pour le Développment (CAFRAD)

Date established: December, 1967

Headquarters: Tangiers (Morocco), P.O. Box 310

Membership: Algeria, Cameroun, Central African Republic,
                        Egypt, Ghana, Ivory Coast, Libya, Mauritania,
                        Morocco, Senegal, Somalia, Sudan, Togo,
                        Tunisia, Zambia.

Observations: The CAFRAD was created under the auspices
                        of UNESCO.

Inter-State School for Rural Engineers
Ecole Inter-Etats d'Ingénierus de l'Equipement Rural (EIER)

Date established: December, 1968

Headquarters: Ouagadougou (Upper Volta), P.O. Box 139

Membership: Cameroun, Congo (Brazzaville), Dahomey,
                        Ivory Coast, Mauritania, Niger, Senegal, Togo,
                        Upper Volta.

Observations: The EIER is a specialized institution of the
                        OCAM.

Afro-Malagasy Council for Higher Education
Conseil Africain et Malgache de l'Enseignement Supérieur (CAMES)

Date established: 1968

Headquarters: Ouagadougou (Upper Volta), c/o Lycée National

Membership: All OCAM member countries plus Mali and
                        Mauritania.

Observations: The CAMES is a specialized institution created under the auspices of the OCAM.

East African Statistical Training Center

Date established: 1965

Headquarters: Dar-es-Salaam (Tanzania), P. O. Box 35091

Membership: All countries in the Eastern African subregion.

Observations: This center was established under the auspices of the ECA to train statisticians from these countries, and works closely with the East African community.

Institute of Statistics and Applied Economics

Date established: 1968

Headquarters: Kampala (Uganda), P.O. Box 7062

Membership: All countries in the Eastern African subregion.

Observations: The institute was created through the initiatives of the ECA and maintains close relations with it.

Regional Institute for Population Studies

Date established: Not yet formally established

Headquarters: Yaoundé (Cameroun)

Membership: All countries in the African region.

Observations: The institute was created under the initiatives of the ECA and caters for all French speaking African countries.

Institute of Statistics and Applied Economics

Date established: 1961

Headquarters: Rabat (Morocco), P.O. Box 406

Membership: All countries in the North African subregion.

Observations: This institute was created under the initiatives
                       of the ECA.

Institute of Statistical, Social and Economic Research

Date established: 1961

Headquarters: Accra (Ghana), P.O. Box 74, Legon, Ghana.

Membership: All countries in the West African subregion

Observations: This institute was established under the ECA
                       initiatives.

Regional Institute for Population Studies

Date established: Not formally established

Headquarters: Accra (Ghana)

Membership: All countries in the African region

Observations: This institute was created under the auspices
                       of the ECA and caters for the English speaking
                       countries.

Cairo Demographic Center

Date established: 1963

Headquarters: Cairo (Egypt)

Membership: North African countries and the Middle East

Observations: The center was established under the ECA
                       initiatives and works closely with the ECA.

VI. TRADE AND CUSTOMS ARRANGEMENTS

Intergovernmental Council of Copper Exporting Countries
Conseil Intergouvernemental des Pays Exportateurs de Cuivre (CIPEC)

Date established: June, 1967

Headquarters: Paris, (France), 3, Avenue du Général de Gaulle

Membership: Chile, Congo (Kinshasa), Peru, Zambia.

Organization of the Petroleum Exporting Countries (OPEC)
Organization des Pays Exportateurs de Pétrole

Date established: 1960

Headquarters: Vienna (Austria)

Membership: Algeria, Libya, Abbu Dahbi, Indonesia, Iran,
                      Iraq, Kuwait, Qatar, Saudi Arabia, Venezuela,
                      Nigeria.

Customs Union Agreement between the Governments of Swaziland, Botswana, Lesotho, and South Africa

Date established: March, 1970

Headquarters: Not established;

Membership: Botswana, Lesotho, Swaziland, South Africa

Observations: The customs union agreement replaced an
                      earlier agreement signed in 1910.

Afro-Asian Organization for Economic Cooperation (AFRASEC)

Date established: 1958

Headquarters: Cairo (Egypt), 4, Midan El Falady, Chambers of
                      Commerce Building, P.O. Box 507

Membership: Membership is spread over 38 countries in
                      Africa and Asia consisting of national federations
                      of Chambers of Commerce, Industry and Agricul-
                      ture.

Observations: There are 8 associate members in similar
                      organizations.

VII: MULTINATIONAL BANKS, MONETARY AND FINANCIAL ARRANGEMENTS

African Development Bank (ADB)

Date established: August, 1963

Headquarters: Abidjan (Ivory Coast), P.O.Box 1387

Membership: Algeria, Botswana, Burundi, Cameroun, Central
                         African Republic, Chad, Congo (Brazzaville),
                         Congo (Kinshasa), Dahomey, Egypt, Ethiopia,
                         Gabon, Ghana, Guinea, Ivory Coast, Kenya, Liberia,
                         Liberia, Libya, Madagascar, Malawi, Mali,
                         Mauritania, Morocco, Niger, Nigeria, Rwanda,
                         Senegal, Sierra Leone, Somalia, Sudan, Swaziland,
                         Tanzania, Togo, Tunisia, Uganda, Upper Volta,
                         Zambia.

Observations: The ADB was created through the initiatives of
                         the ECA and works closely with it, but is an
                         autonomous organization.

Central Bank of the States of Equatorial Africa and Cameroun
Banque Centrale des Etats de l'Afrique Equatoriale et du Cameroun
   (BCEAEC)

Date established: 1962

Headquarters: Paris (France), 29, Rue du Colisée

Membership: Cameroun, Central African Republic, Chad,
                         Congo,(Brazzaville), Gabon.

Observations: The BCEAEC was established to replace the
                         Institute of Issue of the French Equatorial
                         Africa (Institut d'Emission de l'Afrique Equa-
                         toriale Francaise et du Cameroun). It has
                         identical membership with the Monetary Union
                         of Equatorial Africa and Cameroun (UMAEC)
                         and works closely with it.

Monetary Union of Equatorial Africa and Cameroun
Union Monétaire de l'Afrique Equatoriale et du Cameroun (UMAEC)

Date established: 1962

Headquarters: Paris (France), 29, Rue du Colisée

Membership: Cameroun, Central African Republic, Chad,
                         Congo,(Brazzaville), Gabon.

Observations: The UMAEC has identical membership with the
                       Central Bank of Equatorial Africa and Cameroun
                       (BCEAEC) and works closely with it.

East African Development Bank

Date established: December, 1967

Headquarters: Kampala (Uganda), 13, Portal Avenue, P.O. Box
                       7928

Membership: Kenya, Tanzania, Uganda.

Observations: The East African Development Bank is a
                       specialized institution of the East African
                       Community.

Central Bank of the West African States
Banque Centrale des Etats de l'Afrique de l'Ouest (BCEAO)

Date established: May, 1962

Headquarters: Paris (France), 28, Rue du Colisée

Membership: Dahomey, Ivory Coast, Mali, Mauritania, Niger,
                       Senegal, Togo, Upper Volta.

Observations: The BCEAO has identical membership with the
                       West African Monetary Union (UMOA) and works
                       in close cooperation with it.

West African Monetary Union
Union Monétaire Ouest Africaine (UMOA)

Date established: May, 1962

Headquarters: Paris (France), 28, Rue du Colisée

Membership: Dahomey, Ivory Coast, Mali, Mauritania, Niger,
                       Senegal, Togo, Upper Volta.

Observations: The UMOA has identical membership with the
                       BCEAO and works in close cooperation with it.

Mutual Aid and Loan Guarantee Fund
Fonds d'Entraide et de Carantie des Emprunts.

Date established: June, 1966

Headquarters: Abidjan (Ivory Coast), P.O. Box 20824

Membership: Dahomey, Ivory Coast, Niger, Togo, Upper Volta.

Observations: The Mutual Aid and Loan Guarantee Fund is an
                       institution created by the Council of Under-
                       standing (Conseil de l'Entente).

Association of African Central Banks

Date established: 1968

Headquarters: Not established (Provisionally ECA secretariat)

Membership: Central Bank of Algeria, Bank of Burundi,
                       National Bank of Congo (Kinshasa), Central
                       Bank of the States of Equatorial Africa and
                       Cameroun (BCEAEC), National Bank of Ethiopia,
                       Central Bank of Egypt, The Gambia Currency
                       Board, Bank of Ghana, Central Bank of Kenya,
                       Bank of Libya, Malagasy Currency Issuing
                       Institute (Institut d'emission Malgache), Reserve
                       Bank of Malawi, Central Bank of Mali, Bank of
                       Mauritius, Bank of Morocco, Central Bank of
                       Nigeria, National Bank of Rwanda, Bank of
                       Sierra Leone, Somali National Bank, Bank of
                       Sudan, Bank of Uganda, Central Bank of the West
                       African States (BCEAO), Bank of Zambia.

Observations: The Association of African Central Banks was
                       created under the auspices of the ECA.

VIII: HEALTH AND SOCIAL SERVICES ORGANIZATIONS

Organization for Coordination and Cooperation in Combatting Major
Endemic Diseases
Organization de Coordination et de Coopération pour la lutte Contre
les Grandes Endémies (OCCGE)

Date established: April, 1960

Headquarters: Bobo-Dioulasso (Upper Volta), P.O. Box 153

Membership: Dahomey, Ivory Coast, Mali, Mauritania, Niger,
                       Senegal, Togo, Upper Volta.

Observations: The OCCGE works in close collaboration with
                       France.

Joint Organization for Bird and Locust Control
Organisation Commune de lutte Antiacridienne et de lutte
Antiaviare (OCLALAV)

Date established: May, 1965

Headquarters: Dakar (Senegal), P.O.Box 1066

Membership: Cameroun, Chad, Dahomey, Ivory Coast, Mali,
                       Mauritania, Niger, Senegal, Upper Volta.

Observations: The OCLALAV works in close collaboration
                       with the International Organization for African
                       Migratory Locust Control (OICMA)

Organization for Coordination and Cooperation in Combatting Major
Endemic Diseases in Central Africa
Organisation pour la Coordination et la Coopération Contre les
Grandes Endémies en Afrique Centrale (OCCGEAC)

Date established: 1963

Headquarters: Yaoundé (Cameroun)

Membership: Cameroun, Central African Republic, Chad,
                       Congo (Brazzaville), Gabon.

Agency for Cultural and Technical Cooperation Between French
Speaking Countries
Agence de Coopération Culturelle et Technique des Pays Francophones

Date established: African countries signed its Convention in
                       March, 1970

Headquarters: Paris (France)

Membership: Membership in this organization is open to all
                       French-speaking countries in the world. The

African members are Burundi, Cameroun,
Chad, Dahomey, Gabon, Ivory Coast, Madagas-
car, Mauritius, Mali, Niger, Rwanda, Senegal,
Togo, Tunisia, Upper Volta.

SELECTED BIBLIOGRAPHY

CHAPTER 1

Hailey, Lord: An African Survey, London: Oxford University Press, 1957.

Hance, W.A.; African Economic Development, New York: Harper & Row, 1958.

Hargreaves, J.D., Prelude to the Partition of West Africa, London: Macmillan, 1963.

Legun, Colin, Pan-Africanism: A Short Political Guide, New York: Frederick A. Praeger, 1962.

Moon, Parker Thomas, Imperialism and World Politics, New York: The Macmillan Company, 1926.

Myrdal, Gunnar, Economic Theory and Underdeveloped Regions, London: Duckworth, 1957.

Nurkse, Ragnar, Problems of Capital Formation in Underdeveloped Countries, Oxford: Basil Blackwell, 1953.

Ritner, Peter, The Death of Africa, New York: Macmillan, 1960.

Rosenstein-Rodan, Paul N., "Problems of Industrialization in South and South Eastern Europe" in The Economic Journal, Vol. LIII, No. 210, London: Royal Economic Society, June–September, 1943.

Shepperson, George and Price, Thomas, Independent African, Edinburgh: Edinburgh University Press, 1958.

Stamp, A.H. Other Nations Colonies, Kent: Courier Printing and Publishing Company Ltd., 1957.

CHAPTER 2

Balassa, Bela, The Theory of Economic Integration, London: George Allen & Unwin Ltd., 1965.

Cooper C.A. and Massel B.F., "A New Look at the Customs Union Theory" in The Economic Journal, Vol. LXXV, No. 300, London: Royal Economic Society, December 1965.

Johnson, Harry G., Money, Trade and Economic Growth, London: George Allen & Unwin Ltd., 1964.

Meade, J.E. The Theory of Customs Union, Amsterdam: North-Holland Publishing Company, 1965.

Mikesell, R.F., "The Theory of Common Markets as Applied to Regional Arrangements Among Developing Countries" in Roy Harrod and D.C. Hague, eds., International Trade Theory in a Developing World, London: Macmillan, 1963.

Viner, Jacob, The Customs Union Issue, New York: Stevens and Sons Ltd, 1950.

CHAPTER 3

Economic Commission for Africa. Annual Report. E/4354. New York, 1967,

_____. Institutional Arrangements for Multinational Decision-making in the Central African Sub-region. E/CN.14/CA/ECOP/12.

_____. Inter-governmental Machinery for Economic Integration Existing in Africa and Other Parts of the World. E/CN.14/NA/ECOP/7 and 8, Rev.1.

_____. Proposals on Inter-governmental Machinery for Sub-regional Cooperation in West Africa. E/CN.14/WA/ECOP/1/Rev.2. 1966.

_____. Report of the Sub-regional Meeting on Economic Cooperation in Central Africa. E/CN.14/351.

_____. Report of the Sub-regional Meeting on Economic Cooperation in Central Africa. E/CN.14/465. Kinshasa, November 1969.

_____. Report of the Sub-regional Meeting on Economic Cooperation in East Africa. E/CN.14/346. Lusaka, December 1965.

_____. Report of the Sub-regional Meeting on Economic Coopera-
tion in North Africa. E/CN.14/354. Tangier, June 1966.

_____. Report of the Sub-regional Meeting on Economic Coopera-
tion in West Africa. E/CN.14/366. Niamey, November 1966.

_____. Report of the West African Sub-regional Conference on
Economic Cooperation. E/CN.14/399. Accra, May 1967.

_____. Review of the Organization and Functions of the Sub-regional
Groupings in Africa. E/CN.14/ECO/13. October 1969.

_____. A Venture in Self-Reliance, 1958-1968. E/CN.14/424.
February 1969.

CHAPTER 4

Economic Commission for Africa. A Survey of Economic Conditions
in Africa, 1967. E/CN.14/409.

Food and Agriculture Organization. African Agricultural Development.
E/CN.14/342. New York, 1966.

_____. Africa Survey. Rome, 1962.

_____. A Report to the Governments of Gambia and Senegal. In-
tegrated Agricultural Development in the Gambia River Basin.
Rome, February 1964.

_____. State of Food and Agriculture. C.65/4. Rome, 1965.

Gaitskell Arthur Gezira, A Story of Development in the Sudan. London:
Faber, 1959.

Kamarck, Andrew, M. The Economics of African Development. New
York: Frederick A. Praeger, 1967.

Nicholls, William, H. "Industrialization, Factor Markets and Agricultural Development." Journal of Political Economy, August 1961.

CHAPTER 5

Economic Commission for Africa. Development of Forest Industries in Africa. E/CN.14/AS/III/3.

_____. Economic Bulletin for Africa. E/CN.14/406, Vol. VII, Nos. 1 and 2.

_____. Economic Conditions in Africa in Recent Years. E/CN.14/435.

_____. Industrial Coordination in East Africa: A Quantified Approach to First Approximations. E/CN.14/INR/102.

_____. Industrial Growth in Africa. E/CN.14/INR/1. December 1962.

_____. Iron and Steel Industry in Africa. E/CN.14/AS/III/23.

_____. Prospects for the Development of Chemical Industry in Africa. E/CN.14/AS/III/22.

_____. Report of the ECA Industrial Coordination Mission to East Africa. E/CN.14/247.

_____. Report of the ECA Mission on Economic Cooperation in Central Africa. E/CN.14/L.320/Rev.1. New York, 1966.

_____. Report of the ECA Mission on Industrial Coordination to Algeria, Libya, Tunisia and Morocco. E/CN.14/248.

_____. Report of the West African Industrial Coordination Mission. E/CN.14/246.

_____. A Scheme for Sub-regional Industrial Promotion Centers in Africa. IND/IF.2/WP/2.

_____. A survey of Economic Conditions in Africa. E/CN.14/401, E/CN.14/409/Rev.1, and E/CN.14/480.

_____. Textile Industries in Africa. E/CN.14/AS/III/24.

Ewing, A. F., Industry in Africa. London: Oxford University Press, 1968.

Mountjoy, A. B. Industrialization of Underdeveloped Countries. London: Hutchinson, 1963.

Simpson, J. T. Financing Industrial Development with Particular Reference to Africa. CID/SYMP.B/11. Paper presented at the Symposium on Industrial Development in Africa, Cairo, 1966.

Stalty, E. and Morse R., Modern Small Industry for Developing Countries. New York: (Stanford Research Institute,) 1965.

CHAPTER 6

Economic Commission for Africa: Africa's Trade Trends, Problems and Policies. E/CN.14/UNCTAD II/1.

_____. Development of Trade in the Central African Sub-region. E/CN.14/CA/ECOP/II. November 1969.

_____. Foreign Trade Newsletter. E/CN.14/STC/FTN/1-23.

_____. Foreign Trade Plans in Selected Countries in Africa. E/Conf. 46/83. March 1964.

_____. Regional Trade Promotion Center Within ECA. E/CN.14/434.

_____. Trade Expansion in Eastern Africa. E/CN.14/EA/EC/2, Parts I and II.

_____. Trade Expansion in Eastern Africa: An Outline for a Program of Action. E/CN.14/EA/EC/2 and Add.1, Parts I and II. August 1967.

Jackson, E. F., ed. Economic Development in Africa. Oxford: Basil Blackwell, 1965.

Johnson, Harry G., Money, Trade and Economic Growth. London: George Allen & Unwin Ltd., 1964.

Nicholas Kaldor. "International Trade and Economic Development." in Journal of Modern African Studies, Vol. II, No. 4 (1964).

Sachs, Ignacy., Foreign Trade and Economic Development of Under-developed Countries. Bombay: Asian Publishing House, 1965.

United Nations Conference on Trade and Development. Trade Expansion and Economic Integration Among Development Countries. TD/B/85/Rev.1. New York, 1967.

CHAPTER 7

Bureau Central d'Études pour les Équipements Paris d'Outre-mer, and Secrétariat des Missions d'Urbanisme et d'Habitat (France). Report on Inter-State Connexions in West Africa.

Economic Commission for Africa. African Transport Development Study, Part I (covering Nigeria, Niger, Dahomey, Togo, Ghana, and Upper Volta). E/CN.14/TRANS/28.

_____. Aspects of Transport Development in West Africa. E/CN.14/INR/118 and Add.1.

_____. Machinery for Coordination of Transport Policies and Planning in the Central African Sub-region. E/CN.14/CA/ECOP/7.

_____. The Problems of Transport Across the Sahara. E/CN.14/194, Add.1.

_____. Study of the Prospects for the Development of Inland Waterways in West Africa. E/CN.14/INR/111.

_____. Transit Problems of African Land-locked Countries. E/CN.14/TRANS/29. February 1966.

_____. Transport Development in the West African Sub-region. E/CN.14/TRANS/31. September 1967.

_____, and Center for Industrial Development. Industrialization, Economic Cooperation and Transport Hypothesis of Work in the Region of the Great African Lakes. E/CN.14/AS/IV/7 and Add.1. Paper presented at the Symposium on Industrial Development in Africa, Cairo, January 1966.

Hailey, Lord., An African Survey. Oxford: Oxford University Press, 1967.

Office de la Coopération au Développement (Belgium). Survey Mission on International Surface Transports in the Central African Sub-region. Vols. I and II.

American Society for International Law. International Legal Materials. Vol. III, No. 6; Vol. VII, No. 4.

Borel, Paul. Economic Cooperation in Central Africa. E/AC.54/L.26/ Add.3. United Nations, March 1968.

East African Common Services Organization. Treaty for East African Cooperation. Nairobi, June 1967.

Economic Commission for Africa. The Kampala Treaty and the Eastern African Common Market. E/CN.14/EA/EC/12. May 1968.

_____. Main Problems of Economic Development and Cooperation in North Africa. E/CN.14/NA/ECOP.4. May 1966.

_____. Report of the ECA Mission on Economic Cooperation in Central Africa. E/CN.14/L.320/Rev.1. New York, 1966.

_____. Report of the Sub-Regional Meeting on Economic Coopera- tion in East Africa. E/CN.14/346. November 1965.

General Agreement on Tariffs and Trade. Treaty Establishing a Cen- tral African Economic and Customs Union. GATT Document No. 12354. February 1965.

_____, Ndegwa, Philip., The Common Market and Development in East Africa. Nairobi: (East African Publishing House, 1965.

Raisman, Jeremy., East Africa, Report of the Economic and Fiscal Commission. London: H. M. Stationery Office Cmnd: 1279, 1961.

Robson, Peter., Economic Integration in Africa. London: George Allen & Unwin Ltd., 1968.

431

Thompson, V., and Adloff, R. The Emerging States of French Equatorial Africa. London: Oxford University Press, 1960.

Thompson, V., and Adloff, R. French West Africa. London: Oxford University Press, 1958.

United Nations Department of Economic and Social Affairs. The Latin American Common Market. E/CN.12/531. New York, 1959.

CHAPTER 9

Azikiwe, Nnandi. The Future of Pan-Africanism. London: Nigeria Information Service, 1961.

Breton, A., "The Economics of Nationalism" in Journal of Political Economy, August 1964.

Chisiza, D. K. Realities of African Independence. London: The Africa Publications Trust, 1961.

Ghana High Commission, Ghana Today London, June, 1961.

Green, Reginald H. and Seidman, Ann. Unity or Poverty? London: Penguin, 1968.

Kenyata, Jomo. Facing Mount Kenya. London: Secker and Warburg, 1953.

Legum, Colin. Pan-Africanism: A Short Political Guide. New York: Frederick A. Praeger, 1962.

Nkrumah, Kwame. Africa Must Unite. London: Heinemann Educational Books Ltd., 1963.

Nyerere, Julius K. Freedom and Unity: A Selection from Writings and Speeches 1952-1965 Dar-es-Salaam: Oxford University Press, 1967.

Onuoha, Bede. The Elements of African Socialism. London: Andre Deutsch Ltd., 1965.

Organization of African Unity. Charter of the Organization of African Unity. Addis Ababa: OAU General Secretariat, 1965.

CHAPTER 10

Caves, Richard, Johnson, Harry G., and Kenen, Peter B., Trade, Growth and the Balance of Payments Amsterdam: North-Holland Publishing Company, 1965.

Economic Commission for Africa, Economic Conditions in Africa in Recent Years, E/CN.14/435.

ECA, Special Measures in Favor of the Least Developed Among the Developing Countries, E/CN.14/WP.I/21: OAU/TRAD/20.

Michael, M. "On Customs Unions and Gains from Trade" in The Economic Journal, Vol. LXXV, No. 299, London: Royal Economic Society, September 1965.

Newlyin, W.T., "Gains and Losses in East African Common Market" in Yorkshire Bulletin of Economic and Social Research. 1965.

Robinson, E.A.G., Economic Consequences of the Size of Nations. London: Macmillan, 1960.

United Nations Conference on Trade and Development, Special Measures to Be Taken in Favor of the Least Developed Among the Developing Countries TD/17/Supp. I.

UNCTAD, Trade Expansion and Economic Integration Among Developing Countries TD/B/85/Rev.I. New York, 1967.

NOTES

CHAPTER 11

Council of Mutual Economic Assistance. Report by N. I. Ivanov, C.Sc. Papers of United Nations First Inter-regional Seminar on Development Planning, Ankara, Turkey, September 1965.

Economic Commission for Africa, Africa's Strategy for Development in the 1970's. E/CN.14/493/Rev.3, February 1971.

Hirschman, A. O. The Strategy of Economic Development. New Haven: Yale University Press, 1958.

433

Kindleberger, Charles P. Economic Development. New York: Mcgraw-Hill, 1965.

United Nations. Planning for Balanced Social and Economic Development (Six Country Case Studies), ST/SOA/56; E/CN.5/346/Rev.1. New York, 1964.

_____. Planning for Economic Development (Report of the Secretary-General transmitting the study of a group of experts). A/5533/Rev.1. United Nations, New York, 1963.

_____. Department of Economic and Social Affairs: Report on the Fourth Inter-regional Seminar on Development Planning. ST/TAO/SER.C/116. December 1968.

_____, Department of Economic and Social Affairs. United Nations Multinational Planning, Economic Integration and Cooperation: The African Experience. ISDP.5/A/R.3. Papers of the Fifth Inter-regional Seminar on Development Planning, Bangkok, Thailand, September, 1969.

_____, Economic and Social Council. United Nations Problems of Plan Implementation: Economic Cooperation in Eastern Africa. (E/AC.54/L.26/Add.1) Report prepared by the Center for Development Planning, Projections and Policies and presented at the Third Session of the Committee for Development Planning, Addis Ababa, 1968.

_____, Economic and Social Council United Nations. Problems of Plan Implementation: Economic Cooperation and Integration in Central Africa. E/AC.54/L.26/Add.3. Report prepared by Paul Borel and presented at the Third Session of the Committee for Development Planning, Addis Ababa, 1968.

_____, Economic and Social Council. United Nations Problems of Plan Implementation: Economic Cooperation in West Africa E/AC.54/L.26/Add.2: Report prepared by the Center for Development Planning, Projections and Policies and presented at the Third Session of the Committee for Development Planning, Addis Ababa, 1968.

_____, General Assembly. United Nations International Development Strategy for the Second United Nations Development Decade. Resolution: A/RES/2626(XXV). November 1970.

Webster Mutharika, now Economic Affairs Officer in the United Nations Economic Commission for Africa, has very wide knowledge and experience in problems of economic cooperation in Africa. For the past five years he has worked on proposals for joint economic development among the African countries. Having worked closely with the African countries Mr. Mutharika has first hand knowledge of the economic problems of Africa. He has written a number of papers and studies for the United Nations relating to trade and economic coopera- tion in Africa. He has traveled extensively in Africa, Europe, and Asia and has represented the Economic Commission for Africa on a number of conferences and seminars on these subjects.

Prior to joining the United Nations, Mr. Mutharika was Adminis- trative Officer in the Government of Malawi from 1963 to 1964 and in the Government of the Republic of Zambia from 1965 to 1966. In both cases he was dealing with policy matters relating to banking, insurance, currency and exchange control regulations, and some aspects of eco- nomic cooperation. In 1965, he was one of the Economic Advisers to the Zambian delegation to the Conference on Economic Cooperation in Eastern Africa organized by the Economic Commission for Africa.

Mr. Mutharika studied economics at the University of Delhi and was attached to the Department of African Studies and the Delhi School of Economics for his post-graduate work.